Government Intervention in the

Government Intervention in the Brewing Industry

by

John Spicer

Chris Thurman MBE

John Walters

Simon Ward

© John Spicer, Chris Thurman, John Walters and Simon Ward 2012, 2013
Foreword © Anthony Hilton 2012, 2013

All rights reserved. No reproduction, copy or transmission of this publication may be made without written permission.

No portion of this publication may be reproduced, copied or transmitted save with written permission or in accordance with the provisions of the Copyright, Designs and Patents Act 1988, or under the terms of any licence permitting limited copying issued by the Copyright Licensing Agency, Saffron House, 6–10 Kirby Street, London EC1N 8TS.

Any person who does any unauthorized act in relation to this publication may be liable to criminal prosecution and civil claims for damages.

The authors have asserted their rights to be identified
as the authors of this work in accordance with the Copyright, Designs and Patents Act 1988.

First published 2012 by
First published in paperback 2013 by
PALGRAVE MACMILLAN

Palgrave Macmillan in the UK is an imprint of Macmillan Publishers Limited, registered in England, company number 785998, of Houndmills, Basingstoke, Hampshire RG21 6XS.

Palgrave Macmillan in the US is a division of St Martin's Press LLC,
175 Fifth Avenue, New York, NY 10010.

Palgrave Macmillan is the global academic imprint of the above companies and has companies and representatives throughout the world.

Palgrave® and Macmillan® are registered trademarks in the United States, the United Kingdom, Europe and other countries.

ISBN: 978–0–230–29857–6   hardback
ISBN: 978–1–137–30572–5   paperback

This book is printed on paper suitable for recycling and made from fully managed and sustained forest sources. Logging, pulping and manufacturing processes are expected to conform to the environmental regulations of the country of origin.

A catalogue record for this book is available from the British Library.

A catalog record for this book is available from the Library of Congress.

10   9   8   7   6   5   4   3   2   1
22 21 20 19 18 17 16 15 14 13

Printed and bound in Great Britain by
CPI Antony Rowe, Chippenham and Eastbourne

Contents

List of Figures and Tables		vii
Notes on the Authors		ix
Acknowledgements		x
Foreword by Anthony Hilton		xii
Timeline		xiv
Introduction		xv
1	The "Big Six" Brewers and the Early Investigations	1
2	Milestones on the Road to a Monopoly Reference	18
3	The State of Affairs in 1985	31
4	The OFT Prepares its Case	41
5	The Conduct of the Inquiry	51
6	The MMC Receives the Evidence	58
7	Radical Change Proposed	73
8	Mixed Reactions to the Report	92
9	The Government Confronts the Recommendations	103
10	The Beer Orders Emerge	119
11	Complying with the Orders	128
12	Four More Reviews	139
13	The Big Brewers Fall into Foreign Hands	152
14	The Regionals React	165
15	Pub Companies and Licensees	173
16	Prices and Choice	184
17	The Beer Market	195
18	The Beer Orders are Revoked	205
19	Pubcos Move Centre Stage	210
20	Summary and Conclusions	221
	What if…?	245

Appendices

Appendix 1.1	The Regulatory Framework	249
Appendix 1.2	History of Inquiries into the Brewing Industry and Licensing Law	252
Appendix 3.1	The European Aspect	253
Appendix 3.2	Industry and Company Statistics	260
Appendix 3.3	Reference Graphs	264
Appendix 3.4	The Participants	267
Appendix 5.1	Companies, Organisations and Others Making Submissions to the Monopolies and Mergers Commission (MMC)	276
Appendix 5.2	Options for Change	278
Appendix 19.1	Major Pub-owning Companies as at July 2010	281
Bibliography		282
Glossary and Abbreviations		285
Index		300

List of Figures and Tables

Figures

3.1	Beer Sales, 1971 to 1985	37
3.2	Sales of Ale/Stout and Lager, 1971 to 1985	38
17.1	UK Beer Sales, 1989–2009	195
17.2	Beer Sales in On- and Off-Trade Channels, 1989–2009	196
17.3	Beer Price Indices, 1989–2009, Adjusted for Inflation	197
17.4	Alcohol Consumption by Type of Drink, 1989	198
17.5	Alcohol Consumption by Type of Drink, 2009	199
17.6	Personal Imports of Beer, 1990–2009	202
17.7	Beer Consumption: UK Sales and Personal Imports, 1990–2009	203

Appendix 3.3

1	Beer Consumption 1960–2009	264
2	Beer Consumption 1971–2009 Analysed by Channel of Trade	265
3	Beer Consumption 1960–2009 Analysed by Type of Beer	265
4	Number of Licensed Premises 1960–2004	266

Tables

1.1	UK Alcohol Consumption and Drunkenness in England and Wales	15
6.1	Number of Beer Brands Per Pub/Bar	59
6.2	Minutes Taken to Earn a Pint of Draught Beer in a Pub or Bar	61
6.3	Beer Price Ratios, 1987	62
10.1	National Brewers' Ownership of Full On-licences as at July 1989 and Freeing-up Requirements	122
13.1	Current Status/Ownership of the "Big Six" Brewing Plants Operating in 1987	163
16.1	Average Pub Price of Draught Bitter, Excluding Duty and VAT, Relative to RPIY	185
16.2	Average Pub Price of Draught Lager, Excluding Duty and VAT, Relative to RPIY	185
16.3	Range of Pub Beer Prices Covering 80 per cent of Sample	188

Appendix 3.2

1	Beer Production and Market Shares in 1985 and Pub Ownership at the End of 1988	260
2	National Pub-owning Brewers' Shares of Beer Production in 1985 and Production Facilities as at 30 September 1985	261

3	Numbers of UK Licensed Premises by Type of Licence, 1986	261
4	Beer Consumption and Proportions by Channel of Trade and Beer Type	262
5	Average Price of Draught Bitter in the Public Bars of Managed Houses, Excluding Duty and VAT, Relative to RPI	262
6	Average Number of Beer Brands in Tied and Free Trade Pubs, 1987	263
7	Financial Results of UK Brewers' Beer-related Activities	263

Notes on the Authors

John Spicer has been associated with the drinks industry for most of his career, first as a sales forecasting analyst with Whitbread, and then as a stockbroking analyst covering brewers and distillers. He worked in finance for 18 years, spending the latter half at UBS Warburg, and for nearly a decade he was rated the No. 1 drinks sector analyst in the Extel Annual Survey and the Institutional Investor European Research Survey. In 1993 he served as Special Adviser to the Parliamentary Agriculture Select Committee during its inquiry into the effect of the Beer Orders, and in 2001 as an expert witness in a trial concerning the beer tie, which went all the way to the House of Lords. He now conducts specialist consultancy work.

Chris Thurman MBE joined the Brewers' Society in 1970 to establish a department responsible for economics and statistics. He was fully involved in the Price Commission, the Monopolies and Mergers Commission (MMC) and other official inquiries into brewing, and attended all the Society hearings of the MMC leading up to the 1989 Supply of Beer report. He received an MBE for services to the brewing industry in 1991.

John Walters was a stockbroker, specialising in the drinks and pubs industries, from 1970 until his retirement in 2002. For 13 years leading up to the City's "Big Bang" he was a Member of the Stock Exchange, and at the time of his retirement was a Fellow of the Securities Institute and an Associate of the Society of Investment Professionals. In retirement he has written two editions, for City readers, of a "Directory of UK Brewing and Pub Companies", and has maintained regular contact with former industry leaders.

Simon Ward has spent most of his working life in the drinks and leisure industry, principally with Whitbread, for whom he worked from 1972 until 2001. During this period he served at various times as Strategy Director, Public Affairs Director and a member of the Executive Committee. Subsequently he has been a consultant and Director of Public Affairs for the pub company, Mitchells & Butlers. Simon has extensive experience of working with Whitehall, Westminster and the UK and EU competition authorities, and from 1999 to 2004 he served on the Government's Better Regulation Task Force.

Acknowledgements

The authors gratefully acknowledge the time and assistance willingly provided by the following, who were either involved in or close observers of the events related in this book, and without whose memories, insights and reflections the account of those events would have been much the poorer.

Tim Amsden	Adam Hogg	Tony Portno CBE
Catherine Bell CB	Sir Derrick Holden-Brown	Jeremy Phillips
Mike Benner	Diana Houghton	Sir Ian Prosser
Keith Bott	Martin Howe CB	Hubert Reid
John Brackenbury CBE	Robert Humphreys	Peter Robinson
Tim Bridge	Chris Hutt	Bill Sharp
John Bridgeman CBE	Peter Jarvis CBE	Brigid Simmonds OBE
Stephen Burbridge CB	Alan Jackson	Sir Brian Stewart
Gerry Carroll	Peter Lawrence	Tony Susman
Tim Clarke	Sir Jeremy Lever QC KCMG	Miles Templeman
Stephen Cox	Mark Leverton	Peter Thomas
John Cryne	Hans Liesner	David Thompson
Janet Dooner	Peter Martin	Andy Tighe
Gus Evans	Richard Martin	The late Alan Tilbury CBE
Arthur Fisher	Tim Martin	
Mike Foster	Richard Matthews	David Treacher
Peter Freeman CBE QC	Rt Hon Francis Maude MP	Ted Tuppen CBE
Anthony Fuller CBE		The late Dave Wickett
Barry Gillham	John Melia	Chris Williams
Edward Guinness CVO	Leif Mills CBE	Bernard Wright
Tony Hales CBE	Sir Paul Nicholson	George Yarrow
Jeremy Hardie CBE	John Overton	Bob Young

The authors also wish to place on record their special gratitude to Pat Spicer, who over a long period devoted many hours to reading and rereading the drafts, and whose criticisms and suggestions for improvement have been invaluable. They would like to thank, too, Palgrave Macmillan, and specifically Paul Milner and Virginia Thorp, for their guidance during the writing; Heather Holden-Brown for her technical advice in the early stages of the project; Tony Pratt for his comments on the initial draft; Shirley Tan, of the editorial consultancy firm, EXPO, who dealt rapidly and efficiently with numerous queries arising during the editing process; Anthony Fuller, Rt Hon Francis Maude, Leif Mills, Sir Ian Prosser, Greene King and Kelham Island Brewery for supplying photographs and other visual material for use in the book; and JD Wetherspoon for giving permission for the use of photographs taken by (author) Chris Thurman of The Blue Boar pub in Billericay, Essex. Finally, the authors would like to thank those relatives and friends who selflessly contributed to the beer brands survey by visiting dozens of pubs and sending in reports from around the country, namely, Will Cockburn, Harold Coe, Matt Cox, John Leaviss, Robert Riggall, Philip Shaw, Richard Smith, Amy Walters and Eddie Wilson.

Foreword by Anthony Hilton

The one certainty in business is that things will go wrong. Human beings, programmed by nature for either fight or flight, are not in general good at dealing with complexity, and modern business is nothing if not complex. There is a dangerous tendency in management, which is often even more pronounced in outside agencies like regulators and legislators, to ignore this complexity because it is simply too difficult to deal with. The result is that complex issues get oversimplified so that they can be made easier to solve. Sometimes this works; sometimes it changes behaviour in ways which make the cure worse than the disease. It is rare indeed for things to evolve exactly as expected.

Partly this is because of a second trap lurking for the unwary. Because business is controlled by numbers – the measurement of inputs and outputs, profits and losses – management thinking assumes that businesses are mechanical. But the most important dimension in any business is the people – those working in it, those supplying it, those buying from it – and they are anything but machines. It is impossible to know how these different crowds will react to any given change in their circumstances or environment, but it is seldom exactly as predicted. We would make life simpler for ourselves if for this reason we thought of businesses as biological rather than mechanical. They evolve, rather than grow, and such growth – or change – is better if it is steered and channelled rather than forced.

The great value of this book is the warning it gives of how effectively the law of unintended consequences operates when such lessons are ignored. By copious use of the Freedom of Information Act to access previously unseen government and regulatory archives, by interviewing in depth many of those involved, and by drawing on their own experience and memories as veterans of the brewing industry the authors chart a unique story of what can happen when politics seeks to change the direction of business. It carries the added irony that the events were shaped in the Thatcher era and carried out by some of the most pro-business politicians to have held power in post-War Britain.

The book follows the course of the 1980s Monopolies investigation into the tied house system, whereby brewers sold beer through pubs which they generally owned and which could stock only their products. The regulatory concern was that this appeared to inhibit customer choice. The Monopolies report recommended radical change and this led in turn to the Beer Orders, which sought to loosen the brewers' grip on these outlets, partly by forcing the break-up of the larger pub estates, partly by widening the choice of beers on sale inside.

The point was to give customers more choice and lower prices. Two decades later, however, the brewing operations of all six of the UK's national brewers have been taken over by overseas competitors. In some cases the name survives, as at Whitbread or M & B, but these businesses are high street food and drink specialists and hoteliers, not brewers in any traditional sense.

Many local brewers, which the Monopolies Commission's recommendations were intended to sustain, have instead succumbed to the competitive pressures caused by the freeing-up of the market, with the loss of many of the beers once available across the country. At the same time, pub prices have soared. But the most dramatic result has been the rise of the pubco. Pubs were reorganised into national chains, which led to a concentration of ownership considerably greater than anything the brewers could have contemplated in their wildest dreams. It was the purchasing power of these new giants which forced the brewers to consolidate or die.

The book charts the triumph of theory over practice, experiment over experience, the destruction of an industry, the unpicking of a social fabric based on pubs, and the demise of local brewers as a pillar of business life in small towns across the country. What started as a practical application of economic theory precipitated – or at least accelerated the onset of – a period of unparalleled social and business change, which saw the end of the pub as the unique centre of community life.

Today we face challenges of business structure, particularly in financial services, and calls for reform far greater than anything the brewers ever faced in their day. In banking it may well be that something has to be done to reshape the industry. But this book should be read as a cautionary tale before anyone sets out on that course.

Anthony Hilton
Financial Editor
Evening Standard
London
April, 2011

Timeline

Timeline 1961–2011
From six major UK-owned brewers to four foreign-owned

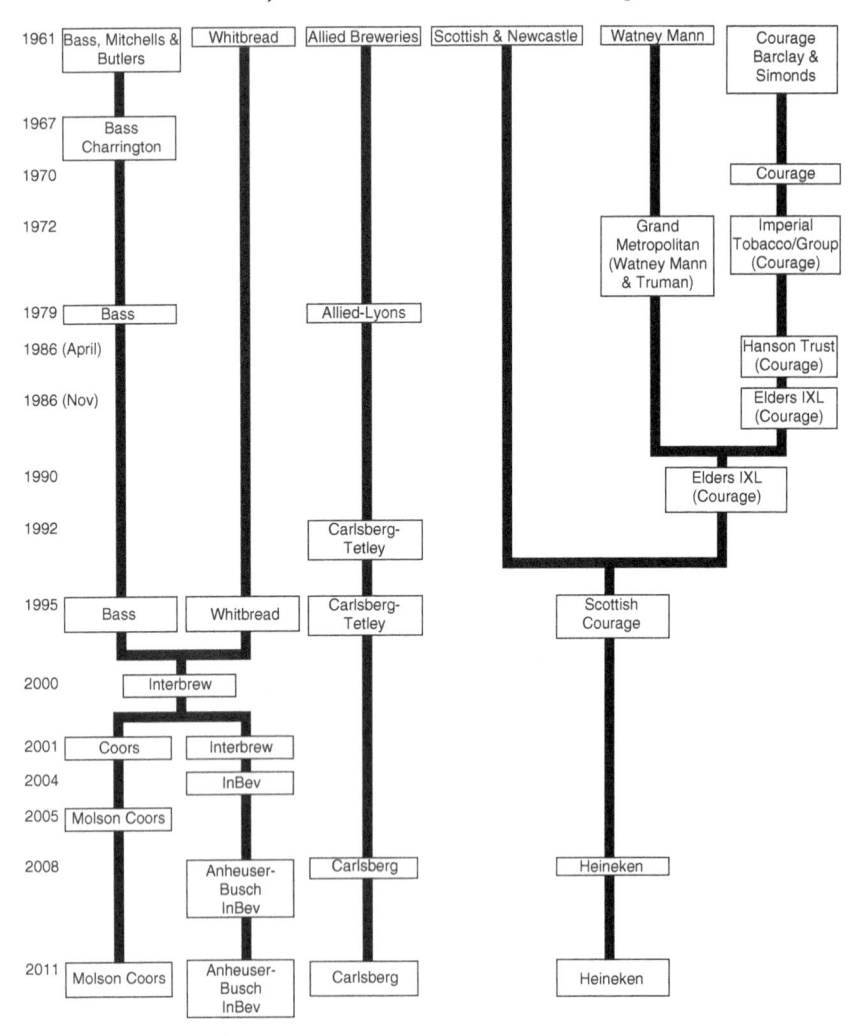

1961	Bass, Mitchells & Butlers	Whitbread	Allied Breweries	Scottish & Newcastle	Watney Mann	Courage Barclay & Simonds
1967	Bass Charrington					
1970						Courage
1972					Grand Metropolitan (Watney Mann & Truman)	Imperial Tobacco/Group (Courage)
1979	Bass		Allied-Lyons			
1986 (April)						Hanson Trust (Courage)
1986 (Nov)						Elders IXL (Courage)
1990						Elders IXL (Courage)
1992			Carlsberg-Tetley			
1995	Bass	Whitbread	Carlsberg-Tetley	Scottish Courage		
2000		Interbrew				
2001	Coors	Interbrew				
2004		InBev				
2005	Molson Coors					
2008		Anheuser-Busch InBev	Carlsberg	Heineken		
2011	Molson Coors	Anheuser-Busch InBev	Carlsberg	Heineken		

Source: Authors' research

Introduction

The seeds of the idea for this book were sown during a conversation early in 2008 between John Spicer and John Walters, two long-serving and retired City drinks analysts, *en route* from London's Waterloo station to the Twickenham rugby ground. The twentieth anniversary of publication of the Monopolies and Mergers Commission (MMC) Report on the brewing industry and the resulting Beer Orders was approaching, and although a number of – mostly learned – papers had been written on the subject, nobody had produced a complete narrative account in business, political and human terms. The idea was mentioned amongst friends, and by the late summer Chris Thurman, erstwhile economist at the Brewers' Society (formerly the industry's trade body), and Simon Ward, who had spent almost his whole career in the brewing industry, mostly at Whitbread, had joined the team. The four had between them accumulated over 120 years of experience of working in or being closely associated with the brewing industry. Chris Thurman had been present at all the Brewers' Society's hearings at the MMC, and Simon Ward had had close and frequent dealings with officials of the UK Government and European Union.

In their research the authors interviewed more than 60 individuals who had been intimately involved in the affair, including two members of the MMC panel that investigated the brewers, former senior industry executives, civil servants, regulators, lawyers, academics, the (then) junior Minister who conducted the post-Report negotiations, licensees' and consumers' representatives, and licensees themselves. Very few requests for interview were denied, and, indeed, a number of interviewees recommended other individuals to speak to. Several remarked that this was a story that must be told. Conversations and events previously unknown to outsiders emerged, and private papers were lent. Archived material and Hansard reports of Parliamentary proceedings were studied and copious amounts of Government documents were obtained through use of the Freedom of Information Act.

The book embraces the great brewery mergers of the 1950s and 1960s, the stream of official investigations into the industry, the genesis of the 1986–89 inquiry, its conduct, the Parliamentary debates and political manoeuvring that followed publication of the Report, and the consequences, both short- and long-term, of the action taken by the Government. The authors believe that the story will be of interest both to lay people and to students of business, economic history, regulation, politics and public policy formulation.

Although few UK industries have been subjected to as much scrutiny by the regulatory authorities as beer and pubs, the official appetite for investigating the pub trade shows no sign of being assuaged, suggesting that the issues and events described here will remain topical. The beginnings of a seemingly unending era of investigation – which is shown in chart form in Appendix 1.2 – can be traced back to 1966, when the National Board for Prices and Incomes (NBPI), in examining costs, prices and profits in brewing, observed that competition in the industry was weak. This led to a major inquiry by the Monopolies Commission (MC), but the latter's well reasoned recommendation when it reported in 1969, namely, that the licensing system should be relaxed, was sidelined by the Government, despite being endorsed in a subsequent official report in respect of England and Wales (by the Erroll Committee). The same year that the MC reported the NBPI took a second look at the industry, and this was followed by four Price Commission probes in the late 1970s, all of them critical of the impact of the industry's structure on competition.

In retrospect, these interventions were mere skirmishes compared with what was to come. Battle was fully joined in 1986, when the Office of Fair Trading (OFT) concluded its own study of the industry by referring it to the Monopolies and Mergers Commission (MMC) for investigation. This was to take two and a half years, and the resulting Report, The Supply of Beer, forms the centrepiece of this book. Its recommendations were seen by many as draconian, and, although diluted by the Government, the resulting so-called Beer Orders, approved by Parliament in 1989, represented an intervention arguably more radical than any in post-nationalisation Britain. But the implementation of the Beer Orders, completed in November 1992, didn't mean that the authorities had lost their appetite for scrutinising the industry. Within months the OFT was on the case again, conducting a confidential review of competition in the new industry structure that was emerging – but taking no action as a result.

In 1995 the European Commission, which had also been taking an interest in the UK beer industry for a number of years, asked the OFT to undertake another review. Brussels then spent much of the rest of the decade ponderously considering arrangements between British brewers and their pub tenants. The OFT returned to the matter yet again in 2000, when it conducted a formal review of the effects of the Beer Orders, as a result of which the Orders were eventually revoked. Meanwhile, during the period 1985–2001 the MMC, and its successor body, the Competition Commission, investigated no fewer than seven proposed transactions involving large UK brewers, with the result that three of them didn't proceed. A further proposed deal was aborted when it was referred to the MMC.

Parliament, too, has been exercised by competition in beer and pubs, and in the 20 years since the MMC's 1989 Report there have been five Select Committee reports involving the industry. Another was planned for 2011. Almost inevitably, given the foregoing multiplicity of investigations, the courts, including the House of Lords and the European Court of Justice, have been obliged to opine on industry competition matters on more than one occasion.

This book attempts to steer a path through the litany of inquiries. But it is first worth examining why there have been so many investigations into an industry in which no one company had ever enjoyed a scale monopoly (defined as a market share of at least 25 per cent) until Scottish & Newcastle acquired Courage in 1995 – a merger which, paradoxically, was waived through without any MMC investigation.

A number of factors contribute to the answer to this conundrum. One important political consideration, at least in decades gone by, was the social and political importance of the price of a pint of beer. Beer has often been described as the "drink of the working man", and acting to exert downward pressure on prices was seen as a vote winner. Nor were attempts to control prices, although perhaps politically motivated, without some economic logic, since for much of the period covered by this book expenditure on beer accounted for some 4 per cent of the basket of goods and services in the Retail Prices Index. Thus the first major post-war inquiry into the industry, by the NBPI, took place when controlling inflation had become an imperative.

At the heart of the competition authorities' long-standing interest in beer and pubs has been the tied house system, in which vertically integrated companies brew beer and own pubs. Under this arrangement, which evolved over generations, brewers let their pubs to tenants, who were obliged, through the "tie", to buy beer, and perhaps other drinks, exclusively from the brewer. In return, the tenant paid a below-market rent. It was a relationship which generally suited the parties well, but it had its critics, and from the 1960s onwards the authorities began to view the tied house system as one that could inhibit competition.

First, they argued, it was difficult, perhaps impossible, for other brewers to sell their beers to pubs tied to another brewer, and, since so many pubs were owned by brewers – 80 per cent of them in 1967 – much of the market was foreclosed. Compounding the problem of access faced by third party suppliers was the brewers' practice of lending money at a soft rate of interest to licensed outlets that they didn't own in exchange for a tie on drinks purchases. The market available to other suppliers was indeed limited. Moreover, the effect of vertical integration went beyond beer, since many brewers had preferred brands of non-beer drinks, such as cider, generally based on ownership or trading agreements.

The difficulties faced by UK and overseas brewers owning few or perhaps no pubs, and by suppliers of non-beer drinks, were for several decades reinforced by the operation of the licensing system. Until relatively recently applications for new licences were considered by local licensing magistrates. They were obliged to take account of the suitability of the applicant and of the premises, but many licensing benches also tried to reach a view on the economic need for a new full on-licence, and thus in effect to second-guess the market: frequently they determined that a new full on-licence wasn't needed and so rejected the application. The need criterion wasn't used in relation to clubs, off-licences or restaurants, and this was reflected in the rapid growth in the number of these outlets. But, for pubs, the way the licensing system was operated acted as a significant barrier to entry, and it wasn't until 2003, a third of a century after the Monopolies Commission had recommended a substantial relaxation of licensing, that the Government took effective action, with the passing of a new Licensing Act.

Two other factors fuelled the authorities' interest in beer. For obvious logistical reasons brewers had historically traded in areas nearest to their breweries, and the consolidation that occurred in the industry in the 1950s and 1960s led to large companies having many local concentrations of pub ownership. In Bristol in 1967, for example, Courage owned 80 per cent of the city's pubs. Second, the suspicions of the regulators were aroused by the way in which vertically integrated brewing companies seemed to pursue very similar trading strategies: apart from some specialist brands, their pubs stocked only their own beers, and they seemed to adopt similar pricing policies. Innovation was unusual.

With the benefit of hindsight, it was probably only to be expected, then, that at some point the Director General of Fair Trading would question the Monopolies Commission's failure in 1969 to recommend effective action against the brewers, and initiate a further inquiry. But despite the fact that the resulting MMC investigation was lengthy and the Report's recommendations wide-ranging and radical, the resulting Beer Orders failed to produce a competitive structure that would satisfy regulators, industry participants and consumers.

Having concluded that a complex monopoly existed in the supply of beer and that this operated against the public interest, the Commission devised what it saw as suitable remedies. The Fair Trading Act 1973 (superseded by the Competition Act 1998) defined a complex monopoly as a situation in which at least 25 per cent of the relevant market was supplied by "two or more persons (not being a group of inter-connected bodies corporate) who, whether, voluntarily or not and whether by agreement or not, so conduct their respective affairs as in any way to prevent, restrict or distort competition". The finding that a complex monopoly existed was by no means unusual in an MMC inquiry, and nor was the conclusion that it operated against the public interest. Thus in 1986, the very year in which the beer inquiry started, the MMC investigated two sectors where it found complex monopoly situations to exist, one in greyhound racing and the other amongst tour operators, and in both instances the Commission believed that the monopoly operated against the public interest. But in both these cases it proposed only modest, non-legislative remedies, such as the strengthening of a voluntary code of practice.

In 1991 the Commission investigated the supply of carbonated drinks, like beer a vertically integrated industry, and, as in the case of beer, it found a complex monopoly to exist, which, it said, operated against the public interest. And, like the panel investigating beer, it considered mandatory asset disposal as a remedy. But, in contrast with that panel, it found this to be too drastic a solution and settled for more moderate remedies.

What makes the 1989 Report on beer so unusual, in fact, is the extent and depth of the changes that it recommended. The proposal – although it was to be heavily modified by the Government – to compel companies to divest legally acquired assets in a situation where none enjoyed a scale monopoly (unlike, for example, in the BAA case in 2009, where the company enjoyed a dominant position in the relevant markets) was possibly unprecedented. So too was the sheer scale of the assets involved, which, as the *Financial Times* pointed out, was easily the biggest that the Commission had recommended in any sector. It was also unusual – as it is now – for retailers, in this case pub owners, to be obliged to permit a product supplied by a competitor to be offered for sale, as was the case as a result of the beer inquiry.

The story of the inquiry into The Supply of Beer – its genesis, its conduct and its consequences – is important not just in its own right but for the wider lessons to be drawn by regulators and politicians. Foremost amongst these lessons are that it is unwise to ignore the law of unintended consequences, and that policy formulated even partly according to political expediency is rarely good policy. Meddling in long established practice carries the risk, perhaps certainty, that events will not turn out altogether as planned and that the results may be not only unwelcome but the opposite of what was sought. Interventionists should therefore tread with caution and humility.

1
The "Big Six" Brewers and the Early Investigations

Decline and consolidation

Prime Minister Harold Macmillan was no doubt right when he told a Conservative party rally in July 1957 that most British people had "never had it so good", and that the country was in "a state of prosperity such as [it had] never had in [his] lifetime". While, however, a nation emerging from post-War austerity was indulging a developing taste for consumer durables and foreign holidays, one UK industry remained in the doldrums: namely, brewing. Thus beer production, which in the last year of the War (12 months to March 1945) amounted to 31.3 million barrels, had by 1950/51 fallen by over 20 per cent, to 24.9 million barrels. It remained at around this level for the next eight years, reaching a nadir in 1958/59 of 23.8 million barrels, down by almost a quarter on 1944/45.

Post-War controls on the supply of materials for the construction or renovation of pubs were not relaxed until the mid-fifties, and run-down bars, together with beer at that time of variable quality, were evidently not greatly to the taste of the newly affluent British consumer. The violent shocks to the "beerage" (a late-19th century slang word conveying the brewers' inherited wealth and political power) which would be administered by Charles Clore, Eddie Taylor and Max Joseph still lay in the future; but even now the brewing industry could not but be aware that doing nothing was not an option, particularly for those companies whose financial and management resources were inadequate to cope with the challenging environment.

The outcome, hastened to some extent by the dilution of family control of companies, was the conventional market solution of industry consolidation, in this case with the aim of taking out excess production capacity and reaping economies of scale through enlarged distribution. Mergers were, of course, nothing new, in brewing as elsewhere, but the pace of amalgamation rose markedly in the brewing sector during the fifties. Thus the number of brewing companies fell by 32 per cent – from 362 to 247 – between 1950 and 1960. What is more, the speed of consolidation was accelerating, with around two-thirds of the 115 brewery mergers and takeovers during the fifties occurring in the second half of the decade. Over the decade as a whole the number of brewing plants fell by 209, from 567 to 358.

It was during this period that the first of the major deals were done that were to lead by the late sixties to the creation of the "big six" integrated brewers and retailers that would dominate the industry for the next 30 years or so. These deals included the acquisition by Courage of Barclay Perkins in 1955; the acquisitions by Ind Coope of Benskin's in 1957 and of Taylor Walker in 1959 (all later to become part of Allied Breweries); and Watney Combe Reid's acquisition of Mann, Crossman & Paulin in 1958, to form Watney Mann (later acquired by Grand Metropolitan Hotels).

Notwithstanding this far-reaching consolidation, attack from without was imminent, and the first major assault on the brewing industry arrived like a bolt out of the blue in the spring of 1959, in the form of a hostile cash bid for a 75 per cent stake in Watney Mann by Charles Clore, who became one of the wealthiest and most powerful British entrepreneurs of the post-War era. During the fifties and sixties he built up a highly successful conglomerate, Sears Holdings, demonstrating during the process a particular skill in identifying underutilised property assets, and it was this that provided the key to his intense interest in Watney Mann.

It is safe to assume that not only the Watney Mann board but the entire industry was deeply perturbed, and that there was – at least in terms of moral support – a closing of the brewing ranks. In fact, the stock market quickly pushed the Watney Mann share price well above the level of Clore's offer and the deal foundered. In the face of what had for years been a stagnating beer market, however, the brewers had now been given a stark warning that they must use their property assets more efficiently or open the way for someone else to do it for them.

Within a year, however, another outsider was to appear on the scene, who would exert considerably more influence than Clore on the development of the UK brewing industry, namely, Eddie Taylor. He was a dynamic Canadian, who had built up the Ontario-based Canadian Breweries and had decided in the early fifties that he would try to sell his Carling Black Label lager in Britain. Concluding after a few years that without a tied estate he would never achieve more than a niche position for a type of beer which was then virtually unknown in this country, he set about building a stake in Hope & Anchor, the tiny Sheffield concern which was brewing Carling. In 1959 he took his stake up to 30 per cent, and then in a whirlwind of dealing acquired during 1960 both Hope & Anchor and a string of small brewers, most of them Scottish, to form United Breweries. This activity precipitated wholesale consolidation in the Scottish brewing industry, culminating within a matter of only months in the creation of Scottish & Newcastle; whilst, both in Scotland and elsewhere, those companies whom

Taylor had approached during his buying spree, or who simply felt vulnerable, hastily sought refuge with a friendly new owner or shareholder.

Not one to let the grass grow under his feet, Taylor then – in 1961 – mounted a hostile bid for Bristol Brewery Georges, which had been formed by merger only five years earlier. Courage, Barclay & Simonds (as it had now become) had for 30 years been picking up brewing companies to the West and South West of its original London base, and it quickly came to the rescue – albeit one undoubtedly based on self-interest – with a counter-offer. Courage's second – and final – offer was almost 60 per cent above the pre-bid level, and helped also by some plausible industrial and commercial arguments, and perhaps by hostility towards someone seen in the conservative world of family brewers as a dangerous intruder, Courage prevailed.

The first steps towards the development of national brewing groups had thus been made, but within weeks a far more important event took place, with the merging, as an unashamedly defensive measure, of Ind Coope – with its bases in Romford and Burton – with the Leeds-based Tetley Walker and Birmingham-based Ansells, to form Ind Coope Tetley Ansells, shortly to be renamed Allied Breweries. Within just another few weeks Bass, Ratcliff & Gretton, of Burton, had merged with the Midlands-based Mitchells & Butlers. In the following year, 1962, yet another major event in the consolidation process took place, with the marriage of the London-based Charrington and Eddie Taylor's United Breweries, to form Charrington United Breweries. The latter then, in 1963, acquired the Scottish lager brewer, J&R Tennent, and finally, in 1967, after a relatively quiet four years in the industry, agreed a merger with Bass, Mitchells & Butlers, to form the UK's largest brewing company, Bass Charrington.

In the meantime, Watney Mann, having escaped Charles Clore's clutches, had in 1960 made three sizeable acquisitions, namely, Phipps & Co., of Northampton, Wilson & Walker, of Manchester, and Ushers, of Trowbridge. Further acquisitions followed during the first half of the sixties, most importantly Steward & Patteson and Bullard & Son, both of Norwich, and Drybrough, of Edinburgh.

Whitbread had already in the mid-fifties taken the first steps in the process which would transform it from London-based regional into one of the "big six" nationals. Its initial strategy was to purchase shareholdings in small companies which felt vulnerable to hostile bids, taking a place on their boards and putting in place reciprocal trading arrangements. Early entrants into what was to become known as the Whitbread "umbrella" included Marston's, Ruddle, Morland and Strong; and these were followed in the sixties by – amongst others – Vaux, Boddingtons, Brakspear, Matthew Brown, Fremlins and Flowers.

These companies saw Whitbread's involvement as providing a degree of protection against hostile bids, and it is generally the case that those of them which traded successfully and wished to remain independent were able to do so. Thus Whitbread famously helped to repulse a bid by Allied Breweries for Boddingtons in 1970. Against this, however, during the sixties Whitbread gobbled up over 20 companies, including Strong, Fremlins, Flowers, J Nimmo and Dutton's.

The consequences of the consolidation that had occurred in ownership and production were quantified in the findings of the Monopolies Commission (MC) investigation into the supply of beer ordered by the Board of Trade in July 1966.[1] [A description of UK legislation relating to competition, price control, licensing and taxation in the brewing industry is provided in Appendix 1.1.] The Commission found that in 1967 the six national integrated brewers and retailers had a combined market share of around 68 per cent, with the non-pub owning Guinness accounting for slightly under 5 per cent. The "big six" were: Allied Breweries; Bass Charrington; Courage, Barclay and Simonds; Scottish & Newcastle Breweries; Watney Mann; and Whitbread. They operated around 70 breweries, representing just 29 per cent of the total – which by now had fallen from 358 in 1960 to 240. Eleven other companies – including such as Greenall Whitley, John Smith's, Truman, Vaux and Wolverhampton & Dudley – accounted for around 14 per cent of production.[2]

The number of pubs owned by all brewers in 1967 was just over 58,000,[3] representing 80 per cent of the country's total pub stock of around 72,400. Of these the "big six" owned 37,340 pubs,[4] around 52 per cent of the total, and in fact, as the MC Report noted, a further 1405 pubs were acquired during 1968 by Bass Charrington and Whitbread,[5] taking the proportion up to about 54 per cent.

One consequence of the rationalisation of production was that delivery runs lengthened significantly, and this played a major role in the promotion of so-called keg beers. These were draught beers which had been conditioned – that is, filtered, pasteurised to halt fermentation, and then carbonated – before delivery. Unlike traditional cask-conditioned beers, they were immediately ready for sale on arrival at the pub (with no requirement to stand and settle), and they had a far longer shelf life than cask.

Inevitably, they had a consistency of appearance and taste – many would say blandness – which at a time when the quality of cask beer was still far from reliable appealed particularly to young consumers. They were successfully marketed as premium products, costing, as the 1969 MC Report found, as much as sixpence (2.5p) a pint more than the same brewer's cask beer – representing, on the basis of the price data collected by the Commission, a premium of more than 25 per cent.[6] And because of these beers' tolerance of travelling they could be distributed nationwide, opening the way for the large-scale development of national draught beer brands (thitherto only bottled beers had enjoyed national distribution – primarily Guinness, Bass and Worthington). Thus product rationalisation followed production rationalisation, countless local brands were abandoned, and unprecedented amounts of money were spent on promoting brands such as Double Diamond from

Allied Breweries, Courage Tavern, Bass Charrington's Worthington E, Scottish & Newcastle's Tartan, Watney's Red Barrel, and Whitbread Tankard.

"The working man's pint"

In February 1965 Harold Wilson's newly elected Labour administration was quick to negotiate a Joint Statement of Intent on incomes and prices with the Trades Union Congress (TUC) and employers' organisations, and in the same month the National Board for Prices and Incomes (NBPI) was established. In September of that year the Government announced an early warning system, under which increases in prices and pay would be pre-notified to the Government for possible examination by the NBPI, during which the proposed increase would be deferred.

During the period 1966–68 Labour pursued a policy of tightly restricting pay and price rises, but, against a deteriorating economic background, in April 1968 legislation was unveiled to freeze wages completely for 12 months. Throughout the first half of 1969 the Government was toiling to enact legislation based on a White Paper introduced by Barbara Castle MP, *In Place of Strife*, which contained proposals for controlling trade union power; but in June it abandoned the project and within days was forced to sign a Letter of Intent to the International Monetary Fund, containing undertakings on public spending and credit control. In December 1969 Labour published its last White Paper on prices and incomes before losing to the Conservatives in the June 1970 Election. It laid down a 2.5–4.5 per cent range for wage increases.

This was, of course, a time when millions of men worked in coal-mining, shipbuilding, steel manufacture, engineering and other strenuous manual occupations, and routinely slaked their thirst in what was known as the public bar, where amenities were inferior to those in other parts of a pub and prices were lower. The widespread perception amongst commentators that Labour politicians of the time regarded "the working man's pint" as sacrosanct was almost certainly true. So it is unsurprising that, against the background of repeated attempts to restrain wages and prices across the whole economy, the brewing industry had received its full share of attention from the NBPI. What would have been considerably more surprising, could it have been known at the time, was that one inquiry would lead to another, and, indeed, that in the remaining three and a half decades of the century there would be only five years during which the brewers, individually or collectively, were not under investigation. [A chart plotting these inquiries is shown in Appendix 1.2.]

For the time being, though, it was the straightforward matter of the cost of a pint of beer that was exercising Ministerial minds. During 1965 a number of brewers had been raising prices, and when proposals by other brewers to follow suit in late 1965 and early 1966 were notified to the Government under the early warning system, the industry was referred to the Board and the proposed price rises deferred, pending the Board's Report. This was the first early warning reference that had been made, and the Board's brief was to examine costs, prices and profits in brewing. It reported in April, and it found that the biggest contributor to increased costs in the industry had been labour costs. It concluded that this couldn't be justified on productivity or competition grounds, and it saw "no justification, at a time when the country is trying to grapple with the wages-prices spiral, for the [brewing] industry's seeking to continue to pass on to the consumer increases in earnings of this magnitude".[7]

The Board made clear that it disapproved of the industry's practice of charging pub tenants a below-market property rent ("dry rent") but higher prices for beer than could be achieved in the free trade ("wet rent"). On the basis of these conventions, the companies covered by the Board's sample had been making a pre-tax return on assets of 33 per cent in brewing and distribution and less than 2 per cent in pub retailing, with the tenanted – as opposed to brewery-managed – pubs actually making a negative return. The Board opined that if – as it recommended – tenants were charged rents and beer prices closer to market levels, the brewers "would have a better guide to the effective use of their assets and would therefore be better equipped to contain rising costs".[8]

The Report concluded that "some pressure should now be put on costs by a check to the movement of prices…that during the next six to nine months there should be no increase in the wholesale price of beer or in its retail price at the public bar except where a company [had] not increased the price of any of its major brands…since 1 January 1964".[9] [Maximum public bar prices in tenanted pubs were at this time set by the brewer, while prices in other bars in the same establishment were set by the licensee.]

This judgment is unlikely to have been well received by the brewers, but should be seen in the context of an imminent general freeze on prices and incomes. What would have seemed more ominous to the industry was the explicit suggestion that the Government might refer the brewers to the Board again if it judged that the aim of tightening pressure on costs in the industry had not been achieved.

Even more significant than this, however, at least in its long-term implications, was the passage in the Report dealing with the industry's structure, as set by the licensing system, which the Board regarded as the fundamental determinant of costs in the industry. At this time licences for new premises were very rarely granted, so that putative new entrants were in the position of needing to obtain outlets for their products from established competitors who had every incentive not to dispose of those outlets. The Board accordingly suggested "that the Government may wish to consider an enquiry into how best it can maintain control over the sale of alcoholic liquor without at the same time impeding the entry of new competitors into the industry".[10]

Stronger criticisms of the tied house system

The Government took the hint, and in July 1966 the Board of Trade referred the industry to the MC. The latter's Report was published on 28 April 1969, and it reiterated the view expressed by the NBPI that competition at retail level was inhibited by the licensing system. It asserted that:

> The implementation of this system of restrictive licensing limits competition. Licensed retail outlets are individually and collectively protected from competition by the restriction on the establishment of new competitors in the licensed trade.[11]

The MC went further than the NBPI, however, in finding unequivocally that within this licensing environment the tied house system – under which pubs owned by brewers (80 per cent of the total) were contracted to purchase their supplies from their brewer-landlord – had a number of disadvantageous effects. It had sustained inefficient brewing capacity; had been detrimental to the creation of rational distribution systems; had hindered the development of independent wholesalers of wines, spirits, and so on, and thus relieved the brewers from any pressure to pass on the benefits of their bargaining power in relation to independent producers and suppliers of such items; had hindered the entry into the industry of new products (other than the brewers' own); and had created a situation where price competition at the retail level was almost non-existent.[12] Thus was a light put to a slow-burning fuse.

The Commissioners asked themselves whether there were "practicable alternative arrangements *within the framework of restrictive licensing* [authors' italics] which would remove the defects of the existing tied house system without creating counter-balancing disadvantages".[13] And it is interesting, in the light of what was to happen 20 years later, to read their reasons for dismissing the various options they identified.[14] First, they considered requiring the brewers to dispose of their pubs; but while expressing their approval for such a change, concluded that the consequential problems would be "so serious"[15] that they couldn't recommend such a course. These problems were that the cost of formulating, implementing and policing the change would be high; the consumer would suffer from the withdrawal of the brewers' expertise in operating pubs and by the interruptions to service at a local level; and the property market would be dislocated by the large-scale disposal of brewers' pub estates. Albeit only in a footnote, the Commissioners also presciently mentioned the possible development of supply agreements between brewers and the new owners of their pubs.

Next, the possibility of allowing brewer-ownership but without a tie was mooted, but not regarded as a realistic remedy, on the grounds that brewers would simply install co-operative tenants, or remove the tenants and install their own managers.

The idea of prohibiting the tie on products other than beer – or even just draught beer – was considered, but dismissed, largely because it could be circumvented in the same way as the complete removal of the tie, but also because, given the preponderance of beer in pub sales, it wouldn't go far in remedying the adverse effects of the tied house system.

Finally, the Commissioners considered the question of "wet rent", condemned by the NBPI in 1966, and which they saw as a disincentive to retail competition in pubs. Somewhat wearily, one imagines, they concluded that prohibiting "wet rent" would on its own produce a negligible advantage, and, again, could be countered by conversions from pub tenancy to management – unless this, too, were prohibited.

Thus it was judged that as long as the current licensing framework existed, no practicable and acceptable remedy would be found to the problems inherent in the tied house system, and consideration must therefore be given to modifying the licensing system itself.[16] Referring to the social objectives of the current system, the Report pointed out that restricting the number of pubs didn't appear to have inhibited excessive drinking; and, furthermore, that the prevailing practice of granting full on-licences only to pubs, rather than to catering establishments, hardly seemed likely to discourage excessive drinking either.[17]

Expanding on this theme, the Commissioners raised the possibilities of flexible opening hours and allowing children in pubs, and suggested that local authorities rather than justices should administer licensing. It speculated that easier availability of full on-licences would result in the free trade – consisting of licensed premises not owned by brewers – growing at the expense of the tied trade, with consequent downward pressure on wholesale beer prices, the elimination of excess brewing capacity and inefficient brewers, the entry of new participants into the brewing industry, and the development of a stronger independent wholesaling sector in wines, spirits, and mineral waters. There could well be some growth in independent pub chains. If demand developed for drinking on premises other than pubs, the proposed relaxation would lead to the establishment of new catering premises and to the sale of drinks in entertainment outlets. The retail trade would become more differentiated in terms of its amenities and prices, and pubs would have to adapt to compete. Thus the merits of the tied house system "would be exposed to the test of the market".[18]

The Report concluded as follows:

> We recommend that, by way of remedy for the defects which we have found in the tied house system in the UK, the licensing system in England

and Wales should be substantially relaxed, the general objective being to permit the sale of alcoholic drinks, for on or off consumption, by any retailer whose character and premises satisfy certain minimum standards.[19]

It was noted in the Report that 86 per cent of full on-licences in England and Wales were brewer-owned, compared with 27 per cent in Scotland, so that it was particularly in the former two countries that the tied system operated against the public interest and that a remedy was required. Brewer-ownership in Scotland had been rising, however, and if this trend were to continue, the authorities would – the Commissioners assumed – conduct a separate review.

Shortly after the MC had reported, the President of the Board of Trade, Anthony Crosland MP, told Parliament that the Commission had made a strong case on economic grounds for relaxing the constraints on competition inherent in the tied house system, but that the far-reaching nature of its proposed remedy required a thorough examination of the social implications. The Government would discuss this question with the brewers, and might consider whether anything else could be done to mitigate the undesirable features of the tied house system. Nothing further was heard from the Government on the subject, however, until December 1970 (by which time a Conservative administration had been in power for six months).

Price increases blocked for over three years

In the meantime, against the background of the Labour Government's anti-inflationary policies the standstill on public bar beer prices which the NBPI had recommended in 1966 for "six to nine months" had proved remarkably durable. Indeed, it was still in place in September 1968, at which point the Government held talks with the brewers resulting in the latter agreeing to hold prices for yet a further 12 months. Just seven months later, however, in April 1969 – the same month in which the MC Report was published – the industry was again referred to the NBPI, which was asked to examine brewers' costs, prices and margins, with special regard to return on capital and the industry's ability to finance investment. The resulting Report was published in November 1969. (Although the anniversary of the further 12-month price freeze on beer which had been agreed in September 1968 had by then passed, the brewers assented to the arrangement continuing in force till after the NBPI Report had been published.)

As the Report starkly pointed out, the continuing operation of the early warning system in respect of price rises, together with the September 1968 agreement, meant that both wholesale prices and public bar prices of beer had effectively been controlled by the Government. Moreover, as far as the larger brewers were concerned, prices hadn't been increased since July 1966 – over three years earlier.

In the brewers' submission to the NBPI they had sought increases of 1.5 old (pre-decimal) pennies (equivalent to 0.625p) per pint on the wholesale price and a further 2 old pennies (0.833p) at the retail level, a total increase to the public bar customer of 3.5 old pennies (1.46p). In most parts of the country a pint of beer in 1967 had cost the equivalent of a little over 9p, so, given that beer duty at the time was around 4p a pint, the ex-duty increase that was being sought – moreover, against an increase in the Retail Prices Index between 1966 and 1969 of just 13 per cent – could fairly be described as very substantial.

The authors of the 1969 NBPI Report were frank in their assessment of their difficulty in reaching a conclusion in the context of the industry's return on capital and its ability to finance investment. "We cannot...identify a precise rate of return on either [pub] retailing or brewing",[20] they stated in their Conclusions and Recommendations, going on to say that it was "difficult to put a figure to the amount of necessary investment"[21] in the industry. They pointed out, however, that available data showed that pub tenants were investing more than their income in their pubs, and that if their rents were raised to a market level, the shortfall would be even greater. From this they inferred that retail margins were insufficient to finance pub investment, and that – as had been found in the 1966 Report – the return on retailing was lower than that on brewing. The Report also accepted, however, that production costs had risen, that its sample of brewing companies had a cash deficiency, and that in the absence of a price increase these companies' long-term investment plans would cause the deficiency to grow.

The recommendation was that wholesale beer prices should be allowed to rise by 0.67 old pennies (0.28p), slightly under half of what the brewers had asked for; and the retail margin in the public bar by 1.33 old pennies (0.55p), which was two-thirds of the figure requested. Thus public bar prices were allowed to rise by 2 old pennies (equivalent to slightly more than 0.8p), which was just over half of what had been requested. On the day the Report was published the Agriculture Minister announced that the Government accepted its recommendations, and said that brewers and licensees had given an assurance that for the next 12 months there would be no further rise in public bar beer prices and that restraint would be exercised in respect of beer prices in other bars.

Brewers' four-point action plan

Following Crosland's statement in the Commons in May 1969, in the wake of publication of the MC Report, officials from the Board of Trade – which was shortly to be assimilated into a newly formed Department of Trade and

Industry – held detailed negotiations with the industry's representative body, the Brewers' Society, with the aim of identifying ways of addressing the detriments that the 1969 Report had identified. [All but the very smallest brewers qualified for full membership of the Brewers' Society and were represented on the Council. Policy was formulated, for approval by the Council, by committees, the most important of which was the Executive Committee. In 1994 the Society became the Brewers & Licensed Retailers Association and in 2001 the British Beer & Pub Association.]

The discussions with the Brewers' Society continued after the change of government in June 1970, and culminated in the publication on 1 December of a statement by the Society. The latter felt justified in pointing out, first, that the MC had made only one recommendation, namely, that the licensing laws should be substantially relaxed; and, moreover, that the MC had said that the disadvantages of any alternative arrangements to the tied house system would outbalance the advantages. The Society said that it had nevertheless been considering options to widen choice within tied pubs, and it listed four action points.

First, the Society had recommended to all its members that brewers should make available throughout their tied estates all wines, spirits and minerals for which there was a reasonable demand, at a price no higher than their normal free trade prices. And if a brewer was unwilling to supply a given brand, the tenant could purchase it elsewhere. This recommendation applied also to cider, except in the case of small brewers who had significant cider interests of their own.

Next, the Society had secured the agreement of its members and the pub trade for the granting of longer tenancy agreements.

In response to the Government's concern about local concentrations of pubs owned by one brewer, the Society would provide the Minister with information on the matter and submit proposals to provide wider consumer choice in such places at an early date. (The 1969 MC Report had touched on this subject, quoting figures that showed that Courage owned over 80 per cent of Bristol pubs and that Allied Breweries and Bass Charrington owned, respectively, 38 per cent and 52 per cent of Birmingham pubs.[22])

Finally, the Society had conducted a survey of all licensed premises voluntarily disposed of by its members over the previous three years, and was considering recommending to its members that, when disposing of licensed premises, they should not impose any covenant which would prevent their use as licensed premises in the future.

It should be noted that the only one of these four matters on which the brewers had actually reached agreement – longer tenancies – had no implications for the point which the statement purported to address, namely, consumer choice. Moreover, of the two most important issues covered in the statement, namely, the weakening of the tie in respect of non-beer beverages and local concentrations of pub ownership, the first was no more than the subject of a recommendation; while the second was evidently only starting to be addressed. And the abolition of restrictive covenants wasn't even a recommendation, but merely something in respect of which a recommendation was being considered. [Such a recommendation was in fact issued in 1972, and in 1983 the Brewers' Society estimated that restrictive covenants were down to only 2–3 per cent of pub sales.]

A week after publication of the above statement the Secretary of State for Trade and Industry, Nicholas Ridley MP, expressed to the Commons his concern about local concentrations. He reported that the Brewers' Society had informed him that it was conducting a study of the matter, and he warned that further action could be taken if he wasn't satisfied with the rate of progress. The Society promptly instructed a firm of industrial consultants, Merrett Cyriax, to conduct an investigation, and they presented their findings in February 1971.

The consultants limited their research to Local Authority Administrative Areas in England and Wales (local concentration not being an issue in Scotland and Northern Ireland) with a population of at least 100,000, of which there were 56. They defined concentration as a situation where a brewer produced 50 per cent of locally sold beer, and they calculated that to reach this market share a brewer would need to own 69 per cent of local pubs. Using this methodology, they identified five areas of local concentration, namely, Bristol (Courage), Ipswich (Tollemache & Cobbold), Northampton and Norwich (both Watney Mann) and St. Helens (Greenall Whitley). In aggregate, the four brewers mentioned owned 853 pubs in these five areas. At the time there were around 63,000 public houses in England and Wales.

In December 1970 Courage and Truman had already done an exchange deal involving 109 pubs, and then in September 1971 Courage exchanged 68 of its Bristol pubs for 85 Watney pubs, including 60 in Northampton and Norwich. But apart from a handful of very small exchanges and outright sales during 1971 and 1972, little came of the Brewers' Society's undertaking in the third point of its December 1970 statement. Ridley doesn't seem to have regarded 69 per cent of local pubs owned by one brewer as an unreasonably high proportion by which to judge whether a concentration existed, and, whether or not he was ever satisfied with the rate of progress in reducing local concentrations, the issue went away – at least for a few years.

The Erroll and Clayson Reports

On the same day that Ridley was raising his concern over concentrations of pub ownership, that is, on 8 December 1970, the Home Secretary, Reginald Maudling MP, reacting to the recommendation in the MC Report that the licensing system be substantially relaxed, announced his proposal to appoint a committee to review the liquor licensing laws of England and Wales. Known as the Departmental Committee on Liquor Licensing, it would examine the social implications of the MC's recommendation, and its Chairman would be Lord Erroll. The same day, the Secretary of State for Scotland announced that a Departmental Committee on Scottish Licensing Law would be appointed to review the situation in Scotland, and that this would be chaired by Dr. Christopher Clayson.

The Erroll Committee was appointed on 1 April 1971, and its Report was published in December 1972. It dealt with three broad aspects of licensing law, namely, the granting of licences to sell alcoholic drinks; opening hours of licensed premises; and the admission to licensed premises of young people and children.

The first of these was clearly the most important as far as the MC's conclusion relating to restricted competition was concerned, and Erroll adopted a radical line, trenchantly criticising the "need" criterion, by which many licensing magistrates, without any legal requirement to do so, had routinely judged – and frequently rejected – applications for new full on-licences. The Report asserted

> the application of the test of 'need' to new applications for on-licences is out of date and unnecessary. 'Need' itself is a meaningless expression which has little or no commercial or economic significance. In our view, the only relevant commercial consideration is that of market demand. A licensing authority is hardly qualified to assess whether such a demand exists, and we see no reason why any licensing process should interfere with the ordinary operation of market forces.[23]

Instead of on the basis of "need", the Erroll Report recommended that licences should be granted or refused simply according to the fitness of the applicant and the premises, and the implications for public order and the local environment.

The Brewers' Society and the pub trade suggested that such a change would lead to a proliferation of licensed outlets and a lowering of standards, but Erroll rebutted this. It was also argued, as it had been at the time of the 1969 MC report, that abandoning the "need" criterion could cause a reduction in pub values. Erroll's stern response to this was broadly the same as that of the MC, namely, that the Committee saw no reason why its conclusions "should be influenced by the need to maintain property values which in effect stem from the semi-monopolistic privileges conferred by the present licensing law".[24]

Having thus dealt with the issue that had principally been in the minds of the 1969 Commissioners, the Erroll Committee turned to the subjects of opening hours and the admission of children to pubs, and in both cases recommended modest and controlled liberalisation. In conclusion, and in words redolent of the MC in 1969, the Erroll Report asserted that in the short term its proposals would encourage the development of new forms of catering and the provision of bar facilities in leisure outlets other than pubs; and that in the medium term they would stimulate the growth of the free trade. It added that its proposals didn't pose a threat to the traditional pub.

The Clayson Committee was appointed the day after the Erroll Committee, but it didn't present its findings till several months after Erroll had reported, namely, in June 1973, and the Report wasn't published until August. Clayson examined broadly the same issues as Erroll, and rejected the "need" test just as firmly, asserting that it was no job of licensing authorities to safeguard against a decline in the condition or conduct of licensed premises which the licensed trade had argued would result from abandoning the concept of "need". The Committee also echoed Erroll in flatly rejecting the idea that a licensing authority was qualified to assess whether a demand existed for any proposed new licensed premises. And it was sceptical of the idea that an increase in the number of licensed premises might harm the moral and social well-being of the community. Using almost precisely the same words as Erroll had used, Clayson recommended that licensing decisions be made on the basis of the fitness of the applicant and the premises and with regard to the implications for the locality. In addition, and like Erroll, he proposed a measure of liberalisation in terms of permitted pub opening hours and children in pubs (though he drew the line at Erroll's suggestion that the drinking age in pubs should be reduced from 18 to 17).

Clayson's principal recommendations were embodied in the Licensing (Scotland) Act 1976, and the longer opening hours were introduced in December. The story in relation to Erroll could hardly be more different. Roy Jenkins MP, Home Secretary of the Labour Government that had been elected in 1974, told the Commons in March 1975 that the Erroll Committee had made "a number of useful recommendations for rationalising and simplifying licensing procedures which [he] should expect to be relatively non-controversial",[25] but he indicated that giving effect to them was not a high priority. Which specific recommendations he had in mind isn't clear, but it is the case that the issue which addressed competition – no requirement to demonstrate "need" – was immediately conflated in the minds of most politicians and interest groups with the questions of opening hours and young people. And this was to prove fatal to Erroll's recommendations.

In April 1977, four months after most of Clayson's recommendations had been enacted, the junior Minister in the Home Office, Dr. Shirley Summerskill MP, told the Commons that the Government had not yet completed its consideration of the Erroll Report, and for almost ten years thereafter questions were sporadically asked in Parliament as to the intentions of the government of the day – either Labour or Conservative – with regard to Erroll. During this period the reasons for non-implementation of the Report were increasingly made clear. Thus in January 1982, in answer to a specific question on the matter, Timothy Raison MP, Minister of State at the Home Office, referred to "a good deal of concern about the extent of heavy drinking, particularly among the young".[26]

Such concern is to some extent understandable in the light of the figures in Table 1.1, which show alcohol consumption growing by 9 per cent in the first half of the sixties, 15 per cent in the second half, and 27 per cent in the first half of the seventies, a cumulative increase between 1960 and 1975 of 58 per cent. Offences of drunkenness in the same period had risen by 53 per cent. Disconcerting as these statistics must have been, it is interesting to note that the drunkenness statistics for Scotland (not included in the table) showed a much bigger rise between 1960 and 1975, namely, one of 76 per cent. In other words, the Government's self-contradictory view seems to have been that the alcohol problem was a reason for not reforming licensing; but the greater was the alcohol problem, the more pressing was the need for reform.

Table 1.1 UK Alcohol Consumption and Drunkenness in England and Wales

Year	LPA* per head of UK population aged 15 and over	Drunkenness offenders in England and Wales
1960	5.7	68,109
1965	6.2	72,980
1970	7.1	82,374
1975	9.0	104,452
1980	9.4	122,259
1981	9.0	108,591
1982	8.7	107,326
1983	8.9	109,724
1984	9.0	90,300
1985	9.1	82,785

*Litres of Pure Alcohol. The factors used to convert volumes of different alcoholic drinks to their pure alcohol equivalent are shown in the British Beer & Pub Association *Statistical Handbook*. This series of statistics is not available in respect of the separate countries of the UK.
Source: British Beer & Pub Association, *Statistical Handbook*.

As Table 1.1 shows, both average alcohol consumption and cases of drunkenness fell in both 1981 and 1982. And in 1983 the Brewing Sector Working Group of the National Economic Development Council published a report in which it expressed its concern about the declining importance of pubs in the beer market and recommended that the Government should consider legislation along the lines of Erroll's proposals in respect of opening hours. Ministers were unmoved, however, and in December 1983 David

Mellor MP, Conservative Under-Secretary of State at the Home Office, reiterated the official view. He said that successive governments had refrained from implementing Erroll's recommendation concerning the "need" criterion on the grounds that it would lead to a proliferation of new licences, thus exacerbating the problem of alcohol misuse – much as the brewers and publicans had unsuccessfully urged on Erroll. But he also expressed the Government's concerns in relation to Erroll's recommendations on opening hours and young people, and it was around these issues that the arguments for and against were mainly deployed in the 15 years following the Report.

In the end, the strength of the medical and anti-alcohol lobbies, the 1976 Blennerhassett Report on the drink/driving laws, and the considerable differences of opinion within Parliament itself, combined to produce inertia amongst ministers. MPs continued right into the mid-eighties to point to the success of the Clayson recommendations in Scotland, where recorded cases of drunkenness fell between 1976, the last year before liberalisation, and 1985 by an astonishing 64 per cent, compared with a 24 per cent decline in England and Wales. MPs also cited the damage being done to the tourist industry in England and Wales by restricted opening hours, the extra employment that would be generated by longer hours, and the plight of children left outside pubs. The Conservative Government, however, like its Labour predecessor, proved impervious to all such argument, and the name of Erroll gradually ceased to be mentioned.

Notes

1. Monopolies Commission (MC), *Beer: A Report on the Supply of Beer*, HC 216 (1969).
2. *Ibid.*, paras. 14–15.
3. *Ibid.*, Table XVII.
4. *Ibid.*, Table XXI.
5. *Ibid.*, Table XXI, footnote (a).
6. *Ibid.*, para. 23 and Table VIII.
7. National Board for Prices and Incomes (NBPI), Report No 13, *Costs, Prices and Profits in the Brewing Industry*, Cmnd. 2965 (1966), para. 53.
8. *Ibid.*, para. 42.
9. *Ibid.*, para. 57.
10. *Ibid.*, para. 56.
11. MC, *Beer: A Report on the Supply of Beer*, HC 216 (1969), para. 340.
12. *Ibid.*, para. 393.
13. *Ibid.*, para. 397.
14. *Ibid.*, paras. 400–5.
15. *Ibid.*, para. 401.
16. *Ibid.*, para. 406.
17. *Ibid.*, para. 409.
18. *Ibid.*, paras. 411–12.
19. *Ibid.*, para. 416.

20 NBPI, Report No. 136, *Beer Prices*, Cmnd. 4227 (1969), para. 71.
21 *Ibid.*, para. 72.
22 MC, *Beer: A Report on the Supply of Beer*, HC 216 (1969), para. 176.
23 *Report of the Departmental Committee on Liquor Licensing*, Cmnd. 5154 (1972), para. 8.34.
24 *Ibid.*, para. 8.36.
25 HC Deb 10 March 1975, Vol. 888, cc5–6W.
26 HC Deb 21 January 1982, Vol. 16, c397.

2
Milestones on the Road to a Monopoly Reference

The Price Commission and pub swaps

In November 1970 the new Conservative Government had announced the winding-up of the National Board for Prices and Incomes (NBPI), indicating that it intended to rely on the market to determine prices and incomes. Almost precisely two years later, however, faced with the failure of its attempt to reach a voluntary agreement with the Trades Union Congress and Confederation of British Industry on fighting inflation, it performed a notable U-turn, and introduced the Counter-Inflation (Temporary Provisions) Bill, under which most prices, pay, rents and dividends would be subject to a 90-day freeze. This was followed in mid-January 1973 by a fully fledged Counter-Inflation Bill, which would lead to the establishment on 1 March of a Pay Board and a Price Commission (PC).

Barely a year later, however, Prime Minister Edward Heath, confronted with the prospect of a second coal miners' strike in three years, called an Election. Although not gaining an overall majority, Labour emerged as the largest single party, leading the Queen to invite Harold Wilson in March 1974 to form a government. In the autumn Wilson called another Election, winning an overall Commons majority of three. The PC continued to function under Labour for two and a half years, with only minor tinkering by the Government, but in July 1977 its powers were significantly amended with the passing of the Price Commission Act.

Until then the Commission had been a blunt instrument, operating according to rigid rules, which were undiscriminating in their application and arbitrary in their effect, and were based on companies' historic pricing policy, with no regard to the merit of that policy. As Roy Hattersley MP, Secretary of State for Prices and Consumer Protection, succinctly put it when introducing the second reading of the Bill in April 1977, "Within the rules every price increase is permissible. Outside them no price increase is permissible."[1] The effect had been in some cases almost to institutionalise inflation, as businesses exploited the rules to the maximum. Certainly, some beer prices had been going up at three-monthly intervals – against the background, it should be borne in mind, however, of a rise in the Retail Prices Index (RPI) between 1973 and 1976 of 68 per cent.

In February 1977, a few months before the Price Commission Act was passed, the Secretary of State had instructed the Commission to report on prices and margins in brewing, and then in March he extended the terms of reference to include margins in retail businesses licensed to sell beer. The Brewers' Society immediately responded with a press release pointing out – *inter alia* – that every price rise in the industry since 1973 had been notified to and examined by the PC, and that it was "ludicrous for it to be argued that there [was] a case for referring the industry's prices to the very Commission which [had] approved them – unless there is some political motive".[2]

In response, the Commissioners investigating the case pointed out in their Report, submitted to the Minister in late July, that "The fact that a company's prices conform with the Code and that its profits are within its reference level means no more than it has complied with the Code. It expresses no view on the reasonableness or otherwise of either its prices or its profits."[3] The authors of the Report added that "the brewers started with a higher level of profits than industry generally and [had] succeeded in maintaining the level of their profits during the period of price control better than almost any other major sector".[4]

In the end, however, the Commission could unearth nothing to justify claims that brewers' prices were unreasonable. Indeed, its main finding was that between June 1974 and June 1977 ex-duty beer prices at both wholesale and retail levels had risen less than prices generally. It didn't seem to approve, however, of variations in prices between different pubs and regions, asserting that "Where unusually high prices or price rises occur, it is no comfort to the customer to tell him that on average prices have not increased unreasonably."[5] As for the premium price of lager, the Commission concluded that brewers were charging what the market would bear, though whether or not it approved of this practice wasn't said.

The Commission then, however, went outside its terms of reference, and, like the NBPI in 1966, took it upon itself to express its disapproval of the industry's structure, as follows:

> The combined effect of high concentration and vertical integration has enabled the brewers to exert a high degree of price leadership and to augment the barrier to entering the industry imposed by restrictive licensing laws. Their direct control of prices in their managed houses has been reinforced by contractual arrangements with their tenants, which broadly restrict the tenants' access to other wholesalers and therefore limit their ability to compete with managed houses on sales of wines,

spirits, soft drinks and packaged beers. The effect of price leadership by managed pubs has been to lead prices up.[6]

High concentration within the brewing industry, significant barriers to entry and the virtual absence of competition from imports, the authors continued, were "the classic conditions for a monopoly which is likely to operate to the detriment of consumers".[7] The Government, it concluded, must answer the question of whether the present situation was in the public interest.

In September the Brewers' Society issued an extremely critical response to the PC Report, pointing out that the latter had gone beyond its terms of reference; that its analysis of returns on capital was "incomplete and inconclusive and, at least in part, without factual support";[8] and that it had ignored a sizeable part of the beer market, namely, clubs and off-licences, as well as the steady decline in the number of tied outlets and the steps being taken to reduce local monopolies. The Society noted that the Commission had omitted information which it had requested from and had been provided with by the industry, and that "what is omitted is generally favourable to the industry's case and unhelpful to that being made by the Price Commission".[9]

But as far as the immediate issue of prices and margins was concerned, there was apparently no case to answer and little to be said. Nevertheless, Hattersley, accompanied by John Silkin MP, Minister of Agriculture, Fisheries and Food, met a high-powered delegation from the Brewers' Society on 16 December 1977 to discuss the Report. Both sides agreed that quarterly price rises were undesirable, but the brewers said that these had been due primarily to the operation of the old Price Code. And they warned that with many beer prices not having been raised for between six and nine months, further applications for increases were likely in the near future. The Government side confirmed that such applications would be for the PC to judge on their merits, without interference.

The Ministers weren't willing to leave it at that, however, and a predictable exchange of views on the industry's structure was entered into. Thus the PC's conclusions on this subject were reiterated, and the issue of local monopolies of brewer-owned pubs (something which had lain dormant since the start of the decade and which the PC Report hadn't actually mentioned) was also raised. Hattersley also warned that the Government was unlikely to look favourably upon future merger proposals in brewing. For their part, the brewers restated the PC's finding that beer had risen less in price than the RPI and was cheaper in tied houses than in free houses. Furthermore, it was cheaper than in most other countries. The major reason for all this was efficiency in distribution, and if the tied system went, this advantage would be lost and prices would rise.

Further discussions would take place between brewers and Ministry officials, but the entrenched views of the two sides were clearly enough illustrated in their separate press releases following these talks. Thus Hattersley expressed the hope "that *the changes the Government looked forward to seeing in the industry* [authors' italics] could be brought about"[10] as a result of the planned discussions; while the brewers, for their part, "welcomed the opportunity to explore the issues *with a view to achieving a better understanding by Government of the operations of the brewing industry*"[11] [authors' italics]. It seemed fairly clear that the *status quo* was still at stake.

Hattersley had told the Brewers' Society representatives that if the brewing industry would like to submit its reasons for claiming that the tied house system operated in consumers' interests and encouraged competition, Ministers would be prepared to consider those reasons. The Brewers' Society duly set out the industry's case in an internal note, "The Tied House System", in April 1978. The note pointed out again that the tied system enabled brewers to obtain substantial economies in both production and distribution, and that no inquiry into the industry had produced any evidence to suggest that these benefits were not passed on to the consumer. In addition, consumers benefited from the fact that brewers had a strong incentive both to spend heavily on pub amenities and to ensure that high standards of cleanliness, service, observance of the licensing laws and acceptable standards of conduct were maintained. Further, licensees with a company behind them were better placed than independent businessmen to resist protection racketeers and other undesirables.

The note went on to assert that the security provided to brewers by the tie enabled them to open pubs in new housing estates well ahead of the development of full economic demand, and to keep open remote pubs which were viable only by virtue of their proximity to their owners' delivery routes and the marginal turnover they provided. The tie also allowed brewers to let pubs at rents which would be unacceptable to property companies, and yet provide their tenants with free technical, management and financial advice, thus enabling tens of thousands of small businessmen with little capital to run their own enterprise.

As for competition, the Society first pointed out that the proportion of full on-licences owned by brewers had fallen from 78 per cent in 1967 to 69 per cent in 1976, whilst the proportion of beer sold in brewery-owned outlets had dropped from 66 per cent to 56 per cent. The declines in these tied proportions reflected, the note said, both the more active management of brewers' tied estates and a more liberal attitude towards the granting of new licences. Thus free houses had risen in number by 40 per cent between 1967 and 1976, and licensed and registered clubs by almost 17 per cent, while the number of "Restricted" on-licences (such as restaurants) had more than doubled. Pubs competed locally, on the basis of the "package" of drink and amenity that they offered, not only with other pubs, but with the free on-trade – including clubs in many areas – and with take-home. Overall, the Brewers' Society felt justified in pointing out that the planned, gradual and evolutionary nature of the changes that had been occurring meant that the situation envisaged by the Monopolies Commission in 1969 was being achieved without harming the traditional British pub or losing the economic benefits of the tied house system.

The tone of the remainder of the brewers' defence of the tie was one of willing cooperation. Yes, there was still an issue with local concentrations of pub ownership, but the Society note pointed out that about 400 pubs had been exchanged in the period 1969–76 and that in September of the previous year a total of 437 outlets had changed hands in a tripartite transaction involving Allied Breweries, Bass Charrington and Courage. The difficulties associated with pub exchanges were outlined, and readers who remember the anarchic state of UK industrial relations in the seventies will not be surprised to learn that the industry advanced as a legitimate consideration the fact that draymen had gone on strike against one proposed exchange. The Society nevertheless recognised the need to continue to improve competition in this way, and would put forward specific proposals to tackle the issue within six months.

On another matter raised by Ministers, the widening of choice within outlets, the note argued that there were many difficulties involved in admitting other brewers' draught ales into pubs, but stated that brewers accounting for 75 per cent of brewer-owned pubs had agreed to explore this possibility. As for the request from some tenants that they should be allowed to buy from elsewhere in the event of a strike halting supplies, the Society warned that its members' trade unions wouldn't allow industrial action to be undermined in this way. Even addressed to a Labour Government, such an argument seems unlikely to have been received with much sympathy.

Hattersley and Silkin met with the brewers on 2 May 1978 to formalise agreement on the various matters that had been discussed over the previous four months, and later that day Hattersley reported back to the Commons. He said that the discussions had been conducted "in a co-operative and constructive atmosphere, which [offered] a promising basis for the future relationship between the Government and the industry".[12] And his warning in December that the Government was unlikely to look favourably on future brewery merger proposals had by now transmogrified into the rather less hawkish statement that such proposals would be examined "with particular care".[13] In retrospect, this seems to have been the high point in Government/brewer relations – and under a Labour Administration.

The industry still had to deliver, however, and the results of its investigations into pub and draught ale exchanges were set out in a confidential paper in October.[14] As in the 1971 analysis of local concentrations, each Local Authority Administrative Area with a population of 100,000 was examined. Whereas, however, in the earlier report concentration had been defined as a situation where one brewer was responsible for 50 per cent or more of total beer in that locality, which was taken to imply 69 per cent ownership of local pubs, the criteria used now were 35 per cent of beer sales and 50 per cent pub ownership. The adoption of these latter numbers obviously put a greater onus on the industry, but was more likely to be acceptable to Ministers.

Eighteen areas of the country were identified as having an excessive concentration of ownership, 11 of which were dominated by a major brewer, six by a regional, and one by a small (unnamed) local brewer with all its pubs in the vicinity of the brewery, which the Brewers' Society didn't accept as amounting to an undue concentration. The named companies included Allied Breweries, Bass Charrington, Scottish & Newcastle, Watney Mann & Truman and Whitbread – in fact, all of the "big six" integrated brewers apart from Courage. The note restated the difficulties involved in pub exchanges, the most serious of which were likely to be in the field of industrial relations. The major companies which had been named would, however, take "all feasible steps"[15] to reduce, by pub exchanges, their ownership of pubs to below 50 per cent in the areas which had been identified. As for the regionals involved, namely, Greenall Whitley, Daniel Thwaites and Tollemache & Cobbold, their relatively small trading areas put them in a particularly difficult position, but they were nevertheless willing to commit themselves to reducing their concentrations by exchanges "wherever possible".[16]

The confidential note dealt more tersely with the question of draught ale exchanges. The companies which had undertaken to explore the matter had concluded that it was possible to increase such exchanges. They would be pursuing the matter, and the note proposed that an audit of the number of pubs which were offering draught ales produced by brewers other than the one owning the pub should be taken in April 1979, and again "at some suitable later date".[17]

On 11 December 1978 Hattersley and Silkin held another meeting with a Brewers' Society delegation, to discuss progress since their May meeting and the contents of the October note. The brewers said that they expected some 1000 pubs to change hands and that the programme would take up to five years. Derrick Holden-Brown, Vice-Chairman of the Brewers' Society, said that the putative ale exchange programme had no clear formula or objective, and that little evidence had emerged of customer demand. He also warned that he didn't expect a large exchange to ensue. But it seems that Ministers were reluctant to mar what had been achieved, and they assented to the suggestion that they meet to address this subject again in six months.

The planned meeting never happened, however, because of the May 1979 Election and change of Government. The Office of Fair Trading (OFT) was subsequently given the task of monitoring the operation of the pub exchange programme, and when responding to a request from the Office in early 1981 for a progress report on that front, the Brewers' Society took the opportunity to state that, because of a lack of consumer demand, ale exchanges were not commercially viable. At a meeting in July OFT officials appeared to accept that there was no point in pursuing the matter, and it faded from the agenda.

The Society informed the OFT in February 1981 that pub concentrations of 50 per cent ownership by a major company had been eliminated in six of the 11 areas which had been identified in the 1978 report, and that in the other five areas the number of pubs in excess of the 50 per cent level had fallen substantially. In only one of the six areas where a regional brewer had had more than 50 per cent pub ownership had the dominant company got the level to below that, but, again, the number of pubs in excess of 50 per cent in the other areas in question was well down. The pub-swapping process continued and in August 1985 the Director General of Fair Trading advised the Government that it had effectively been completed – a matter, however, on which within less than a year an internal OFT paper was to express a rather less favourable view.

Three more price investigations – and renewed criticisms of the tie

Since the passing of the Price Commission Act in July 1977 companies had been required to give the Commission 28 days' notice of a proposed price increase, and the Commission had the power to investigate such specific proposals, and restrict – or even freeze – individual price increases for up to a year.

It was only a matter of time before the first brewing company was subjected to examination, and that company was Allied Breweries, which notified the PC in December 1977 that it proposed to raise wholesale beer prices by an average of 7.42 per cent and the prices of food, drink and accommodation in its managed pubs by an average of 7.34 per cent. In August 1976 the Campaign for Real Ale (CAMRA) had submitted a detailed request to the Director General of Fair Trading (DGFT) for Allied to be referred to the Monopolies Commission (MC) on the grounds of its dominance of the pub market in Hertfordshire, Buckinghamshire and Bedfordshire. CAMRA, which had been founded in 1971 to campaign for the preservation of cask-conditioned ales, but which had broadened its activities to campaign more generally on behalf of pub users, had shown that Allied's purchase in 1972 of The Aylesbury Brewery Company had taken its local market share of pubs to around two-thirds, "grossly in excess of the 25 per cent required to establish a monopoly under the [Fair Trading 1973] Act".[18]

Nothing came of this, but, in any case, around three weeks after Allied's notification the PC advised the company that it had recommended to the Minister that an investigation should be carried out. The company promptly applied, as it was entitled to do under the regulations, for interim price rises, and was granted the beer price increase in full and an increase of 6.85

per cent in managed house prices; the latter was subsequently increased to the full figure which had been requested.

Consistent with the record of earlier Government-appointed bodies investigating the brewers, however, the PC strayed from its brief, observing in its Report that, "A full examination of the consequences of the tied house system has been made elsewhere and is outside the scope of this investigation. However, we note and agree with the conclusions of other studies that the system does to some extent shield the brewers from the rigours of competition."[19] And the Commission also took the opportunity to declare its views in relation to the industry as a whole that future price increases should be weighted towards pub retailing and away from brewing; and that progress towards commercial "dry" rents and the elimination of "wet" rents should continue, thereby allowing the brewers to free tenants from the tie in respect of wines, spirits and so on.

In January 1979 Bass Charrington (shortly to become Bass) notified the PC of its proposal to raise wholesale beer prices by a weighted average of 7.94 per cent and beer and other prices in its managed houses by 7.90 per cent. Again, the PC recommended an investigation and again it used its discretionary powers to allow interim price rises. By the middle of May the company had been granted four increases in managed house prices, cumulatively amounting to the 7.90 per cent that had been notified, and two increases in its wholesale beer prices, together amounting to 6.27 per cent – about four-fifths of what the company had proposed.

The Commission explained in its Report that it had found Bass to be well managed and efficient, but that it had two concerns, namely, that higher prices might be used to buy industrial peace through spurious productivity schemes; and that profits were being invested in expanding the company's free trade loan book – that is, tying in free trade through loans on attractive terms, which the Commission saw as a way of inhibiting competition. In allowing a smaller increase in wholesale than in retail prices, the Commission was acting in line with one of the recommendations in the Allied Report. Nor did the Report neglect to criticise the tied house system: "The extensive ownership of public houses by brewers and the operation of UK licensing laws provide some degree of protection from competitive market forces."[20] And it concluded with the suggestion that the "potentially anti-competitive nature"[21] of free trade loans might merit further examination.

Just two days after the Bass Charrington notification, Whitbread announced its intention to raise the wholesale prices of all its drinks products by an average of 5.65 per cent and the prices of drinks, food and accommodation in its managed pubs by an average of 8.82 per cent. In three steps, the company was allowed to raise both its wholesale and managed pub prices by the full amounts requested. In the same way that the Commission had justified withholding part of Bass Charrington's proposed price increase, it justified depriving Whitbread of an estimated £5m of revenue (by partly postponing the increase) by reference to the company's expenditure on free trade loans. The – by now – customary objection to the industry's structure appeared, although in slightly less dogmatic terms than elsewhere. Thus "To some limited extent, therefore, the operation of the licensing laws protects Whitbread's tied estate, as well as the tied estate of other brewers, from the full rigours of a competitive market."[22] Finally, and using almost precisely the same words as had appeared at the end of the Bass Charrington Report, the Commission raised the question for the future of a specific examination of the free trade loan business.[23]

Within a couple of weeks of the Conservatives' Election victory on 4 May 1979 the new Prime Minister, Margaret Thatcher, announced the abolition of the PC. The free operation of market forces was, of course, at the heart of the Thatcher philosophy, but it was in fact just before the Election that the issues of full-line forcing and tie-in sales had been referred to the Monopolies and Mergers Commission (MMC). Together, these comprised the practice of requiring anyone to whom goods or services were supplied to purchase other products as a condition of that supply, and the investigation wasn't to be confined to one industry.

The authors of the Report, which came out in March 1981, included Dick Smethurst, who was to chair the 1986–89 MMC inquiry into the supply of beer, and it included a chapter devoted to brewers and petrol suppliers. This began by stating that "Tenants of brewery-owned public houses are subject to a number of tying conditions relating to the supply of beer and, sometimes, wines and spirits, minerals and soft drinks, and other products such as tobacco and amusement machines."[24] The Report also pointed out, however, that these conditions were contained in tenancy agreements, and the authors concluded that the latter were outside their terms of reference. The Commissioners considered that free trade loans were relevant to the practice being investigated, and they stated that such loans, sometimes with a tie attached, could put small brewers lacking the financial resources to compete in this market at a disadvantage. They nevertheless concluded that they were unlikely to be against the public interest, provided that any associated tie ceased on repayment of the loan.

Perhaps ominously, however, the Commissioners seemed reluctant to abandon their point of contention, and this section ended with the assertion that "Ties in tenancy agreements, which are outside the terms of our reference, appear to be much more significant [than free trade loans] from the point of view of the public interest."[25] So with free trade loans given a clean bill of health and with tenancy agreements outside the Commission's terms of reference, no action was required of the industry after the Report. But once again the issue of the tie had been highlighted.

Continuing consolidation and the Matthew Brown bid

Following the development of the "big six" integrated brewers during the 1960s, consolidation continued over the next 30 years, albeit on a rather more modest scale than previously. Thus the late sixties and the seventies saw the acquisition by five of the "big six" – Scottish & Newcastle stood aside during this period – of well known companies such as Stones, John Smith's, Brickwoods, Webster and Lorimer's. At the same time, the larger regional brewers, such as Boddingtons, Matthew Brown, Greenall Whitley and Vaux, were mopping up the smaller, often family-owned brewers. This period also saw the first acquisitions of brewing businesses by companies from outside the industry, with Grand Metropolitan Hotels (one of the two ancestors of the modern Diageo) buying Truman Hanbury & Buxton in 1971 and then the much larger Watney Mann the following year (to form Watney Mann & Truman). In 1972, also, Imperial Tobacco acquired Courage, while the shipping company, Ellerman Lines, bought JW Cameron and Tollemache & Cobbold.

Throughout the sixties and seventies, too, the "big six" integrated brewers were acquiring businesses involved in the manufacture, wholesaling and retailing of wines, spirits and soft drinks. These included names such as Victoria Wine and Showerings (Allied Breweries), Old Bushmills (Bass, Mitchells & Butlers), Saccone & Speed (Courage), Charles MacKinley (Scottish & Newcastle), International Distillers & Vintners, or IDV (Watney Mann), and Threshers, R White and Long John International (Whitbread). Except in the case of Watney, which bought IDV in an unsuccessful attempt to render itself unpalatable to Grand Metropolitan Hotels, the motivations for these purchases were partly to exploit what were seen as areas of growing demand, but also to capture a larger share of the business in both the brewers' own tied trade and also in the free trade.

Takeover activity amongst brewers during the first half of the eighties was largely confined to the regionals, with Boddingtons, Matthew Brown, Greenall Whitley, Mansfield Brewery, Marston's, Wolverhampton & Dudley and the privately-owned Robinsons and Thwaites all emerging as predators. It was only when Scottish & Newcastle (S&N) decided that it too must expand that the regulatory authorities decided to take an interest. S&N's first target, in 1984, was its local neighbour in the North East, JW Cameron, but an agreed merger was aborted when the proposed deal was referred to the MMC. Turning then to the North West of England, it mounted a hostile bid for Matthew Brown in April 1985, and this too was referred to the MMC, but was nevertheless pursued by S&N.

Matthew Brown strenuously argued the case against the deal on a number of grounds, including the adverse effect on competition in two of its development areas, North and West Cumbria and the North East. The Report found, however, that in the former region S&N had virtually no tied trade, and that its considerably bigger share of the free trade there was of no special significance in terms of competition.[26] As for the North East, Matthew Brown had not yet developed a significant presence in the region and the Report doubted whether it would do so in the foreseeable future.[27]

The company's two biggest shareholders, Brittanic Assurance and Whitbread Investment Company (WIC), told the Commission that they would like to see Brown remain independent, and Charles Tidbury, a former Chairman of Whitbread and a venerable figure within the industry, wrote that he was personally opposed to the deal. Regional brewers, he said, "provided a greater variety of beer at cheaper prices than the nationals", and the merger "could open the way to a spate of further takeovers by the big brewers. This would decimate the British brewing industry and thus prevent a gradual adjustment through the formation of more regional companies which would ensure enhanced competition to the major brewers and better service to the public."[28] Given the continuing existence at that time of the Whitbread "umbrella", Tidbury's strongly stated view was hardly surprising, but would nevertheless have had a hollow ring to it for those who remembered that Whitbread had itself demonstrated a voracious appetite for small brewers just a couple of decades earlier. Dick Smethurst participated in this investigation, too, adding further to his stock of knowledge of the brewing industry.

By far the most significant contribution to the inquiry, however, at least as far as the long term was concerned, seems to have come from Guinness. Except in the case of WIC, the Report didn't attribute any of the evidence it received to a named company. But it is highly unlikely that any pub-owning brewer would have argued that "The proposed takeover of Matthew Brown must be viewed against the existing structure of the brewing industry, the increased purchasing power wielded by those major brewers in whose hands were concentrated the retail outlets, and the degree of parallel retail pricing between them. In addition to restricting the launch of new products and distorting consumer choice, particularly in the on-trade, the effect had been unwarranted rises in the prices paid by consumers."[29] Nor would any of the tied estate brewers have complained that the merger would "further squeeze independent suppliers".[30] Such sentiments could, of course, have been expressed by a non-beer supplier, but since they appear in the section of the Report dealing specifically with the views of other *brewers*, the former can be discounted.

In the end the Commission found in favour of S&N, albeit perhaps grudgingly, because, just as in the case of the *Full-Line Forcing and Tie-In Sales* Report, it managed to convey that perhaps it hadn't been asked the right question. Thus it concluded, "We discern no material advantages to the public interest arising from the proposed merger; but the question before us is whether the merger may be expected to operate against the public interest, and in our view there are not sufficient grounds for such an expectation."[31] And earlier in the Report the authors had taken the opportunity to reproduce part of the conclusions of the 1977 PC Report on the industry, in which the effect of the industry's structure on the consumer interest had been roundly criticised.[32]

In the short term the Commission's decision to allow the S&N/Brown deal proved to be academic, because, thanks to an extremely energetic defence operation, which included direct telephone calls by the Chairman to individual small shareholders, the bid failed (though the respite wasn't to last for long).

Hostile takeover bid from overseas

In the meantime, the first assault on a UK brewer from overseas since Eddie Taylor had blazed his trail in the early sixties had been made. Early in 1985 interests associated with Elders IXL, an acquisitive multi-national conglomerate based in Australia, whose interests included Foster's lager, started to buy shares in Allied-Lyons. In October Elders announced a takeover bid for Allied, but on 5 December the Department of Trade and Industry (DTI) referred the bid to the MMC. The DTI's press release made clear that the point at issue was the financing of the proposed acquisition.

The Commission had initially been instructed to report by the end of July but was granted a five-week extension. The Report[33] pointed out that, unusually in such an investigation, the merger in question didn't appear to involve any material competition issues. It accepted that in the immediate aftermath of the merger capital gearing would be considerably higher – and interest cover considerably lower – than was usual in the UK, but it convinced itself that for a number of reasons, such as Allied's strong cash flow and the backing and track record of the bidder, that the financial arrangements were unlikely to present problems. The Commission thus concluded that the Elders bid for Allied could not be expected to be against the public interest.

By this time, however, Allied had taken protective action by acquiring the Canadian spirits manufacturer, Hiram Walker, and it was able to see off the bid. Anyone who assumed, though, that the UK – and specifically the regulatory authorities – had seen the back of Elders was mistaken.

Notes

1 HC Deb 27 April 1977 Vol. 930 c1256.
2 Brewers' Society press statement, 10 February 1977.
3 Price Commission (PC), Report No. 31, *Beer Prices and Margins* (1977), para. 2.17.
4 *Ibid.*, para. 2.19.
5 *Ibid.*, para. 6.1(b).
6 *Ibid.*, para. 6.5.
7 *Ibid.*, para. 6.6.
8 Brewers' Society, *Beer Prices and Margins – Response to the Price Commission* (1977), para. 1.2.

9 *Ibid.*, para.1.7.
10 Department of Prices and Consumer Protection press notice, 16 December 1977.
11 Brewers' Society press statement, 16 December 1977.
12 HC Deb 02 May 1978 Vol. 949 c45W.
13 *Ibid.*
14 Brewers' Society, "Local Concentrations of Ownership of Public Houses: Exchanges of Draught Ales", October 1978.
15 *Ibid.*, para. 15.
16 *Ibid.*, para. 18.
17 *Ibid.*, para. 22.
18 Campaign for Real Ale, "Request for a Reference to the MMC of a Local Monopoly in the Supply of Beer", August 1976, para. 3(ii).
19 PC, *Allied Breweries (UK) Limited – Brewing and Wholesaling of Beer and Sales in Managed Houses*, HC 415 (1978), para. 12.
20 PC, *Bass Ltd – Wholesale Prices of Beer and Prices in Managed Houses*, HC 109 (1979), para. 5.2.
21 *Ibid.*, para. 5.20.
22 PC, *Whitbread and Company Limited – Wholesale Prices and Prices in Managed Houses of Beer, Wines, Spirits, Soft Drinks and Ciders*, HC 110 (1979), para. 2.14.
23 *Ibid.*, para. 6.6.
24 Monopolies and Mergers Commission (MMC), *Full-Line Forcing and Tie-In Sales: A Report on the Practice of Requiring Any Person to Whom Goods or Services are Supplied to Acquire Other Goods or Services as a Condition of that Supply*, HC212 (1981), para. 8.1.
25 *Ibid.*, para. 8.5.
26 MMC, *Scottish & Newcastle Breweries PLC and Matthew Brown PLC: A Report on the Proposed Merger*, Cmnd. 9645 (1985), paras. 7.6–7.8.
27 *Ibid.*, para. 7.10.
28 *Ibid.*, para. 6.36.
29 *Ibid.*, para. 6.15.
30 *Ibid.*, para. 6.15.
31 *Ibid.*, para. 7.31.
32 *Ibid.*, para. 2.27.
33 MMC, *Elders IXL Ltd and Allied-Lyons PLC: A Report on the Proposed Merger*, Cmnd. 9892 (1986).

3
The State of Affairs in 1985

The phoney peace

Notwithstanding the Elders/Allied situation, old hands in the brewing industry may well have concluded in the autumn of 1985 that, at least for the time being, the industry's structure and trading practices were safe from further investigation and interference. During 20 years of inquiries little in the way of specific fundamental change had ever officially been proposed, and the industry continued to function apparently to the reasonable satisfaction of most consumers, licensees and shareholders.

Thus the lengthy 1969 Monopolies Commission (MC) Report had made only one recommendation, namely, that the licensing system be relaxed in order to stimulate competition. And the 1972 Erroll Report had recommended little more than that market forces rather than licensing authorities' perception of need should determine the provision of new licences; and even this idea had been shelved. More recently, the tricky matter of interbrewer draught ale exchanges seemed to have disappeared from the agenda of the Office of Fair Trading.

For their own part, and as foreshadowed in the Brewers' Society's four-point statement of December 1970, all brewers had either removed non-beer beverages from the tie or incorporated into their tenancy agreements those provisions of European Community Regulation (EEC) No 1984/83, which gave tenants choice in their supplier of such products. [A note on European competition law and its interaction with the UK brewing industry is given in Appendix 3.1.] They had started to make longer tenancy agreements available (although 10- or 20-year leases were still a rarity), and had introduced – and on three occasions updated – a Tenants' Code of Security. They had addressed the issue of local concentrations of pubs owned by one brewer. And restrictive covenants on pub sales had fallen from virtually 100 per cent of sales in the sixties to 2–3 per cent in 1983.

There was the unarguable fact that the proportion of full on-licences – which include pubs, hotels, restaurants and so on – owned by brewers had fallen from 78 per cent of the total in 1967 to 58 per cent. And adding to the feeling of confidence was the knowledge that Regulation 1984/83, which also had the effect of endorsing the UK tied house system in respect of the supply of beer, would run till 1997. What was more, with the election of Mrs Thatcher's Conservative Government the spectre of price controls seemed to have been banished.

But, perhaps most encouragingly, the Director General of Fair Trading, Sir Gordon Borrie, had written to the Brewers' Society in August 1985 to say that he had advised the Minister for Consumer and Corporate Affairs – and the latter had accepted – that the pub exchange programme initiated in 1978 was regarded as having been completed. Borrie also reported that the Minister had noted the significant reduction in the incidence of restrictive covenants in contracts for the sale of licensed premises. He even referred to the fact that the range of beers in pubs had been widened, thereby in part achieving the increase in consumer choice that draught ale exchanges had been meant to achieve. Surely the industry could not have wished for a more welcome and significant sign of official approval than this letter; surely the letter drew a line under all the inquiries and changes of the preceding 20 years.

Such an attitude, however, failed to take into account a suspicion in some official minds that the economic benefits provided by the tied house system flowed wholly – and unfairly – to the brewers. In fact, it seemed that as long as successive reports failed to lead to major change, and in particular as long as the Erroll recommendations went unheeded, the potential for further investigation would be ever-present.

If there was, indeed, a degree of prejudice towards the industry amongst the authorities, it was, first, because the official reports of the previous two decades had never seemed to land any real blows, and, second, because these reports had frequently strayed outside their terms of reference to express more general criticism of the brewers and the regulatory framework within which they operated. Thus, as we have seen, the 1966 Report of the National Board for Prices and Incomes, overtly concerned with beer prices, ended by suggesting an inquiry into the licensing system. On the other hand, the resulting 1969 MC Report, while finding several serious disadvantages inherent in the tie, including what it saw as an almost complete absence of retail price competition, didn't recommend any direct action to deal with the tied house system.

Then in 1977 the Price Commission (PC) – having been asked to investigate brewers' prices and margins, and having, as we have seen, found nothing wrong with beer prices – decided to wade into the wider debate, talking of "the classic conditions for a monopoly" and inviting the Government to consider whether such a situation was in the public interest. In its 1978 Report on price rises requested by Allied Breweries, the PC, having approved them in full, went on to observe that the tie partly shielded the brewers from the rigours of competition. Just over a year later the PC awarded Whitbread all, and Bass Charrington almost all, of the price increases that they had proposed, but in both cases supplemented its reports by floating the idea of an examination of free trade loans. In 1981 the authors of the Monopolies and Mergers Commission (MMC) Report on *Full-line Forcing and Tie-in Sales* adopted an ambivalent stance in relation to such loans, finding that they were not against the public interest, but that they could disadvantage small brewers. They conceded that the tenants' tie in respect of beer, and sometimes other products, didn't fall within their terms of reference, but this didn't stop them highlighting it and asserting that it was far more significant in public interest terms than the matter of free trade loans.

Various official bodies had thus been keeping the pot simmering for 20 years, and any Minister or regulator minded to re-examine the industry at this time could point to a number of grounds for thinking that competition was only partly working. Thus the price of beer in the pub had been rising in real terms in the first half of the eighties, even after allowing for a near doubling of excise duty in that period. Furthermore, the brewers tended to announce price rises annually, creating a suspicion that prices were driven not so much by costs and competition as by the exercise of market power.

Another issue was that suppliers without tied estates which wished to sell in the on-trade – Guinness and Bulmer were prime examples – had to do so through other brewers. The latter had limited interest in selling a competitor's offering, except on the basis of a high profit margin, and this obviously inhibited demand. And the suppliers' negotiating position was made permanently difficult by the purchasing brewer's ability at any time to delist the product or products in question. Overseas brewers were in a similarly disadvantaged position, but because of their need for local brewing capacity, chose in almost all cases to enter licensing agreements with individual UK brewers, thereby providing access at least to one major tied estate. Even so, it was usually the UK brewer which controlled marketing strategy and pricing and therefore the product's competitive position.

Through shareholdings in consortia such as Taunton Cider, Squires Gin and Britvic Soft Drinks, or through subsidiaries such as Showerings, IDV and Saccone & Speed, the major brewers also had substantial commercial interests in cider, wine, spirits and soft drinks, and their natural inclination to promote these in preference to competitor brands meant that the latter's access to the pub trade was highly restricted. European legislation, as mentioned earlier, had empowered pub tenants to choose which brands of these non-beer beverages they stocked, but because they didn't enjoy the same rights and protection under the law as other business tenants, they were normally reluctant to offend their brewer/landlords by rejecting the latter's own offerings.

Against this background, the Report on the proposed takeover by Scottish & Newcastle (S&N) of Matthew Brown, complete with its potentially significant interventions by Guinness and the senior industry figure of Charles Tidbury, was completed on 18 October 1985 and published a few weeks later. From then on the pace of events was to quicken.

Changes since the 1960s

Before examining the momentous changes that were about to get under way, it is worth taking stock of the size and structure of the UK brewing and pub industries in the mid-eighties. [Where possible, statistics used in this description relate to 1985, that is, the last year before the reference of the industry to the MMC, and the authors believe that where figures in respect of other years have had to be used, the differences between these and the 1985 figures are not material. Throughout this section there are references to Appendix 3.2, in which the statistics being referred to appear in numerical form. Some of these statistical series, together with some others, and covering a longer period, are shown in graph form in Appendix 3.3.]

The composition of the brewing industry in the mid-eighties would have been easily recognisable to those who had served on the 1966–69 MC investigation. Thus the same six pub-owning companies which had dominated the industry then were still dominating, and, indeed, through acquisitions had by 1985 raised their share of the market by almost seven percentage points from the 67.8 per cent which they had been found to account for in 1967. Again like their predecessors, the Commissioners on the 1989 Report identified 11 leading regional brewers; but with several from the old list having been taken over, the new group of top regionals had a market share of only 11 per cent, down from 14 per cent in 1967. But considerably more stark was the collapse in the importance of the smaller brewers, which by the end of the eighties had more than halved in number, from 93, with a similar decline in market share from the 13 per cent or so they had held in 1967.

The UK brewing industry in 1985 thus comprised the following:

(1) The "big six" national pub-owning brewers, namely, Allied Breweries, Bass, Courage, Grand Metropolitan, Scottish & Newcastle and Whitbread;
(2) 11 regional pub-owning brewers, of which the most important were Boddingtons, Greenall Whitley, Greene King, Marston's, Vaux and Wolverhampton & Dudley;
(3) Around 40 local pub-owning brewers, including the London-based Fuller Smith & Turner and Young & Co., and names such as Adnams, Belhaven, Hardys & Hansons, Morland and Shepherd Neame;
(4) Three brewers without a tied estate (BWTE), namely, Carlsberg, Guinness and the Northern Clubs Federation Brewery co-operative; and
(5) Around 160 so-called "micro brewers", about half of which owned at least one pub, in which in many cases the brewery itself was located.

These brewers accounted for less than 1 per cent of national beer production.

Beer production and market shares, together with the numbers of tenanted and brewery-managed pubs, accounted for by each of the above categories (except for the micro-brewers) and by each of the "big six" are given in Appendix 3.2, Table 1. This table shows that the biggest brewer, Bass, produced around 23 per cent of the UK's beer and the smallest, Courage and Grand Met, slightly under 9 per cent each. Although the seven largest brewers – including Guinness, with an estimated share of production of around 6 per cent – had a combined share of just over 80 per cent in 1985, the UK industry was by international standards relatively fragmented. Thus the Brewers' Society was to claim in its submission to the MMC that the four biggest UK brewers had an aggregate market share of 58 per cent, compared with equivalent figures of between 79 per cent and 99 per cent in Australia, Canada, Denmark, France, Japan, the Netherlands and the US.

And at this time not only the UK brewing industry as a whole but the brewing capacity of the individual big brewers was fragmented. Reflecting the creation of the "big six" through mergers and takeovers across the land, in 1985 these companies were still brewing in a combined 39 locations – though this was well down on the 70 operating in the mid-sixties. Guinness, which had grown organically on the back of its eponymous brand of stout, had only one UK brewery. The locations and ownership of the national pub-owning brewers' production facilities and their share of UK beer production are shown in Appendix 3.2, Table 2.

Statistics in respect of UK brewing capacity are not generally compiled, partly for the good reason that it is hard to attach much meaning to them. This is because they are influenced by factors such as the styles of beer being produced; whether it is draught, bottled or canned; the number of days/shifts worked; whether a plant operates high gravity brewing (in which beer is brewed to a high strength and diluted at a later stage); the availability of storage capacity; and so on. In 1989, however, capacity utilisation was estimated in the Elders/Grand Met MMC Report to be 75 per cent across the brewing industry as a whole, consisting of 80 per cent amongst the national brewers and 59 per cent amongst the regional brewers; and given that a handful of breweries had closed during the late eighties, while output during that period had risen slightly, one can state with certainty that capacity utilisation had been lower than this in 1985.

There were also at this time large differences amongst the major brewers in terms of the degree of fragmentation of production. Thus it can be calculated from the production figures and numbers of breweries shown in Appendix 3.2, Tables 1 and 2, that in 1985 average output, for example, from Courage's breweries was slightly more than double that from Grand

Met's and Whitbread's, and that S&N's average output was double that of Bass's.

Major reduction in tied business

As stated earlier, the proportion of full on-licences owned by brewers fell from 78 per cent in 1967 to 58 per cent in 1985; and in 1986 it fell to 57 per cent. In terms of numbers, brewer-owned full on-licences declined from 58,525 in 1967 to 46,200 in 1986. Using these figures, and others published in the 1969 MC Report[1] and in the 1989 MMC Report,[2] it is possible to say that brewer ownership of pubs – as opposed to other forms of full on-licence – fell between 1967 and 1986 from 58,000, or 80 per cent of all pubs, to 42,000, or 72 per cent. [The sizeable discrepancy between this figure of 42,000 and the 45,782 brewer-owned pubs as at the end of 1988 shown in Appendix 3.2, Table 1, is explained by the fact that, as stated below that table, the higher figure relates not to pubs but to brewer-owned full on-licences. This becomes apparent in Table 2.26 of the MMC Report, where the number of brewer-owned full on-licences in 1986 is shown as slightly under 46,100, which would be compatible with 45,782 a couple of years later.]

The numbers in Appendix 3.2, Table 1, show that at the end of 1988 S&N had slightly under 3 per cent of all UK full on-licences, while the other five big integrated companies each owned between 6 per cent and 9 per cent. As a proportion of brewer-owned full on-licences S&N accounted for 5 per cent and the others for between 11 per cent and 16 per cent. The composition of the total number of premises licensed for the sale of intoxicating liquor in 1986 is shown in Appendix 3.2, Table 3.

The British Beer & Pub Association (BBPA) estimated throughout the mid-eighties that 72 per cent of brewer-owned pubs were tenanted and 28 per cent directly managed, and the MMC reported that on average across the country managed pubs sold 91 per cent more beer than tenanted ones.

The MMC was to find that in 1985 48.4 per cent of beer sales went through brewer-owned outlets, a further 18.5 per cent through outlets tied to a brewer by a loan or similar arrangement, 17.4 per cent to the free on-trade, and the remaining 15.5 per cent (differences due to rounding) to so-called national accounts – including supermarkets – and to independent off-licences.[3] Thus two-thirds of beer sales went to customers who were tied in one way or another to a brewer. Compared with the 48.4 per cent figure just quoted, the 1969 Report had found that 66 per cent of beer supplied in the UK was sold through brewer-owned outlets.[4]

Beer market back in decline

As noted at the start of this book, UK beer production in the 12 months to March 1959 had fallen to its lowest level since the end of the War. In the following year, however, it rose by an extraordinary 10 per cent, and, what is more, then went up in every year of the sixties, registering cumulative growth over the period 1959/60 to 1969/70 of 26 per cent. Production continued to grow strongly through the seventies, helped by exceptionally dry and hot summers in 1975 and 1976, which also gave a considerable fillip to the trend towards lager. The rise in production in this decade, however, was not quite uninterrupted, and, perhaps more significantly, there was a marked slowdown in growth towards the end of the period, with production increasing by only a little over 3 per cent between 1976/77 and 1979/80.

By this time, of course, in the aftermath of Labour's Election defeat and Margaret Thatcher's appointment as Prime Minister, the UK was entering a period of economic recession, which, moreover, was particularly deeply felt in the country's heavy industries. Added to this, the rate of Value Added Tax, which in the case of alcoholic drink was levied on duty as well as on the underlying price, was raised in June 1979 from 8 per cent to 15 per cent, helping to push up the average price of beer in the public bars of managed houses by around 42 per cent between 1978 and 1980, compared with rises of 38 per cent in the ex-taxes price and 35 per cent in the Retail Prices Index (RPI). Beer production fell for three years at the start of the eighties, before stabilising.

The figures for beer consumption, which include imports and exclude exports, are less volatile than those for production, and differ also in that they are calculated on a calendar year basis, but both series display similar long-term trends. Table 4, in Appendix 3.2, shows the course of total beer consumption for the 15 years up to 1985, together with the – at this time – fairly gentle decline, from 90.4 per cent to 84.4 per cent, in the proportion accounted for by on-trade consumption (that is, in licensed premises,

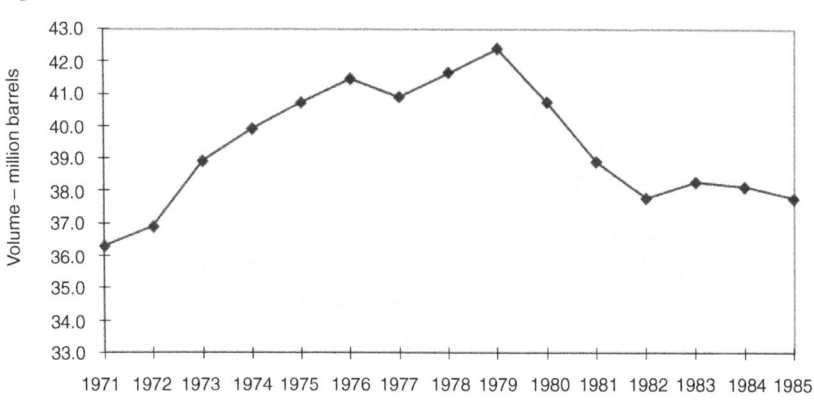

Figure 3.1 Beer Sales, 1971 to 1985

Source: Derived from statistics from British Beer & Pub Association, *Statistical Handbook*.

Figure 3.2 Sales of Ale/Stout and Lager, 1971 to 1985

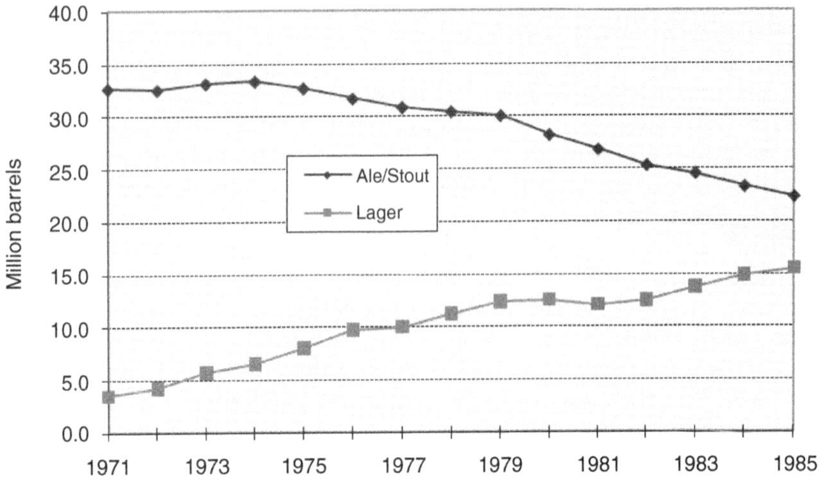

Source: Derived from statistics from British Beer & Pub Association, *Statistical Handbook*.

as opposed to away from such premises) and the much more rapid decline, from 90.1 per cent to 59.1 per cent, in the importance of ale and stout, as lager flourished. These movements are also shown in Figures 3.1 and 3.2.

Rising prices and profits

Until 1988 the Brewers' Society, one of the predecessors of the BBPA, for many decades published estimates of the average price of draught bitter and lager in the public bar of a managed pub, and since then the data have been provided by the Office for National Statistics. The BBPA *Statistical Handbook* warns, however, that the figures – from both sources – are "for indicative purposes only", and it is certainly the case that they have been subject to restatement from time to time. The MMC nevertheless availed itself of the data, which showed that the ex-taxes price of bitter, after falling marginally in real terms between 1973 and 1977, rose in real terms by just over 14 per cent between 1977 and 1985. The relevant figures are shown in Appendix 3.2, Table 5.

As to customer choice of beer within pubs in the mid-eighties, the best source of information is the survey of licensees conducted by the MMC in connection with the 1986–89 investigation. Most of the fieldwork for this was carried out in the summer of 1987, and the sample was 1383 licensees. Within the tied category, tenants (as opposed to pub managers) were found to stock on average 15.2 different beer brands, of which an average of 3.1 – falling to 2.5 in respect of the national brewers – were brands not produced by their landlord brewer; but these brands from other companies were normally bottled or canned, and usually lager rather than bitter. It must be assumed that Guinness stout was also frequently one of the "foreign" beers on offer. The results in respect of beer alone (the survey also covered other drinks) are summarised in Appendix 3.2, Table 6.

Finally, the brewing industry which the MMC was to investigate seemed to be in rude financial health. Using information obtained from the individual companies, the MMC produced aggregated financial data for the period 1983/4–1985/6 in respect of the companies' brewing, beer wholesaling and licensed retailing activities. The main features of these data are given in Appendix 3.2, Table 7, and they show that between 1983/84 and 1985/86 the industry's turnover grew by 17 per cent and profits before interest by 32 per cent. As the MMC noted, the rise in profits represented an increase in real terms over the two years of more than 18 per cent. Return on assets, however, fell during the period from 12.9 per cent to 12.2 per cent.

Summary

This, then, was the state of affairs in the UK brewing industry immediately ahead of the reference of the supply of beer to the MMC. It was an industry in which the six largest companies had increased their combined share of the beer market over the previous couple of decades, largely through acquisition, but which nevertheless comprised one of the most fragmented beer markets in Europe. The brewers' share of ownership of the country's pubs and other licensed premises had declined significantly, and the proportion of beer sold through brewer-owned premises had fallen from two-thirds to less than half. Beer production by the six biggest companies was carried out in 39 breweries, of greatly varying size, and it seems likely that the industry as a whole was brewing at less than 75 per cent of capacity. For eight years starting in 1978 average pub prices of beer had been rising in real terms without interruption. Within pubs there was a wide choice of brands, but little choice between different brewers' products, particularly in the largest segment of the market, namely, draught ale. And the industry was growing its profits considerably faster than inflation.

As we shall see, well before 1985 had come to a close, discussions were already taking place which would set in train a sequence of events that would involve scores of distinguished individuals from many branches of public life, and ultimately bring about enormous change. [Background details on those who played the most significant parts in these events are provided in Appendix 3.4.]

Notes

1 Monopolies Commission (MC), *Beer: A Report on the Supply of Beer*, HC 216 (1969), para. 168 and first two footnotes to Table XVII.

2 Monopolies and Mergers Commission, *The Supply of Beer: A Report on the Supply of Beer for Retail Sale in the United Kingdom*, Cm 651 (1989), para. 2.108.
3 *Ibid.*, Table 2.17.
4 MC, *Beer: A Report on the Supply of Beer*, HC 216 (1969), para. 43.

4
The OFT Prepares its Case

Borrie's bombshell

When Sir Gordon Borrie, Director General of Fair Trading, told the Brewers' Society in August 1985 that he had advised the Government that the task of reducing local concentrations of pub ownership had been effectively completed, the Society believed that a long saga had ended. Thus it was remarked in its Annual Report for the year to September 1985 that "This was an extremely satisfactory position and represented a closing of the files on matters which had caused the industry concern since the days of the Monopolies Commission (MC) inquiry in 1966."[1]

What the Society didn't know was that the OFT still had major reservations about the value of the pub-swapping exercise. This has now become clear from an internal document of June 1986, seen by the authors, which recalled that "The Office had advised the Government and [name redacted, but presumably Brewers' Society] in 1985 that the programme had been effectively completed. In coming to this conclusion the Office recognised that the position was not entirely satisfactory."[2]

Circulation of the Brewers' Society's Annual Report was followed by the Annual General Meeting on 11 December, at which the outgoing Chairman, Ewart Boddington, who was succeeded in the post by Edward Guinness, reviewed the past year. Only five days earlier, however, a bombshell had been dropped, in the form of a speech by Borrie to the Leicester Chamber of Commerce. The Director General had referred to several industries, but dealing specifically with the brewing industry he said:

> The tied house system makes it difficult for drink producers who do not themselves own pubs to get their product into pubs and through to the customers in fair competition with the products of the major brewers.

Consumer choice, which is so important in the drinks market where tastes vary so much, is reduced and price leadership by managed houses has caused prices to go up.[3]

He added that the brewers were "technically in a monopoly situation" and that he needed to consider carefully the case for a referral to the Monopolies and Mergers Commission (MMC). He also referred to the 1969 Report by the MMC's predecessor body, the MC, which had found the tied house system to be against the public interest; and he noted that its preferred solution, a relaxation of the licensing laws, had not happened.[4] Amongst the list of possible questions, together with suggested answers, that Borrie's officials had prepared ahead of his speech was the following:

Q. Is it usual for the Director General to "trail" [a] possible monopoly reference?

A. No. It is not but there is nothing to stop him doing so and, of course, giving notice of how his mind is moving does allow Sir Gordon to trawl for outside opinions from all sectors affected by a possible reference – opinions that will be helpful when he comes to make a final decision.

What has only now come to light, as the result of access to an internal OFT paper dated 21 November 1985, is that at the time of Borrie's speech the OFT was already considering in detail the possibility of another reference to the MMC. This note[5] opened by informing its recipients that the Director General had asked his officials to review the 1969 MC Report and in particular to establish whether its "reasoning against any direct action to deal with the tied house system could be adequately challenged".[6] It will be recalled that instead of "direct action" the Commission had recommended liberalisation of the licensing regime, and the OFT memorandum acknowledged that there was little likelihood of change in this respect. The MC had seen merit in more fundamental change, such as enforced pub disposals, but had argued that it would cause an unacceptable degree of upheaval. The memorandum rejected this view, contending that disposal by the brewers of all – or a substantial proportion – of their pubs could be managed over a reasonable timescale, "say, ten years".[7] The note concluded that "because the alternative remedy [licensing reform] is not available...*it seems reasonable to refer the problem to the MMC again*" (authors' italics).[8]

Lobbying by Guinness

As we have seen, everything seems to suggest that Guinness was the company behind the strong representations made to the MMC at the time of the Scottish & Newcastle/Matthew Brown merger inquiry, describing the problems created for suppliers and consumers by the structure of the brewing industry. But what is now also known is that Guinness wasn't content to leave matters solely to the MMC, but also lobbied the OFT. Thus the June 1986 OFT paper referred to earlier confirms the key role played by a third party in stimulating talk of a reference. The paper states, "*As a result of* [name redacted] *representations to the Office* at the time of the proposed Scottish & Newcastle and Matthew Brown merger...it was decided that the case for a new reference of the supply of beer and the tied-house system to the MMC should be considered" [authors' italics].[9] The authors have been told that this party was Guinness.

The authors have also learnt that later that year – and before Borrie's Leicester speech – senior executives of Guinness, including Ernest Saunders, the Chief Executive, followed up the complaints that the company had made to both the MMC and the OFT with a fresh approach to the latter. An integral part of Saunders's corporate strategy was to broaden Guinness's drinks portfolio away from stout and lager, and underlying his continuing agitation was frustration at the company's inability to get its new alcohol-free lager, Kaliber, into the majors' pubs. At a time when low alcohol/no alcohol beers seemed to have a bright future, the pub-owning national brewers had been introducing their own products, and so were reluctant to stock Kaliber, even though, according to Guinness, it was a superior brand.

Guinness's presentation of its case to the OFT was apparently altogether more professional than the OFT was accustomed to, and this would probably have been helpful to officials in putting together an authoritative case to the Director General. Guinness – and Saunders in particular – at this time relied heavily on management consultants Bain & Company. It was Bain that marshalled many of the arguments put to the OFT, and the company went so far as to offer the services of its team of consultants to the Office to help in preparing a case against the brewers.

Saunders disclosed the engagement with the OFT to very few of his senior executives. This was not altogether surprising, given that the company would have been susceptible to reprisals from its major customers – for example, in the shape of raising the retail price of Guinness stout, or, *in extremis*, de-listing the brand – if its actions had become more widely known. Certainly, it is plain from the OFT papers that this fear preoccupied Guinness.[10] Yet it might be argued that if the other brewers had been aware that Guinness had provoked the OFT to review the tied house system, then retaliatory behaviour on their part could only have served to nourish suspicions held by the OFT, and play into Guinness's hands.

Secrecy seems to have been a feature of Saunders's management style, as was to be dramatically demonstrated in what became known as "the Guinness Affair", which broke in December 1986. This was the notorious share support operation aimed at artificially inflating the Guinness share price and thereby facilitating a £2.7 billion bid for the Scottish drinks company, Distillers. Saunders, together with four others, none of them Guinness employees, was tried, and all but one received prison sentences. The investigation by the Department of Trade and Industry (DTI) which led to the trial revealed that the illegal arrangements put in place by Saunders had not been disclosed to – let alone sanctioned by – the Guinness board.

Officials working on the industry case made efforts to gather information from other interested parties, notably the Campaign for Real Ale (CAMRA). One of them wrote to CAMRA in December expressing an interest in receiving an "update on CAMRA's views on how competition is being affected by the tied house system". The official added that the Office would be interested to receive CAMRA's thinking on how the tied house system "might be modified *or even dissolved*" [authors' italics]. This invitation to contemplate the end of the tie might be judged as both radical and a case of leading the witness; and, as we see later, it wasn't the last time the OFT would take the organisation into its confidence.

Engagement with the Brewers' Society

After the Leicester speech, the Brewers' Society contacted the OFT to ask for a meeting to help the industry to understand Borrie's criticism of the tied house system. The meeting took place on 13 January 1986 and involved three Society staff members – Desmond Mangham, Alan Tilbury and Chris Thurman [one of the authors] – and Borrie and his team. Alan Tilbury was the Society's Secretary, and his report on the meeting recorded that the OFT had said that the industry was more concentrated than in 1968; that there was the possibility of further concentration as a result of a new wave of mergers; and that while there had been a decline in the relative importance of the tied house system, it was still reinforced by trade loans. The OFT was particularly concerned with price and with the problems faced by third party producers in selling to tied houses.

Shortly after the meeting, and at the request of the Society, an official sent a letter to Mangham on 21 January 1986, setting out the Office's concerns. It read:

> The main areas of concern to which the Director General referred were:
> (a) that the industry supplied a high proportion of its products through retail outlets tied to the brewers and that therefore the usual conditions of competition do not operate;
> (b) that independent suppliers face difficulties in marketing their products through the major brewers;
> (c) that consumer choice is limited because tied houses have to concentrate on selling products supplied by their brewers; and

(d) that efficiency gains in the industry do not seem to be passed on to the consumer in the form of lower prices.

The OFT then set about collecting data to establish whether there was a case for a referral. It used brewing companies' Annual Reports and a financial survey carried out by Inter Company Comparisons, an independent agency. It also received a memorandum from the Brewers' Society pointing to the changes which had occurred between 1969 and 1986, such as the reduction in the number of premises owned by brewers and in the proportion of draught beer accounted for by these premises.[11]

The OFT also issued a questionnaire to nine brewers – the six nationals and three regionals (Vaux, Greenall Whitley and Greene King) – asking for turnover, volume and profit of own draught beers and bought-in draught beers, costs, and top selling brands of beer in managed houses and to the off-trade. It also requested capital expenditure data and details of the top selling brands of different types of spirits, stout and cider.

There is an apparently innocuous but in fact significant comment in the OFT's subsequent review of the results of this survey. The Brewers' Society had been consulted on the drafting of the OFT questionnaire and on 28 April 1986 it had submitted a commentary, identifying areas in which it thought that "the responses might be misleading". Prior to submitting a paper such as this, it would have been Society policy to circulate a draft to its members for comment and subsequent agreement. The following remark appears in the OFT paper:

> [name redacted] which saw a copy of the [name redacted] representations in draft, questioned whether it was inappropriate as [name redacted] suggested to draw the inference from the information.[12]

The conclusion one reaches is that, unbeknown to the Society's staff or other members, one member of the Brewers' Society was questioning the validity of the latter's representations and thereby giving assistance to the OFT in its pursuit of a reference.

More evidence collected

During the next few months the OFT developed the case for referring the brewers to the MMC through internal staff work and by receiving submissions from third parties. This certainly included more input from Guinness, but other organisations, including representatives of pub tenants, came forward. While Bulmer and Guinness are not specifically named in these OFT papers, there are references to a major stout and a major cider producer, which leave little or no doubt as to the identities of the two companies, since Guinness was the only major stout company and the other major cider producers were owned by the brewers. It should be noted that the authors have no direct evidence that Bulmer itself made representations to the OFT at this time; details about its situation could have been derived from other sources.

Bulmer faced perhaps an even more difficult barrier than Guinness in penetrating the pub estates of the national brewers. For although Guinness complained that the latter pushed up the price of its draught stout unreasonably, the fact remained that the Guinness brand had no real competitor of stature. It was close to a "must stock" brand, so that threats by the nationals to withdraw it rang hollow. The same did not apply to Bulmer, which, although a market leader, did have credible alternatives – the most important of which were owned by the brewers.

In May 1986 the OFT received some timely help from CAMRA in the shape of a 50-page report entitled *Abuse of Monopoly in the Supply of Beer to the County of Norfolk by Grand Metropolitan PLC 1986*. This thoroughly researched and detailed report had been prepared especially for the OFT, and seemingly at the latter's suggestion. It followed similar surveys conducted in 1976 and 1977 in which CAMRA had examined concentrations in Avon, Gloucestershire, the Mid-Chilterns, Norfolk, Northamptonshire and the West Midlands, all of which were sent to the OFT. CAMRA's latest report drew attention to a reduction in brand choice, high prices and brewery closures, and it provided a detailed village-by-village analysis of pub closures, some of which had deprived villages of their last pub.

By June the Competition Division of the Office was in a position to put forward a paper demonstrating inadequate competition in the brewing industry and recommending a reference.[13] In the first place, it was asserted, the dominance of the "big six" brewers had grown since the 1969 MC Report. Collectively they now owned a greater proportion of tied pubs than before. And the free trade loan market had also grown, to the extent that it was estimated that no more than a third of free houses were now completely free of ties. All in all, and taking owned and loan-tied pubs into account, it was estimated that tying arrangements accounted for over half of total beer sales.[14] As for the MMC's conclusion in its 1981 report on *Full-line Forcing and Tie-in Sales*,[15] namely, that free trade loans were not against the public interest, the OFT paper merely noted, without comment, that it had been reminded of this finding in one of the submissions it had received.

Next, the paper turned to the problems faced by independent suppliers, articulating the position expressed by Guinness, Bulmer and others.[16] Bulmer, it said, had suffered declining market share in the estates of Bass and Courage after those brewers had taken a financial interest in Taunton Cider. In spirits too it was demonstrable that where a brewer owned or had an agency relationship with a brand, that brand had a larger share of sales in the brewer's tied houses than in the free on-trade or in take-home. A soft drinks supplier had described a similar picture.

The choice of drinks available in pubs reflected the owning brewer's marketing policies rather than consumers' wishes, the OFT claimed, adding that the majority of the major brands sold in tied houses were either manufactured or distributed under agency arrangements by the pub-owning brewer. In a few sentences, officials next sought to deny that there had been very much significance in the letter from the Director General, referred to at the start of this chapter, in which he had declared that the pub swap programme had been completed, and which had so heartened the brewers. It was now claimed that the brewers' approach to the programme had been "dilatory", and there were still districts where one brewer owned more than half the pubs.[17]

Representations from individual publicans and from the [redacted, but assumed to be tenants'] organisation suggested they were suffering some constraint in respect of their newly gained freedom to buy some products outside of the tie, as embodied in Regulation 1984/83. Allegations of insidious threats by brewers to withhold investment if a tenant did not co-operate were noted.[18]

Drawing on data from its questionnaire, the Office found at least some evidence of retail prices having increased faster than the general rate of inflation. Moreover, prices varied from region to region, and by more than might be justified by differences in operating costs. The Chairman of Wolverhampton & Dudley Breweries was quoted as saying that such differences were not justified. The suspicions aroused amongst officials by real price increases were reinforced by evidence of widening brewer margins.[19] Officials who had scrutinised the data found no evidence that the "big six" earned below-average returns; and, indeed, there was some evidence that Bass and Scottish & Newcastle enjoyed excess profits, they said. Arguments put forward by the Brewers' Society to counter such points and urging caution in the interpretation of the data met with little sympathy.[20]

As if the foregoing conclusions were not serious enough for the brewers, the paper's authors proceeded to recount allegations of collusion between brewers on matters such as the timing and quantum of price increases and the level of discounts for free trade customers. Names of those alleged to have colluded have been redacted in the OFT paper, but it may be that the OFT thought that the alleged collusion had taken place within the Brewers' Society. The paper's authors observed, however, that the Office's Legal Division felt that there was insufficient evidence to bring any action under the Restrictive Trade Practices Act.[21]

Divestment of pubs deemed feasible

The paper next turned to the question of possible remedies. Conceding that this would be a matter for the MMC, should there be a reference and should the Commission then find public interest detriment, the authors of the paper sought to give some reassurance that the most obvious remedy, divestment of tied pubs, was feasible. The 1969 Report had feared that this would cause damaging upheaval which could be detrimental to consumers. This time officials at the OFT had consulted two independent surveyors, and both thought that a period of five to ten years for disposal would be sufficient to avoid disruption. The European Commission had been consulted and reported that it saw no reason why enforced divestment would fall foul of European regulation. But "the Director responsible expressed sympathy with the existing arrangements taking the line that it would be necessary to ensure that any remedy was not worse than the evil it was seeking to cure".[22]

There was one *caveat* not included within the main paper, but which is referred to in notes passing between senior staff, and it concerned rural pubs. The problem was recognised by an OFT official, but then dismissed, as follows:

> Maybe the tied house system does allow the brewers to keep going uneconomic pubs which serve a useful social purpose...but...the particular issue of rural pubs should not concern us at this stage.

Concluding, and noting that the brewers would not like it and would probably offer "ineffective palliatives" to support the *status quo*, the Competition Division said that the case for a complex monopoly reference was a strong one, and recommended that a reference be made.[23]

A reference is made

On 13 June, three days after this paper had been produced, Borrie held a meeting with his top officials. There appears to have been no serious disagreement with the paper's conclusions, and the Director General summed up by saying that, subject to the "usual rounds of consultations", he was minded to make a reference by the end of July.[24] This statement is somewhat at odds with a handwritten note from Borrie to the Head of Competition Policy dated the same day: "I agreed today, following the meeting, a reference should be made", he had written. The die was cast; consultation would be a formality.[25]

On 25 June an official wrote to the Secretary of the Brewers' Society advising that Sir Gordon intended to refer the industry to the MMC, but indicating that he was willing to meet a Brewers' Society delegation before making a reference. The letter, referred to the "high degree of concentration and vertical integration", pointing out that:

> The Director-General has noted four possible effects of the tied-house system:

(a) Because the brewing industry supplies a high proportion of its products through outlets tied to the brewers competition is restricted;
(b) Because of the brewers' hold over retail outlets, independent suppliers face difficulties in marketing their products;
(c) In view of (b), consumer choice, particularly in the on-trade is limited. Tied houses concentrate on selling products supplied by the brewers which own those houses; and
(d) Prices, margins and profits within the industry appear to be high.

The brewers took up the invitation to see Borrie, and a meeting was held on 9 July 1986. The Brewers' Society team consisted of Edward Guinness (Chairman), Anthony Fuller (Vice Chairman), Sir Derek Palmar (Bass), Sir Derrick Holden-Brown (Allied-Lyons), Allen Sheppard (Grand Met), Desmond Mangham (Director) and Alan Tilbury (Secretary). There was, presumably, still hope in the industry that the delegation might persuade Sir Gordon to stay his hand, but, having seen many of the relevant papers, the authors have concluded that this was a remote possibility.

On 23 July the Director General again met with senior officials to review comments about the proposed reference. Neither the DTI nor the Ministry for Agriculture, Fisheries and Food was convinced of the need for a reference, but this didn't deflect the meeting, which closed with the Deputy Director General asking for final confirmation that this would not conflict with European law.[26] The representations made by the Society had had no effect, and on 25 July 1986 a senior official wrote to Tilbury, advising that Sir Gordon had decided to refer the industry to the MMC. This letter, much of which was identical to that of 25 June, gave the reasons for the referral in some detail.

On the same day an OFT official wrote to the Chairman of CAMRA,[27] stating that the Director General had decided to make a reference, and adding that the Office was grateful for the advice which CAMRA had given. The letter mentioned the likely date when the reference would be made. Briefing CAMRA in advance was a remarkable step to take. This information was without doubt potentially price sensitive, but not only did the letter fail to point this out, but so far as can be seen, the advance warning to CAMRA came ahead of any notification to the Stock Exchange.

And so on 4 August 1986 Sir Gordon Borrie wrote to the MMC referring the brewing industry for an inquiry into the supply of beer. He did this under the powers given to him in Sections 47(1), 49(1) and 50(1) of the Fair Trading Act 1973. The letter was formal and didn't refer to any of the OFT's concerns. Thus the events were set in motion which would lead to the Beer Orders and to the vast structural changes in the industry. With the benefit of hindsight, a further reference to the MMC was always a distinct possibility once the 1969 Report had decided that the tied house system "may be expected to operate against the public interest" and no direct action was taken.

Notes

1. Brewers' Society Annual Report for the year to September 1985, p. 9.
2. Office of Fair Trading (OFT) paper "Possible Monopoly Reference: The Supply of Beer and Tied Houses", 10 June 1986, paras. 27–8.
3. Sir Gordon Borrie's speech to the Leicester Chamber of Commerce, 6 December 1985.
4. Monopolies Commission, *Beer: A Report on the Supply of Beer*, 216 (1969).
5. OFT memorandum "Beer and Tied Houses", 21 November 1985.
6. *Ibid.*, para. 5.
7. *Ibid.*, para. 7.
8. *Ibid.*, para. 8.
9. OFT paper "Possible Monopoly Reference: The Supply of Beer and Tied Houses", 10 June 1986, para. 1.
10. *Ibid.*, para. 2.
11. Brewers' Society paper, 28 February 1986.
12. OFT paper "Possible Monopoly Reference: The Supply of Beer and Tied Houses", 10 June 1986, para. 39.
13. *Ibid.*
14. *Ibid.*, paras. 8–10 and 15.
15. Monopolies and Mergers Commission (MMC), *Full-Line Forcing and Tie-In Sales: A Report on the Practice of Requiring Any Person to Whom Goods or Services are Supplied to Acquire Other Goods or Services as a Condition of that Supply*, HC212 (1981).
16. OFT paper "Possible Monopoly Reference: The Supply of Beer and Tied Houses", 10 June 1986, paras. 18–20 and 22.
17. *Ibid.*, para. 28.
18. *Ibid.*, paras. 33–5.
19. *Ibid.*, paras. 41–3, 45 and 60.
20. *Ibid.*, para. 46.
21. *Ibid.*, para. 59.
22. *Ibid.*, paras. 75–7.
23. *Ibid.*, paras. 82 and 84.
24. OFT "Minutes of the meeting held on 13 June to discuss a possible reference of beer and the tied house system", 17 June 1986.
25. OFT memorandum "Tied houses", 13 June 1986.
26. *Ibid.*, para. 6.
27. OFT letter to J. Scanlon, 25 July 1986.

5
The Conduct of the Inquiry

The two teams assemble

Following receipt of Sir Gordon Borrie's letter, the Monopolies and Mergers Commission (MMC) established a panel to undertake the beer inquiry, announcing its members on 8 September 1986. The Chairman was to be Dick Smethurst, who had been a Commissioner since 1978 and a Deputy Chairman since 1986. An economist at Worcester College, Oxford, he was to leave the Commission a few months after the publication of the report of this inquiry.

The other members of the group were Dan Goyder, a solicitor, later to become a Deputy Chairman of the MMC; David Thomson, a banker from Lazards; Percy Flint, who had been with Imperial Chemical Industries (ICI); Leif Mills, a trade union official; and Bob Young, another industrialist (who, alone amongst them, was participating in his first inquiry). The case officer assigned to the inquiry was Bernard Gravatt and the MMC's senior economist was Robin Aaronson.

Three of the panel members had been involved with other MMC inquiries dealing with the brewing industry. Dick Smethurst had participated in the 1981 investigation into full-line forcing,[1] and the Scottish & Newcastle/Matthew Brown merger inquiry of 1985,[2] while Goyder and Thomson had been members of the group that had investigated the proposed merger between Elders IXL and Allied-Lyons in 1985–86. Both Smethurst and Young were later to be appointed to the group examining the proposed merger between Elders and Scottish & Newcastle, Smethurst once more as Chairman. Coincidentally, at the time when the beer group was selected, four of them were working on the same inquiry (into British Waterways), with Smethurst acting as Chairman of that group.

Very soon after the inquiry was established advertisements were placed in several newspapers and magazines inviting submissions from interested parties. 69 companies, organisations and associations, together with 80 individuals, made one or more submissions, and a list of the former group is given in Appendix 5.1. Easily the most substantial of these came from the Brewers' Society. Some submissions were only in writing but several companies and organisations also attended hearings. Documents in the possession of Leif Mills show that 176 written submissions, comprising 560 separate papers, were received, and that there were 20 hearings. The panel was to meet 59 times.

The MMC spent the first few months of the inquiry time getting to know the industry. It held meetings with the Brewers' Society, and during the autumn of 1986 and in the spring of 1987 members of the panel visited breweries owned by Bass, Arkell, Greene King, Shepherd Neame, Eldridge Pope, Vaux and Whitbread.[3] The Commission mainly obtained its information, however, through questionnaires. The first one, issued on 31 December 1986, went to the brewers themselves; it was 84 pages long and its coverage was extensive, embracing beer sales, production details, pubs and financial data. The Commission subsequently issued several other questionnaires, both to brewers and to companies producing, importing and selling other alcoholic and soft drinks.

In addition, during the period June to September 1987 the MMC commissioned a number of efficiency studies, covering areas such as employment and wages, production, research and development, primary and secondary distribution, packaging and marketing. Data were gathered mainly by interview with senior personnel in the companies concerned, which comprised a mix of national, regional and small brewers.[4] Also in the summer of 1987 research into pubs was conducted on the Commission's behalf by an independent market research company, which investigated – in respect of tenanted, managed and free houses – the number of brands on sale for each type of drink, nearest competitors (pubs and others), size of pub, price increases, numbers of suppliers and so on.[5]

Soon after the announcement of the MMC inquiry the Brewers' Society established an MMC Steering Committee, chaired by Ian Prosser of Bass, to represent the industry at the hearings. Prosser gave monthly progress reports to both the Executive Committee and Council of the Brewers' Society, and all submissions to the MMC were agreed by the Council.

In due course the membership of the Steering Committee comprised Anthony Fuller of Fuller Smith & Turner (and Chairman of the Brewers' Society), Richard Martin of Allied-Lyons, John McGrath of Grand Met, Peter Jarvis of Whitbread, Paul Nicholson of Vaux (representing the regional brewers) and Peter Robinson of Frederic Robinson (representing the small brewers). At first Michael Cottrell of Elders IXL (owners of Courage) was a member but he resigned when his company made a takeover bid for Scottish & Newcastle. Subsequently, Tony Portno of Bass joined the Committee; he was the Chairman of the Society's Technical Committee and his appointment reflected the fact that technical questions had been raised during the course of the hearings.

The Brewers' Society retained several advisers. Lead Counsel was Jeremy Lever, QC, assisted by Stephen Richards; the solicitor was Peter Freeman, of Simmons and Simmons; and the economists were Derek Morris, George Yarrow, John Vickers and Jeremy Hardie. Rightly or wrongly, the brewers decided that the Society, aided by its professional advisers, should present the industry's case. Contact between the Brewers' Society and the MMC took place by formal correspondence, by written submissions from the Society, by documents such as the Public Interest Letter (see below) and by hearings before the MMC panel. The initial submission from the Society was dated 1 June 1987 and it argued that the nature of the market and the intensive competition between brewers led to the inevitable conclusion – and this was the key issue – that a complex monopoly didn't exist.

The MMC was initially suspicious of the role of the Society, and it later became known, in fact, that the MMC had considered but decided against including the Brewers' Society in the potential finding of a complex monopoly. The MMC's first concern was that the Society might put pressure on its members to ensure that they kept to the agreed line, but the Society made clear to the MMC in an exchange of correspondence between March and May 1987 that members had the right to make their own submissions and express their own views. Indeed, while the pub-owning brewers all agreed that the then system of vertical integration was in the public interest, and should be strongly supported, there were bound to be differences, reflecting variations in size and operating area: the composition of the Society's MMC Steering Committee was in fact chosen to reflect these nuances. Most members of the Society did make submissions on their own behalf, the longest – which took up several pages of the final Report – coming from one of the non-integrated companies, namely, Guinness.

The MMC's second concern was that the Society might itself be involved in anti-competitive practices, and in September 1987 it despatched a solicitor to the Society's offices. He took away photocopies of several hundred pages of documents, such as minutes and committee papers, but these showed that the MMC's fears were groundless. One Commissioner involved in the inquiry has told the authors that, once the Commission's fears regarding the Society had been put to rest, it welcomed the participation in the inquiry of a single entity to present the industry's case.

The hearings

The Society's first hearing before the MMC panel was on 17 June 1987. On one side of the room sat the MMC group. In the centre was the Chairman, Dick Smethurst, and beside him sat the MMC Secretary, Stephen Burbridge (who attended all the hearings but played little or no role in the proceedings), and the MMC case officer, Bernard Gravatt. Two members of the panel (usually Dan Goyder and Leif Mills) sat to Smethurst's left and the other three to his right. In the second row, behind the panel, sat the MMC staff members, foremost amongst them being the MMC's chief economist Robin Aaronson. Opposite them sat the Brewers' Society team. In the centre was Ian Prosser, who was flanked by Jeremy Lever, QC, and the Society's Director, Desmond Mangham, while the other brewers sat on either side of them. In the second row were Peter Freeman and colleagues from Simmons and Simmons, together with Alan Tilbury and Chris Thurman of the Society's staff. The economic advisers sat in either the second or third row.

Sir Paul Nicholson described one of the hearings in his book, *Brewer at Bay*:

> The commission sat appropriately in Carey Street. The case was heard by a panel of commissioners chaired by an academic, a Professor Smethurst, with panel members largely drawn from former 'apparatchiks' of major companies such as an ex-secretary of ICI. The most sensible and perceptive of the panel members was the trade unionist Lief (*sic*) Mills of the Inland Revenue Staff Federation, who from his questions at the formal hearings, at least seemed to understand what he was talking about.
>
> The whole atmosphere was unreal, certainly one, if not two of the commissioners seemed asleep during much of the proceedings. From where I sat, the only factor relieving some of the tedium was watching the comings and goings of the 'bouncing Czech' – Robert Maxwell's – helicopter on the Mirror building some few hundred yards away.[6]
>
> [*Carey Street, in London, is where the bankruptcy court used to be situated. Leif Mills was from the Banking, Insurance and Finance Union.*]

There were no representatives at the hearings from any other interested organisation, or from the press, and the minutes of meetings were kept confidential within the two bodies. So too were those of hearings between the MMC and individual companies and organisations. Certainly no details of hearings were ever released to the press.

Virtually all the questions were asked by the Chairman, although occasionally another member might raise an issue; panel member Goyder, for instance, made clear his concern over the tenants' situation. Lever often dealt with the questions in the first instance but he was usually supported by one or more of the brewers. It was unusual for anyone sitting behind the main Brewers' Society team to speak, but sometimes notes were passed from those in the second row to those in front. Among matters discussed at this first hearing were the major issues which would be considered during the course of the inquiry, such as access to tied estates by third party suppliers, local concentrations of pub ownership, the position of independent wholesalers, and general market trends.

The Public Interest Letter

On 10 December 1987 the Secretary of the MMC, Stephen Burbridge, wrote to the Brewers' Society and to all the affected companies, stating that the Commission had provisionally concluded that a complex monopoly existed. Under the provisions of the Fair Trading Act 1973 a complex monopoly existed when two or more unconnected entities, together supplying at least 25 per cent of a specified market, acted in such a way as to prevent, restrict or distort competition in connection with the production or supply of goods or services in that market. The existence of a complex monopoly didn't, however, in itself imply that the practices of the named parties operated against the public interest, or were in any sense illegal. [See also Appendix 1.1.]

Attached to Burbridge's letter to the Society was a list of those of its members that the MMC believed were implicated, which were all those companies that owned pubs or made trade loans (including Guinness, which made trade loans, mainly in Northern Ireland). The letter itself was known as the Public Interest Letter (PIL), and wasn't shown to the public or the press; and once it was issued, the pace of activity changed significantly. Attached to the PIL were three substantial annexes, as follows:

- Annex 1 contained the results of the MMC's data collection, analysed by market/economic activity. It comprised 160 pages, including appendices.
- Annex 2 reported the MMC's provisional finding that there was a complex monopoly and it listed 22 public interest issues.[7] These issues included the price of beer generally, lager pricing, regional price variations, barriers to entry created by tied houses and trade loans, treatment of wholesalers and tenants, horizontal integration, involvement in non-beer drinks, efficiency and capacity, and the use of transfer prices between production and retailing in a vertically integrated industry. The annex recognised the possibility that mitigating countervailing benefits might be found, but just one factor was presented as possibly acting in the public interest – the way in which the tied house system enabled medium and small brewers to exist. This annex was six pages long.
- Annex 3 contained a summary of the submissions received by the MMC from companies and organisations. Among these were brewers, including Guinness; consumer bodies, including the Campaign for Real Ale and the Consumers' Association; other drinks manufacturers, including Bulmer; wholesalers; and individual pub tenants and the National Union of Licensed Victuallers. Annex 3 comprised 37 pages.

The Economist was later to say of the PIL: "Incredibly, this monster of a document arrived a full year into the investigation."[8]

On 22 February 1988 the MMC issued its first addendum to the PIL, which contained further material on costs and margins, transfer pricing and profitability, and was linked to one of the public interest issues. The Society's response to the PIL was also in three volumes and was submitted at the end of April 1988. Thereafter there was a considerable increase in the amount of discussion and volume of documentation between the Society and the MMC. The reference had specified that the inquiry should be completed in two years, that is, by 4 August 1988, but by July it had become clear that the original timetable was inadequate. The Commission accordingly requested more time, and the Secretary of State, using his powers under the Fair Trading Act 1973, extended the period for completion by six months, that is, until 3 February 1989.

That same month a second addendum to the PIL was issued, and it dealt with a range of possibilities for structural change. These included banning brewers from owning pubs or limiting the number they could own; giving pub tenants greater purchasing freedom; banning free trade loans or changing the terms on which they could be made; compelling brewers to publish wholesale prices and discounts; banning restrictive covenants on pubs being sold; and improving security for tenants.[9] [See Appendix 5.2.] The Society gave its detailed response to these items in October 1988.

As described in the next chapter, the MMC's agenda for much of the last few months of 1988 was dominated by further consideration of financial issues, including the reworking by the Brewers' Society of financial data which had originally been submitted over the course of the previous two years. During the second half of 1988 the last formal hearings took place between the MMC and the Brewers' Society: on 8 July, 18 July, 23 August, 8 November and, finally, 8 December.[10] It was said of the last hearing, in the Brewers' Society's Annual Report for the year to September 1989, that "the Society's representations team also took the opportunity to complain about the bias appearing in numerous passages of purportedly factual material which had been prepared for inclusion in the Commission's report and sent to the Society for comment".

Amongst the last acts of the inquiry were fact-finding visits to the USA and to Belgium by members and staff of the Commission.

Notes

1 Monopolies and Mergers Commission (MMC), *Full-Line Forcing and Tie-in Sales: A Report on the Practice of Requiring Any Person to Whom Goods or Services are Supplied to Acquire Other Goods or Services as a Condition of that Supply*, HC 212 (1981).
2 MMC, *Scottish & Newcastle Breweries PLC and Matthew Brown PLC: A Report on the Proposed Merger*, Cmnd 9645 (1985).
3 Brewers' Society papers.
4 Ibid.
5 MMC, *The Supply of Beer: A Report on the Supply of Beer for Retail Sale in the United Kingdom*, Cm 651 (1989), Appendix 2.1, paras. 4–17 and 2.60; tables 2.12–2.13, 2.16, 2.35, 2.41–4, 2.57 and 2.59–60.

6 Sir Paul Nicholson, *Brewer at Bay* (Memoir Club, 2003), p. 160.
7 MMC, *The Supply of Beer: A Report on the Supply of Beer for Retail Sale in the United Kingdom*, Cm 651 (1989), paras. 5.92–5.189.
8 *The Economist*, p. 39, 17 June 1989.
9 MMC, *The Supply of Beer: A Report on the Supply of Beer for Retail Sale in the United Kingdom*, Cm 651 (1989), paras. 5.195–5.237.
10 Brewers' Society files.

6
The MMC Receives the Evidence

The Brewers' Society

From the start of the inquiry the brewers were convinced that they had a strong case. The industry then comprised six national brewers, two major specialist companies without a tied estate (Guinness and Carlsberg), 11 regional brewers and dozens of local brewers. And by contrast with the situation in several leading beer-producing countries, there was no question of a brewer having a scale monopoly, that is, a market share of 25 per cent or more. But nor did the brewers accept that a complex monopoly existed.[1]

Brewers' ownership of premises with a full on-licence had fallen from 78 per cent of the total in 1967 (the date used in the 1969 Monopolies Commission (MC) Report) to 57 per cent in 1986, while their share of combined full on-licences and clubs was down from 58 per cent to 40 per cent.[2] Sales of beer through brewers' outlets had also been declining in both absolute and relative terms during this period and by 1986 accounted for 46 per cent of total beer sales and 54 per cent of sales for consumption on the premises, including clubs.[3] [Clubs at this time, although starting to decline in popularity, were still providing very strong competition to pubs, so it was rational to combine them with full on-licences in measuring the size of the market.]

The brewers firmly believed that through the tied house system the industry was providing the consumer with plenty of choice and good value for money, and their arguments can be summarised under four headings: choice between pubs, choice within pubs, responsiveness to changing market conditions, and price and value for money – the price/amenity package.

The first of these, the existence of choice – and therefore competition – between pubs, was a central argument on the brewers' part. For many years the Brewers' Society had commissioned the market research company, Market and Opinion Research International (MORI), to carry out surveys of public attitudes to pubs and beer, based on various criteria, such as the brands of beer offered, the comfort of the venue, whether it offered food, and whether it was where the customer would meet congenial company. The industry believed that this and other research suggested that regular pub visitors often had a repertoire of preferred pubs, which they used according to the circumstances of the visit.

MORI found, *inter alia*, that 60 per cent or more of respondents who had visited a pub in the previous 12 months had consistently over recent years expressed satisfaction with the choice of pubs near their home; and that, amongst a selection of social, eating and drinking venues, pubs scored highest in terms of popularity as measured by frequency of visit. The brewers claimed that this research demonstrated that a visit to a pub matched more closely than any other activity the average person's idea of the ideal evening out.

Moving on to their second argument, the brewers pointed out that, because part of the overall experience lay in product choice, it was essential, if pub operators were to compete effectively, that they keep a full range of beers, wines, spirits, cider and soft drinks. At that time a pub would normally offer a choice of draught ales, a choice of draught lagers, and a draught stout, as well as a range of bottled or canned beers, including some of the more specialist lines, such as barley wine, strong ales, sweet stout and strong lagers. There would also be a wide range of non-beer drinks. The industry believed that this range of beers was wider than that available in other countries, and asked Research Bureau Limited (RBL), to investigate. Its findings, which are summarised in Table 6.1, confirmed this view.

Table 6.1 Number of Beer Brands Per Pub/Bar[4]

	England and Wales	West Germany	France	Denmark	Ireland
Draught	6.5	2.2	1.9	0.6	8.5
Packaged	9.8	1.7	4.7	8.5	9.2
Total	16.3	3.9	6.6	9.1	17.7

Sources: RBL; Brewers' Society.

The figures in Table 6.1 appear to suggest that the best choice was in Ireland. But the Irish market had relatively few brands, and the same draught beers – nine in number – were available in half the pubs surveyed in Ireland. The total number of draught brands recorded in Ireland was 18, compared with 133 in England and Wales, with only one draught brand [clearly Guinness stout] showing a similar widespread penetration to that seen in Ireland.

The brewers' third point was that that they had responded well to the dramatic changes in the market place that had occurred since the 1969 MC

Report. As real incomes and leisure time had grown, there had been a widening in the range of on-licensed premises, particularly in relation to the popular eating-out market. By the time of the Monopolies & Mergers Commission (MMC) inquiry food had already become a very important element in the running of many pubs, and, indeed, the Brewers' Society estimated in 1988 that 40 per cent of consumer expenditure on eating out occurred in pubs.

There had also been a rapid response, the brewers said, in a competitive market, to consumers' demands for new beer brands, particularly in the fastest growing segment, namely, lager, which necessitated investment in new plant. The brewers had concluded that the best way of competing effectively in this growth market was to introduce into the UK well known overseas brands (mostly European or Australian, although one of the major lager brands from the start was Carling, which originated in Canada). Another important trend was the growing importance of beer sales in supermarkets, which fuelled the growth of beer in cans and therefore necessitated investment in new canning lines.

The fourth strand of the brewers' case was that they competed in terms of the price-amenity package that they offered. Unlike beer purchased in a supermarket, the price of beer bought in a pub or other on-licensed outlet contains three elements – the product itself, service, and the amenities of the venue. The amenities can vary from simple wooden chairs to comfortable armchairs, from bare flooring to plush carpets, and in numerous other ways. But throughout the MMC inquiry the industry had a major problem in trying to convince the Commissioners of the validity of the concept that the price of beer was a function of both the product and the surrounding amenities.

The brewers told the MMC that, with pubs not only in competition with other leisure activities, but serving as the shop window for the brewer's beer, it was vital that the quality of the buildings be maintained, if not enhanced, and that this was reflected in the large sums they had invested in their pubs. Capital expenditure on their estates in the period 1980 to 1986 had amounted to £2.7 billion at 1986 prices, equivalent to £10 a barrel in tenanted pubs and £35–40 in managed pubs. The pace of investment had latterly accelerated, they added.[5] [£2.7bn is around £6.4bn in 2011 terms.]

The industry believed that pub beer prices were set in a competitive market place and were reasonable, and it set out to demonstrate this by means of some international comparisons. RBL collected data from a number of countries in respect of prices in pubs and bars in residential areas, thus excluding, for instance, tourist spots and the centres of major cities. Since a significant element in price was – and still is – tax (and there is a tax-on-tax situation, with excise duty levied according to alcoholic strength and VAT levied on the price including duty), figures were collected both including and excluding tax. The results are shown in Table 6.2.

Table 6.2 Minutes Taken to Earn a Pint of Draught Beer in a Pub or Bar[6]

	England and Wales	West Germany	France	Denmark	Ireland
Average price – pence per pint	101	143	171	268	135
Price – net of tax	70	122	143	195	62
Minutes worked to earn a pint of beer	14	14	26	21	19
Minutes – net of tax	9	12	21	16	9

(Earnings base = gross hourly earnings of a male manual labourer in manufacturing industry.)
Sources: RBL; Eurostat; Brewers' Society. (February 1988 exchange rates.)

The brewers believed that these price statistics, whether viewed in absolute terms or in relation to earnings, offered two strong arguments to support their contention that prices in the UK were reasonable.

A second test was to compare the on- and off-trade prices in the UK with other countries, and the Brewers' Society duly arranged for a survey to be carried out of the differences between on- and off-licence beer prices in a number of countries. As explained in a paper written by George Yarrow and submitted to the MMC,[7] this test had the advantage of nullifying the otherwise distorting effects on the comparisons of different standards of living, exchange rate fluctuations and varying beer strengths. It was important, of course, for the validity of the exercise, that UK off-trade prices were fully competitive, but this was not in doubt. Thus a significant number of brewers, including national, regional and some local brewers, competed to supply this market; whilst, by contrast, the buying side was dominated by a small number of large supermarkets, which, because of the scale of the volumes purchased, were able to extract low prices from their suppliers. Furthermore, there was nothing to stop an overseas brewer selling to these chains: in other words, barriers to entry into this segment of the market were low.

Again, tax had to be taken into account in order to derive valid conclusions from this test. Excise duties were (and still are) higher in the UK than in the other countries in the sample, and thus ratios calculated from tax-inclusive selling prices will show a smaller premium in respect of on-trade compared with off-trade prices in the UK. Table 6.3, which contains the findings, therefore gives the ratios with and without tax, and, as can be seen, on either measure the on-off ratio is lower in the UK than in any other country in the sample.

Table 6.3   Beer Price Ratios, 1987[8]

Country	Ratio of on-trade to off-trade prices	
	With tax	Without tax
Belgium	3.1	3.2
France	3.5	3.6
Italy	3.8	3.8
USA	2.3	2.4
West Germany	3.5	3.6
UK	1.7	2.0

Sources: Brewers' Society, from data produced by ERC Statistics International Ltd; CBMC/EBIC combined statistics.

In his paper Yarrow concluded that:

The data are therefore consistent with the view that vertical integration and tying arrangements in Britain have broadly pro-competitive effects, and contradict "the market power hypothesis" that these characteristics of the British market tend to restrict competition in the on trade and thereby raise consumer prices.[9]

To show that the relatively low price of beer in British pubs wasn't down to an inferior level of amenity, the Society submitted the results of two other surveys, which found that a clear majority of both Britons and foreign visitors preferred British pubs to foreign pubs; and that British pubs had far more entertainment facilities – television, pool, juke box and so on – than pubs in a selection of other European countries, as well as offering a much wider choice of beer.[10]

Vertical integration the issue

Well though the brewers may have presented an evidence-based case on matters such as choice, price and amenity, the central issue for the MMC was the degree of vertical integration within the industry – vertical integration being the situation where a company has an interest in more than one level in the production and distribution chain. Thus most brewers not only brewed beer, but wholesaled it (along with other producers' beers and drinks), and then sold it to the public in their pubs, whether managed or tenanted.

In December 1988 the Brewers' Society submitted two papers on vertical integration. The first one, prepared at the Commission's request and written by Derek Morris and George Yarrow, both leading Oxford economists and advisers to the Society, gave a theoretical underpinning to the then structure of the brewing industry.[11] The second paper outlined in less technical terms how vertical integration operated in the UK brewing industry.

The brewers also pointed out that DG1V, the section of the European Commission dealing with competition, had considered the structure of the brewing industry throughout Europe, and that it too had concluded that vertical integration could benefit the consumer. That was why it had issued the Block Exemption (Regulation (EEC) No 1984/83), which exempted qualifying contracts, such as the UK tied tenancy, from its general prohibition of restrictive agreements.

The Brewers' Society contended that vertical integration had beneficial effects on the amenity/price package offered to consumers and a positive effect on the number of outlets in operation. This was because, when investing in pubs or setting prices, brewers benefited from margins on extra beer sales (driven by better amenities or lower prices or both) at both the retail and wholesale levels, and the latter – wholesale – effect provided the stimulus for higher retail investment and lower retail prices than would otherwise have been the case. In assessing the arguments for keeping a rural pub open the brewer would look at the returns it produced at both retailing and wholesaling levels, which might be more than sufficient to justify its existence in commercial terms when retailing returns alone would be insufficient.

The brewers went on to claim other positive consequences of vertical integration:

(a) It provided a means of economic access by small brewers to consumers and enabled them to compete effectively with the national brewers.
(b) It enabled brewers to apply important managerial and other skills at the retail level; and to accelerate the pace of improvement of full on-licensed premises.
(c) It provided an efficient way of facilitating, by means of tenancies, the participation of large numbers of small businessmen in retailing.
(d) It enabled brewers to control the conditions in which draught beer was sold.[12]

The Brewers' Society, in the light of what it saw as these manifest benefits, argued that any interference in the integrated system would be detrimental to consumers in terms of the price/amenity package or higher prices or both.[13]

An issue which took up an inordinate amount of time towards the end of the inquiry was the analysis of much accounting data dealing with the costs of production of beer, and, more importantly, transfer prices.[14] The debate on transfer prices started with the publication in December 1987 of the Public Interest Letter (PIL), which contained a list of public interest issues and described this particular one as follows:

> The practice of the industry in operating its brewing, wholesaling and retailing businesses on an integrated basis with transfer not conducted on an arms length basis and whether this obscures the relative profitability and returns from the individual segments and has resulted in:
> (i) cross-subsidisation of individual segments of the businesses; and
> (ii) cross-subsidisation of particular products.[15]

Then on 22 February 1988, the MMC issued its first addendum to the PIL, drawing "attention to the possibility that the present structure of pricing provides for the main contribution from beer sales to be taken at the wholesale level", and referring once again to the potential for cross-subsidisation.[16] As the Brewers' Society pointed out in its evidence, the essence of the Commission's hypothesis was that beer prices charged to the free trade were excessive, that this was supported by the Commission's calculation that integrated brewers took most of their profit at the wholesale level, and that on the basis of wholesale list prices brewers' managed houses operated at "minimal profit".[17]

The concept that prices to the free trade were too high was rejected by the Society, which argued that the free trade sector was growing rapidly, that there were many buyers, including supermarket chains with plenty of bargaining muscle, and many suppliers who wished to sell their beers in to this sector. It was a very competitive market, in which it would be impossible to maintain artificially high prices.

The MMC's original questionnaire in 1986 had requested financial data for the various sectors of a brewer's operation, but it was later felt that this was inadequate and that more detailed data were required. The MMC therefore issued further questionnaires, in September 1988, namely, Segmented Costs and Profits and Beer Brands Costs and Profits. In fact, much of the second part of 1988 was concerned with an analysis of financial data.

The Society was critical of the way the MMC had analysed the data, particularly its use of wholesale list prices as a basis for calculating managed house profits, and the way in which it allocated managed house costs, sometimes wholly or substantially to beer rather than across all managed house operations including food. The net effect of the MMC's calculations was to show that brewers achieved a return on capital employed of 21.2 per cent in brewing and only 8.9 per cent in retailing – a conclusion that would prove crucial in the Commission's deliberations.

The industry rejected this view and set about producing its fresh calculations, employing the accountancy firm, Arthur Andersen, under the direction of Jeremy Hardie and George Yarrow. The team reworked all the MMC data, making use of the confidential figures submitted by individual companies. The main difference between the Society's new calculations and those used by the MMC was that the former, instead of using wholesale list prices to estimate transfer prices to managed houses, now used the – much lower – market prices actually charged to the untied free trade (excluding national accounts).

On this basis, "If brewers made the whole of their sales of beer to the managed and tenanted estates on similar terms to those to the free on-trade, brewers' return on the capital employed in production and wholesaling would not be abnormally high (10.4 per cent); and further, if managed houses paid for their beer on the same terms as the free on-trade, they would achieve an adequate return on their capital employed (10.9 per cent)".[18] Thus wholesale profitability was neither excessive nor disproportionate, while the fact that brewers continued to invest in managed pubs demonstrated that they couldn't be unprofitable.[19]

The MMC, however, in turn rejected the industry's recalculations. The industry and the Commission had reached an impasse and, as will be seen, the Commission's interpretation of the returns from brewing and retailing would significantly influence its final conclusions and recommendations. The reaction of companies to the regulatory regime that was to ensue would be one way of judging the wisdom of this thinking.

To sum up, the industry believed it had presented a compelling justification for retaining the *status quo*. Brewing was a very competitive industry, supplying many thousands of outlets, of which the brewers owned only 24 per cent (including off-licences and restricted on-licences). Furthermore, the brewers' outlets accounted for only around 46 per cent of total beer volume, a figure that, moreover, was falling, as other channels of trade, particularly supermarkets, became increasingly important. There was a choice of well over 1000 beer brands, and the industry had been responding to consumers' expectations of higher levels of amenity, and satisfying the accelerating growth in demand for the provision of food in pubs, through major capital investment. Finally, the comparisons with other countries in terms of price, beer choice and amenity demonstrated that the level of price-amenity provided in UK pubs was without equal. [The Brewers' Society's detailed arguments appear in Chapter 5 of the MMC Report, which also gives the Society's views on each of the public interest issues and on the addendum to the public interest letter dealing with Options for Change.]

Guinness

Most of the submissions received by the MMC, apart from those made by the pub-owning brewers, were critical of the operation of the tied house system in one way or another. These came from brewers without a tied estate, some small brewers that were not members of the Brewers' Society, non-beer drinks suppliers, independent wholesalers, consumer representative bodies and individuals (including licensees and small businessmen). Some of the arguments deployed in these submissions are described below.

Guinness was unique amongst those making submissions, by virtue of being hostile towards the tied house system (and, indeed, listed in the MMC Report as a brewer without a tied estate), yet in the MMC's eyes a participant in the complex monopoly. This was on account of its use of trade loans, particularly in Northern Ireland, where it had a strong market position. The company sold more beer than any of the regional brewers, but less than the smallest of the nationals. Much of this was brewed at the Park Royal brewery in London (now closed) but there were also substantial imports from the company's Dublin brewery. The only other brewer with national distribution but without a tied estate was Carlsberg, but, unlike Guinness, it wasn't held to be part of the complex monopoly because it didn't use trade loans. Furthermore, and unlike Guinness, Carlsberg was not critical of the tied house system.

Guinness's submission to the MMC was longer and more detailed than any of the others,[20] and, in a nutshell, its case was that it should be given a fair chance to compete on price, range and quality of product and service. The company's main brand was Guinness stout, which has a distinctive bitter taste, and which was – and remains – a unique product, with a considerable following: in the judgment of most licensees, in fact, a "must stock" item. To compensate for its lack of retail outlets Guinness has relied on heavyweight advertising – traditionally both imaginative and memorable – to maintain and enhance its position in the market.

Guinness stout had originally been delivered in bulk to other brewers, who bottled it and undertook the wholesale distribution of the beer to their own and other outlets. The company believed that in this way it gave pub-owning brewers an incentive to take its beer, as they received benefits at the bottling, wholesaling and retailing stages. In its MMC submission Guinness noted that sales of all types of bottled beer were in decline, and that bottled Guinness was no different. In fact, figures from the British Beer & Pub Association (BBPA) show that bottled beer fell from 29 per cent of the market in 1967 to 9 per cent in 1985.[21]

In 1960 the company had started selling its stout in draught form, packaging it itself. It was concerned that limitations on the amount of space available in bars for draught beer pumps might dissuade pub-owners from stocking the product. While such fears were understandable, the fact was that draught Guinness stout also became a "must stock" brand, with a growing number of consumers preferring it to the bottled version: any pub not stocking it was thus likely to be at a disadvantage to its competitors. Nevertheless, the possibility that a pub-owning brewer – particularly a large one – might de-list what was the company's main product was a continuing concern for Guinness management.

Guinness produced two other beers, namely, Harp lager and Kaliber non-alcoholic lager. One of the first lagers to be brewed in the UK, Harp had been launched during the early1960s by Guinness in alliance with three national pub-owning brewers. In 1977 the Harp Lager consortium comprised Courage, Guinness and Scottish & Newcastle, each with 32.03 per cent, and Greene King and Wolverhampton & Dudley, each with 1.96 per cent, but by December 1987 it was owned 75 per cent by Guinness and 25 per cent by Greene King. Throughout the 1970s and 1980s lager sales grew very rapidly, generating intense competitive activity.[22] Harp was sold in the pubs of those brewers that produced it, normally – but not exclusively – members of the consortium; but it was rarely seen in the pubs of other brewers, and Guinness argued that this was discriminatory.

Kaliber had been launched in 1985 into the emerging market for no alcohol and low alcohol beers (NAB/LABs). At the time of the MMC Report this was thought to be a market segment with considerable growth potential, based on concerns over drinking and driving, as well as alcohol consumption in general. In the event, this optimism proved to be misplaced, with sales peaking in 1988 at 1.1 per cent of the beer market, falling to 1.0 per cent in 1989, and then declining steadily.[23] The point is, however, that a number of pub-owning brewers introduced their own NAB/LABs, thereby excluding Kaliber from a very large part of the market. Guinness argued that this was another instance of the tied house system putting it at a competitive disadvantage – an argument with which, as we shall see, the MMC was later to be very impressed.

During the 1970s Guinness had diversified into many different areas of activity, but the new management of the early 1980s sold most of these businesses and took the strategic decision to become a major force in the spirits sector. First, in 1985, the company bought the whisky distiller, Arthur Bell, and then came the battle for the Distillers Company, with Guinness finally gaining control in April 1986. The circumstances surrounding this latter takeover were to lead, by 1990, to arrests, court action and imprisonment for a number of the leading participants, but for the time being the relevance of the two acquisitions was that Guinness came into direct competition with those pub-owning brewers that had their own spirits interests.

A pub customer ordering, for example, a Scotch whisky would be served, unless he specified otherwise, with a brand from one of the optics – devices attached to bottles which automatically dispense a single measure. A pub owner naturally supplied through optics his own spirits if he had them, or those of a supplier with whom he had a contractual relationship. Guinness argued that optics held the key to selling spirits in a pub and that its own brands were put at a significant disadvantage in a large number of pubs.

The arguments put forward by Guinness regarding access to pubs for its spirits brands were thus similar to its arguments regarding Kaliber and Harp. But it also drew attention to other issues. Guinness was in the unusual position of being in competition with its customers, in that every one of its products that was sold in a brewer-owned pub represented a lost sale of the pub owner's own product – a loss for which the pub-owning brewer would seek means of compensation. A way of achieving this was to set the retail prices of Guinness products higher than the pub owners' own equivalent brands. Thus Guinness was able to demonstrate that its share of the retail price of its draught stout had fallen from 28 per cent in 1965 to 19 per cent in 1986, while the proportion taken by VAT and excise duty had remained pretty constant, at 31 and 32 per cent, meaning that the share taken for wholesaling and retailing had risen from 40 to 49 per cent.[24] The MMC Report stated that in its evidence to the Commission

> Guinness acknowledged the need to provide an adequate retail mark-up in public houses, from which the costs of public houses, and so forth, were funded. But where the retailer/wholesaler margin was merged, structural problems are created for the independent supplier by:
> (i) making it inevitable that a brewer's own products would appear more profitable than an independent's; and
> (ii) creating a potential price premium at the wholesale level for the independent product.[25]

Bulmer

Another company which had several pages in the MMC Report devoted to its comments on the tied house system was the cider maker, Bulmer.[26] The company said that the tied house system was detrimental to its business and it complained about the effectiveness of Regulation (EEC) No 1984/83, which supposedly gave tenants the right to buy non-beer products, including cider, from a supplier other than their brewer-landlord. It also highlighted the difficulties of getting into the pubs of brewers which owned, wholly or in part, a cider producer or had a long-term trading relationship with one.

A particular problem, Bulmer said, was the ownership by brewers of its principal competitor, Taunton Cider, whose shareholders in 1985 included Bass and Courage, with 41.6 per cent each, Scottish & Newcastle, with 9.6 per cent, and Greene King, with 3.3 per cent, with the 3.9 per cent balance held by other brewers. Bulmer believed that the competition it faced from the Taunton consortium was discriminatory and had largely been responsible for its loss of market share during the 1970s. Bulmer also referred in its evidence to the cider interests of Allied-Lyons and Greenall Whitley, although, ironically, during the course of the inquiry it actually bought the latter's cider business. Echoing the point made by Guinness, it said that even when a brewer decided to sell its draught cider, the problem arose of the pub-owning brewer setting its bar price above those of its own beers, in order to provide some safeguard to the latter.

Bulmer complained too about the concentration of pub ownership in some areas, particularly the Midlands, by brewers from whose outlets its products were excluded, and it said that this reduced the effectiveness of its television advertising in such areas, which also had adverse consequences in terms of new product launches. It said that the exclusion of its products extended to the off-trade, since a number of major brewers owned large chains of off-licences, where they gave priority to their own products; this represented another obstacle to the introduction of new products. Towards the end of its evidence the company asserted that the major brewers were inhibiting consumer choice through their stocking and pricing policies.

Other submissions

Most of the comments from companies other than the pub-owning brewers were of a similar nature, highlighting the difficulty of gaining access to brewers' pubs and off-licences. Trade loans were mentioned by more than one respondent, who claimed that they tied the best outlets and could well be linked to the supply of non-beer drinks. The co-operative brewer, the Northern Clubs Federation, referred to the fact that while the proportion of tied pubs was much lower in Scotland than in England, it was nevertheless difficult to penetrate the Scottish free trade because a considerable proportion of it was tied through loans.[27]

Smiles,[28] a very small brewer, complained about the market power of the national brewers, which, it said, "manipulated consumer demand"[29] and "exercised control of the property market by owning the bulk of licensed property".[30] Smiles added that many of the untied pubs were low-barrelage houses and widely dispersed, which made for high distribution and servicing costs.

Wholesalers pointed out that their brewer suppliers were also their competitors, and that they were therefore affected by the brewers' pricing and discount policies. As became apparent when the MMC Report was published, the evidence of the wholesalers carried considerable weight with the Commission.

Surprisingly, nothing was heard from organisations concerned with alcohol abuse. One of the arguments advanced by such organisations at that time – as today – was that the price of alcoholic drinks was too low. They thought that excise duty should at the very least be increased annually in line with the Retail Prices Index (RPI), but preferably ahead of it, for example, in line with the growth of average earnings. Their silence is surprising, given that the MMC's endgame could well include proposals aimed at reducing the price of beer and/or increasing competition between pubs – in both cases quite obviously the opposite of what the anti-alcohol lobby wished for.

There were two organisations which were supportive of the tied house system in general, although critical of certain aspects. One was the National

Licensed Victuallers Association, which believed that consumer choice in public houses was wide, and argued that if pubs went to free traders choice would not necessarily improve. It was nevertheless critical of the high level of rents, poor security of tenure, and the share of revenue from amusement with prizes machines taken by brewer-landlords. While relations with senior brewery executives were often good, local managers could be overzealous. Some individual pub tenants made submissions, and the MMC also obtained licensees' views through its questionnaire to a sample of 1395 of them. This showed that 38 per cent of tenants claimed to have experienced some sort of problem with their landlord, of which almost a quarter related to rental issues and two-thirds to problems with getting maintenance and repair work done.[31]

The second organisation which supported the tied house system was the Campaign for Real Ale (CAMRA), which believed that without it the industry would become increasingly monopolistic and concentrated. On the other hand, it was concerned about what it saw as the limitations on choice created by local concentrations of pub ownership by one – or a few – brewers; and it therefore recommended that no brewer should own more than 33 per cent of pubs in any licensing district. It was critical of brewery takeovers, loan ties and the way it believed that brewers were able to manipulate the market by heavy advertising, notably of nationally distributed lagers. It referred to regional variations in prices, pointing out that that prices were lower where a number of strong independent local brewers were in competition, and that prices rose when these independent companies were taken over. And it recommended that every pub tenant and manager should be allowed to stock one draught beer of his choice in addition to those available from his brewer.[32]

Unlike CAMRA, the Consumers Association (CA) didn't go so far as to express support for the tied house system, but nor did it call for its end. It felt that since the 1969 MC Report the "extent of the monopoly" and concentration had increased. The growth sector of the beer market, lager, presented particularly difficult barriers to entry and had become dominated by the big brewers. Retail prices had risen faster than inflation, and new entry at the retail level was inhibited by the application of the licensing system, which also had the effect of concentrating pub ownership in fewer hands. The "pervasive influence" of the national brewers was evident in the choice of non-beer drinks available in their pubs.

On the other hand, some of the findings from CA's own research, carried out amongst a sample of 2000 consumers, supported elements of the brewers' case. So, for example, it said that consumers didn't "go to the pub for the beer. Public houses [are] a major social centre and meeting place for adults". This was borne out by the research finding that very few respondents chose which pub to visit on the basis of the drinks on offer or their prices.

The organisation's principal remedies were to prohibit the use by licensing magistrates of the "need" criterion, to restrict the tying of pubs by any one brewer to no more than a third of all those in a licensing district, and to allow tenants to introduce a draught beer of their own choice.

Time to reach a verdict

By the end of 1988 the inquiry team had received a mass of evidence. It had conducted its own research and requested information from many parties. It had made fact-finding visits not just to breweries and pubs in the UK, but to the USA and Belgium. Staff had carried out copious analysis of the data. And the time had now come for the Commissioners to reach their conclusions and finalise their report.

Notes

1. Brewers' Society submission to the Monopolies and Mergers Commission (MMC), June 1987, p. 3.
2. British Beer & Pub Association (BBPA), *Statistical Handbook*.
3. MMC, *The Supply of Beer: A Report on the Supply of Beer for Retail Sale in the United Kingdom*, Cm 651 (1989), para. 5.44.
4. *Ibid.*, Appendix 5.1, Table 10.
5. MMC, *The Supply of Beer: A Report on the Supply of Beer for Retail Sale in the United Kingdom*, Cm 651 (1989), paras. 5.31, 2.132 and 5.101.
6. *Ibid.*, Appendix 5.1, Tables 15–17.
7. Brewers' Society submission to the MMC, April 1988, Vol. 3 of the response to the Public Interest Letter (PIL), Appendix 7; G. Yarrow, *Differentials Between Prices in On- and Off-Licences*.
8. MMC, *The Supply of Beer: A Report on the Supply of Beer for Retail Sale in the United Kingdom*, Cm 651 (1989), Appendix 5.1, para. 7.
9. Brewers' Society submission to the MMC, April 1988, Vol. 3 of the response to the PIL, Appendix 7; G Yarrow, *op. cit.*, para. 5.
10. MMC, *The Supply of Beer: A Report on the Supply of Beer for Retail Sale in the United Kingdom*, Cm 651 (1989), Appendix 5.1, paras. 15–20 and 24–33.
11. *Ibid.*, Appendix 5.2.
12. *Ibid.*, para. 5.19(b)–(e).
13. Brewers' Society submission to the MMC, October 1988, dealing with Possibilities for Structural Change, p. 3, para. v.
14. MMC, *The Supply of Beer: A Report on the Supply of Beer for Retail Sale in the United Kingdom*, Cm 651 (1989), Appendices 3.1–3.4 and 3.6–3.11, comprising the financial questionnaires, studies and reworking of the data by Arthur Andersen.
15. *Ibid.*, para. 5.136.
16. *Ibid.*, para. 5.138.
17. *Ibid.*, para. 5.150.
18. *Ibid.*, para. 5.160.
19. *Ibid.*, para. 5.164.
20. *Ibid.*, paras. 6.156–6.190.
21. BBPA, *Statistical Handbook*.
22. *Ibid.*
23. *Ibid.*

24 MMC, *The Supply of Beer: A Report on the Supply of Beer for Retail Sale in the United Kingdom*, Cm 651 (1989), para. 6.163.
25 *Ibid.*, para. 6.167(k).
26 *Ibid.*, paras. 7.2–7.20.
27 *Ibid.*, para. 6.191.
28 *Ibid.*, paras. 6.194–6.203.
29 *Ibid.*, para. 6.194.
30 *Ibid.*, para. 6.196.
31 *Ibid.*, paras. 9.1–9.19.
32 *Ibid.*, paras. 10.2–10.23.

7
Radical Change Proposed

The complex monopoly

The Monopolies and Mergers Commission (MMC) Report, *The Supply of Beer*,[1] was completed early in 1989, and confidential copies were sent to the Lord Young of Graffham, Secretary of State for Trade and Industry, and Sir Gordon Borrie, the Director General of Fair Trading (DGFT), on 3 February 1989. The Report was signed by five members of the panel, the sixth, Leif Mills, having written a Note of Dissent. The panel had said in their opening Summary:

> Eloquently though the industry's case has been put, we are not persuaded that all is well. We have confirmed our provisional finding that a complex monopoly position exists in favour of the brewers with tied estates and loan ties.[2]

The work of the MMC panel was done, and its members would play no further part in the matter.

The Commission's principal finding was that a complex monopoly, within the meaning of sections 6(1)(c), 6(2) and 11 of the Fair Trading Act 1973, existed in the supply of beer for retail sale in licensed premises.[3] The monopoly was found to exist in favour of 72 brewers, which were listed in an Appendix to the Report, and which comprised virtually the entire brewing sector, including two brewers – Guinness and the Northern Clubs Federation Brewery – without a tied estate.[4] It might be seen as ironic that Guinness, the company which added weight to the pursuit by the Office of Fair Trading (OFT) of a reference during the period 1985–86, was now deemed to be one of the monopolists. It should be noted that the Commission did not find a scale monopoly – a situation in which one supplier accounts for at least 25 per cent of the market – to exist in the case of beer.

The finding that a complex monopoly existed may have been unwelcome to the brewers, but it shouldn't have come as a surprise, given that in

December 1987 the MMC had told both the Brewers' Society and individual brewers in its Public Interest Letter that it had provisionally reached such a conclusion, and, indeed, had subsequently asked the Society and its members to comment on a range of possible remedies[5] [as listed in Appendix 5.2].

The specific practices which led to the conclusion that competition could be prevented, restricted, or distorted were the tying of managed and tenanted houses to beer brewed by the brewer that owned the property, and/or making loans to non-owned outlets in exchange for some form of restriction in their choice of beers. One effect was that suppliers without a tied estate and independent wholesalers were prevented from competing freely.[6] The Commission acknowledged that it must demonstrate some detriment to the public interest if it was to reach a position where it could make recommendations for change, and this it set about doing, first making some observations on the state of the market.

Reviewing major changes since its last monopoly report on beer, in 1969, the Commission highlighted the small increase in the number of full on-licences as compared to the growth in restricted and off-licences; a tendency towards concentration in production, although to a level below that in many other countries; the diversification of some brewers into other business areas; and the lack of growth in the independent wholesaling sector, because the brewers had their own distribution networks and controlled access to their own estates and loan-tied outlets. There had, however, been some growth in the number of very small (or micro-) brewers, and an improvement in facilities in pubs.

The growth in lager sales had disadvantaged regional and local brewers, who didn't regard capital investment in lager production as worthwhile, and couldn't afford the sums needed to create brand support. The need felt by many independent retailers to stock a national lager, coupled with the national brewers' practice of competing by supplying cheap finance rather than on price, was equally unhelpful to regional and local brewers. Sales of draught cider were also on the increase, and no alcohol and low alcohol beers (NAB/LABs) had recently arrived on the scene, and the Commission speculated that, as with lager, these latter categories of beer would come to rely on heavyweight marketing support for a few national brands.

The Commission was eager to examine the economics of brewing, and it refuted the Brewers' Society's contention that there was no material overcapacity. It also dismissed the brewers' assertion that much of the difference in retail price between lager and ale could be explained by higher production costs, claiming that the data submitted by individual brewers showed that the cost difference amounted to no more than one-third of a penny per pint. Wholesale price lists for the same brewer often varied by region, and they didn't provide information on discounts or rebates for collection.

The brewers had contended that vertical integration brought efficiency gains, and perhaps more importantly, that the input price to an integrated retailer was lower than that to a non-integrated retailer, and that this enabled the former to charge a lower price and invest in amenity, and led to lower retail prices generally in the market. Far from accepting this argument, the Commission believed that, if anything, vertical integration acted to *increase* both the marginal and the average cost of production, thus in effect acting as a disincentive to rationalise production. In addition, the subsidies offered to tenants by way of sub-market rents and to loan accounts in the form of lower interest rates were costs that had to be recouped in higher wholesale prices.[7]

The position of Guinness was plainly influential in the Commission's thinking. Guinness had claimed that the fact that 60 per cent of its sales were through the national brewers made it vulnerable to sanctions that the latter might apply, including, ultimately, the threat of delisting. It had backed this up by describing the difficulty which it had experienced in getting its no alcohol beer brand, Kaliber, to market (echoing the representations that it had made to both the MMC and OFT in 1985). The Commission concluded that Guinness exemplified the difficult position of any brewer without a tied estate trying to enter the market.[8]

The Commission turned to the financial information supplied by the brewers – in so doing criticising what it saw as the relative lack of sophistication of their accounting systems. It found that return on capital employed was 13.3 per cent for the national brewers, 6.9 per cent for the regional brewers, and 1.8 per cent for local brewers. The Commission chose to make no comment as to whether these figures were evidence of detriment or not (although one then Chairman of a national brewer in conversation with the authors memorably described these returns as "niggardly"). It did however, point to certain features of the industry, namely, over-capacity, the fact that nearly all brewers produced a perhaps needlessly large range of beers, and possible over-investment in pubs, as consequences of the complex monopoly, which meant that "costs are higher than they need to be".[9]

In its concluding remarks on the market the Commission made plain that it was not impressed with the state of competition therein. Everything pointed to competition being inhibited by the complex monopoly: the position of independent wholesalers and of brewers without tied estates, the struggle of micro-brewers to gain distribution, the price of lager, the inefficiencies in brewing, the absence of a significant independent retail sector, the limitations of the licensing system, regional differences in wholesale pricing. Indeed, all of the evidence examined seemed damning.[10]

> We do not deny that there is competition between the brewers but we consider that the practices set out in the complex monopoly have led to

a muted and stylized form of competition. In particular, most brewers, and certainly all the nationals, are pursuing the same strategy at the retail level of higher price and higher amenity.[11]

The group concluded, "Taking account of all these factors we have therefore found that the integrated businesses of the brewers are not subject to the test of free competition at the manufacturing, wholesaling or retailing stages in respect of on-licensed outlets."[12]

Eleven public interest detriments identified

Having found a complex monopoly to exist, the Commission, in accordance with its terms of reference, moved on to consider whether the monopoly was being exploited and if so by what uncompetitive practices. In fact, the Commission's conclusions were so critical and strongly expressed as to make it seem almost inevitable that several detriments would be found, and deemed to be operating against the public interest. Eleven such detriments were identified.

To start with, the Commission pointed out that between 1979 and July 1986 the average price of a pint of beer in the public bar of brewers' managed houses had risen by 15 per cent in real terms, excluding the effects of duty and VAT changes. It asserted that tenancies and free trade outlets followed the price leadership of managed houses – in effect, that brewers set the retail market price. Wholesale prices too had risen over the period.

The brewers had cited inflationary wage increases and the cost of financing improvements to pubs as mitigating factors, but the Commission didn't accept these arguments, claiming that the general retail environment had improved and that this was captured in the Retail Prices Index. In reality it was the complex monopoly, limiting inter-brewer competition, and high wholesale prices, inhibiting the ability of tenants and loan-tied accounts to compete on price, that were driving real increases, and this was against the public interest.[13]

The retail price of lager in on-licence outlets in 1987 was on average some 10 pence per pint higher than that of ale. The Commission asserted that its investigations didn't support the brewers' contention that this reflected higher production and financing costs. Nor was it persuaded by the brewers' argument that advertising costs were higher for lager. Lager was now well established in the market and it was no longer possible to argue that prices had to be set higher to recover initial investment. Tellingly, said the Commission, margins on lager were higher than on ales, and this was attributable directly to the complex monopoly, and was not in the public interest.[14]

Retail prices for beer showed quite significant differences between regions, the Commission noted, with London and the South East being the most expensive. Average prices for the same beer were as much as 20–30 per cent less in the Midlands than in Greater London. The brewers cited different operating and property costs, as well as differing standards of living from region to region. The Commission felt, however, that the variations were too great to be explained in this way, and it pointed out that, in any case, there were also differences in wholesale prices from one region to another, which couldn't be attributed to differences in retailing costs. It was significant, the Commission said, that in the Midlands and the North West a number of regional brewers had kept their wholesale and retail prices relatively low, which had had the effect of restraining the overall retail price in the market. And in the off-trade, where vertical integration was less prevalent, regional price differences were much less marked. The Commission concluded that, whilst small regional price variations might be explained by cost factors, there was more to it than this, and that the complex monopoly was at work and causing public interest detriment.[15]

The nature of the relationship between brewery and pub tenant, the Commission argued, was extremely important for both brewers and consumers. The paternalism that had typified the relationship at the time of the 1969 Report lingered on in some local brewing firms, but in the case of regional and national brewers the relationship had become more impersonal and subject to a significant degree of control by management. The tenant's stocking obligations were specified in detail in the tenancy agreement, and the initial rent was determined by the landlord on the basis of an anticipated level of business, with an increase likely if actual business exceeded this. If the tenant failed to achieve the expected level of sales the rent might still be increased, or the tenancy terminated. Arbitration was available, but rarely used, and given also that tenants of licensed premises were not included within the provisions of the Landlord and Tenant Act 1954, they had only limited security. Nor were tenants generally able to capture goodwill by improving a business and selling it on; although the Commission noted that some brewers had begun to offer longer terms, notably as with the Inntrepreneur 20-year assignable lease, which had been introduced by Grand Metropolitan in 1988.

Under Regulation (EEC) No 1984/83 tenants could buy some products, notably soft drinks, from suppliers other than their brewer, and some brewers had extended this freedom to wines and spirits. Yet many tenants continued to buy these products from the brewer, and the MMC felt that the main reason for this was pressure felt by tenants to demonstrate loyalty to their brewer for fear of sanctions, such as reduced money for repairs or higher rent. A degree of protection was afforded to tenants under the Brewers' Society Code of Practice, but this was not legally enforceable, and, as argued by the National Licensed Victuallers Association, was therefore inadequate. Concluding, the Commission said that the lack of security meant that brewers could "significantly limit the independence" of tenants, and that this was against the public interest.[16]

In the nationals' managed and tenanted houses nearly all of the drinks offered were selected from the brewer's wholesale list. Many local and regional brewers supplied draught lager from other companies, and most brewers took one or more bottled beers from other brewers. Guinness stout was exceptional in that most brewers sold both the bottled and draught form in their pubs. There was, said the Commission, "no doubt" that consumer choice, not just in beer but also in cider and soft drinks, was restricted. The restriction also extended to loan-tied outlets.

The submissions from the Campaign for Real Ale (CAMRA) and the Consumers' Association had expressed concern about the limitations on choice, especially where the effects of the tie were combined with a high local concentration of outlets in the hands of one brewer. Their views were echoed by drinks producers, notably Guinness and cider maker Bulmer. The Commission said that many tenants would like to respond to consumer demands and offer more choice, and it concluded that the limitations on choice arising from the effects of the tie were against the public interest.[17]

The Commission observed that an important feature of the industry during the previous decade had been the way in which national and regional companies had expanded into the ownership or joint ownership of major suppliers of cider. Bulmer had claimed that the situation had been exacerbated by the takeover of some local brewers by national brewers, which had led to the company's products being excluded from the pubs affected. Bulmer's major competitors were the Taunton Cider Company, jointly owned by Courage, Bass, and Scottish & Newcastle, and Showerings, owned by Allied-Lyons, and the Commission found that a significant proportion of the draught cider sales of these two companies were to the estates owned by their shareholders. The brewers' argument that, prior to the advent of Taunton and Showerings, Bulmer had enjoyed a near monopoly didn't impress the Commission. In off-licences, where price and consumer choice were more important, Bulmer enjoyed a higher market share than in the on-trade, even in off-licences owned by brewers with a shareholding in the two rival cider producers. The Commission concluded that the brewers with an interest in Taunton and Showerings were exploiting the monopoly situation and that this was against the public interest.[18]

The case mounted against certain brewers regarding soft drinks was similar to that in respect of cider. During the course of the inquiry Britvic Corona, supplier of – *inter alia* – Pepsi Cola and Britvic, came under the ownership of three of the national brewers. The Commission drew attention to the way in which, in the wake of this realignment, the products of Coca Cola Schweppes Beverages Ltd had been withdrawn from the estates of the brewers concerned, affecting the competitive balance between the two major suppliers. As mentioned above, Regulation (EEC) No 84/83 gave tenants freedom to purchase soft drinks outside the tie, but the Commission was not sufficiently comforted by this, and concluded that the brewers with a participation in Britvic Corona were exploiting the monopoly situation and, again, that this was against the public interest.

The Commission accepted that, for owners of independent pubs and for club committees seeking capital to finance improvements to their premises, the offer of a loan at a low rate of interest, in return for an agreement to purchase beer, could be attractive. It also appreciated that such arrangements were equally attractive to brewers, both in their own right and because the brewer supplying the beer could normally expect also to secure the customer's cider, soft drinks, and wines and spirits business. The Commission also found, however, that although strong competition existed between national brewers for such business, many regional and local brewers were excluded from the market because they lacked sufficient financial resources and couldn't supply a nationally supported lager. The Commission argued that if discounts were to be offered instead of loans, retailers could offer lower prices. The brewers had countered that many free trade outlets would suffer, and their customers with them, if loans were not available.

In 1981 the MMC had produced a report on the subject of *Full-Line Forcing and Tie-In Sales*,[19] and the group that worked on that investigation included the Chairman of the 1989 inquiry, Dick Smethurst. In 1981 the Commission had concluded that loans were unlikely to be against the public interest, but in 1989 it said, "on this occasion we have conducted a much wider review, focused on the brewery industry as a whole, and we have been able to take into account the overall effect of the loans and the other forms of tying". As a consequence, it concluded that the practice of offering loans acted as a restriction on competition and was against the public interest.[20]

Moving on through its list of detriments, the Commission observed that in many markets there was a flourishing independent wholesaling sector, which supplied smaller retailers and provided a route to market for smaller producers. Yet this could not be said of the UK beer market, where there were relatively few independent wholesalers, providing only limited competition to the wholesaling operations of brewing companies. The Commission argued that the brewers were restricting wholesalers to a relatively small part of the market by practices such as refusing to supply large keg sizes and cask-conditioned beer or making supply conditional on not selling to tenants of the brewer concerned. It was convinced that "the reason why most brewers are at best neutral and at worst hostile to independent wholesalers is the threat that they perceive would arise to their own wholesaling and retailing activities if a strong independent wholesaling force came into being". So it was no surprise that the Commission concluded that this behaviour represented exploitation of the complex monopoly and was against the public interest.[21]

At this time a pub sold by a brewer was often subject to a continuing tie in respect of supplies. The Brewers' Society had suggested that this occurred in only 25–30 per cent of instances and that because the sale was thus encumbered, pubs could be sold at a lower price than would otherwise pertain, making for easier market entry. The Commission saw it otherwise. Such an arrangement meant that the new proprietor was restricted in the choice that he could offer and had little opportunity to price his products competitively. All this added up to exploitation of the complex monopoly and was against the public interest.[22]

Finally, the Commission found that in the past brewers had sometimes imposed a covenant when selling on-licensed premises which prevented their future use as a public house. The Brewers' Society had pointed out that it had issued a recommendation in 1972 that such covenants should not be imposed, and that since then they had only rarely been imposed, but the Commission nonetheless decided to make clear that they were against the public interest.[23]

The Commission had examined the part played by amusement with prizes (AWP) machines in the profitability of pubs, and it felt that the conditions imposed on pub tenants by their landlords in this area were often onerous, and provided for large profits for the brewers. And although the Commission concluded that the brewers' actions weren't the result of the complex monopoly or its exploitation, it nevertheless believed that the DGFT should consider further action, under the Fair Trading Act 1973 or the Competition Act 1980. In the event, no such action was taken, but the contractual relationship between tenants and landlords concerning AWP machines was to prove a controversial one over the following decades.[24]

Further considerations

Before tabling its recommendations as to how the detriments might be remedied, the Commission dealt briefly with licensing law, possible countervailing benefits, and European law. On the first of these, it was noted that the 1969 inquiry had recommended a relaxation of licensing laws as the best way to open up competition. The 1989 Commission took the view, however, that the climate of opinion surrounding alcohol consumption made growth in the number of public houses unlikely, so that the detriments identified were very unlikely to be mitigated by new entrants at the retail level.[25]

The Commission looked at countervailing benefits of the vertically integrated structure, but concluded that "in our view these benefits are significantly outweighed by the detriments". In reaching this view the Commission dismissed the results of three surveys commissioned by the Brewers' Society. The Society had said that these demonstrated that the on-trade price premium was smaller in British pubs than in pubs and bars in other countries, that British pub users and foreign visitors to Britain alike preferred British pubs, and that British pubs scored more highly than foreign pubs on a number of measures, including brand choice and beer prices. The Commission found fault with all of these surveys and said that it could place no reliance on them.[26] Perhaps it was significant that the Brewers' Society had not consulted the Commission in designing its research, the latter later commenting:

> The surveys were arranged by the Brewers' Society without reference to the Commission and we were not given the chance to comment on the questions asked or the construction of the sample.[27]

The Commission's rejection of the surveys, all of them supportive of the brewers' case, and its implicit criticism of the lack of consultation, are to be contrasted with the fulsome praise that it heaped on the Society elsewhere in the Report, declaring:

> Throughout our inquiry we were struck by the vigour and thoroughness of The Brewers' Society's response to the many questions we asked and the points we put back to it. There is no doubt in our minds that the Society is formidably effective.[28]

Concluding its brief audit of the benefits of the tied system, the Commission considered that although competition might often be fierce, it took place on terms set by the brewers, especially the large brewers. "Competition is structured by producers rather than driven by the demands of consumers," it argued. Hence there could be no question of sufficient countervailing benefit in the *status quo*.[29]

In drawing up its recommendations, the Commission was careful to explain that it had taken account of the relevant provisions of European law. Regulation (EEC) No 1984/83 provided for a Block Exemption for tying agreements in the brewing sector, subject to the agreement meeting certain conditions, and the Brewers' Society had contended that any modification of the exemption by the UK authorities would place the UK in breach of its obligations under the Treaty. The Commission rejected this view, citing Article 14, which allowed for an exemption to be withdrawn in certain circumstances. Moreover, it said, a member state was permitted to consider what action should be taken to remedy adverse effects of European legislation.[30]

The Commission acknowledged that there was an issue as to whether a member state could adopt national legislation imposing more stringent restrictions than required under Community law, but argued that this wasn't a matter for the inquiry group, but one for the Secretary of State.[31] As will be seen, the possible conflict between the MMC's recommendations and European law would later become a major headache for the Secretary of State.

The Commission's recommendations

Having established that 11 practices in the brewing industry were detrimental to the public interest, the Commission's next duties, under the Fair Trading Act 1973, were to consider what action, if any, should be taken to remedy the detriments, and, if thought fit, to make recommendations accordingly.

The Commission dismissed the Brewers' Society's claim that change was already occurring and that the market should be allowed to develop without Government intervention. The detriments that had been found were structural and of long standing, it asserted, and although change was evident, property and loan ties were still in place. Furthermore, changes over the previous decade had tended only to entrench the position of the large brewers.[32] Accordingly, if the adverse effects were to be addressed, structural change would be necessary. This would require a far greater number of public houses to be independent of the brewers, and whilst this could perhaps be achieved by requiring all brewers to divest all their pubs, it would jeopardise the position of local and regional brewers, who played a crucial role in providing choice.[33]

It was therefore recommended that no company with brewing interests should be allowed to own or lease more than 2000 on-licensed outlets. This figure was proposed after taking account of several factors: amongst these, that it wouldn't affect the regional and local brewers; that it was enough both to support an efficient national distribution system, as demonstrated in the case of Scottish & Newcastle, which had only around 2300 pubs, and to allow economies of scale in production; and that the number of properties to be divested – some 21,900 – "should be capable of being handled without undue difficulty by the property and capital markets" within the proposed three-year timetable.[34]

The Commission envisaged that the properties would be bought by companies owning groups of pubs, by individual licensees or groups of licensees, and by local and regional brewers. Such purchasers would be able to achieve substantial discounts to the wholesale price list. In order to prevent the tie being reimposed by brewers and retail chains in concert, it was further recommended that when a pub was sold in order to achieve compliance with the disposal recommendation, no brewer should be permitted to enter into an exclusive beer supply agreement of more than one year's duration. "Coupled with our recommendations on wholesaling, this considerable structural change should increase consumer choice and reduce beer prices," the Commission said.[35]

Turning its attention to the position of tenants, the Commission expressed an ambition to give them more choice in the products that they stocked, and it proposed that, in order to achieve this, "the Secretary of State take such steps as may be necessary to effect changes in the present arrangements permitted under Regulation 1984/83" so as to permit tenants to stock at least one brand of draught beer from a supplier other than their landlord.[36] This idea was very much along the lines of the suggestion made by CAMRA,[37] and it came to be known as the guest beer provision. In addition, the tie should not encompass non-alcohol or low-alcohol beers, wines, spirits, ciders, soft drinks or mineral waters.

And because – as the Commission had found – tenants were not able fully to act as independent businessmen, or fully to take advantage of all of the freedoms afforded by the Regulation, it was regarded as essential that their position should be legally protected.[38] The Commission therefore recommended that tenancies should be brought within the provisions of the Landlord and Tenant Act 1954. This would safeguard their independence and enable them to take advantage of the proposed freedom to purchase products from suppliers other than their brewer, and would also mean that rent reviews would be subject to the same well-established court procedures that applied to the great majority of other business premises.[39] It was further recommended that the non-statutory Brewers' Society Code of Practice should be revised in negotiations led by the DGFT, to provide tenants with enhanced security in a number of specified circumstances, and that the Code should be binding on both parties.[40]

The Commission feared that the pub divestment programme it was recommending might increase the extent of loan-tying, a practice which it considered to be an instrument of the complex monopoly. So it also recommended, in the same terms as before, that "the Secretary of State take such steps as may be necessary to effect changes in the present arrangements permitted under Regulation 1984/83", such that the loan-tie be abolished in its entirety. Existing loans should be allowed to continue until the end of the contract. It was argued that the abolition of loans would bring about a much greater use of discounts, which, together with the expected availability of capital from third party lenders, would enable free trade outlets to compete more effectively with the brewers' own pubs.[41]

The Commission recommended that the Government should prohibit covenants made when a pub was sold either specifying a product tie or containing a prohibition on future use as a pub.[42]

It was recommended that brewers should be required to publish price lists which detailed prices and quantity discounts available. The discounts should be available to all on-licensed customers, but the brewer should be able to negotiate further discounts or surcharges. In order to encourage the growth of independent wholesalers, it was further proposed that brewers should be required to supply beer at their breweries or depots at a price which took account of the saving in delivery cost.[43]

Finally, the Commission pointed out that the growth of small brewers would be encouraged, thereby benefiting competition and consumer choice, if a sliding scale of duty were introduced such that smaller brewers paid a lower rate than large brewers.[44]

The Commission then briefly, and without going into detail, set out its vision of the future, in which its recommendations would "bring important benefits to consumers". The national brewers would be forced to compete more vigorously for the business of the greatly increased number of pubs that would be owned by genuinely independent retailers and smaller brewers, which, in combination with greater transparency in wholesale pricing, would yield lower wholesale prices. Crucially, the Commission expected "this reduction in wholesale prices to bring about lower prices to the final consumer". At the same time, the advent of new competition from independent wholesalers and retailers would widen consumer choice. On the other hand, it warned, if no changes were made, "it was inevitable that a small number of national brewers [would] increasingly dominate not only the manufacture of beer but also the wholesaling of beer and non-beer alcoholic and soft drinks and [would] continue to dominate beer retailing".[45]

Thus did the MMC set out its model of the ways in which its recommendations would affect the market, and thereby establish the criteria by which the success or otherwise of those recommendations would be judged.

The dissenting voice

The Note of Dissent, by Leif Mills, appears in the Report immediately after the recommendations of the majority, but – significantly or otherwise – is not mentioned in the Report's list of contents.[46]

Mills was a life-long trade unionist. At the time of the Report he was General Secretary of the Banking, Insurance and Finance Union and a member of the General Council of the Trades Union Congress (TUC); later, from 1994 until 1995, he was the TUC's President. He served on the MMC from 1982 to 1991, and the beer inquiry was the only one on which he served where he dissented from the majority view.

According to Mills, he was unusual amongst the panel members and officials working on the inquiry in that he was a regular pub user and a "real ale" enthusiast. His colleagues, he has said, were generally neither of these. "X was a sweet sherry man", and "Y only ever drank at the tennis club", he has recalled, and to his mind this was significant, in that they lacked real experience of the pub. His dissent sprang not so much from a theoretical dispute with the majority view – he agreed that a complex monopoly existed and that in some regards it acted against the public interest – but rather from a pragmatic view that the recommendations of the majority were by no means certain to improve matters. Indeed, he thought that they could well make things worse.

His Note first detailed the conclusions and recommendations with which he agreed, namely, that public interest detriments were manifest in the limited independence of tenants and in the imposition of ties or restrictions when properties were sold by brewers.[47] And he endorsed the recommendations put forward to remedy these detriments.

Mills also agreed that detriments arose in the higher price of lager relative to ale, in the fact that consumer choice of beers and other drinks was restricted, and in the restrictions placed on independent wholesalers. But he found the remedies proposed too drastic. He didn't agree that any public interest detriment arose in relation to real increases in the price of beer; the level of differences in regional and wholesale prices; the exclusion or partial exclusion of independent cider or soft drinks manufacturers from the estates of brewers with interests in cider or soft drinks companies; or the practice of offering loans.[48]

Mills supported the proposal for guest beers, believing that it would on its own be enough to remedy the detriment and could be achieved without the "major structural upheaval"[49] that would occur if the majority had its way. He was relatively unconcerned as to whether a tenant might choose a local or a national beer in exercising the right to a guest beer, regarding this as a matter of commercial judgment. Nor did he believe that rents would rise significantly where a guest beer was taken. The implementation of the guest beer recommendation might also help to improve the position of the independent wholesaler, he thought; but he did not endorse the other recommendations concerning wholesalers.[50]

Mills reserved his sharpest criticism of the majority recommendations for the proposals to limit the number of pubs owned by brewers and to abolish the loan tie. He found the remedies neither desirable nor necessary, asserting that, if implemented, they could make the market less competitive, reduce choice and create public interest detriments of their own. He was concerned that not all of the pubs that would need to be sold would remain as pubs, but could end up put to alternative use, perhaps becoming "just pieces of real estate to be bought and sold". Moreover, individuals and local brewers could find it difficult to secure suitable financing to buy the pubs even if they wanted to, particularly at a time of high interest rates. Nor was it clear from the evidence submitted to the MMC by local and regional brewers that they all wished to expand their tied estates. Given the upheaval during the sales process that Mills expected, he was particularly anxious about the future of tenants unwilling or unable to buy their pub, fearing that they could become unemployed.[51]

The key question, Mills asserted, was whether the industry could be changed in ways that would bring about greater choice and lower prices. These were the issues that had driven the majority to propose such a radical set of recommendations, and he set about examining the evidence of detriment and considering the possible effects of the proposals. He thought that the availability of six different draught beers offered by the average pub was enough to provide a reasonable degree of choice. Besides, the new owners of pubs divested by the national brewers might prefer to offer the big brands marketed by those same companies, rather than local and regional brews, in which case choice might not be enlarged. There was a physical limit to the number of draught beers that a publican could offer, and a guest beer would in itself represent an increase.[52]

Turning to prices, and the above-inflation increase in the price of a pint, he agreed that there had indeed been real increases in the period leading up to the Report, but he observed that there had been improvements in the standard and quality of pubs alongside this, and that it was virtually impossible to assess whether prices had risen more than costs. He agreed that it was against the public interest that lager was more expensive than ale, but he found the remedy misdirected. He foresaw that a mass disposal of pubs could result in the new owners merely perpetuating higher retail margins on lager rather than reducing prices.[53]

If the enforced sale of pubs wouldn't necessarily lead to lower prices and more choice, the same could be said of the proposed abolition of loans. Were loans to be prohibited, businesses could find it difficult to refinance themselves, and certainly not without an increase in cost, with banks adopting a very different stance from brewers. In all likelihood, he thought, loans would be replaced by volume-related discounts.[54]

Mills was keen to see what he regarded as the correct lessons learnt from international comparisons. Yes, vertical integration in brewing seemed a particularly British phenomenon, but he thought it no coincidence that there was no institution comparable to the British pub. Nor was it insignificant that the price of beer in overseas bars was often higher than in the UK, whilst ambience was frequently inferior. Citing the United States as an example, he noted that concentration in brewing seemed to be higher in countries where there was no vertical integration in the industry. Perhaps the existence of the tied estate limited the number of takeovers in brewing.[55]

It becomes clear that Mills thought the analysis and conclusions of the majority overly theoretical. In the real world, he observed, competition must necessarily always be imperfect. Recommendations in this case should be judged against their likely practical impact on choice and price, and not on any theoretical construct of competition. The theoretical approach, he remarked, "smacks a little of the academic question 'the brewing industry may work well in practice, but does it work in theory?'"[56]

Moving towards his conclusions, Mills drew on his personal experience:

> As a frequent consumer of real ale, I have to say that the British public house is unique, that its product makes it unique and that there is more choice of beers available in this country than in almost any other country. I believe that there is a correlation between the nature and popularity of the British public house and the existence of the tied estate and the availability of the loan tie: and the lack of similar public houses in other

countries is perhaps linked to the absence of that tied estate and that loan tie.[57]

In concluding, he reasserted his support for the recommendations concerning guest beer and improved security for tenants. He finished with a flourish, talking of an "unnecessary leap in the dark", quoting from Aristotle, and finally remarking:

> Warts and all, imperfections and all, the tied estate and the vertical structure that this supports, and the involvement of brewers in the free trade through loan ties, give the consumer reasonable value for money and reasonable choice. The tied estate and the loan tie should be left to continue as they are and the brewing industry should be left to change and develop as it is already doing.[58]

The Note of Dissent was to be much quoted by those opposing the MMC's recommendations, becoming a weapon with which to attack Government support for the recommendations. Mills's dissent perhaps bore a further curious legacy. In the ensuing years three out of the four MMC/Competition Commission reports involving beer – Allied-Lyons/Carlsberg in 1992, Bass/Carlsberg-Tetley in 1997 and Bass/Interbrew in 2001 – included a dissenting voice. Proposals concerning beer and pubs would continue to be controversial and to attract disagreement.

Borrie's advice to Young

The beer Report was to be made public on 21 March, giving Lord Young less than seven weeks in which to decide how to respond, before the start of what could be expected to be a lively public debate. Section 86 of the Fair Trading Act 1973 obliged Sir Gordon Borrie to advise the Secretary of State as to how he should react to the Report's recommendations, and this he did in a confidential letter dated 16 March. Together with annexes, it ran to 44 pages, its length prompting Borrie to observe that it was "inescapably long and detailed".[59]

So Sir Gordon's officials at the Office of Fair Trading (OFT) didn't have much time in which to produce their draft advice on a Report which had taken two and a half years to compile and comprised 501 pages. How much critical scrutiny it received from officials, and whether the Note of Dissent was seriously considered, are not known, but in any case Sir Gordon's letter endorsed the Commission's conclusions. Indeed, his support might be said to have been enthusiastic:

> This is an impressively thorough and well-researched report. Although one member has dissented from most of the recommendations, I find

the MMC's conclusions on the operation of the tied house system entirely convincing.

Borrie observed that the Report was unusual in three ways:

> For the strength and pervasiveness of the adverse effects the MMC have found; for the far-reaching remedies they propose; and for the complex interaction of EC and national competition law which complicates any attempt to put those remedies in place.[60]

The central advice to the Secretary of State was that he accept the MMC's findings and state that he was "minded to implement" its recommendations. But the greater part of the advice was concerned with a detailed examination of the inter-relationship of the recommendations and European competition law. Put simply, would implementation of the recommendations be compatible with European law? The MMC, having considered the question, had concluded that, although this was an issue, a case could still be made to Europe, and in any event, it was a matter for the Secretary of State. Borrie, however, was more cautious, warning that Regulation (EEC) No. 1984/83, the Block Exemption, "vastly complicates" implementation. This Regulation specifically exempted arrangements such as the beer tie from a general prohibition, provided that they enhanced efficiency and benefited consumers, thus raising the possibility in the minds of OFT officials that the brewers would take a case to the European Court of Justice based on the possible incompatibility of the MMC's recommendations with the Exemption.

In fact, several of the recommendations worried the OFT. Borrie was of the opinion that the most radical recommendation, namely, that the national brewers divest large numbers of properties, didn't fall into this category, but he warned that that might not stop the brewers mounting a case, which, although likely to fail, could delay matters. He was more concerned about the proposals concerning loan ties, the lifting of the tie on a guest beer and on non-beer drinks, and the prohibitions on product tying agreements on properties sold by brewers and on exclusive supply agreements of over one year on such premises – all of which he thought might successfully be challenged. And he didn't see any realistic prospect of the European Commission modifying the Block Exemption to accommodate the UK.

Despite these misgivings, Borrie's advice to Young remained that he should say that he was minded to accept all the recommendations, but that he should have a fallback position, not to be made public, which was that those recommendations which might involve a clash with European law should apply only to the large brewers. Borrie suggested that, if this course was followed, Article 14 of the Exemption, which allowed the Commission to withdraw the exemption where the necessary conditions were not satisfied, might be relied upon. As it turned out, the notion of exempting all but the largest brewers from most of the proposals was one that was to play a key part in resolving the difficulties that the Report presented for the Government.

Help for the Government from Europe

Whilst the OFT was preparing its advice, officials at the Department of Trade and Industry (DTI) also began to wrestle with the Report. It soon became obvious that this would be a complex and controversial file and that the Competition Division was under-resourced for the task ahead of it. Accordingly, a Principal Officer was drafted in from elsewhere in the Department to manage the file, and throughout the following months senior officials at the DTI paid close attention to the matter, their involvement testifying to the importance attached to the case.

Like staff at the OFT, officials at the DTI reached the view that they should advise Young to say that he accepted the Report's findings and was minded to implement the recommendations in full. An internal DTI paper written in 1990 with the aim of identifying lessons from the Department's handling of the case reveals, however, that even at this stage some officials regarded the recommendations as "draconian" and likely to have far-reaching consequences,[61] and foresaw that Ministers might baulk at the prospect of enforced property divestment.

But officials were fighting on more than one front, and they also had to turn their attention to Europe and the Block Exemption. In the post-mortem paper referred to above it was recorded that Sir Leon Brittan, the European Commissioner for Competition, had swiftly made known to the DTI his view that the MMC's recommendations did not fall foul of European Community competition law. This would have been of considerable comfort, as too would have been Brittan's announcement on 16 March that he intended to investigate the European brewing industry. The paper stated that the announcement was *"as a result of representations from the UK"*[62] (authors' italics), thereby apparently vindicating suspicions that the European review was initiated in order to help the UK Government, by perhaps concluding that the UK market was insufficiently competitive.

The announcement of Brittan's investigation, coming just days before the expected release of the MMC's Report, came as an unwelcome bolt from the blue for UK brewers. The review would, according to the announcement, cover – inter alia – the "workings of the Block Exemption". Two months later the European Commission started to collect information from member state brewing organisations. For the UK brewers this couldn't have come at a worse time, preoccupied as they were with the UK competition authorities. It was to be a further 12 months before the European cloud lifted and Brittan announced the results of his review, which turned out to have only limited consequences for the UK [as described in Appendix 3.1].

Notes

1. Monopolies and Mergers Commission (MMC), *The Supply of Beer: A Report on the Supply of Beer for Retail Sale in the United Kingdom*, Cm 651 (1989).
2. *Ibid.*, para. 1.18.
3. *Ibid.*, para. 11.24.
4. *Ibid.*, Appendix 2.3.
5. Second Addendum to the Public Interest Letter, July 1988.
6. MMC, *The Supply of Beer: A Report on the Supply of Beer for Retail Sale in the United Kingdom*, Cm 651 (1989), paras. 11.17 and 11.20.
7. *Ibid.*, paras. 11.32–11.35, 11.38–11.39, 11.45–11.48, 11.50, 11.54, 11.57 and 11.83.
8. *Ibid.*, paras. 11.64–11.67.
9. *Ibid.*, paras. 11.72–11.73.
10. *Ibid.*, paras. 11.87–11.88.
11. *Ibid.*, para. 11.91.
12. *Ibid.*, para. 11.92.
13. *Ibid.*, paras. 12.2–12.8.
14. *Ibid.*, paras. 12.10–12.11 and 12.14.
15. *Ibid.*, paras. 12.17, 12.18 and 12.21.
16. *Ibid.*, paras. 12.36–12.39, 12.42–12.44 and 12.47–12.48.
17. *Ibid.*, paras. 12.53–12.54 and 12.57–12.59.
18. *Ibid.*, paras. 12.61–12.65.
19. MMC, *Full-Line Forcing and Tie-In Sales: A Report on the Practice of Requiring Any Person to Whom Goods or Services are Supplied to Acquire Other Goods or Services as a Condition of that Supply*, HC212 (1981).
20. MMC, *The Supply of Beer: A Report on the Supply of Beer for Retail Sale in the United Kingdom*, HC 651 (1989), paras. 12.74–12.76 and 12.80–12.81.
21. *Ibid.*, paras. 12.82, 12.85 and 12.88.
22. *Ibid.*, paras. 12.95 and 12.97.
23. *Ibid.*, paras. 12.98–12.99.
24. *Ibid.*, paras. 12.49–12.52.
25. *Ibid.*, paras. 12.91–12.93.
26. *Ibid.*, paras. 12.104–12.105 and 12.121.
27. *Ibid.*, Appendix 5.1, para. 2.
28. MMC, *The Supply of Beer: A Report on the Supply of Beer for Retail Sale in the United Kingdom*, Cm 651 (1989), para. 1.17.
29. *Ibid.*, para. 12.109.
30. *Ibid.*, paras. 12.113 and 12.117–12.118.
31. *Ibid.*, para. 12.119.
32. *Ibid.*, paras. 12.123–12.124.
33. *Ibid.*, paras. 12.126–12.127.
34. *Ibid.*, paras. 12.129–12.131.
35. *Ibid.*, paras. 12.133–12.134.
36. *Ibid.*, para. 12.137.
37. *Ibid.*, para. 10.17.
38. *Ibid.*, para. 12.138.

39 *Ibid.*, paras. 12.141–12.143.
40 *Ibid.*, paras. 12.144–12.146.
41 *Ibid.*, paras. 12.147, 12.149 and 12.152.
42 *Ibid.*, para. 12.154.
43 *Ibid.*, paras. 12.158–12.159.
44 *Ibid.*, para. 12.161.
45 *Ibid.*, paras. 12.162–12.164.
46 *Ibid.*, pp. 296–303.
47 *Ibid.*, Note of Dissent, p. 296, para. 4.
48 *Ibid.*, p. 296, paras. 5–6.
49 *Ibid.*, p. 297, para. 9.
50 *Ibid.*, p. 297, paras. 8–13.
51 *Ibid.*, pp. 297–8, paras. 14–19.
52 *Ibid.*, pp. 299, paras. 24–5 and 27–8.
53 *Ibid.*, pp. 299–300, paras. 29 and 31.
54 *Ibid.*, pp. 300–1, paras. 37 and 40.
55 *Ibid.*, pp. 301–2, paras. 44–7.
56 *Ibid.*, p. 298, para. 22 and p. 301, para. 43.
57 *Ibid.*, p. 302, para. 53.
58 *Ibid.*, p. 303, paras. 56–8.
59 Letter from Sir Gordon Borrie to Lord Young, 16 March 1989.
60 Section 86 advice, 16 March 1989, pp. 3–4.
61 Department for Trade and Industry untitled internal paper, February 1990.
62 *Ibid.*

8
Mixed Reactions to the Report

Enthusiastic support from the press

The Brewers' Society issued a detailed press statement on the day that the Report was published. It dismissed both the criticism of the industry and the recommendations put forward by the Monopolies and Mergers Commission (MMC), declaring that the Report's remedies were "a charter for chaos", and, *pace* Leif Mills, represented "an unnecessary leap in the dark".[1]

In spelling out the likely consequences of implementation of the recommendations, the Society made some prescient predictions. Concentration in brewing would increase, perhaps fuelled by some large brewers exiting brewing to concentrate on retailing. Many of the pubs to be sold could be bought up by retail chains that would concentrate future investment on the most profitable pubs, to the detriment of smaller, mostly rural, pubs. Forced to operate fewer pubs, the brewers would be obliged to make their retained pubs larger, making the "mega pub" a feature of the future. The whole tenanted system would be undermined, and consumers would suffer reduced choice and higher prices.

The press gave the Report wide and prominent coverage – which, as far as the authors have been able to ascertain, was without exception favourable. *The Times* led, "Brewers may lose monopoly of tied houses",[2] and suggested in its editorial comment that the competition authorities, with 16 brewing industry reports already behind them, "seem finally to have scored a direct hit".[3] But the paper also went on to quote the Brewers' Society's characterisation of the Report as "an academic and arbitrary solution to a theoretical problem", and reported the National Licensed Victuallers' Association (NLVA) as being "seriously concerned" at the effects of the recommendations.[4]

The *Financial Times* similarly made the MMC's Report its top story, but with a characteristically neutral headline, "Brewers may have to sell quarter of Britain's pubs."[5] [The reference by the *Financial Times* to a "quarter" is mistakenly based on the country's 82,000 full on-licences, rather than on the number of pubs.] The editorial column pointed out that thitherto the

MMC had "never, in its 40-year history, recommended significant divestments by companies abusing their market position"; and it opined that it was "refreshing to see the British competition authorities taking a tough stand in a monopoly case".[6] The writer of the paper's *Lex* opinion column speculated, however, that some brewers might sell off their brewing interests and concentrate on retailing and that this might benefit shareholders.[7]

The popular newspapers were unequivocally enthusiastic, the *Daily Mail* reporting on its front page that "The big brewers' stranglehold on Britain's pubs is to be broken after a damning report yesterday accused them of using their power to force up prices."[8] The *Daily Express* went a little further, confidently asserting in its front-page headline, "Price of a pint to fall in big purge", adding below that this followed "a damning Government report on the beer barons".[9] In its business comment the paper marvelled at the Government's willingness to confront vested interests: "Today the brewers join the doctors, nurses, Citizens of Kent and the Gentlemen of the Inner Temple [effectively a barristers' trade union] as the latest bunch to have their collective noses knocked out of joint"; and it concluded, "the tied house system has finally been rumbled".[10] *The Daily Telegraph* carried on its front page the story line, "Young welcomes proposals to bring down price of beer",[11] thereby lending further credibility to the official line on the MMC Report.

Three rebuttals from the Brewers' Society

Within weeks the Brewers' Society had followed up its initial press statement with the publication of two papers, one entitled *Report of the Monopolies and Mergers Commission on "The Supply of Beer" – A Critique*, and the other *The recommendations made by the MMC and their likely consequences*. They were largely written by George Yarrow, of Hertford College, Oxford, one of the team of economists whom the Brewers' Society had engaged at the start of the inquiry. Both were sent to members of the Brewers' Society, politicians, civil servants and the news media. In addition, Yarrow was sole author of a third paper, *The MMC's use of economic analysis in the Report on the supply of beer*.

The first paragraph of the *Critique* was straightforward and hard-hitting. Thus "The Society's fundamental criticisms of the MMC's Report are that the MMC has failed to recognise the nature of competition in the UK beer supply industry and thus failed to perceive its strength; that the MMC's recommendations are misconceived, illogical and disproportionate; and that implementation of the recommendations would severely prejudice consumer interests."[12] Thereafter, the paper tended towards the academic in tone, but made clear its authors' opinions that the MMC's recommendations were incompatible with Commission Regulation (EEC) No. 1984/83 (the Block Exemption); that the MMC's finding that a complex monopoly existed was a legal technicality, and its apparent view that such a situation was inherently detrimental to competition was flawed; and that the interests of non-vertically integrated drinks manufacturers and wholesalers had been given precedence over those of consumers.

The paper went on to accuse the MMC of "serious errors of economic analysis",[13] and of disregarding the significance of facts which testified – *inter alia* – to the low level of concentration in brewing and pubs, intense competition at the retail level, the dwindling share of beer sold through the tied trade, and the low price of beer, net of duty, compared with other countries.[14] It pointed out that all these disregarded facts were confirmed by material within the Report itself, and it drew attention to the fact that the MMC, while rejecting the efficiency of the vertically integrated model, had conceded that "vertical integration has advantages in the supply of beer".[15] As for the MMC's allegation that beer prices in the free trade loan business were excessive, the paper asserted that the MMC had totally failed to show how the use of loans by competing brewers could enable them to put up prices beyond a competitively determined level.[16]

The *Critique* also took issue with the MMC's "desire to interpose in the present industry structure a separate wholesale tier for its own sake – that is, without correctly analysing the reasons for present industry structure being as it is, and without correctly assessing whether or not this operates in the interest of consumers".[17] Individual brewers, it said, used independent wholesalers or carried out their own distribution on the basis of an assessment of their own economic self-interest – which couldn't be described as anti-competitive.

As we have seen, the MMC had rejected the results of all three of the international surveys that the Brewers' Society had commissioned in its attempt to demonstrate the benefits to the British pub user that resulted from vertical integration. The panel had suggested – *inter alia* – that the sample used in the price survey was too small; and that higher on-trade prices outside the UK reflected the higher proportion of more expensive packaged – as opposed to – draught sales, as well as the higher incidence of waiter service and perhaps higher retail wage costs. Yarrow, in his *Critique*, remarked that "The MMC, without even attempting itself to investigate the matter, dismissed the results of the survey on the flimsiest of grounds."[18]

On the MMC's proposed ceiling of 2000 pubs per company, the *Critique* drily observed that the Commission had "wholly failed to show why the considerations which make vertical integration pro-competitive up to a limit of 2000 owned houses make it anti-competitive thereafter".[19] It also pointed out that the MMC appeared not seriously to have considered the possibility that the national brewers might avoid disposing of any pubs by selling their brewing businesses, thereby possibly increasing concentration in beer production, without reducing it in the pub sector. It is worth noting at this point that the

Critique said nothing about the prospect of concentration in pubs developing through the formation of large pub companies.

The guest beer proposal, the *Critique* argued, would probably result in tenants adding to their offering a nationally promoted, high margin lager, which would thereby enjoy a free ride on the back of another brewer's investment in his pubs. This, together with the proposals on tenants' security, and the exclusion from the tie of non-alcohol and low-alcohol beers and other drinks, was likely to make tenancy "a very unattractive form of business" for the brewer, thereby leading to closures or reduced investment in refurbishment, to consumers' detriment.[20] Furthermore, a number of the MMC proposals, including those on guest beers and the abolition of loan ties, were in conflict with the Block Exemption, in that they sought, "through prohibiting agreements and conduct expressly permitted by the block exemption...to impose a restrictive competitive regime in the UK only, i.e., to distort competition in the common market".[21]

As for the Note of Dissent by Leif Mills, the authors of the *Critique* didn't accept his approval of the guest beer proposal, which they believed resulted from a misunderstanding of how it would work in practice. They nevertheless asserted that his Report cast "serious doubts on the main conclusions of the majority".[22] Indeed, Yarrow has remarked to the authors that "in a very short space he [Mills] got to the heart of the issues"; and that his note was "as good as anything the MMC has ever written".

The Brewers' Society's second paper, *The recommendations made by the MMC and their likely consequences*, which was circulated to members on 26 May and then more widely, was a briefer and more accessible document than the *Critique*, and, indeed, came to be known as "The Layman's Rebuttal". It pulled no punches in forecasting dire developments should the MMC recommendations be implemented, and it again warned that some major brewers would simply give up brewing and – presciently – that "a large part, or even most, of the brewing capacity in the UK would fall into foreign hands".[23]

In such an environment, it argued, competition would be concentrated on building major national beer brands, mainly lager, which under the guest beer proposal could become cuckoos in the nests of smaller companies' pubs. The MMC's apparent view that tenants would choose local cask ale was "sentimental". The damage thus wrought on smaller companies would in the long term reduce competition, and as the profitability of small pubs, urban and rural, declined, they would close. At the same time "Britain's rich variety of ales would disappear".[24]

The abolition of free trade loans would leave many clubs and free houses with no source of capital with which to start a business or finance improvements to premises; or, at best, would leave them at the mercy of banks, which were not as well placed as brewers to assess the viability of such businesses, and in any case would charge a commercial interest rate. The result would be fewer free trade outlets, generally lower standards of amenity, a diminution in competition between free and tied outlets, and thus higher prices.[25]

The paper accepted that the Society's voluntary Code of Practice in respect of tenants' rights might no longer be fit for purpose, given the trend towards non-integrated pub companies, whose tenants were not covered by the Code; and that there was therefore an argument for giving tenants some statutory security of tenure. The MMC's proposals, however, went "far beyond what is sensible",[26] and "would kill the tenancy system because the total package of security of tenure...would reduce the brewery's own interest in the pub almost to vanishing point. Once let, a brewery would probably not be able to regain possession of the premises ever again. They would have very little control over the identity of the tenant and the 'partnership' would be destroyed".[27] Bigger pubs would be taken into management, but many small, particularly rural, pubs would close.

The last few pages of this paper consisted of a barrage of facts either contradicting, or putting into perspective, various MMC findings, and in a number of cases reiterating points that had already been made by the Brewers' Society either to the Commission or in its report, *Leading Leisure in Britain*. These included the fragmented state of the UK brewing industry, the low level (by historic standards) of brewers' ownership of pubs, and the huge choice of beer brands in the UK. And the paper explained that lager was more expensive than ale because of the cost of installing substantial new brewing capacity, and because, as a growth sector, it attracted a greater marketing and advertising spend.

Yarrow's paper, *The Monopolies and Mergers Commission's use of economic analysis in the report on the supply of beer*, was a learned discussion paper, whose broad thrust was that the MMC had either ignored or misunderstood the developments that had occurred in economic analysis and in the practice of European Community competition policy since the 1969 Report. More specifically, the paper criticised the fact that throughout the Report there were references to "the monopoly situation when, in fact, the existence of a monopoly situation in any real sense [had] never been established".[28] In addition, the MMC had failed to understand that, as recognised by the European Commission, apparently anti-competitive trading agreements could improve supply conditions and benefit consumers.[29] The MMC's reasoning on vertical integration, was based partly on long-abandoned conventional wisdom and partly on "a wholly original, but unfortunately incorrect, rewriting"[30] of the relevant economic theory. On vertical supply agreements, Yarrow went on to point out that the MMC had completely missed the point that to the extent that tenancies and cheap loans facilitated participation in the retail beer market, their effect was actually to increase retail competition. The Commission's conclusions were consequently "flawed, dated and idiosyncratic [and] not even consistent with its own findings in previous investigations, let alone with the EC approach to these matters".[31] Most seriously, the paper argued, the MMC had failed to appreciate the efficiency of tenancy agreements and loan ties "in reconciling the trade-off between incentives and risk sharing in brewer-retailer relationships".[32] Its analysis of vertical agreements consequently "dissolves into virtually total incoherence".[33]

As mentioned above, Yarrow noted that the MMC had contradicted one of its own earlier findings. This was its opinion, expressed in the 1981 Report on *Full-line Forcing and Tie-in Sales*, that free trade loans were unlikely to be against the public interest. Yarrow observed that the MMC had thereby exhibited again "that propensity for inconsistency" for which it had been criticised over recent years.[34] The Report, he concluded, was "a very weak piece of work", with "dinosaur-like characteristics",[35] whose recommendations, if implemented, would have anti-competitive effects, and by damaging the supply side of the market would mainly harm smaller retailers and brewers in the short term and consumers in the long term.[36]

Qualified approval from consumer organisations

Less cerebral than Yarrow's papers for the Brewers' Society, but equally forthright, was the reaction from the Campaign for Real Ale (CAMRA). The latter had been agitating for a reference for some time before 1986, essentially on the grounds that there should be a greater choice of beers within pubs and easier market access for cask ale producers. In a brief letter dated 5 May 1989 Iain Dobson, CAMRA's Chief Executive, wrote to Lord Young, approving of the MMC Report and enclosing his organisation's formal response.

This 14-page document dealt with six issues arising from the Report and made three supplementary points. On the property tie, it welcomed a limit on the number of tied outlets owned by a brewer, and argued that numerous buyers and adequate finance were available to ensure that divestment would not lead to closures. But it regarded as "misguided" the decision to apply the 2000 limit only to brewers, warning that a small number of large pub owners would come to dominate the market in the same way as the "big six" currently did. Indeed, some of the latter could themselves become pure retailers, with "no limits on growth", buying up the pubs divested by other majors, and also acquiring small integrated brewers, and – as they would have to do – disposing of the latter's brewing capacity. Both brewing and retailing would thus become more concentrated, and the major retail chains might pursue a policy of selling a small range of competitively priced national products, jeopardising the survival of a wide range of beers.[37]

Still on the property tie, CAMRA said it assumed that the MMC's proposals would force the break-up of Whitbread Investment Company (WIC), thus removing from a number of regional brewers the protection provided by WIC's "umbrella" shareholdings and immediately rendering them vulnerable to takeover. It therefore recommended that transitional provisions be put in place to protect them from any takeover threat created by the MMC's proposals; though what these provisions might consist of wasn't said. Returning to the general question, CAMRA believed that "an excellent solution" for the companies to adopt would be for them to break themselves up into a number of truly independent and locally competing integrated companies.[38]

Moving on, the paper welcomed the proposals to prohibit product-tying covenants when pubs were sold and covenants preventing their future use as pubs, and it believed that unless a pub was sold to another brewer, the sitting licensee should have the first opportunity to buy it. Any pub for sale must be on the market with licence and at a reasonable price for at least a year before it could be closed and de-licensed.

CAMRA dealt considerably more briefly with the remaining four issues. It supported both the ending of free trade loans, on the basis that the market would thereby be opened up to many small brewers, and the proposed changes to the product tie, namely, the guest beer provision and the abolition of the tie for non-beer beverages. It also welcomed the recommendations that brewers must issue wholesale price lists, detailing volume discounts, and discounts for collection. Finally, CAMRA favoured the idea, mooted by the Commission, of introducing a sliding scale of beer duty, which would help the microbrewers.

As stated above, CAMRA took the opportunity to put forward three recommendations of its own. First, it wanted the Office of Fair Trading to re-examine those geographical areas which the MMC had identified as having a local monopoly (about which the Commission had made no recommendations), and to monitor local build-ups in concentration of pub ownership, which CAMRA feared could result from the divestment programme. Second, it proposed that the domination of the beer market by national brands should be curtailed by a ban on mass media advertising. And, finally, it wanted all takeovers in the brewing and pub industries to be prohibited – or at least to be automatically referred to the MMC, with the onus always on the bidder to demonstrate that the deal would be in the public interest.

A surprising omission from CAMRA's comments on the product tie was the expression of any concern over the possibility – which, as mentioned earlier, the Brewers' Society had commented on in its *Critique* – that, if tenants were given a completely free choice of guest beer, the great majority of them would opt to expand their selection of nationally promoted lager brands. The other striking feature of the submission was the way in which, after several pages of thoughtful, sensible and far-sighted analysis and discussion, it lapsed at the end into a futile attack on the advertising of alcoholic drinks and a call for takeovers in the industry to be banned.[39]

On 23 May the Chairman of the Consumers' Association (CA), Rachel Waterhouse, wrote to Young, welcoming the Report and endorsing the finding that a complex monopoly existed in beer supply. It was clear, she said, that many consumers were "not happy with the present system"; and she told Young that in its evidence to the MMC the Association had cited five symptoms of the lack of competition.

First there was the regularity of above-inflation price rises. Then there were the marked regional price differences, which the CA regarded as indicating a "lack of price competition in the market generally". Next, in areas where a big brewer had many pubs it generally also had the strongest presence in the free trade. The Association thought this was "probably a result of loan-tying" and "indicative of lack of local as well as national competition". Point number four was that brewers were unresponsive to customers' wishes. Thus people would like to see the introduction of no-smoking rooms in pubs, a ban on loud music and noisy games, and more seating, especially outside; but the brewers took no notice. Finally, the CA pointed out that the normal market solution for customer dissatisfaction, namely, the entry of new competitors, was unavailable because of the operation of the licensing system. This had, of course, repeatedly been alluded to in the industry literature of the preceding 20 years.

Moving on to the CA's reaction to the Report, the Chairman said the Association was disappointed that the Commission hadn't recommended curtailing the power of licensing justices to refuse applications, and that criteria for assessing local demand hadn't been statutorily defined. It strongly supported the 2000 pub limit, and believed that even if this led to the development of large pub-owning companies, these would be more responsive to the consumer than largely brewer-owned pubs. No reason was given for making this assertion. Like CAMRA, the CA was concerned about the development of local concentrations of pub ownership, and felt that no brewer should own more than 33 per cent of full on-licences in any Petty Sessional Division (PSD). Although the MMC had not made any recommendations on this issue, it had found that one brewer owned over one-third of full on-licences in 29 per cent of the 600+ PSDs and more than half in 6 per cent.[40]

The Association presented as a cogent argument in favour of relaxing the tie the fact that in its survey only 10 per cent of respondents considered that tied pubs should not be allowed to buy drinks outside the tie. It had found evidence of high prices and lack of choice in tied pubs amongst non- and low-alcoholic drinks; but it believed that the ending of loan ties should help in this respect. The CA thus seems to have been under the erroneous impression that tenants were recipients of trade loans. The Association insisted that tenants should be able to choose a guest beer, but on the other hand it feared that "the MMC recommendation could be implemented by national agreements between a few large brewers to offer each other's beers *if their tenants so request it*" [authors' italics]. In any case, the letter illogically argued, offering a nationally known ale as a guest beer "would not greatly add to consumer choice within a pub".

A couple of weeks later the CA issued a press release, setting out its arguments and ending with a rallying cry: "It's also very worrying that the brewers can spend millions of pounds on newspaper advertisements putting their point of view...No consumer representatives have that kind of money... The MMC's report lifts the lid on an industry which...works against the public interest. Its conclusions...should not be ignored". Finally, the CA's Parliamentary Officer produced a briefing paper, in the form of a series of questions and answers, of which a short example will illustrate the shortcomings in the case the Association had presented:

Q: Do the MMC recommendations mean the death of the pub as we know it?

A: No – and yes! Many pubs at present are imprisoned in the retailing patterns of the past: a strait-jacket of too strict regulation and control of retailers by producers whose main interest is to push up beer sales has led to a fall in regular pub-going. This is the real "threat" to the British pub.

Serious concerns amongst licensees

Neither of the two licensees' representative bodies, the National Association of Licensed House Managers (conventionally abbreviated to NAHLM, not NALHM) and the tenants' body, the National Licensed Victuallers Association (NLVA), submitted a formal response to the MMC Report. A reading, however, of the licensees' newspaper, The *Morning Advertiser*, for the months following the Report, and of the NLVA Annual Reports and conference reports of the time, suggests that there wasn't much enthusiasm for the MMC's recommendations within either body. NAHLM's almost immediate reaction to the Report, in fact, was to dismiss the remedies proposed by the MMC to address the detriments to the public interest as unacceptable. In April 1989 it requested a delay in the implementation of the recommendations, and then in May it came out specifically against the idea of a ceiling on the number of pubs a brewer could own. But on the whole not much was heard from NAHLM.

The NLVA involved itself considerably more in the lobbying process – not surprisingly, given that not only its members' incomes but their places of abode were possibly at risk. Within two weeks of publication of the MMC Report the union had a meeting with officials at the Ministry of Agriculture, at which it stressed that its overriding priority remained total security for its tenants. At first the NLVA also supported the recommendations on guest beer, wholesale price lists and tenants' terms and conditions, but opposed those in respect of the major issues of enforced pub disposals and the abolition of free trade loans. Later, however, the union seems to have become more pragmatic, re-emphasising that security of tenure and compensation when pubs were taken back by the brewers were paramount, and warning that full implementation of the MMC's proposals could render the tenancy system so unattractive to brewer landlords as to bring about its demise. Even if this didn't happen, the pub disposal programme would cause intolerable disruption to the union's members.

The Trades Union Congress (TUC) didn't make a submission to the Department of Trade and Industry, but on 22 May the TUC General Secretary, Norman Willis, wrote to Lord Young. The authors haven't seen this letter, but Young told the Lords on 10 July that Willis had said in a letter that the TUC opposed the idea of the brewers having to dispose of any of their pubs, and that unrestricted access to soft drinks supplies by tenants could discourage investment by brewers in their pubs, to the detriment of workers in the industry: all the recommendations of the MMC should be completely ignored. The unions' intervention was, in fact, of considerable use to the Government in enabling it to demonstrate that the parliamentary Opposition and its supporters were far from united in their criticism of what some were later to see as a surrender to the brewers.

Notes

1 Brewers' Society press release "Monopolies Report a Charter for Chaos", 21 March 1989.
2 *The Times*, p. 1, 22 March 1989.
3 *Ibid.*, p. 15.
4 *Ibid.*, p. 1.
5 *Financial Times*, p. 1, 22 March 1989.
6 *Ibid.*, p. 20.
7 *Ibid.*, p. 24.
8 *Daily Mail*, p. 1, 22 March 1989.
9 *Daily Express*, p. 1, 22 March 1989.
10 *Ibid.*, p. 39.
11 *The Daily Telegraph*, p. 1, 22 March 1989.
12 Brewers' Society, *Report of the Monopolies and Mergers Commission on "The Supply of Beer" – A Critique* (1989), para. 1.1.
13 *Ibid.*, para. 2.1.
14 *Ibid.*, para. 2.2.
15 *Ibid.*, para. 2.7, quoting Monopolies and Mergers Commission, *The Supply of Beer: A Report on the Supply of Beer for Retail Sale in the United Kingdom*, Cm 651 (1989), para. 12.105.
16 *Ibid.*, para. 2.22.
17 *Ibid.*, para. 2.40.
18 Brewers' Society, *Report of the Monopolies and Mergers Commission on "The Supply of Beer" – A Critique* (1989), para. 2.23.

19 *Ibid.*, para. 4.10.
20 *Ibid.*, paras. 4.12–4.15.
21 *Ibid.*, para. 4.1.
22 *Ibid.*, para. 1.10.
23 Brewers' Society, *The Recommendations Made by the Monopolies and Mergers Commission and Their Likely Consequences* (1989), p. 3.
24 *Ibid.*, p. 5.
25 *Ibid.*, p. 7.
26 *Ibid.*, p. 8.
27 *Ibid.*, p. 10.
28 George Yarrow (Hertford College), *The Monopolies and Mergers Commission's Use of Economic Analysis in the Report on the Supply of Beer*, May 1989, para. 4.
29 *Ibid.*, para. 9.
30 *Ibid.*, para. 13.
31 *Ibid.*, para. 17.
32 *Ibid.*, para. 21.
33 *Ibid.*, para. 22.
34 *Ibid.*, para. 23.
35 *Ibid.*, para. 24.
36 *Ibid.*, para. 25.
37 *The Monopolies and Mergers Commission's Report into the Supply of Beer: The Campaign for Real Ale's Response* (May 1989), paras. 3.1.3–3.1.7.
38 *Ibid.*, para. 3.1.13.
39 *Ibid.*, paras. 4.3 and 4.4.2.
40 Monopolies and Mergers Commission, *The Supply of Beer: A Report on the Supply of Beer for Retail Sale in the United Kingdom*, Cm 651 (1989), para. 12.26.

9
The Government Confronts the Recommendations

Young forced on to the defensive

On 21 March the Monopolies and Mergers Commission (MMC) Report was made public, and Lord Young, acting on the advice of both Sir Gordon Borrie and his own officials, said that he accepted its findings and was "minded to implement" the recommendations in full, a choice of words that was to haunt him.[1] In his autobiography, *The Enterprise Years,* Young gives only the briefest account of the beer Report, but acknowledges that it had been a mistake to say this.[2] A more guarded response would certainly have proved less of a hostage to fortune. That same day Young wrote to Brittan, requesting talks about the inter-relationship between the MMC recommendations and the Block Exemption. He also wrote a "Dear Colleague" letter to Members of Parliament (MPs) commending the Report and announcing his disposition to implement it – but omitting to mention the Mills Note of Dissent.

As the weeks passed, officials at the Department of Trade and Industry (DTI) could have been forgiven for thinking that the Government was losing control of events. In the first place, the Brewers' Society had started a vigorous media and political campaign highlighting what it saw as the negative consequences of implementing the Report's recommendations. Brewery employees and tenants were encouraged to write to MPs, and officials found themselves dealing with a huge postbag of letters from constituents to MPs. Some backbenchers didn't hide their personal feelings. One Conservative London MP, replying to a constituent on whose behalf he had raised some questions about the Report with Lord Young, said that the latter's response (a copy of which he enclosed) "did not resolve matters"; he added "very considerable pressure is being exerted on him [Young] to modify the proposed action in the MMC Report and I hope he will come forward with more acceptable proposals".[3]

Meanwhile, an Early Day Motion (EDM) critical of the MMC Report was tabled, eventually attracting the support of over 100 backbench Conservatives. An EDM is a device used by MPs to attract publicity to an issue or cause, and once sufficient Members have been found to sponsor the Motion any Member may add his or her name in support of it; but EDMs are very rarely debated. This EDM read:

> That this House, whilst taking note of the MMC Report on the supply of beer, also notes that Britain enjoys lower prices and greater choice than almost any other country in the world; congratulates this highly competitive industry on the enhanced quality of the British pub, which contributes so much to the national way of life and to vital tourist earnings; and further calls on HM Government to take no steps to implement the recommendations of the Report until much further consideration has been given to the weight of evidence available that implementation could threaten the existence of many of the 33,000 tenancies, could lead to the possible closure of many breweries both large and small and of many rural pubs with consequent job losses in the industry, could damage the financial arrangements of the 36,000 independently owned pubs and 34,000 clubs, and would be likely to result in less choice and higher prices for the consumer.[4]

If Ministers were disturbed by signs of backbench dissent, they would have been equally unsettled by emerging press reports that several of the national brewers might sell their breweries rather than their pubs if forced by Government to choose. This, of course, was not the outcome that the MMC had foreseen: indeed, as the author of the DTI post-mortem paper referred to in an earlier chapter tartly observed, "oddly, after 30 months of investigation, the MMC had not considered this possibility".[5] If Ministers and Officials were inclined to dismiss such an outcome as mere press talk, they were quickly disabused of the idea when John Elliott, Chief Executive of Elders IXL, met Lord Young just a couple of weeks after the Report's publication. Elliott said that if the recommendations were implemented, the Government would need to accept and manage a greater degree of horizontal concentration, with at least some of the major brewers seeking to sell their brewing assets in order to focus on retailing. He indicated that Courage, the UK subsidiary of Elders, was likely to try to acquire such assets and become a brewer on a scale to rival Bass. In a changed market structure with less vertical integration, the Government might need to allow mergers such as that just rebuffed by the MMC between Elders and S&N.[6]

After Elliott had left, Young remarked that he had been "very impressed by some of [his] arguments...in particular the point about the restructuring of manufacturing".[7] Officials began to analyse the implications of such restructuring, a matter on which the MMC Report provided no help. As one official remarked, in something of an understatement, "whilst some features of the industry structure which the MMC wished to promote are clear, the Commission's vision is not articulated in the Report".[8] They nevertheless realised that policy might need to embrace greater concentration in production, and they wondered who else but other large brewers might buy the beer businesses of companies exiting brewing. The political flak that would result if they were sold to foreign companies was an unpleasant prospect.

The Department would also have been dismayed that, far from causing division amongst the brewers, the MMC's remedies seemed to have united them. This was demonstrated when on 26 April an open letter to Lord Young signed by 48 regional and local brewers castigating the recommendations appeared in several national newspapers:

> Far from being an enhancement of our unique, much-loved and prized public house system, these recommendations would mean the end of the pub as we know it.[9]

Yet what perhaps disturbed officials most was the lack of contact from the brewers. The latter seemed to have prepared the ground well, for example placing a two-page advertisement in the *Financial Times* on 9 February, many weeks before the Report emerged, extolling the competitive virtues of the beer and pub sector, and they were now rapidly making the most of their media and political contacts.[10] The brewers had cultivated a stock of potential allies and were now mobilising this resource, holding meetings to put their case with no fewer than 250 MPs by the second week in May. A note to Young from his special adviser, Peter Luff, warned that the brewers were trying to isolate the DTI within Whitehall by directing their lobbying at other departments, notably the Ministry for Agriculture, Fisheries and Food (MAFF).[11]

In mid-April DTI officials met their counterparts at MAFF, who felt that the proposed remedies were "not proportionate to the public interest detriments".[12] The consequences of such large-scale change had not been thought through and they were especially concerned at the prospect of "uniquely disadvantaging UK brewers on the international stage". Equally discouraging was the position of the Department of the Environment (DoE), which had responsibility for the Landlord and Tenant Act 1954 and adamantly opposed anything that went beyond giving pub tenants basic security under the Act.[13]

If things were not going smoothly for the DTI within Whitehall, the news from Brussels was more encouraging. Young met Brittan in Brussels on 21 April, and it seemed, at least from a DTI perspective, that there was "a will on the Commission's part to seek solutions which would allow the UK to implement the MMC recommendations".[14] When Young reported this development to Borrie, who was pressing for swift action to implement the recommendations in full, the Director General made it plain that he thought that the Government should if necessary challenge the Commission should its support evaporate. Alarmingly from Young's viewpoint, he also said that he thought that the brewers would be "bound to litigate",[15] on the grounds that the MMC's recommendations flouted the European Block Exemption.

The brewers were, indeed, considering this course, and obtained an Opinion from a leading practitioner in European Community law, Professor Michael Waelbroeck of the Brussels Bar. The Opinion confirmed the supremacy of Community law over national law and stated that there was potential conflict between some of the Report's recommendations and Community law. The recommendations in question coincided with those that Borrie had warned Young about, namely the ending of the loan tie, the removal of the tie on one guest beer and on non-beer drinks, and the prohibitions on licensed premises sales by brewers being conditional on a product tie or accompanied by an exclusive supply agreement of more than one year's duration. The Professor also opined, as had Borrie, that the enforced divestment proposal presented no conflict with Europe. The brewers released a paper, based on Waelbreck's Opinion, spelling out what they saw as the conflict between European law and the Report's recommendations.[16] Events over the next few months, however, were to persuade the brewers not to litigate.

During April the Brewers' Society was busy reaching agreement amongst members on some key issues, and at a meeting of the Executive on 26 April several major decisions were taken. First, any thought of mounting a judicial review of the Report was rejected as carrying no prospect of success. And although all aspects of the Report would continue to be opposed, the hope of avoiding any Government action was deemed negligible.[17] It was decided, therefore, that a start should be made on considering areas for negotiation. But meanwhile, in public at least, the attack on the recommendations would continue to be uncompromising.

Indeed, towards the end of April the brewers began an advertising campaign in the national press and on poster sites aimed at mobilising public support. The campaign featured deliberately provocative headlines, such as the one appearing alongside a picture of the Albert, a pub situated opposite the offices of the DTI in Central London: "It survived the Luftwaffe. It survived the property developers. But it may not survive the Monopolies Commission".[18] The campaign used a common strapline, "Be vocal, it's your local". The adverts were changed from day to day, and Peter Jarvis, Chief Executive of Whitbread, recalls meeting his opposite number at Grand Metropolitan, John McGrath, at Waterloo station early one morning to sign off the following day's copy. The campaign was to provoke controversy, no doubt as intended, and was condemned by, amongst others, Lord Young, Bryan Gould MP – who was the Opposition spokesman on trade and industry – and the National Licensed Victuallers Association (NLVA).

By the beginning of May Young had become troubled by backbench dissent and wanted to act. He had been given a rough ride at an unusually well attended meeting of the Conservative Back Bench Trade and Industry Committee, when only two out of the 60 MPs present appeared to support the MMC's proposals.[19] He was left in no doubt that he had a fight on his hands.[20] In contrast, the Committee had given a very sympathetic hearing to Whitbread representatives, who had damned the report.[21] Young emerged equally bloodied from a meeting of the 1922 Committee. Eric Forth MP, a junior DTI Minister, told Young that he had never encountered such a uniformly hostile reaction to a government proposal. Finally, he was told by the Chief Whips of both the Commons and the Lords that the strength of feeling was such that they could not guarantee getting the proposals through either House.[22] Compromise now seemed unavoidable.

Compromise

Young's officials began to draw up a list of possible concessions. It included the idea of restricting the guest beer entitlement to the tenants of national brewers, concessions on the loan tie, and, most importantly, an increase in the number of pubs that the national brewers might be allowed to keep.[23] But first Young needed to get the brewers to talk. He decided to signal his willingness to listen to alternative remedies in a speech on 3 May: "if you don't like the MMC proposals, then write to me and make your own," he declared, whilst making it plain that he could not ignore the MMC's findings.[24] Just a few hours earlier a letter had been delivered by hand to the Brewers' Society proposing talks.

The brewers had planned to run the advertising campaign for three to four weeks, but dropped it after little more than a week. Many within the industry felt that it had succeeded in putting pressure on the Government, and within the Brewers' Society the decision to call a halt aroused controversy, with several chief executives loudly and angrily venting their disagreement. In conversation with the authors twenty years later, some described the decision as "a big mistake", believing that continuing with the campaign could have forced the Government to make more concessions than it eventually did. The Society's 1989 Annual Report recorded that "the advertising campaign was discontinued after six advertisements, the Society receiving a message from Lord Young offering to discuss the whole matter and consider alternative proposals for rectifying the alleged disadvantages of the existing system".[25] There is more than a hint of a behind-the-scenes deal having been struck, involving a more accommodating stance on Young's part in exchange for the cessation of the campaign.

In contrast to the bullishness about the campaign felt by some in the industry, officials in Whitehall considered that it had backfired and antagonised the public. The February 1990 DTI paper argued that "factual errors and tendentious selectivity of fact led the press and the public to question the Brewers' Society's position and its campaign".[26] This official view of the campaign may have encouraged Young to conclude that, while he had to negotiate, his hand had in fact been strengthened.

News of Young's offer evidently reached the licensees' newspaper, the *Morning Advertiser*, which on 6 May led with a story under the headline "Olive Branch from DTI",[27] noting that the Secretary of State had written to the Brewers' Society calling for constructive dialogue. The phoney war was over, and on 8 May DTI Ministers and officials met and agreed that a package of measures should be negotiated with the brewers. During the discussion it became obvious that Young's unease was growing. It was recorded that he said that he accepted the Report insofar as detriments were concerned, but "on implementing [its] recommendations he remained unconvinced. Forced disposal of pubs...was the recommendation on which he was least keen".[28]

Later that evening an Adjournment Debate in the Commons gave the Government an opportunity to hint at its new flexibility. [An Adjournment Debate is a means of enabling Parliament to debate a subject without considering a substantive motion.] The debate was led by Conservative backbencher, Graham Riddick MP, whose criticism of the MMC's Report was comprehensive. Riddick asserted that the Report's recommendations would, if implemented, "lead to enormous fundamental upheaval in the industry". He thought that such a radical intervention in the free market was unwarranted, and declared himself "horrified" at the prospect of enforced disposal of assets "legally and enterprisingly built up over many decades". He saw no evidence of consumer dissatisfaction. "The most stunning omission from the Report," he continued, "is its failure to examine exactly what effect the proposals will have on the industry."[29] He predicted pub closures, concentration in brewing and difficulties for free houses and clubs financed by brewery loans if the Government went ahead.

Francis Maude MP, Parliamentary Under-Secretary of State at the DTI, responded for the Government. He recited the public interest detriments that the MMC had found and which the Government couldn't ignore, and he criticised the brewers' "extraordinary" advertising campaign, which, he claimed, hadn't attempted to "argue through the issues in any thorough sense at all". Other organisations, he said, such as the Campaign for Real Ale (CAMRA) and the Small Independent Brewers Association (since 1995 the Society of Independent Brewers, but still known as SIBA), had welcomed the Report, and he argued that the Brewers' Society would have been better talking to the DTI than spending some £200,000 a day on advertising, all of which had to be paid for by the beer drinker. But, striking a more conciliatory tone, he went on to suggest some flexibility. "We are not wedded to every word of every recommendation the MMC has made. There may well be consequences of some recommendations that were not previously foreseen".[30]

Negotiations and lobbying

The opportunity for negotiation came on 15 May, when the first of many meetings between Ministers, officials and brewers took place. Lord Young led for the Government, and the Brewers' Society was represented by its Chairman, Anthony Fuller, Paul Nicholson of Vaux, John McGrath of Grand Metropolitan, and Richard Martin of Allied-Lyons. Young aired the idea of alternative solutions and proposed that the difficult issue of enforced disposals be left till last. The brewers undertook to "examine aspects of the recommendations with a view to determine if there were any proposals they could make to meet some of the criticisms in the report".[31]

The following day the *Morning Advertiser* led, "Lord Young is Adamant", declaring that Young had stuck to his guns during the meeting with the brewers. The bodies supporting implementation of the recommendations were becoming more organised, and "a massive counter-campaign" was announced by CAMRA, the Consumers' Association (CA) and a hundred small brewers, who were organising a programme of writing to MPs.[32] [The hundred small brewers mentioned here are different from the 48 – larger – regional and local brewers, who, as referred to earlier, had signed an open letter to Lord Young on 26 April.]

Over the next six weeks a series of meetings were held between the Government, represented by Maude and his officials, and the Brewers' Society. Maude also met a number of individual companies, including Allied-Lyons, Bass (twice), Greenall Whitley, Morrells, Sam Smith, Eldridge Pope and Hall & Woodhouse, all of whom expressed criticism of the Report's recommendations. The Minister also met the NLVA, which seemed preoccupied solely with the issue of security for tenants; the CA, which wanted licensing reform above all else; and SIBA, The Committee of Registered Clubs, and Bulmer, all of which wanted implementation of the recommendations in full. But it was a meeting with CAMRA that was to prove the most important in setting the course eventually steered by Ministers. CAMRA representatives said that regional and local brewers should be protected from measures better targeted at the nationals, but they also warned that the enforced disposal of so many pubs by the nationals could be destabilising, and they floated the notion that there should be no limit on the number of pubs a brewer could own but that only 2000 could be tied.[33] This was an idea that was to gain ground in Whitehall.

Another interested party that met Ministers and officials – several times, in fact – was Guinness, whose position was unusual, in that it was a member of the Brewers' Society, but keen to see the MMC's recommendations substantially implemented. Accordingly, it was extremely anxious to conceal its engagement with the Government from other members of the Society. On 16 May some of its senior executives met Young to state their position on the Report, but they went a step further, telling him that the company was prepared "to offer the DTI, on a confidential basis, an interpretation of moves in the debate"; it was recorded that Young was "most grateful".[34] The authors have learnt that this offer meant relaying to the DTI information about discussions within the Brewers' Society. So concerned was the company to preserve secrecy, that clandestine meetings between its executives and DTI officials were held at neutral venues. The intelligence gleaned was powerful and helped to persuade the DTI that, while the brewers presented a united front in public, behind closed doors there were tensions.

Maude received further evidence that the brewers' unity was not solid from another member of the Brewers' Society. David Thompson, Managing Director of Wolverhampton & Dudley Breweries, had publicly voiced his support for most of the MMC's recommendations, objecting to what he saw as the confrontational stance taken by the Society and arguing for negotiation with the Government. He didn't shrink from making his views known in public, even appearing on Radio 2's Jimmy Young Show, to declare that the MMC proposals could mean cheaper beer.[35] Thompson met Maude and conveyed his views, reinforcing the latter's belief that there was not unanimity amongst the brewers.[36]

Officials and Ministers concluded that it would be advantageous to bring about a real and public fracture in the brewers' supposed unity, with a view to isolating the big brewers. This strategy was implemented on 8 June, when Maude told the House of Commons that the Government had decided that some of the proposed measures, namely, the guest draught beer provision and the abolition of the tie on non-alcoholic and low alcohol beers (NAB/LABs), ciders, wines, spirits, and soft drinks, would apply only to the big brewers. The definition of guest beer was to be narrowed such that only cask-conditioned beers would qualify. The Landlord and Tenant Act would, however, and as recommended, be amended so that the licensed premises of all brewers came within its ambit; but the Government didn't intend to impose a mandatory code of practice, as the MMC had recommended.[37]

The unmistakable thrust of the announcement was that the national brewers were to be picked out, whilst the others received only a limited dose of medicine. But there were other points of significance in the statement. Thus the restriction of the tenants' guest beer entitlement to a cask-conditioned beer represented a further attempt to benefit regional and local brewers, since tenants would otherwise probably have opted for one of the nationally advertised lagers, all of which were produced by one or other of the national brewers. Now smaller brewers would have the chance to penetrate the estates of the national brewers, whilst, of course, the pubs of the regional and local brewers were to be closed to guest beer. Significant by its absence from the statement was anything on the question of free trade loans. The Government was still deliberating on the matter, as became evident a few days later in a debate in the House of Lords, but in private officials and Ministers were beginning to fear that any help from the European Commission might be so late in coming as to be worthless.

The Government's attempt to split the brewers was not without success. Greene King, for example, declared that it strongly welcomed the Government's revised position and was writing to all MPs in East Anglia, its trading area, telling them this. But some regional brewers maintained their opposition. As the *Morning Advertiser* pointed out, a number of brewers still wanted to fight the proposals concerning the proposed ban on loan tying and the amendments to the Landlord and Tenant Act.[38] The Brewers' Society welcomed the protection of local and regional brewers from the impact of some of the recommendations, but didn't soften its position.

Hostility in the Lords

Within a few days, on 14 June, Parliament was again preoccupied with the MMC Report, this time in the House of Lords.[39] It was to prove the most substantive Westminster debate on the matter during the entire episode, with 17 of their Lordships, including a bishop, two earls and three viscounts contributing. Throughout the debate speakers were overwhelmingly critical of the Report, and criticism came from across the political divide, with Conservative, Labour and crossbench peers inveighing against the report.

The debate was initiated by Lord Kimball a former Conservative MP. He foresaw the likelihood of foreign takeovers of large UK brewers, pub closures, and financial difficulties for clubs, should the recommendations be implemented.[40] Other speakers rehearsed the, by then, familiar arguments against the Report. The MMC's examination of overseas beer markets had been scanty; rural pubs in particular would be placed in jeopardy, threatening community life, a particular anxiety of the Bishop of Truro; and the whole tenanted system would be at risk if brewers were obliged to sell large numbers of pubs. The price of a pint was only one factor motivating a pub-goer to select a particular pub, and, in any case, the MMC had failed to demonstrate that its remedies would bring prices down. Choice was at least reasonable, and besides, the real competition was between pubs, rather than within the pub. A Labour peer, Lord Williams of Elvel, predicted that some large brewers would sell their breweries and exercise their new retail power to exploit the brewers. Lord Thomas asserted that some of the recommendations fell foul of the European Community's Block Exemption, a possibility that wouldn't have been news to Lord Young.[41]

Several speakers commended the Note of Dissent from Leif Mills, the "lone voice of sanity", according to one. Crossbencher Lord Harris of High Cross drew attention to Professor Yarrow's *Critique* of the MMC, describing it as "devastating" and quoting Yarrow's judgment that "the MMC's analysis of the effects of vertical agreements dissolves into virtually total incoherence". In a dig at his own profession, he added "even amongst economists, this is a fairly unfriendly observation".[42]

The Opposition spokesman, Lord Peston, another economist, was the only speaker fully supporting Young. He said it was undeniable that there had been real increases in the price of beer and this demanded some remedy. He rejected the view that the rural pub was at risk and denied that the pub-going experience had improved as much as some claimed. He scorned the brewers' public relations campaign, paid for by their "monopoly profits".[43]

Lord Young put up a stout defence of the Government's position, whilst adopting a more conciliatory tone than hitherto. He was keen to have the debate, he stressed, and to listen to the various views expressed. He drew attention to the support shown for Government action in independent surveys amongst both pub-goers and licensees, but made plain that he was alert to concerns that a ban on loans could threaten the existence of many clubs. The Secretary of State made a further important announcement: thenceforth he would no longer engage in discussions with the Brewers' Society, but would talk only with the big brewers themselves.

For the Government the debate no doubt reinforced the view that opposition ran across the political spectrum, and that some form of compromise was going to be necessary. The brewers could content themselves with the fact that their position was supported by members of both major parties, the aristocracy, and even the Church of England.

The Government's final position

Discussions between the DTI and the big brewers continued, and the Chief Executive of one national brewer wrote to Maude, putting forward a package of measures which he thought the big companies would be prepared to accept, the centrepiece of which was a reduction in local pub concentrations. But with the *Morning Advertiser* reporting on 23 June that "MMC talks [were] nearing the end", it is difficult to avoid the conclusion that such initiatives were too late, and that the endgame was approaching.[44]

So it proved. On the afternoon of 6 July Lord Young held a meeting with the chairmen of the big brewers and proposed a series of measures, including some concession on the number of pubs to be released from the tie. Within Whitehall there had been some hope that agreement could be reached to implement the measures through voluntary undertakings by the brewers, obviating the need for a Parliamentary majority and eliminating the risk of litigation from the industry. Although the chairmen roundly rejected this idea, and the meeting broke up with little prospect of agreement, Young asked the brewers to meet him again the following Monday.[45]

Immediately afterwards officials were summoned to Young's office, where, the authors have been told, they found the Secretary of State in a dark mood. A Government reshuffle was imminent and Young would have been keen to reach an accommodation with the brewers before that happened. It was agreed that the situation couldn't be allowed to drift, and that, with no agreement in prospect, the scheduled meeting with the brewers should be cancelled and the Government's decision announced as soon as possible. Accordingly, officials were set the task of producing a Ministerial statement, which the Prime Minister approved over the weekend, and on Monday 10 July Young announced the Government's response to the Report in the Lords,[46] whilst simultaneously the Chancellor of the Duchy of Lancaster, Tony Newton MP, made the same statement in the Commons.[47]

It confirmed earlier Government announcements, namely, that the guest beer provision and restrictions on the tying of non-beer drinks would apply only to the large brewers; and that licensed properties would be brought within the scope of the Landlord and Tenant Act. Other recommendations designed to afford greater protection to tenants, including the proposed binding Code of Practice, would not be implemented. The Government noted the uncertainty which the delay in settling the position of tenants was causing and said that it envisaged that all tenancies with three or more years to run from the date of the statement would fall within the scope of the Act. Other tenancies would come within the Act's scope with effect from three years after the date of the statement or with effect from the first rent review after the legislation was passed. These transitional arrangements, it was asserted, should be sufficient to allow those brewers who had issued their tenants notices to quit to withdraw such notices.

The Government had earlier signalled its unease over the idea of prohibiting loans, and now announced that it had decided against this. Instead, all loans should be capable of termination, without penalty, at no more than three months' notice. Large brewers making loans would be allowed to tie for beer only, and the borrower would be permitted to stock a guest beer. Given the opposition that the proposal had aroused, the Government may have been happy to retreat from this MMC recommendation, but the conflict with Europe's Block Exemption and the European Commission's failure to provide timely support probably gave it little choice.

The issue of licensing didn't escape attention. The 1989 Report had made no recommendations in this regard, but the Government now announced that it would look into the matter – making it clear, however, that there would be no wholesale liberalisation as a result.

As far as the big brewers were concerned, the most important decision concerned any enforced disposal of pubs. The MMC had recommended that no brewer should own more than 2000 pubs, but Ministers and officials had determined several weeks before the debate that this number was too low. Young had pointed out in private discussions within Whitehall that such a limit would penalise those who had been successful in building up an estate. And he would have been bolstered in this view by the intervention of the Chancellor of the Exchequer, Nigel Lawson MP, telling Young that he was opposed to the enforced sale of assets.

Although figures higher than 2000 had been floated in DTI discussions, the Secretary of State couldn't simply pluck a figure out of the air, but felt obliged to make his decisions using the starting point of the MMC's recommendations. Thus had an official at the DTI come to devise the seemingly odd formula, partly mooted by CAMRA, that was now announced. Brewers would be allowed to retain all of their pubs, but must free completely from the tie 50 per cent of the number they owned above 2000. This had the effect of softening the blow to the brewers, a necessary political expedient, whilst allowing the brewers with the most pubs at the outset to maintain a tie over the most.

Young pilloried

In the relatively brief Parliamentary debates that took place following the Government statement, reaction was, to say the least, mixed. Opposition spokesmen enjoyed themselves decrying the *volte face*, as they portrayed it, from Young's "minded to implement" statement back in March to the Government compromise a few months later. Colourful phrases such as "a ragged and humiliating retreat" (Lord Williams of Elvel)[48] and "craven and complete capitulation" (Bryan Gould MP)[49] were deployed. Backbenchers continued to split on non-party lines, and the Government found at least some support for its decisions on loan ties, guest beer, reducing the number of pubs to be freed from the tie, and the proposed review of licensing. On the other hand, it was criticised by others for not implementing the recommendations in full, or – conversely – for demanding any pub disposals at all, as well as for not making protection for tenants immediate.

As a symbol of the way in which the entire episode divided political opinion and crossed party lines, the authors offer the following question put to Tony Newton MP in the debate in the Commons:

> As there is no evidence of a monopoly or of collusive price fixing by the six large brewers, does the Right Hon. Gentleman agree that the MMC report was extraordinarily ideological?[50]

Was this a Conservative free-marketeer posing the question? Far from it; the speaker was old Labour stalwart Peter Shore MP.

The broadsheet press, while not employing words such as "humiliating" and "craven" in relation to the Government's compromise solution, was nevertheless as critical of it as the Parliamentary Opposition, but without in any way expressing sympathy for the brewers. The *Financial Times* said

"Young backs down on radical proposals for brewing industry", and declaimed that the Government had "bowed to intense pressure from its own MPs and the brewing industry".[51] The writer of the paper's influential Lex column bemoaned the fact that the Government had been thwarted by a "vested interest", which had deployed "the most intense and sophisticated lobbying there has ever been against an MMC report".[52]

Others were equally unkind to Young. *The Times* remarked that

> Three months after announcing he was "minded to implement" a report by the MMC....Lord Young has retreated. It is never attractive to see Ministers backing off in the face of powerful commercial interests. Lord Young has played his hand badly. The brewers, by contrast, have demonstrated their traditional mastery of political lobbying. The Minister jumped too quickly to endorse the MMC report. From that point he could only walk backwards.[53]

The populist *Daily Express* was just as scornful, complaining that the Government had "protected its traditional friends".[54]

Lord Young had reason to regret acting on the advice of Sir Gordon Borrie and officials, in saying that he was "minded to implement" the recommendations, a phrase that made it all too easy to characterise his final actions as a retreat. Reflecting on the episode in *The Enterprise Years*, Young talked ruefully of both the backbench revolt that had prompted what many portrayed as a U-turn and the political influence of the brewers, complaining that the public had favoured the MMC's proposals but that the brewers had used their influence at a constituency level to prevent their implementation.[55]

Following the Government statement, substantive opposition from the brewers seems to have ended. Certainly, no legal challenge was mounted despite the rather encouraging Opinion about possible conflict between the MMC proposals and European law received by the Brewers' Society in April. Reasons behind the absence of litigation are a matter of speculation. Of course, the brewers had made some gains since the Report was published. The Government had emasculated the MMC's recommendation on loans, and the proposal that the brewers had seen as the most pernicious, the enforced disposal of 22,000 pubs, had been moderated, even though the Opinion had been that the proposal was not in conflict with Europe. Moreover, the regional and local brewers had not only been exempted from most of the proposals, but theoretically stood to gain from the guest beer provision. This meant that the big brewers were isolated, a scenario which Borrie, in his initial advice to Young on the question of European law, had said provided the best chance of resisting legal challenge. It seems that, weighing all this up, the "big six" concluded that they had had enough. They wanted to get on with running their businesses and formulating strategy in the light of the changes. Any legal manoeuvre could only prolong the already lengthy period of uncertainty.

An important postscript to the brewers' decision came in the form of an answer in the European Parliament to a question about the Beer Orders from Anne McIntosh, a British Member of the European Parliament. The answer came on 11 March 1992.

> Before the UK Supply of Beer Order was passed, the matter was discussed between the UK authorities and the [European] Commission. The Commission made sure that this Order, in the form in which it was adopted, did not affect the essential conditions of the block exemption Regulation No 1984/83. The Commission therefore considers that the UK Government's Supply of Beer Order is compatible with this regulation.[56]

The expected Cabinet reshuffle was duly announced within days of Young's statement. Nicholas Ridley MP was installed as Secretary of State at the DTI and Young became Chairman of the Party. But this manoeuvring didn't stop some Parliamentarians seeking to cause Young more discomfort.

First, Opposition spokesman Lord Williams taunted the outgoing Secretary of State in the Lords, mockingly asking what plans the Government had for winding up the MMC, and asserting that the Commission's credibility had been undermined by the Government's handling of the beer Report. In the Commons the attack was led by Graham Riddick MP, one of the sternest Conservative critics of the MMC Report. Bryan Gould MP, for the Opposition, stirred the pot by referring to announcements of price increases for beer made that very day, no doubt, he said, to pay for the brewers' "costs of successfully campaigning against the MMC's recommendations".[57]

The final act before the summer adjournment took place in the Agriculture Select Committee. Shortly after the Ministerial statements the Committee summoned Young and Richard Ryder MP, a MAFF Minister, to a hearing. The role of a House of Commons Select Committee is to examine the expenditure, administration and policy of the relevant government department, in this case MAFF, which – *inter alia* – then acted as sponsor for the brewing industry within Whitehall. The Committee was distinctly unsympathetic to Young and seemed determined to accuse him of acting in haste and without due thought. When its report came out on 26 July, it was critical on two fundamental grounds.

First, the MMC Report had been "defective in a number of important respects". It had purported to help the small brewer, but most of them had opposed the Report. The MMC had simply been wrong in concluding that the brewers made most of their profits from making beer. Why, the Committee asked, had no one visited Australia, where a duopoly producing 95 per cent of all beer had resulted from the enactment of similar proposals? Second, Young's proposals were being pursued "at a pace which does not allow for adequate consultation or consideration". Other Government colleagues had been inadequately consulted, and the proposed timetable didn't allow for sufficient Parliamentary scrutiny. Licensing should have been reviewed *before* the Government settled on its course of action, "rather than at some undefined point in the future".[58]

In accusing Young of acting with undue haste, the Committee may have felt that he seemed intent from the outset on closing the matter rapidly. The degree to which the Committee was fair in this criticism is difficult to judge, but any sense of urgency on Young's part could have had a variety of causes. As suggested earlier, the approach of a Cabinet reshuffle may have played a part. But he would in any case have wanted to stub out the embarrassing backbench revolt as quickly as possible, and would have been motivated by the wish to end uncertainty in a reasonable timescale. But whatever the reasoning, arguably the most radical and far-reaching Report ever produced by the MMC was translated into legislative proposal in just a few months. Be that as it may, attention would now focus on giving legal effect to the Government's decisions.

Notes

1. HL Deb 21 March 1989 vol 505 c675WA.
2. Lord Young, *The Enterprise Years* (London: Headline Publishing, 1990), p. 319.
3. Letter dated 20 May 1989.
4. EDM 833 May 1989.
5. Department of Trade and Industry (DTI) untitled internal paper, February 1990.
6. DTI memorandum "Note of meeting between Lord Young and John Elliott", 5 April 1989.
7. *Ibid.*, para. 9.
8. DTI paper "MMC report on beer: implications for mergers", 19 April 1989.
9. *The Times*, p. 7, 26 April 1989.
10. *Financial Times*, pp. 4–5, 9 February 1989.
11. Memorandum from Peter Luff to Lord Young, 13 April 1989.
12. DTI memorandum "Beer: meeting with MAFF", 14 April 1989.
13. DTI memorandum "MMC report on beer", 18 April 1989.
14. DTI paper "Implementation of MMC report on Beer: Compatibility with EU law", 17 April 1989.
15. DTI memorandum "Secretary of State's meeting with Sir Gordon Borrie 24th April: Beer", 25 April 1989.
16. Brewers' Society, *Further Critique – Conflict with EC Law of the Report of the MMC on "The Supply of Beer"*, May 1989.
17. Minutes of Brewers' Society Council meeting, 10 May 1989.
18. For example, *Financial Times*, 3 May 1989.
19. Minutes of Brewers' Society Council meeting, 10 May 1989.
20. Lord Young, *op. cit.*, p. 319.
21. Memorandum from Peter Luff to Lord Young, 2 May 1989.
22. Lord Young, *op. cit.*, p. 319.
23. DTI memoranda "Beer: Action points", 3 May 1989, and "Beer", 5 May 1989.

24 Speech by Lord Young to North Warwickshire Patrons Club, 3 May 1989.
25 Brewers' Society Annual Report for the year to 30 September 1989.
26 DTI untitled internal paper, February 1990, p. 4.
27 *Morning Advertiser*, 6 May 1989, p. 1.
28 DTI memorandum "Beer: Meeting between Ministers and officials, 8 May", 10 May 1989.
29 HC Deb 08 May 1989 Vol. 152 cc697–699.
30 *Ibid.*, cc702 and 704.
31 Brewers' Society press release, 15 May 1989.
32 *Morning Advertiser*, 16 May 1989, p. 1.
33 DTI memorandum "Note of meeting between Mr. Maude and CAMRA on 22nd May", 23 May 1989.
34 DTI memorandum "Beer: Meeting with [name(s) redacted] of Guinness May 16th", 18 May 1989.
35 Reported in the *Morning Advertiser*, 16 June 1989, p. 1.
36 DTI memorandum "BEER: Note of meeting between Mr. Maude and [name redacted] of Wolverhampton & Dudley Breweries PLC", 8 June 1989.
37 HC Deb 08 June 1989 Vol. 154 c229W.
38 *Morning Advertiser*, June 23 1989, p. 1.
39 HL Deb 14 June 1989 Vol. 508 cc1427–1477.
40 *Ibid.*, cc1428–1430.
41 *Ibid.*, cc1435–1440 and 1458.
42 *Ibid.*, c1462.
43 *Ibid.*, c1474.
44 *Morning Advertiser*, p. 1, 23 June 1989.
45 DTI memorandum "Secretary of State's meeting with the national brewers, 6 July", 7 July 1989.
46 HL Deb 10 July 1989 Vol. 510 cc7–18.
47 HC Deb 10 July 1989 Vol. 156 cc685–697.
48 HL Deb 10 July 1989 Vol. 510 c12.
49 HC Deb 10 July 1989 Vol. 156 c688.
50 *Ibid.*, c691.
51 *Financial Times*, 11 July 1989.
52 *Ibid.*, p. 17.
53 *The Times*, p. 2, 11 July 1989.
54 *Daily Express*, p. 8, 11 July 1989.
55 Lord Young, *op. cit.*, p. 319.
56 No. 117, Official Journal 3-416/192-3.
57 HC Deb 19 July 1989 Vol. 157 c328.
58 Agriculture Select Committee, Fourth Report of Session 1988–90, *Supply of Beer*, 26 July 1989.

10
The Beer Orders Emerge

Government's position formalised

The principal recommendations of the Monopolies and Mergers Commission (MMC) Report had been set out in the first chapter of the Report, under six broad headings, which, to reiterate, were: (1) no brewer to own more than 2000 on-licensed outlets; (2) covenants on premises being sold either specifying a product tie or precluding future use as a pub to be prohibited; (3) no new free trade loans to be made; (4) all tenants to be allowed to stock at least one guest draught beer and to be free from tie in respect of all beverages except beer above 1.2 per cent alcohol by volume; (5) all tenants to be given the protection of the Landlord and Tenant Act 1954 Part II, and a revised and binding Code of Practice to be negotiated with the Director General of Fair Trading and incorporated into all tenancy agreements containing a beer tie; and (6) all brewers to publish wholesale price lists, including details of quantity discounts and further discounts available for collection from the brewery by independent wholesalers.[1]

Within the body of the Report were three other recommendations, namely, that brewers should not be allowed to enter into exclusive beer supply agreements of more than one year in respect of premises specifically disposed of to comply with the limit on pub ownership;[2] that small brewers be charged a reduced rate of duty on part of their beer output;[3] and that any company with brewing interests making an acquisition taking it over the 2000 pub limit must immediately divest itself of the excess.[4] This last recommendation was presumably made principally to prevent Greenall Whitley, which had almost 1700 pubs (more than twice as many as the next biggest integrated brewer) from taking itself over the limit with impunity.

Following the months of negotiations and Parliamentary debates, draft legislation was published in August 1989, incorporating the principal changes from the MMC's recommendations which had already been announced.[5] Thus, most importantly, brewers need not dispose of any premises at all but must free from tie half of the excess over 2000. Next, the guest beer provision and relaxation of the tie wouldn't apply to the tenants of regional and small brewers. The guest beer itself must not only be in draught form, as recommended by the MMC, but must be cask-conditioned (thus excluding stouts – importantly Guinness – and lagers). Free trade loans would not, after all, be prohibited, but borrowers must be able to repay at three months' notice without penalty, and recipients of loans from a major brewer must have the same right as the latter's tenants to a guest beer and freedom from tie in respect of non-beer supplies. And the proposal for a binding Code of Practice for pub tenants had been abandoned.

The MMC recommendation not to allow exclusive beer supply agreements of more than one year involving pubs disposed of under the freeing-up recommendation had early on been dropped on the advice of Sir Gordon Borrie. He believed that such a prohibition would be open to challenge by Europe, and he may in any case have surmised that the brewers could easily circumvent such a prohibition by arranging, say, 95 per cent supply agreements.

So much was already known; but the draft legislation also contained a number of other changes and refinements, as well as the dates for compliance. Thus a provision appearing for the first time required that premises freed from the tie must be let at a market rent, with no repairing obligations on the brewer. This was to prevent brewers from retaining any leverage over the tenant which might be used to induce the latter to continue to stock his brewer-landlord's beer. Also new were the stipulations that brewers must not charge more than advertised wholesale prices, and must not withhold supplies unless there were reasonable doubts about payment, the return of containers or the treatment of the beer.

The proposal to ban product tying covenants in respect of pubs sold by brewers had been allowed to lapse, having effectively been neutralised by the fact that any pub sold with such a covenant would count towards the vendor's tied estate. And the "Greenall Whitley clause" had been rendered irrelevant by the decision not to limit pub ownership, and had been replaced by a provision stating that any brewer owning a prohibited interest in tied pubs as a result of the acquisition of shares after 1 May 1991 must regularise the situation within six months. The guest beer provision and release from the tie on non-beer beverages would take effect on 1 May 1990, and the untying exercise in respect of half the excess over 2000 pubs was to be completed by 1 November 1991.

Of specific interest to two companies, Whitbread and Whitbread Investment Company (WIC), it was now stipulated that "brewery groups" must also comply with the provision relating to the limit on tied house ownership. Such a group was defined as the combination of one company with every other company in which the former controlled at least 15 per cent of voting shares, as long as one member of the group was a brewer. This clause was probably inserted to prevent brewers from evading the limit on number of tied premises by restructuring themselves as separate but related entities. Given, however, the existing cross-shareholdings between Whitbread and WIC, and both these companies' holdings in regional brewers, another effect of the 15 per cent rule (although this wasn't finally clarified till almost two years later) was that the estates of some of these regionals counted towards Whitbread's total number of premises. Given that the Department of Trade and Industry (DTI) took it as read that protecting the regionals was central to benefiting the consumer, its lawyers took great care to draft the Orders in a way that meant that only the shareholding company, and not the companies in which the shares were held, was directly affected by the aggregate tied limit on pub numbers.

Interested parties were invited to submit representations in respect of the draft proposals by 10 October, as a result of which Nicholas Ridley MP, who had succeeded Lord Young as Secretary of State for Trade and Industry at the end of July, told the Commons on 31 October that, following further consultation, the date for complying with the pub freeing-up requirement would be postponed by 12 months from the 1 November 1991 deadline which had appeared in the draft Orders.

The Beer Orders

In December the Secretary of State laid two Statutory Instruments before Parliament. These are the principal means by which delegated – or secondary – legislation is made. Delegated legislation is so called because it is made under powers given to the executive by primary legislation, and it enables a minister to make changes to a law without pushing through a completely new Act. Statutory Instruments can be accepted or rejected by Parliament, but not amended. These particular Instruments came commonly to be known as the Beer Orders.

Statutory Instrument number 2258, The Supply of Beer (Loan Ties, Licensed Premises and Wholesale Prices) Order 1989, was laid on 4 December. Commonly abbreviated to LTO, it dealt with the right to repay loans at three months' notice, the prohibition of clauses in pub sale contracts preventing the pubs from continuing as such, and the publication of wholesale price lists; and it applied to all brewers. The Order differed from the draft version only in that it specified the date for compliance, namely, 1 May 1990.

Far more significant, of course, was Statutory Instrument number 2390, The Supply of Beer (Tied Estate) Order 1989, which was laid before Parliament on 6 December. Known as the TEO, it dealt with the limit on ownership of tied licensed premises and the changes to the tie, and it didn't differ in any significant way from the draft Order, except in respect of Ridley's postponement until 1 November 1992 of the date for complying with the freeing-up requirement (which also applied to the clause relating to the ownership of a prohibited interest in tied pubs through the acquisition of shares).

The number of premises to be untied was based on the highest number of pubs held at any time on or since 10 July 1989 – when the untying formula had first been announced. These numbers were never published, although each national brewer was notified of its own permitted tied house total, and in Table 10.1 the authors have used the figures as at July 1989 quoted in Table 3.17 of the MMC Report of July 1992 on the Allied-Lyons/Carlsberg brewing merger.

Table 10.1 National Brewers' Ownership of Full On-licences as at July 1989 and Freeing-up Requirements

Company	Number	Excess over 2000	Number to be freed	To remain tied
Allied-Lyons	6,858	4,858	2,429	4,429
Bass	7,476	5,476	2,738	4,738
Courage	5,000	3,000	1,500	3,500
Grand Metropolitan	5,266	3,266	1,633	3,633
Scottish & Newcastle	2,354	354	177	2,177
Whitbread	6,628	4,628	2,314	4,314
All national brewers	**33,582**	**21,582**	**10,791**	**22,791**

Source: Monopolies and Mergers Commission, *Allied-Lyons PLC and Carlsberg A/S: A Report on the Proposed Joint Venture*, Cm 2029 (1992), Table 3.17.

Thus, as things stood at the start of 1990, almost 11,000 licensed premises would have to be freed from a major brewer's tie, representing just under one-third of the major brewers' combined tied estate. And the way the freeing-up formula operated meant that the larger the tied estate that a brewer owned, the greater was the proportion of the estate that had to be freed from tie.

Pub tenants to be protected by legislation

Before leaving this part of the story, two loose ends need to be tied up. First, the MMC's recommendation on tenants' security of tenure was to be put into effect by primary legislation, namely, the Landlord and Tenant (Licensed Premises) Act 1990. And, second, its idea of charging small brewers a lower rate of duty than the large ones was finally acted upon in Gordon Brown's Budget of April 2002. The implementation of the first of these recommendations was, as we are about to see, marked by strongly expressed views.

One result of the discussions between the Brewers' Society and the DTI following the 1969 Monopolies Commission Report was that the Society secured the agreement of its members and the pub trade for the granting of longer term tenancies than the traditional annual contract. The Society subsequently recommended that brewers should specifically consider offering three-year contracts. Most companies, including all the majors, implemented the recommendation, but tenants' organisations, aware that not all their members wished to commit to three-year terms, started to highlight the fact that pub tenants were excluded from the protection offered to business tenants by the Landlord and Tenant Act 1954 Part II.

The reasons for this were bound up with the operation of the licensing laws. The view taken by the authorities at the time of the 1954 Act had been that a brewer-landlord must – effectively in contravention of the Act – not only be able to evict at short notice a tenant whose licence had not been renewed, but must also be allowed to take such action in relation to a tenant whose conduct of his business made non-renewal likely. Otherwise, the continuity of the licensed status of the premises could be jeopardised. Following discussions between the Brewers' Society, Government departments and licensees' organisations, a Code of Practice on Tenants' Security was introduced in 1973. This sought to provide tenants, by voluntary means, with the same level of protection as they would have received under the 1954 Act, with machinery put in place for independent adjudication on matters such as rent and termination or non-renewal of a tenancy. All the interested parties except for some of the smaller brewers accepted that, properly applied, the Code could provide adequate protection. As a result of representations by the National Union of Licensed Victuallers (NULV), a number of amendments to the Code had been introduced in 1981, and it was this amended version which was submitted to the MMC in June 1987.

The MMC was unimpressed, however, and recommended that tenants of licensed premises be given the same protection as other business tenants, and, moreover, that a new Code of Practice be introduced. On 8 June 1989 Francis Maude MP, Parliamentary Under-Secretary of State at the DTI, told the Commons that "while it would be appropriate to amend the Landlord and Tenant Act 1954 to remove the present exception for licensed premises, it would not be right to go further and require additional provisions for tenants' protection in a mandatory brewers' code of practice".[6] On 10 July 1989, when setting out the Government's overall response to the Report, Lord Young announced that amendments to the Landlord and Tenant Act 1954 would be brought forward. To this end, on 14 December, his successor, Nicholas Ridley MP, moved the Second Reading of the Landlord and Tenant (Licensed Premises) Bill. The legislation would take effect three years after Young's announcement, and Ridley told the Commons that, under transitional arrangements, tenancy agreements entered into up to the date of the July announcement and due to end in the three years following it would not be affected.

It is interesting to note that John Redwood MP, who had taken over from Maude as Parliamentary Under-Secretary of State, and who assisted Ridley during the debate, had seven months earlier been one of the signatories to an Early Day Motion (EDM) that was hardly supportive of the Beer Orders.[7] Indeed, the Motion was unstinting in its praise for the British brewing industry and its pubs, and urged the Government not to implement the MMC's recommendations without further consideration.

Worrying developments for tenants

Within a couple of weeks of publication of the MMC Report, in March 1989, Bass had announced that it had frozen investment plans for its tenanted estate and stopped recruiting new tenants in the North and Midlands, while at the beginning of May it was reported that Courage was to slow down the pace of investment in its tenanted estate. But much more worryingly for tenants, some brewers had quickly responded to the Report by issuing notices to quit. Thus by the end of April three small brewers, Charles Wells, Burtonwood and Mansfield, had served notice on their tenants, and in May Robinsons wrote to its tenants warning that their jobs had been put at risk by the MMC. Robinsons was not surprisingly accused of scaremongering, but many other companies were to send out notice letters.

In April 1989 the National Licensed Victuallers' Association (NLVA) had appointed Stan Crowther MP as its Parliamentary adviser, and he played a prominent part during the passage through Parliament of the Landlord and Tenant legislation. Another Labour MP who took a close interest in the matter was the Opposition spokesman on trade and industry, Doug Henderson MP. He unsuccessfully moved an amendment on 26 February 1990 that would have prevented mutually agreed contracting-out of the specific terms of the Act. Henderson, Crowther and others feared that brewers might otherwise pressurise tenants into foregoing their rights, but the Government argued that without the contracting-out option the balance between the two parties' interests would be upset and the availability of pubs to rent reduced.

On 22 October 1990 Redwood, for the Government, moved that the Commons approve a Lords amendment to the legislation, which closed a loophole by ensuring that protection would apply to tenants who had received notice to quit ahead of the introduction of the Act in July 1992. Redwood, Crowther and Henderson all paid tribute to the lobbying and advice that had been provided by the NLVA in this matter, and the amendment was approved.

In June 1991 Crowther tabled an EDM in the Commons calling for an immediate review of the Beer Orders by the Office of Fair Trading, compensation for displaced tenants and independent arbitration on rents.[8] On 11 July he asked the Leader of the House, John MacGregor MP, to arrange for a debate before the summer recess. MacGregor suggested that the matter could be raised in the summer Adjournment Debate, scheduled for 22 July. Crowther duly grasped the opportunity. He opened his speech by reporting that 121 Members had now signed his EDM, he pointed out that the future for thousands of tenants was very insecure, and he requested that the Government admit it had made a mistake in respect of the MMC's recommendations and take swift action to repair the damage. Peter Lilley MP, who had by this time taken over from Ridley as Secretary of State for Trade and Industry, was sufficiently influenced by the degree of support for the Motion to receive a deputation from the NLVA and then to call in the major brewers for talks on tenants' concerns. The brewers agreed to introduce rent arbitration procedures but showed little willingness to move on the issue of compensation for tenants displaced by managers.

The brewers' position

In September, in an attempt to set the record straight on the subject of pub tenants and the Tied Estate Order (TEO), the Brewers' Society issued a briefing note for the benefit of MPs and other opinion formers. It pointed out that the Order required that pubs let free of the tie must be let at an open market rent and on a full repairing basis, but that once the new Landlord and Tenant legislation took effect, in July 1992, it might well be impossible to alter the terms of leases to comply with those requirements. Given also that July 1991 had in many cases been the last date at which notice having effect in July 1992 could be given, tenants likely to be affected had already had to be served notice and new leases put in place. To make matters worse, the scale of the freeing operation was such that in many cases the brewers had issued notice not because they had reached a decision to free a particular pub but because they hadn't had time to make up their minds. [The Agriculture Select Committee, in its 1993 Review of the Beer Orders, was to vindicate the national brewers, stating that they "had no reasonable alternative course of action" but to issue notices to quit, and that the Government's claim to have been concerned about the notices was "disingenuous".[9] The smaller brewers, who, as described above, were the first to serve notice, would presumably have argued that, at the time – that is, before it became clear that they weren't subject to the TEO – they felt that they had no choice either.]

The Society's note pointed out that, in any case, whether a pub was to be tied or not, the forthcoming application of the Landlord and Tenant Act to pubs meant that it would be appropriate for leases to be offered on longer terms than the traditional maximum three-year basis. And it added that there had been a trend towards granting longer leases even before the MMC Report, and that this had been driven by demand from licensees, who stood to benefit both from greater security and from the right to assign the lease, thereby crystallising any goodwill they had built up. Given also that long leases in the licensed trade normally gave lessees the right to retain the profits from amusement-with-prize machines, and that the lessees of the major brewers now had the right to stock a guest ale and to buy low alcohol beer and non-beer drinks in the open market, it was inevitable that rents would rise.

Review of Beer Orders "a matter of the utmost urgency"

Two months later, on 14 November, Crowther initiated another Adjournment Debate, again drawing attention to the upheaval in the industry since the Beer Orders, and his opening salvo in the Commons that day is worth setting out in full, as an indication of the sense of shock and disillusionment that the Beer Orders and the new Landlord and Tenant Act had engendered amongst tenants. He declared:

> There can hardly ever have been a piece of legislation that has so utterly failed to achieve its stated objectives. We were told that the Orders were introduced with the intention of increasing competition, thus providing more choice for consumers and holding down prices. In fact, competition has been reduced, prices have rocketed, thousands of public house tenants have been forced out of the trade and thousands more have felt that they have no reasonable option other than to accept the terms being imposed upon them by the brewers and accept long leases at enormously increased rents, with full responsibility for repairs. The brewers have decided to destroy the traditional tenancy system. It is on its way out.[10]

Later on he said, "I am not especially critical of the brewers. They operate in a hard commercial environment. They are looking after their commercial interests".[11] He quoted Grand Met as having told him that 40 per cent of its tenants had left the trade since the Beer Orders; and he suggested that roughly the same figure applied amongst all the major brewers.

Towards the end of the debate, Redwood conceded that he and Ridley were worried about the notices to quit that the major brewers had been issuing, but he declared that most of the notices had been issued to allow for the renegotiation of existing agreements and that few would lead to eviction. He went on to reiterate one of the points made in the Brewers' Society's briefing note, namely, that the timing of notices had been determined by the fact that all tenants would be protected by the new Landlord and Tenant legislation by July 1992. He referred to a letter which Ridley had sent to MPs, pointing out that it would be unrealistic to expect the removal of all differences between brewers and their tenants. But he reported too that the NLVA had said in its most recent letter to the Secretary of State that the reaction of the big brewers to their meetings with Lilley and himself "would initially seem to be both positive and encouraging".[12]

On 27 November, almost two years after the laying of the Beer Orders, Crowther made his final contribution to the matter, when he tabled another EDM. It read, "That this house views with alarm the hardship faced by thousands of pub licensees and the damage being done to the interests of consumers and to the industry as a whole; and calls upon Her Majesty's Government to review the 1989 Beer Orders as a matter of the utmost urgency."[13] The motion attracted cross-party support and 189 signatures – an unusually high number.

Notes

1. Monopolies and Mergers Commission, *The Supply of Beer: A Report on the Supply of Beer for Retail Sale in the United Kingdom*, Cm 651 (1989), paras. 1.25–1.30.
2. *Ibid.*, para. 12.134.
3. *Ibid.*, para. 12.161.
4. *Ibid.*, para. 12.129.
5. *The London Gazette*, 22 August 1989, p. 9726.
6. HC Deb 08 June 1989, Vol. 154 c229W.
7. HC 1988–89 EDM 833.
8. HC 1990–91 EDM 1035.
9. Agriculture Select Committee Fourth Report of Session 1992–93, *Effects of the Beer Orders on the Brewing Industry and Consumers*, 21 April 1993, para. 50.
10. HC Deb 14 November 1991 Vol. 198 c1327.
11. *Ibid.*, c1329.
12. *Ibid.*, c1334.
13. HC 1991–92 EDM 285.

11
Complying with the Orders

Elders bid for Scottish & Newcastle blocked

The reference of the brewing industry to the Monopolies and Mergers Commission (MMC) in August 1986 had brought about a slowdown in the rate of corporate activity within the industry, but by no means a complete cessation. Thus, just a couple of weeks after the announcement, Scottish & Newcastle (S&N) bid for Nottingham-based Home Brewery, at the invitation of the family owners, and then in the following year it made a second, this time successful, attempt to acquire Matthew Brown. By the end of 1986, however, events which would ultimately prove rather more significant for S&N were in train.

Courage had been bought by Imperial Tobacco in an agreed deal as far back as 1972, and after the latter had been taken over in April 1986 by the corporate-raiding conglomerate, Hanson Trust, Courage found itself being sold in November to Elders IXL, just a couple of months after the failure of the latter's bid for Allied-Lyons. In hindsight, the acquisition by Elders of a leading and very long established participant in the domestic beer and pub markets can be seen as the harbinger of the great international takeover of UK brewing that was to follow the Beer Orders.

In fact, if Elders had had its way, another large step in that process would have been taken well before the MMC had even reported. For in February 1987 – as it later transpired – Elders, having established a UK base, suggested a merger with S&N. It was rebuffed, and towards the end of that year started buying shares in its prey, accumulating by February 1988 a 2 per cent stake. Over the next few months Elders made a number of unsuccessful attempts to persuade Scottish to merge, and in October, having increased its holding to 9.5 per cent, it announced a bid, which was immediately rejected.

Three weeks later the bid was referred to the MMC, and the resulting Report[1] was completed in March 1989 and published in the afternoon of the same day that the industry Report *The Supply of Beer* came out. Its authors confirmed that they had seen the industry Report during the later stages of their inquiry, but that they had been able to reach their conclusions on the basis of their own evidence. In fact, two Commissioners, Dick Smethurst and Bob Young, served on both investigations, the former as Chairman in both cases. Given that the industry Report expressed such deep concerns about competition and concentration in brewing, it would have appeared extremely odd if the Commissioners in the Elders/S&N case had reached any other conclusion than to recommend prohibiting the merger: having a Chairman and another member in common made it virtually inconceivable.

And so it turned out. The Commission found that the merger could be expected to have serious adverse effects on competition and that there were no mitigating benefits. More specifically, it argued that both Courage and S&N were major suppliers to the free trade, and that the loss of independence of one of them would reduce choice and competition. It considered that the merger would reinforce the Bass/S&N duopoly in Scotland, and by creating a UK competitor the same size as Bass would lead to reduced competition. Finally, the Commissioners expressed concern – thereby displaying a somewhat unusual interpretation of the public interest – that Elders might dispose of some S&N businesses, "which would affect the spread of interests which attaches to S&N's position as an independent company directly managed in Scotland".[2] In the light of these words, and what was to happen several years later, it is hard not to concur with the view – stated by outsiders both at the time and since – that skilful political lobbying by S&N and the influential Scottish establishment played at least some part in the reference, if not the outcome of this takeover attempt. In any case, the Government accepted the MMC's conclusions, and the proposed merger was blocked.

Courage deal with Grand Metropolitan allowed

When the Beer Orders passed into law in December 1989, the "big six" companies were given until 1 November 1992 to comply with the most onerous requirement, namely, that if they wished to continue as integrated brewers and retailers, they must release from tie half of their licensed premises over 2000. The remainder of this chapter describes how the majors initially reacted to this requirement, and thus how the process got under way which would ultimately result in six integrated brewers and pub operators, of which five were UK-owned, becoming four non-integrated brewers, all foreign-owned.

The first companies to show their hands were Courage and Grand Metropolitan. Against a background during the second half of the eighties of stagnating beer sales and soaring property prices, Grand Met had already been considering the future direction of its brewing and pub interests. In 1986 it had established a separate property division to manage its pub estate, with the aims of trying to ensure that the pubs earned an appropriate return on capital, and were not regarded merely as outlets for its beer. In brewing, the company had decided that with a UK beer market share of 11 per cent, and a brand portfolio that was regarded as the weakest amongst the majors, it must either get bigger or get out of the industry. Following publication of the MMC recommendations and the resulting Beer Orders, Grand Metropolitan minds were made up, and with the twice-thwarted Elders, owners of Courage, still hoping to strengthen its UK brewing base, a deal was beckoning.

In fact, a "pubs-for-breweries-swap" agreement was announced just three months after the Beer Orders, in March 1990. Under the terms of the transaction Grand Met would transfer its brewing business to Courage, and all the pubs of both companies except for the majority of Grand Met's managed pubs would be put into a new company, to be owned 50:50 by the two participants, and to be known as Inntrepreneur Estates Limited (IEL). Both IEL and Grand Met's managed pubs would enter into ten-year beer supply agreements with Courage. Grand Met, having given up brewing, would thus be free of the Beer Orders, but Courage, by virtue of its being both a brewer and a major shareholder in IEL, was still subject to them.

Towards the end of April, just two days before the scheduled completion date, the deal was referred to the MMC.

On 30 July the two parties put forward a number of proposals to meet concerns expressed by the Commission during discussions. Grand Met's withdrawal from brewing would in any case mean that its 1730 managed pubs were no longer tied for the purposes of the Beer Orders, but the parties now offered to free from the tie 1067 more IEL premises than would be required by the Beer Orders absent the transaction. Thus, compared with around 3150 premises (out of over 10,000) which the two companies between them would have to free without the deal, roughly 5950 would be freed if the deal was allowed. In addition, the parties offered to terminate the Courage beer supply agreement with Grand Met's managed pubs by November 1992, rather than running it for ten years; undertook to deal with local concentrations of IEL and Grand Met outlets; and offered not to seek to renew Grand Met's interest in Carlsberg brands when the licensing arrangement came to an end the following year, thereby reducing the enlarged Courage market share from 20 per cent to 18 per cent.

The MMC Report was published on 16 October, and in the opening summary its authors baldly stated their concern that allowing a reduction in the number of national brewers from six to five "would significantly increase concentration". Within the body of the Report they noted that the Elders/S&N Commissioners had referred disapprovingly to a potential combined market share, together with Bass, of over 40 per cent, and they pointed out that much the same applied in this case. They concluded that the proposed merger would lead to higher wholesale prices and local concentrations of retail interests, and that benefits arising from it would not suffice to outweigh these adverse effects.

Accordingly, they recommended that the merger should be allowed to proceed only subject to certain conditions. One of these, namely, that 1067 more pubs must be released from the IEL tie than was required under the Beer Orders, had already been offered by the parties; while two other MMC conditions, relating to local concentrations of pubs and the length of the supply agreement with Grand Met's managed estate, were actually less demanding than those proposals. While there was thus much common ground between the two sides, the MMC also wanted the combined beer market share to be brought down to 15 per cent, through brand and probably capacity disposals, and the supply agreement with IEL to operate for only five years, rather than ten.

In response to the MMC's recommendations, Peter Lilley MP, Secretary of State for Trade and Industry, announced that he was prepared to waive the beer market share condition, meaning that all that remained was for the length of the IEL supply contract to be negotiated. In discussions with the OFT a supply agreement lasting till 1998 (that is, for seven years) was finally settled on, but in an unexpected twist the supply agreement with Grand Met's managed pubs – which the MMC had wanted to run until 1995, but which the merger partners had offered to terminate in 1992 – would, indeed, operate until 1995 (that is, for four years).

Both the MMC Report and the Minister's comments were interesting for what they revealed about current thinking on competition and regulation in the industry. Thus in the Report itself, written less than a year after the laying of the Beer Orders, we find its authors explicitly drawing attention to the limitations, in terms of enhancing competition, of the guest beer and tied pub ownership rules.[3] They go on to say, "There is little support for the parties' view that the national brewers' competitive position has materially changed since the Beer report or is likely so to change in the foreseeable future".[4] This and other passages show that the Commissioners were preoccupied with the need to maintain competition at the brewing and wholesaling level. As far as pub retailing was concerned, their unease seemed to be restricted to considerations of local concentrations of ownership.

Lilley, on the other hand, indicated in his statement that he was opposed not so much to concentration *per se*, either in brewing or in retailing, as to the vertical links between them, "which magnify the effects on competition of any increases in concentration". Concentration was unwelcome unless "counterbalanced by major weakening of these vertical links"; and "there should be moves to free the retail business from the influence of the brewer so that they may respond to consumers' preferences". Finally, in order not to be seen as setting ground rules for possible future mergers in the industry, he stressed that reducing vertical integration as part of such deals would not guarantee that they would be approved; and, indeed, that the greater the degree of existing concentration, the more reluctant he would be to allow increases in market share by acquisition. The deal was completed in March 1991, and IEL set about the agreed task of freeing from the tie around 4200 outlets. Roughly half were let on free-of-tie leases, and half were sold, the most important disposal being of the former Grand Met subsidiary, Ushers Brewers, consisting of 433 pubs together with the local brewery.

Allied-Lyons/Carlsberg brewing merger allowed

Allied-Lyons was widely regarded as having a mediocre beer brand portfolio, with a particular problem in lager, and for years it had slowly been losing market share. It is no secret that at some point in the early nineties it discussed a brewing merger with Whitbread – an idea which came to nothing. In any case, in October 1991, still less than two years after the Beer Orders, but against the background of an already increasingly competitive wholesale beer market, Allied and the Danish brewer, Carlsberg, announced that they had agreed to merge their UK brewing interests in a joint venture, Carlsberg-Tetley Limited (CTL), in which each would hold a 50 per cent share. Allied would continue to own its pub estate, and had agreed to take all its beer requirements, up to 15 per cent of which could be non-CTL brands, from the joint venture for seven years. The merger would enhance Allied's lager brand portfolio, while providing Carlsberg – whose licensing agreement with Grand Met had recently come to an end – with access to a substantial distribution network and customer base. The merged brewing business would have a market share the same as the newly enlarged Courage.

On 9 March 1992 the deal was referred to the MMC. The Commission's Report was published in July,[5] and not for the first or last time in a brewing industry inquiry there was a dissenting voice. The conclusion reached by the majority was that the merger would have both positive and detrimental effects on competition. In the deal's favour, CTL would be able to compete more vigorously with the two biggest brewers, Bass and (now) Courage. But, against this, there would be three large brewers (which would account for 67 per cent of the lager market, compared with 46 per cent for Bass and Courage, and 59 per cent of the total beer market, compared with 43 per cent).

The majority on the inquiry finally adopted the second of these views, asserting that the removal of Carlsberg as an independent supplier would harm competition and that the deal should not proceed unless three conditions were satisfied: namely, that CTL undertake not to worsen the terms of supply to Carlsberg's small brewer and wholesaler customers; that the length of the supply agreement with Allied be reduced to five years; and that Allied allow its tenants, after two years, to be freed from the tie with CTL in respect of half of their lager requirements.

The Note of Dissent was written by Professor ME Beesley, a Managing Trustee of the free market think-tank, the Institute of Economic Affairs. He supported the view expressed by the parties to the merger that recent trends in the industry – the growth of the free on-trade and take-home trade, the decline in the importance of tied estates, the growth in pub chains and the existence of spare brewing capacity – meant that the beer market was highly competitive and that competitive pressures would continue to increase. To him, supply agreements and loan ties were "methods by which rivalry is now pursued"; if lager brands disappeared from the market, "this is a result of competition in it";[6] and if some independent wholesalers lost trade, "that is the price of increased rivalry among the larger players".[7] Towards the end of his Note he succinctly addressed his colleagues' unease over the concept of allowing three – rather than two – companies to dominate the market, as follows: "There is also a concern that regional and local brewers will be adversely affected through the loss of Carlsberg as an independent supplier and the increased competitive strength of CTL…But one cannot have one's cake and eat it. An inevitable side effect of confronting the larger players more vigorously will be difficulty for other players".[8] The Professor concluded that the effects of the deal, either pro- or anti-competition, were minor, which in itself "should induce caution in finding against a merger", but that the likely favourable effects outweighed the unfavourable. The merger should therefore be allowed.[9]

Discussions with the regulatory bodies continued until December, when Michael Heseltine MP, President of the Board of Trade, announced his decision to allow the merger, subject to three conditions. The first was the same as the MMC's first recommended condition, except to make clear that the undertaking required from CTL not to change the terms of supply to existing Carlsberg customers would not apply to non-CTL brands. Next, Heseltine also demanded compliance with the MMC's second condition – that the life of the supply agreement be reduced from seven years to five years. And, third, Allied would have to free from the tie, over four years, 400 more pubs than required by the Beer Orders. The MMC's own third condition, concerning a loosening of the tie for Allied tenants in respect of lager, was dropped completely. With all obstacles having thus been cleared, the two parties now quickly completed the merger and CTL began trading on 18 January 1993.

In the meantime, the process of complying with the second Beer Order as it related to freeing outlets from the tie hadn't gone entirely smoothly for Allied. In addition to the 400 outlets to be freed in connection with the Carlsberg deal, the company was required to free 2429 of its 6858-strong estate, and it finally achieved this with a combination of around 1000 free-of-tie leases and 1400 outright sales.[10] Purchasers and lessees included the pub company Sycamore Taverns (308 pubs) and regional brewers Fuller's, Gales, Greene King, Marston's and Shepherd Neame.[11]

A significant interruption in the process occurred, however, when in the early summer of 1992 Allied somewhat disingenuously entered into a deal with Pubmaster whereby the latter leased 734 pubs from Allied and entered into a seven-year agreement to take a minimum barrelage from Allied equivalent to 62 per cent of its estimated annual beer sales. What was cheeky about this on Allied's part was that the leased pubs accounted for only around 38 per cent of Pubmaster's total requirements. The Director General of Fair Trading (DGFT) wasn't impressed and announced that he would probably not regard the 734 pubs as having been freed from tie for the purpose of complying with the Tied Estate Order (TEO).

Negotiations were entered into, and a month before the deadline for compliance it was agreed that for the first three years of the supply agreement the minimum contractual obligation would be limited to the equivalent of 29 per cent of Pubmaster's requirements. On the basis of these arbitrary numbers, and what appeared to be just a short-term fix, the 734 pubs would after all be regarded as having been freed from Allied's tie. Even then, after this reprieve, Allied was pronounced by the DGFT in March 1993 as not having been compliant with the Order by the due date – though he also said that he had been assured that the company had subsequently become so.[12]

"Beer wars"

For the time being, the other three majors – Bass, S&N and Whitbread – got down to the task of complying with the Beer Orders, but otherwise carried on as before. According to the MMC figures, Bass owned 7476 outlets and therefore had to free from tie 2738. The company, having commissioned some work by management consultants, McKinsey, quickly decided to remain an integrated brewer and retailer. At a later stage it decided on a long-term strategy of owning only 2000 pubs, which would all be managed by the company; and it is worth noting, in this context, that within a year or so of the November 1992 deadline Bass had already disposed of around 500 more outlets than required by the Beer Orders.

At the same time, the company had no intention of leasing pubs free of tie in order to comply with the TEO: as it somewhat tartly observed in its evidence to the Agriculture Committee in 1993, it didn't regard collecting rents as a core activity.[13] If a pub couldn't be tied, it didn't want it. It considered the possibility of circumventing the Order by breaking itself up into a number of regional companies, but rejected the idea as incompatible with the management's ambition to develop an international beer business. It also held discussions about selling the unwanted outlets in one block to the international private equity firm, KKR, but these came to nothing, possibly because – as was suggested to the authors by a former Bass executive – the company was unwilling to include the pubs' senior management in the deal.

The company's federal structure of regional fiefdoms meant that implementation of the Beer Orders was not as orderly and coherent as it might have been, but Bass nevertheless achieved compliance on time – by selling parcels of pubs to the emerging multiple pub operators, to regional brewers and to individuals. These disposals included the sale of 368 outlets to Enterprise Inns, 203 to Centric Pub Company, 185 to Century Inns and 170 to Marr Taverns. Regional brewers which purchased pubs from Bass included Greene King, Vaux, Charles Wells, Hardys & Hansons, Thwaites and Shepherd Neame.[14]

Bass had long been extremely proud, and fiercely protective, of its position as the country's biggest and most successful brewer, and as part of its response to the Beer Orders and to the Courage/Grand Met brewing merger in March 1991, it embarked on an all-out strategy of growing market share, with a target rate of one percentage point *per annum*. The pubs which Courage had had to free from the tie represented an obvious potential source of market share growth, and while Courage naturally did all it could to retain this business, Bass competed for it extremely aggressively. Both companies blamed the other for starting a price war. In addition, the 15 months during which the Carlsberg-Tetley deal was in gestation provided a good window of opportunity for all the other majors to compete for new business – a process which, moreover, didn't end when the new company started trading at the beginning of 1993.

Bass let it be known that it was aiming for a 30 per cent market share by the year 2000, and, indeed, a belief developed amongst commentators – a belief which Bass did nothing to discourage – that it intended to become the UK's equivalent of America's Anheuser-Busch (which had a domestic market share of 45 per cent). Be that as it may, the industry as a whole, and Bass and Courage – by now the two biggest brewers – in particular, waged a battle royal for volume, characterised by price discounting and generous free trade loan offers – the "beer wars". So much for the conclusion reached by the MMC that the Courage/Grand Met merger would lead to higher wholesale beer prices.

Radical moves at Whitbread

Whitbread, like Bass, took the decision after the Beer Orders that if a pub wasn't tied, it didn't want to own it; but, unlike Bass, it was willing to "park" these unwanted outlets with free-of-tie lessees until the market improved. For this was certainly a time of depressed pub prices, with the problems posed by the arrival on the market, for disposal within a narrow timeframe, of many thousands of pubs being exacerbated by the economic recession and property market collapse. As a company in its own right Whitbread was required to free from tie 2314 out of 6628 outlets, and it did so by selling around 1400 and leasing around 900.[15] It is interesting to note in passing that while both Allied and Whitbread sold roughly 1400 outlets, only 650 of Allied's were bought by individuals, but between 1100 and 1200 of Whitbread's – although only around 200 of the latter were purchased by the sitting tenant. Very few of the 900 pubs leased free of tie went to individuals. Corporate buyers of Whitbread pubs included Shepherd Neame and Adnams, while lessees included Pubmaster, Scorpio Inns and Paramount.[16]

As described earlier, however, Whitbread wasn't operating just "in its own right", because the TEO provided that companies with shareholdings of 15 per cent or more in other companies would have the latter's pubs aggregated with their own for the purposes of calculating the number of pubs to be freed from tie. This was clearly targeted at Whitbread and Whitbread Investment Company (WIC), with their extensive brewery investments (the "umbrella"), but, according to Whitbread, it wasn't until the autumn of 1991 (that is, almost two years after the Beer Orders were laid) that this interpretation of the relevant provision of the Orders was confirmed.

WIC was the main custodian of the "umbrella", with stakes in around 20 brewing companies, including 15 per cent or more of Boddingtons, Devenish, Marston's and Morland. In June 1992 it reduced its holding in Morland to below 15 per cent; and then in September it also reduced its holdings in the other three to below this level. For its own part, Whitbread sold a substantial portion of its holding in Brakspear. Although WIC retained shareholdings in all four of the aforementioned companies, and Whitbread in all but Morland, the effect of the divestments was that both Whitbread and WIC were compliant with the Beer Orders by the required date.

Matters could have rested there, but senior figures at Whitbread were keen both to dismantle the company's archaic share structure and to end the interlocking relationship with WIC, which together effectively rendered the company bid-proof. Accordingly, in November 1993 Whitbread took over WIC, at the same time scrapping its own "A" and high-voting "B" shares. The principal consequence of the takeover was that Whitbread found itself with holdings of just over 21 per cent in Boddingtons, Marston's and Brakspear (Devenish having meanwhile been acquired for cash by Greenalls). The Beer Orders allowed Whitbread six months within which to reduce the three relevant holdings to 15 per cent, but in keeping with its modernising mood it not only – in March 1994 – sold the two biggest holdings (Boddingtons and Marston's) in their entirety, but also completely divested itself of its stakes in Greenalls, Greene King, Morland and Vaux. It also took its holdings in Brakspear and Fuller's (previously 18 per cent) down to below 15 per cent.

Scottish & Newcastle had only 2354 licensed outlets at the relevant date, and so although it came within the scope of the second Beer Order, complying with it was a relatively straightforward job. The company had either to sell or untie 177 outlets, but it chose to dispose of the whole of the excess over 2000, and by completing the process before 1 May 1990, which was the date by which the majors had to free tenants from the tie in respect of non-beer beverages and allow them a guest beer, it was able to escape these requirements.

The *Publican* magazine estimated that of the roughly 11,000 outlets sold or leased free of tie to comply with the second Order at least 8000 went to the new multiple pub operators, or pubcos – most of which were started by former executives of the major brewers, which no longer needed their services as they slimmed down their estates. The authors believe, however, that only around 6000 went to pubcos, with 3000 going to entrepreneurial individuals and 2000 to small brewers. Few seem to have been taken up by sitting tenants, who generally couldn't raise the capital required to compete even in what was a depressed market.

Guest beers

Guest beers proved to be fairly popular amongst tenants of the majors, and both Allied and Whitbread ensured that a wide choice was made available. The former introduced to its price list around 40 cask ales brewed by other companies, normally four or five of which would be stocked by each depot, selected after consultation with tenants' representatives on the basis of local demand. Allied estimated that three years after the guest ale provision had been implemented around three quarters of its tied tenants stocked a guest beer. Whitbread operated in a similar way, but with a smaller selection – 26 – of cask ales on its "slate".

Bass naturally complied with the guest beer provision, but left its tenants to deal direct with the third party of their choice. In the inimitable words of the Bass director, Charles Darby, giving evidence to the Agriculture Committee in March 1993, "we left it entirely up to them...we have always prided ourselves – and I suppose we would say this anyway – that we had an unbelievably good range of cask beers, and so why should anyone want to buy others?... My view is that, basically, we were satisfying our customers previously...the actual purchasing customer is remarkably conservative and views any change with deepest suspicion." As mentioned above in relation to Allied and Whitbread, however, guest beers were popular – except, that is, among the tenants of small brewers, who found themselves excluded from a scheme which had been intended by its architects to benefit those very same small brewers.

Notes

1 Monopolies and Mergers Commission (MMC), *Elders IXL Ltd and Scottish & Newcastle Breweries PLC: A Report on the Merger Situations*, Cm 654 (1989).
2 *Ibid.*, para. 1.10.

3 MMC, *Elders IXL Limited and Grand Metropolitan PLC: A Report on the Merger Situations*, Cm 1227 (1990), paras. 8.39–8.40.
4 *Ibid.*, para. 8.42
5 MMC, *Allied-Lyons PLC and Carlsberg A/S: A Report on the Proposed Joint Venture*, Cm 2029 (1992).
6 *Ibid.*, Note of Dissent, para. 4.
7 *Ibid.*, Note of Dissent, para. 6.
8 *Ibid.*, Note of Dissent. para. 7.
9 *Ibid.*, Note of Dissent, para. 9.
10 Agriculture Select Committee Fourth Report of Session 1993, *Effects of the Beer Orders on the Brewing Industry and Consumers*, HC 402, p. xii, para. 18.
11 Authors' research.
12 Agriculture Select Committee Fourth Report of Session 1993, *Effects of the Beer Orders on the Brewing Industry and Consumers*, HC 402, p. xii, para. 18.
13 *Ibid.*, p. 78, para. 1.
14 Authors' research.
15 Agriculture Select Committee Fourth Report of Session 1993, *Effects of the Beer Orders on the Brewing Industry and Consumers*, HC 402, p. xii, para. 18.
16 Authors' research.

12
Four More Reviews

Second reference to MMC mooted

The Beer Orders were not fully operational until November 1992, but even before then there had been mounting disquiet about the initial impact of the measures. As we have seen, such doubts had surfaced in Parliament as early as June 1991, when Stan Crowther MP put down an Early Day Motion (EDM) bemoaning the disruption to the licensed trade.[1] He hadn't left it at that, securing an Adjournment Debate in November, in which he lambasted the Beer Orders,[2] and following this up with another EDM, calling for their immediate review.[3] Crowther was primarily concerned with the position of tenants in a rapidly changing world, but he also lamented what he saw as the impact on consumers in the shape of rocketing prices and reduced competition.

Concern was not confined to the Commons, however, and behind the scenes both the Department of Trade and Industry (DTI) and the Office of Fair Trading (OFT) were becoming anxious. Confidential papers show that a meeting between the two parties took place on 19 August 1991, at which DTI officials briefed the OFT on discussions which Ministers had held with the National Licensed Victuallers Association (NLVA) and subsequently with the major brewers.

Much of the meeting between officials was occupied with detailed discussion of arbitration between tenants and brewer-landlords and the position of tenants approaching retirement, but the most significant exchange came when DTI representatives revealed the Government's more general disillusionment with the Orders. It was explained that Ministers, whilst accepting that it wouldn't be possible at that stage to change the Orders, "had continued, and increasing, doubts about whether the action taken on the MMC [Monopolies and Mergers Commission] Report had been correct".[4]

Damagingly for the credibility of the Report, such doubts seemed to go to the very heart of the MMC's analysis:

> Ministers were sceptical about the concern expressed over the level of vertical integration in the brewing industry, and this was affecting their

views on other monopoly reports where vertical integration was an issue, for example soft drinks.[5]

This was a reference to the recently published MMC Report *Carbonated Drinks: A Report on the Supply by Manufacturers of Carbonated Drinks in the UK*.[6] It is to be noted too that in 1990 the MMC had investigated the supply of petrol, also featuring a vertically integrated industry, but had found a fully competitive market to be operating.[7] George Yarrow, one of the economists who advised the brewers during the beer inquiry, had observed that many of the arguments put forward by the Brewers' Society in the case of beer had also been deployed in the petrol inquiry.[8]

So, within two years of announcing the Beer Orders, and even before they had been fully implemented, the Government had privately reached an entirely different view of the MMC Report, to the extent that competition policy in the broad was being affected. This was the signal for the OFT to become embroiled in the beer market once again, as officials concluded that a review of the situation was too urgently needed to wait until that by the Director General of Fair Trading scheduled for 1993. Accordingly, during the closing months of 1991 and into 1992 officials held meetings with various interested parties, gathering information about the state of the market. In fact, quite a few organisations seem to have relished the opportunity to get across their point of view, and by now any semblance of unity amongst the members of the Brewers' Society seems to have gone, as the changes stimulated by the Beer Orders led to a growing divergence of interests. The prime example of changing commercial objectives was provided by Courage, the UK brewing subsidiary of the Australian conglomerate, Elders IXL.

As described earlier, Elders and Grand Metropolitan announced a deal in March 1990 whereby Courage would acquire Grand Met's brewing business, whilst Courage's pubs and Grand Met's tenanted pubs would go into a joint venture, Inntrepreneur Estates Limited (IEL). Following negotiations with the MMC, Courage was allowed a seven-year supply contract with IEL and a four-year contract with Grand Met's managed pubs division (GMR). As a further condition of regulatory clearance the parties had agreed to free from the tie over 1000 more pubs than required under the Beer Orders.[9]

By late 1991 Courage had had time to contemplate a future in which it would need to operate without these supply contracts, and in November its representatives met with OFT officials and made a full presentation on the state of the market.[10] The Beer Orders were in large part not achieving their aim, they said: the national brewers had increased their share of the market, retail prices were still rising and independent wholesalers remained marginalised. Worse, supply contacts between national brewers and the emerging retail chains meant that the market was not being freed up in the way that the MMC had expected. And these chains weren't passing on to tenants the discounts they had negotiated from the brewers. Courage said that it wanted a level playing field, with supply agreements limited to one year from, say, January 1996. It is to be noted that Courage's supply contract with GMR was due to expire in 1995 and that with IEL in 1998. Furthermore, the company saw no reason for the permitted total of tied pubs being set at 2000 plus 50 per cent of the number above this figure. It thought the major brewers shouldn't be allowed to tie any pubs and that 400 pubs for a regional brewer and 150 for a local brewer were sufficient. OFT officials could scarcely have failed to spot the self-interest in the presentation.

To add to officials' unease, several complaints had been made to the Office, and the trade press was reporting disaffection with events. The suspicions amongst officials would also have been strengthened by the injudicious public boasting on the part of one of the nationals that it had succeeded in retaining over 70 per cent of beer sales in pubs that it had divested.[11] This reinforced the view that the scope of vertical links was showing no sign of decline, whilst it was plain that horizontal concentration had increased. None of the detriments identified by the MMC regarding vertical integration were being resolved, and some officials proposed that the industry be referred to the MMC again. Others were more cautious, questioning what new remedies a fresh inquiry might put forward, and arguing that it would make more sense to gather new information before deciding what action to take.[12] The latter view prevailed, but, even so, the Director General of Fair Trading (DGFT) was warned by his officials that such an exercise could perhaps lead to a further reference.[13]

A request for information was sent to all the national brewers and two selected regionals, the data to be gathered falling under the headings of beer prices, rents and long-term supply agreements. The very tight timetable, with Christmas falling within it, would not have pleased the recipients of the letter, but its tone would have disturbed them more. The fact that the move to more market-related rents had not been matched by advantage to the tenants, the brewers were told, indicated "at least market power if not abuse of power".[14] And long-term supply agreements were being substituted for the tie in those pubs being freed up. The fact of this OFT inquiry was not made public.

The Office took soundings from various interested parties. Representatives of the two regional brewers, Fuller's and Vaux, were especially critical of long-term supply agreements. Anthony Fuller thought that they drove "a coach and horses" through the aims of the Beer Orders,[15] while Paul Nicholson, of Vaux, said that the emerging pub companies were pushing up retail prices.[16] The Campaign for Real Ale (CAMRA) drew attention to rising retail prices and said that long leases and associated rent increases were responsible for higher prices in tenanted pubs. It was concerned about the development of large retail chains and their supply agreements with large brewers, noting that discounts paid to the chains were not being passed on to their licensees. New entry into the pub market was being held back by the restrictive licensing laws.[17]

Gathering information from the brewers and holding discussions with other parties took much longer than planned. The idea had been to produce a paper with recommendations for the DGFT by the end of January, but by the end of March the paper was still only in draft, and by this time radical solutions such as a fresh reference to the MMC or some modification of the Beer Orders were no longer under consideration.[18] In the event, officials were able to avoid any further work on the matter because on 9 March 1992 the Secretary of State referred the proposed merger of the UK beer interests of Allied-Lyons and Carlsberg to the MMC. This inquiry would itself necessitate a full examination of the beer market and the changes that had occurred since the laying of the Beer Orders, so a halt was called to further analysis by the OFT.

The work may have been aborted, but it was not wasted and in fact was put to use when on 11 April the Director General, Sir Gordon Borrie, addressed the Annual General Meeting of CAMRA in Bristol. He took the opportunity to sound warnings about some of the developments taking place in the beer market, and was particularly stern in his threat to use his powers if he thought that long-term supply agreements were being used "to frustrate the loosening of the tie that has been set in train". Betraying his frustration at the slow pace of change and concerns about rising prices, he called upon publicans and consumers to take up the opportunities afforded to them by the Beer Orders. The overall message was that the OFT was on the case,[19] and although it once again shelved its file on beer, it certainly didn't close it. And the major brewers probably never knew how close they were to being subjected to another MMC reference in 1992. But it was only a matter of months before an inquiry of a different sort was announced.

Agriculture Select Committee critical of Beer Orders

Following full implementation of the Beer Orders towards the end of 1992, the Agriculture Select Committee decided to review how effective the Orders had been. It conceded that the deadline for the Tied Estate Order had only just passed, and it would have been aware that the OFT was scheduled to conduct a more formal review later in 1993, but it thought that a preliminary judgment could nevertheless be made. The Committee was chaired by Conservative backbencher, Sir Jerry Wiggin MP, and had ten other members. [John Spicer, one of the authors, was a specialist adviser to the Committee.]

It took written evidence from a wide variety of witnesses and asked a number of parties to attend hearings. The witnesses included representatives from all the major brewing companies, smaller brewers, CAMRA, licensees' organisations, the DTI and the Home Office. The hearings began on 19 January 1993, and the attendees included Michael Heseltine MP, President of the Board of Trade, Neil Hamilton MP, Parliamentary Under-Secretary of State for Corporate Affairs, and two officials from the DTI.

Sir Jerry set out his stall very early in the proceedings, when in his introductory statement he said:

> We have collected a substantial amount of evidence which, in due course, will be published, almost none of which is in any way complimentary about the effects of the Beer Orders. I think the very worst fears have been reflected; the number of brewers reduced; the number of public houses has almost certainly reduced; the choice of beer may have gone up slightly; but prices of beer have also gone up very, very much. Certainly on an initial study of the written evidence the picture is not a particularly happy one.[20]

Heseltine's response took the Committee completely by surprise:

> A considered assessment of the impact of the Orders can only be undertaken in the longer term. The overriding need now is, in my view, for a period of stability in which brewers can get on with running their businesses, and tenants their pubs, within the regulatory framework that has been created by the Orders. I believe it is appropriate, therefore, that I should tell the Committee, before you begin your questioning, that I have decided not to ask the Director-General of Fair Trading to carry out a review of the effects of the Orders later this year. Accordingly, I would like to let you know of the statement that I am making this afternoon to the House by way of a written question.[21]

This statement pre-empted perhaps the most important conclusion that the Committee was hoping to reach. But the Committee nevertheless resolved to adhere to its timetable and proceeded to conduct a series of hearings.

A number of interesting statements emerged from the written submissions and interviews. CAMRA was the only consumer association to give oral evidence and was the first party to be called, following Heseltine. In its submission[22] CAMRA stated its belief that Government intervention had been justified, but it also highlighted several areas of concern. These included beer prices in pubs rising faster than inflation, increased concentration in brewing, and the long-term supply agreements of the pub companies. It made a number of recommendations, including limits on supply deals, a halt to further brewing concentration, reform of the licensing system, and a reduction in excise duty for very small brewers. The NLVA was also concerned about the new pub-owning companies and their supply agreements, claiming that they weren't truly independent.

Adnams wanted loan ties to be prohibited and the Association of Licensed Multiple Retailers wished to see the introduction of dual licences, a system whereby separate licences would apply to the premises and the licensee. Three of the major brewers, Allied-Lyons, Bass and Whitbread, adopted a common theme, asking merely for a period of stability – as did Scottish & Newcastle, whilst pointing out, however, that since its disposal of around 300 pubs it wasn't subject to the same conditions as the others. Grand Metropolitan and Courage now adopted different positions from the ones they had held during the MMC inquiry. The former was anxious to point out that, having disposed of its breweries in 1991, it was no longer in the same situation as the major brewers, while Courage considered that the Beer Orders hadn't gone far enough, and therefore that the beer industry certainly shouldn't be left alone. The change of stance by Courage drew a rapid response from Allied, Bass and Whitbread in the form of supplementary memoranda drawing attention to the former's *volte face*. A number of the questions put to Grand Met and Courage concerned IEL, showing the already existing – but growing – concerns of its licensees about the new leases.

The Committee concluded that it was very difficult to identify which of the changes that had occurred were due to the Beer Orders, which to the economic climate, and which represented a continuation of previous trends; but it shared the view expressed by a number of witnesses that the Orders had accelerated structural change within the industry. There were, however, two areas where it was very simple to see the direct effect of the Orders: the reduction in vertical integration caused by pub disposals, and the right of tenants of the major brewers to sell a guest beer.

The Committee found that there was no firm evidence that loan-tying had been used by the brewers on any significant scale to re-tie pubs which had been untied to comply with the Orders. It reported that guest beers had found widespread approval from almost all areas of the industry and recommended that this provision should remain. It didn't recommend the introduction of a sliding scale of beer duty, but, rather, that the Government should lower rates to bring them more into line with those in the rest of Europe. As far as licensing law was concerned, it proposed that the grounds on which licences could be refused should be laid down in statute.

The Committee was critical of the MMC, and whilst supportive of the Government's position regarding the cancellation of the OFT's review, it didn't consider that conditions in the industry were ideal. It concluded, however, that the industry should be spared the uncertainty of renewed regulatory intervention in the short term, especially, perhaps, as it estimated the cost to the industry of compliance with the Orders to have been around £500 million.[23]

Consumer bodies disillusioned

Early in 1995 another Select Committee, this time the one concerned with Trade and Industry matters, announced an inquiry that involved beer. The scope of its investigation, however, went beyond beer and into the whole question of how suspected monopoly situations were tackled by the competition authorities.[24] The MMC's 1989 Supply of Beer Report was examined by the Committee as one of four case studies. It is noteworthy that only one brewer – Adnams – made a submission. But important written evidence was supplied by the Brewers & Licensed Retailers Association (BLRA), CAMRA and the Consumers' Association (CA), and the BLRA and CA also appeared as witnesses before the Committee. [One of the authors, Chris Thurman, gave verbal evidence on behalf of the BLRA.]

The BLRA was scathing of both the Commission's procedures and its conduct during the beer inquiry. The MMC was prosecutor, judge and jury, it said. After publication, it wasn't accountable, and there was no forum for challenging or even debating its conclusions. As to the particulars of the beer case, it had been "approached on an academic basis...the impression given was of a prejudicial approach, reflecting preconceptions". Evidence had been used selectively to support the preconceptions. The Secretary of State had compounded the defects by declaring that he was "minded" to accept the recommendations. The industry was "condemned from then on".[25]

The attack on the MMC by the CA – whose letter to Lord Young in May 1989 had begun with the words, "Consumers' Association warmly welcomes the MMC report and its main conclusion" – was no less severe. "There is wide agreement that the MMC's proposals were far more interventionist than was necessary", it said, and "the period since 1989 has been disastrous for the brewing industry". It felt that a much more modest package of measures, built around licensing reform and an attack on local concentrations of pubs, could have yielded more of a stimulus to competition without the "degree of trauma" suffered by the industry. It pointed out that since the beer report the authorities had become more tolerant of vertical restrictions, as evidenced in the inquiries into new cars and recorded music.[26] CAMRA saw some good coming from the beer report, pointing out the success of guest beers. But it shared the BLRA's view that the report had pursued an academic approach, which had led to flawed recommendations. The Commission's "abstract model conflicted with certain common sense ideas about the way the industry works". Perhaps its most telling criticism was that "after a two and a half year investigation into a major industry, the MMC made a proposal [regarding divestment] without understanding what its logical consequences would be".[27]

The Committee's report was published on 17 May 1995, and it made 11 recommendations, at least two of which were relevant to the beer inquiry.

These were that the MMC should produce "a detailed assessment of the result they foresee should their proposals be implemented"; and that the DTI should consult on remedies after the publication of an MMC report.[28] Either recommendation, had it been in place some six years earlier, would almost certainly have produced a different set of remedies from those that were adopted. Neither of them, however, was taken up by the Government.

Differential wholesale pricing cleared by OFT

At almost exactly the same time as the Trade and Industry Select Committee announced its inquiry, the brewing industry received rather less welcome news when on 7 February 1995 the OFT announced that it was to mount an inquiry into brewers' wholesale pricing policy.[29] This inquiry came at the request of the European Commission, in its pursuit of a case dating back to July 1992. It was then that IEL had notified its standard lease agreement to the Commission, seeking confirmation that it benefited from the Block Exemption rather than being caught by the general prohibition on restrictive agreements.[30] A year later the Commission declared that it intended to grant such comfort to IEL by way of a retrospective exemption, but allowing one month for third party comment.[31] The announcement was accompanied by a brief review of the market, which according to the BLRA was ill-informed and inaccurate: the Commission, for example, described the UK brewing industry as "highly concentrated", whilst the BLRA pointed out that it was, after Germany's, the least concentrated in the European Community.[32]

The Commission was wrong-footed when it received an unexpected number of representations arguing against its intention to grant an exemption. As Lord Hoffman put it in a judgment by the House of Lords more than a decade later, "the notice stirred up a hornet's nest of disaffected Inntrepreneur tenants".[33] Not only did the latter object to an exemption, but some urged the Commission to take action against IEL. The Commission became bogged down, with no visible sign of progress, over the next year. Then in May 1994 Whitbread sought an individual exemption for its own lease agreements.[34] As far as the Commission was concerned, the matter was becoming more complex, and on 19 December 1994 – some two and a half years after IEL's notification – it wrote to IEL to say that, in the light of objections, it was having second thoughts about granting an exemption, and felt unable to proceed.[35] It concluded that a proper investigation of the position of lessees in the UK was called for, that it shouldn't be restricted to IEL alone, and that the OFT was best placed to carry it out.

The OFT duly announced its investigation in February 1995. The announcement referred to the Commission's concerns that IEL tenants were obliged to buy beer from Courage at prices significantly higher than those charged to free trade customers, and that other large brewers appeared to operate similar pricing policies, leading the Commission to question whether lessees had been placed in a position where they couldn't compete.

In some ways the brewers were fortunate that the Commission had ceded the case back to the UK. In the first place, the OFT had built up a body of information and knowledge of the industry, whilst the Commission's somewhat inept description of the UK market in its 1993 announcement had betrayed considerable ignorance. Crucial too, was the fact that the OFT said that it would conclude its investigation in three months; the Commission, in contrast, had spent 18 months achieving little observable progress. All the same, the industry would have been wary of the outcome, its unease heightened by the prospect of another reference to the MMC should the Office find detriment.

The Office sent questionnaires to each of the national brewers, and to selected regional brewers and pub companies. The brewers were asked about list prices, discounts, net prices and price differentials between different categories of wholesale customers.[36] The Office wanted to know who was benefiting and who was losing out from such differentials, and how they affected consumers. The questions put to pub companies centred on beer purchasing arrangements, prices charged to tenants, retail prices and price differentials.[37] The OFT's terms of reference were as follows:

> To collect evidence on the prices charged by the larger brewers to their tied tenants and to free trade customers, with a view to determining whether any differential between the prices charged to the two classes of customer may lead to an adverse effect on tied tenants' ability to compete effectively in the retail market. The assessment will need to take account of factors such as any countervailing benefits (e.g., lower rents) enjoyed by tied tenants under the terms of their leases and the extent to which consumers benefit from price competition among the larger brewers.[38]

The prime concern of the brewers was to convince the authorities that any wholesale price differential between tenants and free trade customers did not put the tenants at a competitive disadvantage. Countervailing benefits, they argued, did indeed exist and offset or more than offset higher input prices. Such benefits mostly came in the form of below-market rent, but were supplemented by purchasing benefits on items such as utilities, and by business advice and training. The tenant benefited from low entry cost, and enjoyed lower risk by virtue of sharing it with the brewer, particularly important at a time of falling pub values. The fact that the wholesale price differential had widened since 1991 demonstrated that the Beer Orders were stimulating more competition in the supply of beer.[39]

Each brewer argued its case, but most of them also attacked IEL, arguing that the inquiry was taking place only because of the way in which the latter was operating – as an out and out property company seeking the maximum return on capital and behaving unsympathetically to its tenants. The fact that the European Commission had been swamped by complaints from IEL tenants proved this.

With the announcement of the results of the inquiry expected in early May, and with the Office still demanding more information well into April, some brewers may have begun to fear the worst. But good news arrived on 16 May, when the OFT announced what amounted to a clean bill of health for the industry in the area of differential pricing. The Director General of Fair Trading, Sir Bryan Carsberg, said:

> While I acknowledge that a minority of tied tenants on long leases have experienced some hardship, I do not believe that the differential wholesale pricing policy of brewers has in general placed the tied trade at a disadvantage to free houses. I therefore do not consider that there are sufficient grounds for me to refer this issue to the MMC.[40]

The OFT had been persuaded that wholesale prices to tenants were fair and that the advent of pub companies had increased retail competition. The Office's detailed findings – which were never made public – would be conveyed to Brussels. The ball which Europe had passed to London was about to bounce back into its own court.

Big brewers' leases approved by European Commission

Receipt of the results of the OFT investigation cleared the way for the European Commission once again to consider IEL's application for an exemption for its standard leases, which would, if granted, confirm that they enjoyed the benefit of Regulation (EEC) No 1984/83. The latter, in accordance with Article 85(3) of the Rome Treaty, gave beer supply agreements – subject to certain conditions being met – a Block Exemption from Article 85(1), which prohibited trading arrangements that prevented, restricted or distorted competition. IEL had lodged its application in July 1992, followed by Whitbread in May 1994, and Scottish & Newcastle (S&N) and Bass in 1996. But it was to be over two years after receiving the OFT's report before the Commission went public on the matter, in the meantime leaving these companies and their tenants – over 15,000 in total – in a state of uncertainty.

The logjam seems to have been unlocked by IEL's decision in March 1997 to withdraw its application and to submit to the Commission its newer style lease, "RetailLink", which was somewhat less restrictive than its predecessor leases. The Commission began to process not only the notifications from IEL, but also those from Whitbread, S&N and Bass, and by late 1997 was issuing 19(3) notices, stating that, subject to third party views, it intended to adopt a favourable position in respect of the various agreements and to grant retrospective exemptions. [A 19(3) notice is a notice publicly issued by the Commission stating that it intends to exempt or clear a notified agreement.]

Another year passed, and in February 1999 the Commission announced a decision to grant Whitbread an exemption – including a retrospective element – for the period 1990–2008.[41] Similar decisions were announced in June 1999 for both S&N, covering 1985–2002,[42] and Bass, covering 1991–2002.[43] But by the time the letters conveying these decisions arrived, the three companies were either selling or had sold most of their tenanted estates.

The position of IEL, which, along with Spring Inns, had in March 1998 become part of the Grand Pub Company (which was set up by the Japanese investment bank, Nomura), was somewhat different. Ultimately the Commission issued two comfort letters in regard to the company's leases, the first dealing with the period before March 1998 and the second with the period afterwards.[44] [A Commission comfort letter is sent to the notifying party confirming informally, and without reasons, either that the agreement fulfils the conditions for an exemption or – in the case of a negative comfort letter – that the Commission would be unlikely to take action against the agreement.]

The Commission's favourable decisions on the large brewers' leases included an assessment of the competitive forces in the market that was, as we shall see, to prove very important in the UK courts in the long-running Crehan case.[45] The Commission concluded:

> an examination of all tying agreements...shows that the brewers' tying agreements had in 1990 and still have today...the cumulative effect of considerably hindering independent access to the market, for new national and foreign competitors.[46]

Thus, almost a decade after the Beer Orders, the Commission evidently still felt that a relatively high proportion of beer sales in the UK were tied and that significant barriers to entry persisted.

Notes

1. HC 1990–91 EDM 1035.
2. HC Deb 14 November 1991 Vol. 198 cc1327–34.
3. HC 1991–92 EDM 285.
4. Office of Fair Trading (OFT) memorandum "Meeting with DTI on 19 August at Ashdown House", 22 August 1991.
5. *Ibid.*
6. Monopolies and Mergers Commission (MMC), *Carbonated Drinks: A Report on the Supply by Manufacturers of Carbonated Drinks in the UK*, Cm 1625 (1991).

7   MMC, *The Supply of Petrol: A Report on the Supply in the UK of Petrol by Wholesale*, Cm 972 (1990).
8   G Yarrow, "Opinion on the Likely Effects of Regulation of the Beer Market", 26 April 1990.
9   MMC, *Elders IXL Ltd and Grand Metropolitan PLC: A Report on the Merger Situations*, Cm 1227 (1990).
10 OFT memorandum "Note of a meeting held on 27 November 1991 with Courage to discuss changes in the beer industry", undated.
11 OFT memorandum, subject redacted, 23 December 1991.
12 OFT memorandum "Beer", 13 November 1991.
13 OFT memorandum "Beer", 4 December, 1991, para. 3.
14 OFT letter, subject redacted, 23 December 1991.
15 OFT memorandum "Note of meeting with Fuller Smith and Turner PLC on 15th January 1992", 22 January 1992.
16 OFT memorandum "Note of a meeting with Vaux Group PLC on 8 January 1992", undated.
17 OFT memorandum "Note of a meeting on 7th January 1992 with the Campaign for Real Ale", 31 January 1992.
18 OFT memorandum "Beer review", 25 March 1992.
19 OFT press release "Borrie on beer", 12 April 1992.
20 Agriculture Select Committee Fourth Report of Session 1993, *Effects of the Beer Orders on the Brewing Industry and Consumers*, HC 402, p. 2, para. 8.
21 *Ibid.*, p. 3, para. 2.
22 *Ibid.*, p. 11.
23 Agriculture Select Committee Fourth Report of Session 1993, *Effects of the Beer Orders on the Brewing Industry and Consumers*, HC 402, p. xiii, para. 9.
24 Trade and Industry Select Committee Fifth Report of Session 1994–95, *UK Policy on Monopolies*, HC 240–1.
25 *Ibid.*, memorandum submitted by the BLRA.
26 *Ibid.*, memorandum submitted by the Consumers' Association.
27 *Ibid.*, memorandum submitted by the Campaign for Real Ale.
28 Trade and Industry Select Committee Fifth Report of Session 1994–95, *UK Policy on Monopolies*, HC 240–1, paras. 68 and 77.
29 OFT press release No. 4/95 "Enquiry into brewers' wholesale pricing policy", 7 February 1995.
30 17 July 1992, Case No. IV/34.387/FS.
31 OJC 206, 30 July 1993.
32 Brewers & Licensed Retailers Association (BLRA) paper "The market", 5 August 1993, p. 3.
33 House of Lords Session 2005–06 (2006) UKHL38 Judgments – Inntrepreneur Pub Company and others (Original Appellants and Cross Respondents) v. Crehan, para. 30.
34 Case No. IV/35.079/FS, 22 May 1994.
35 House of Lords Session 2005–06 (2006) UKHL38 Judgments – Inntrepreneur Pub Company and others (Original Appellants and Cross Respondents) v. Crehan, para. 30.
36 OFT "Questions for Brewers", 7 February 1995.
37 OFT "Questions for Retail Pub Chains", 7 February 1995.
38 OFT press release No 4/95 "Enquiry into Brewers' Wholesale Pricing Policy", 7 February 1995.
39 Internal BLRA paper "OFT Survey", 31 March 1995.

40 OFT press release No. 22/95 "Carsberg Announces Results of Enquiry into Brewers' Wholesale Pricing Policy", 16 May 1995.
41 OJL (1999) 230/EC.
42 OJL (1999) 188/28/EC.
43 OJL (1999) 186/1/EC.
44 Negative comfort letters, 24 January 2000 and 29 June 2000.
45 Inntrepreneur Pub Company and others v Crehan [2006] UKHL 38.
46 OJL (1999) 230/EC para. 127.

13
The Big Brewers Fall into Foreign Hands

The demise of Courage

As a result of the Courage/Grand Met and Allied/Carlsberg deals, a brewing industry consisting at the beginning of 1991 principally of the mighty Bass plus five others had by early 1993 become one consisting principally of three more or less sizeable companies – Bass, Courage and Carlsberg-Tetley, with a combined market share of 59 per cent – plus two others, namely, Whitbread and Scottish & Newcastle (S&N), each with a share of 11–12 per cent.

As described in an earlier chapter, the early nineties saw an intensification of competition for market share, based on both price discounting and generous – some would say reckless – free trade loans. And these "beer wars" were to prove far from ephemeral, as the industry sailed through what would nowadays be described as "the perfect storm". First, beer consumption was declining at an alarming rate – by almost 10 per cent between 1990 and 1993. Second, complying with the Beer Orders meant that, as intended by the regulators, much of the major brewers' tied on-trade business had become free trade. In addition, the withdrawal from brewing of some regional companies meant that another source of erstwhile tied business had become exposed to the competitive demands of the free trade. And, finally, the lower margin take-home trade was continuing its rapid growth. According to a piece of stockbroker's research, the result of all this was that tied trade as a proportion of total beer sales fell from 44 per cent in 1989 to only 29 per cent in 1993; the free on-trade rose from 36 per cent of sales in 1989 to 46 per cent; and take-home went up from 20 per cent to 25 per cent.[1] The British Beer & Pub Association doesn't provide estimates in respect of tied and free on-trade percentages, but it estimated that take-home was 19 per cent in 1989 and marginally over 23 per cent in 1993.[2]

What would also have been exercising the minds of brewing company managements at this time, however, was the fact that the beer supply agreements that had been put in place as part of the freeing-up process and associated corporate restructuring would start to expire in 1995. The first to go would be Courage's contract with Grand Met, to be followed over the next four years by – *inter alia* – the agreements between Courage and IEL; between Carlsberg-Tetley and Allied-Lyons (shortly to become Allied Domecq), Greenalls and Pubmaster; between Bass and Greenalls, Enterprise Inns and Century Inns; and between Whitbread and Devenish. In addition, albeit unconnected with the Beer Orders, the supply contract between Whitbread and Boddingtons, following the former's purchase of the latter's brewing interests, was to expire as early as 1994. The volume represented by these supply contracts was equivalent to 13–14 per cent of the total beer market.

As a pure brewer, Courage had good reason to hope that the process of freeing up the market would go further; and, indeed, as we have seen, the company had in November 1991 lobbied officials at the Office of Fair Trading (OFT) to that effect. For its supply contracts with Grand Met and Inntrepreneur Estates Limited (IEL), due to expire in 1995 and 1998, respectively, accounted for around 40 per cent of its volume, and companies with substantial – albeit much reduced – tied estates would clearly be in a considerably stronger position than Courage itself from which to compete for that business once it became free. Courage's pleadings fell on deaf ears, however, and, already weakened by the punishing trading conditions that had obtained since its brewing merger with Grand Met, and with its parent, Elders IXL, not in the best of financial health, the company was in effect put up for sale in 1994.

Bass, S&N and Whitbread were all interested in acquiring the Courage business, and its management, aware of the company's parlous state, urged the authorities not to intervene in any bid. Bass was advised that the chances of its gaining regulatory approval were low, but both S&N and Whitbread – the two smallest national brewers – were given unofficial guidance by the OFT that bids from them would not be opposed, as long as no serious and unexpected objections were raised by a third party. The fact that the authorities were thus apparently willing to overlook the geographical concentrations that would have resulted, particularly in the South and West of England, from a Whitbread/Courage merger testifies to their acceptance of Courage's arguments. In the end, Whitbread was unwilling to accede to the demand by Elders for a £50m premium to take account of the risk of a reference to the Monopolies and Mergers Commission (MMC) which Elders still saw in the event of a bid from that quarter, and in May 1995 S&N announced that it had reached agreement to acquire the company, including its supply agreement with IEL.

This proposed deal placed the Government and regulators in what might be described as an interesting position, given that in 1989 the MMC had unequivocally recommended – and the Government had accepted – that the bid by Elders, owners of Courage, for S&N, which would have created a UK brewing business with a 20 per cent market share, would seriously affect competition, would provide no mitigating benefits, and should therefore not be allowed. Since then, of course, Courage had acquired Grand Met's brewing interests, thereby taking its own market share up to 20 per cent or so, and the combination with S&N would create a brewer with a – by UK standards – massive market share of around 30 per cent. It therefore came as something of a surprise when the Department of Trade and Industry (DTI) decided not to refer this deal to the MMC.

Sir Bryan Carsberg left the post of Director General of Fair Trading (DGFT) the day after the deal had been announced, and towards the end of June Jeffrey Preston, the acting DGFT, sent his advice in relation to the proposed merger to Michael Heseltine MP, Secretary of State for Trade and Industry – or, as he was known, President of the Board of Trade. Notwithstanding earlier confidential guidance, Preston now recommended that the takeover be referred to the MMC.

Nor was he half-hearted in his advice to the Minister, pointing out that the proposed merger constituted "the most significant structural change to the market since the beer orders were made",[3] and that smaller changes had in the past been referred to the MMC and had resulted in adverse reports and requirements to weaken vertical ties in the industry. He warned that a decision not to refer would be seen, in his opinion rightly, "as marking a significant shift in Government policy towards the brewing industry"[4] – an opinion in which he was supported by both the Treasury and MMC representatives on the OFT's Mergers Panel.[5] Preston said, moreover, that he feared that the merger might trigger further moves, creating an even tighter oligopoly.

With an evident lack of enthusiasm, he reiterated to Heseltine the arguments that officials at the DTI had put to him, including the one that a reference would effectively prevent anyone buying Courage. In this connection, Preston pointed out that although the company's owners "took a bleak view of Courage's future",[6] its latest half-year results showed an improvement – on the basis of which an MMC official claimed, somewhat immoderately, that "the failing firm argument seemed to have collapsed".[7] The acting DGFT's overall stance seems to have been informed by two basic beliefs, namely, that increased concentration in brewing should be accompanied by a compensating reduction in vertical integration (as Peter Lilley had argued in relation to the Courage/Grand Met deal); and that the loss of Courage, as a brewer without a tied estate, would inevitably be detrimental to competition.

Heseltine's response, dated 4 July, makes clear that, as far as the DTI was concerned, a reference to the MMC was not an option. In fact, Heseltine's letter mainly consisted of a request to Preston to identify undertakings acceptable to S&N which would obviate the need for a reference but meet the acting DGFT's concerns – concerns which he said he recognised (a term implying, one feels, less than whole-hearted agreement). He further made clear his view that immediate termination of the Courage/IEL supply agreement, due to expire in March 1998, would be "too traumatic for the industry";[8] but he said he was attracted by the idea of the early release of some IEL pubs from the agreement, and the freeing from tie of a proportion of S&N's own pubs. This must have been one of the last letters that Heseltine signed as President of the Board of Trade, as he left the post the following day, to become Deputy Prime Minister.

On 21 July the DTI announced that the acting DGFT had recommended that Jonathan Evans MP, Competition and Consumer Affairs Minister at the DTI, should ask the acting DGFT to seek undertakings from S&N with a view to meeting competition concerns. These undertakings consisted of the disposal by Scottish within one year of 115 of its 2739 tied outlets (it had gone back to over 2000 mainly as a result of purchasing the Chef & Brewer chain from Grand Met in 1993); the capping of S&N's tied estate at the reduced number of 2624; and the freeing of 1000 IEL pubs – out of 4350 – from the Courage supply agreement earlier than originally agreed. Interested parties were given only a week within which to make submissions in respect of these undertakings, but this didn't prevent 33 bodies and individuals making representations, mostly lobbying for a reference. Preston nevertheless declared himself satisfied that the undertakings constituted sufficient remedy to the competition concerns that had arisen. Evans announced on 14 August that the deal would not be referred to the MMC, and it was rapidly completed.

It was rare for the Secretary of State flatly to go against the recommendation of the OFT; and one has to ask why S&N was given such an easy passage in respect of the biggest ever UK brewing merger. There was, of course, little or no geographical overlap between the two companies. But that doesn't start to explain why a deal formerly regarded as being against the public interest was now to be allowed, even though the market share involved had risen substantially.

Some conspiracy theorists have blamed – as they had at the time of the Elders/S&N inquiry – the putative influence of the "Scottish lobby". It is a fact, for example, that Ian Lang MP, who succeeded Heseltine as President of the Board of Trade shortly after the deal was announced, had, in his previous post of Secretary of State for Scotland, supported S&N's proposal, and, indeed, the Scottish Office representative on the OFT's Mergers Panel spoke out against a reference.[9] But it is also the case that, because of his earlier backing for the takeover, Lang delegated the matter to John Taylor MP, a junior Minister at the DTI.

The issue of market share couldn't, of course, be ignored by the authorities, and it is interesting to note that in its May announcement of the takeover agreement Scottish stated that the combined market share of the merged group would be around 25 per cent. This is the figure above which, under the Fair Trading Act 1973, a monopoly situation could be deemed to exist, allowing the competition authorities to intervene if it was felt to be justified. The difference between 25 per cent and the 30 per cent mentioned above was accounted for by substantial volumes of other brewers' beers which Scottish sold to its customers in its role as wholesaler. Even the 25 per cent share was, however, comfortably above the 20 per cent which had been deemed unacceptable six years earlier.

One is left to conclude that the Government was extremely concerned about the gravity of Courage's financial situation, realised that it was unlikely to be able to survive on its own, and sacrificed principle for pragmatism. With Carlsberg-Tetley having come into being little more than two years earlier, and apparently not bedding down very successfully, with Whitbread dropping out of the bidding, and with the prospect of a takeover of Courage by Bass testing pragmatism beyond breaking point, the agreed deal which had been announced was the only one available. Another explanation – probably there was something of both behind the DTI's stance – is that Heseltine, as a former businessman, and very much his own man, was unsympathetic to the DGFT's consumerist philosophy, and believed that the development of major national companies was in itself a legitimate aim, which shouldn't be inhibited by formulaic competition concerns. Whatever the reason(s) for Heseltine's decision, it served to create even more uncertainty than had already existed in relation to Government policy towards the brewers, and, as would be seen, gave no guidance whatsoever as to the fate of other proposed deals.

Bass takeover of Carlsberg-Tetley blocked

It seems that the announcement of the S&N/Courage deal in May 1995 immediately spurred Bass into consideration of its own position, for in August 1996 it was announced that, after 15 months of negotiations, Bass had purchased Allied Domecq's 50 per cent stake in Carlsberg-Tetley, and, subject to regulatory approval, would merge its own brewing interests with those of Carlsberg-Tetley and acquire a further 30 per cent stake in the enlarged business. Carlsberg would have the remaining 20 per cent shareholding.

The background to the deal was that Allied had taken the decision to leave brewing; Carlsberg felt that its business would decline if it didn't have a pub-owning partner, and that Bass would be the most appropriate partner; and Bass was keen to acquire a lager of international status (Carlsberg) and a market-leading ale (Tetley Bitter), as well as some additional brewing capacity. Bass at this time had a market share of 23 per cent and Carlsberg-Tetley 14 per cent, meaning that, if the deal went ahead, the Bass Carlsberg-Tetley and Scottish Courage combines would together account for around 65 per cent of the market. This was evidently too much for the regulators to stomach, and, the DGFT, now John Bridgeman, advised Ian Lang to refer it to the MMC, which he did in December 1996.

As instructed, the MMC produced its Report[10] in March 1997, but Lang decided to hold it back until after the May General Election, which was won by Labour. On 19 May Bridgeman sent his confidential advice to the new Secretary of State, Margaret Beckett MP. He reported that the MMC had concluded that the merger would significantly reduce competition in the wholesale beer market, to the detriment of the public interest; but that the majority on the panel thought that it should nevertheless be allowed, subject to implementation of a package of remedies. The principal remedy was that Bass should own no more than 2500 tied houses, which would entail the disposal of around 1900; and the others were concerned with such matters as the size of parcels of pubs to be sold, their geographical concentration, and the prohibition of any pressure on a buyer to enter into a tying agreement. One of the Commissioners, Professor Newbery, dissented from the majority view, arguing that the proposed divestment of pubs wouldn't adequately counterbalance the adverse effects of the further concentration in brewing.

Bridgeman informed Beckett not only that he agreed with the MMC's assessment of the effect of the merger, but that he also shared Newbery's view that the proposed remedies were inadequate. Non-interventionists may well allow themselves a wry smile at Bridgeman's suggestion that the new owners of pubs divested by Bass probably wouldn't change supplier, "not least because consumers may prefer Bass beer".[11] At any rate, the DGFT concluded that Bass would benefit from the elimination of one of its major brewing competitors, from a stronger brand portfolio and from an enhanced position in wholesaling, which together had the potential to lead to increased retail prices; and that the deal should therefore be prohibited.

Beckett didn't take long to decide to acquiesce in Bridgeman's advice, announcing towards the end of June 1997 not only that she regarded the remedies demanded by the MMC as inadequate, but, moreover, that she was not open to offers of further remedies, such as increased pub sales or brand disposals. S&N, as quoted in the MMC Report, had argued fervently against the merger, but it seems unlikely that the "Scottish lobby" was influential in any of this, and, indeed, the Scottish Office actually supported the merger (on the grounds that, without it, employment in Scotland could suffer). Probably the decision not to go along with the MMC's recommendation was at least partly based on the newly elected Labour Government's wish to send an early signal to the City that it intended to adopt a tough stance in relation to competition issues. Certainly, if the brewers had interpreted the waving through of S&N's takeover of Courage as indicating a more liberal attitude towards the industry, they had been abruptly disabused of the idea.

As allowed under the fall-back arrangements, Bass now sold its 50 per cent stake in Carlsberg-Tetley to Carlsberg. Three months later the latter, which had been losing market share for some time, announced a major scaling-down of its activities, including sacking 40 per cent of its workforce and closing three of its five breweries. The company's Danish Chief Executive blamed Margaret Beckett for the extent of the redundancies and closures, claiming that the regulation of competition in the UK was politically driven. About six weeks later it emerged that Bass had agreed to purchase one of the Carlsberg-Tetley breweries earmarked for closure, namely, the Burton plant. This was adjacent to Bass's own Burton brewery, and the acquisition, together with the closure of two of Bass's other breweries, would yield significant efficiency gains. Carlsberg-Tetley was left with two breweries, at Northampton and Leeds. In 2004 it changed its name to Carlsberg UK, and in 2008 it announced that the Leeds brewery, one of only two survivors of the six breweries operated by Allied Breweries before the 1989 MMC Report, would close in 2011. The other survivor – albeit in different hands, namely, Molson Coors – was Burton.

The transformation of Whitbread

Whitbread had throughout the eighties and nineties been regarded as being more interested in pub retailing than in brewing, and by the second half of the nineties, having failed to do its own brewing deal, and with its beer business having become increasingly dependent on licensed brands (Heineken and Stella Artois), the company concluded that the only viable option open to it was to leave the industry completely.

The corollary of this was that it would further expand its pub, restaurant and leisure activities. In autumn 1993 it had lost out in the contest to buy the coveted Chef & Brewer chain of 1600 managed pub restaurants from Grand Met, and although it had made a number of acquisitions of restaurant chains in the mid-nineties, none of these could be described as transformational. Then, towards the end of May 1999, it was announced that the company had reached agreement to buy Allied Domecq's estate of some 3500 pubs. Within weeks, however, Punch Taverns, a private equity-backed pub company which had been formed in 1997 with the acquisition of 1400 pubs from Bass, announced that it intended to make a superior offer for the Allied estate, and that Bass would provide a substantial portion of the cash to finance Punch's bid, in return for 600–700 selected ex-Allied pubs.

On 28 June Whitbread put out a statement, perhaps a little rashly, to the effect that in its discussions with the OFT it had not been made aware of any substantive concerns to prevent its offer being completed. The OFT promptly announced that it had advised Whitbread that the proposed deal was to be considered by its Mergers Panel, pointedly adding that the latter didn't meet unless there were substantive competition concerns. On 1 July, the Panel having met, the DGFT – still John Bridgeman – sent his confidential advice to the Secretary of State for Trade and Industry, by now

Stephen Byers MP, and recommended that the Whitbread/Allied deal be referred to the Competition Commission (CC) (which had replaced the MMC in April 1999).

Whitbread had told the OFT that, to achieve compliance with the Tied Estate Order (TEO), it planned to float off its beer business as a separate company, Whitbread Brewing; and that the latter would have a five-year contract to supply the enlarged estate, New Whitbread Retail Company, with the same volume of beer as it currently supplied to the pubs in question – both Whitbread and Allied. The former Allied pubs would additionally remain subject to their existing supply agreement with Carlsberg-Tetley.

Bridgeman's concerns about the merger were threefold, the first being the resulting increase in concentration at the retail level. In this respect, the DGFT pointed out that the merger would give rise to a tied estate of some 7400 on-licences, which was far bigger than those of Bass (2450) and S&N (2660), and 2870 more than would be permitted by the 1989 TEO if Whitbread Brewing weren't sold. In addition, it would substantially increase the level of concentration of Whitbread pubs in specific locations. Bridgeman accepted that Whitbread might address the latter issue through disposals. But this didn't alter the fact that with 7400 pubs Whitbread would be, by a considerable margin, the largest pub company in the country (the pubcos Enterprise Inns and Punch Taverns were at this time still in their infancy). Whether Bridgeman ever pondered the fact that Whitbread would still own only 12 per cent of UK pubs, while the two biggest brewers had around 50 per cent of the beer market between them, one cannot know.

The DGFT's second concern related to beer, specifically, the possibility that once the five-year beer supply agreement between Whitbread Brewing and New Whitbread Retail expired, the brewing company, as a purely free trade operation, would struggle to provide effective competition within the market. Indeed, he questioned the long-term viability of such a business, quoting the example of Courage, and expressed his fear that, with the number of major brewers already down to four, the proposed float of Whitbread Brewing might lead to yet further concentration.

Third, although supply agreements had been operating since the start of the decade, Bridgeman questioned their propriety in this case, specifically in view of the size of the pub estate affected, arguing that the deal might "simply have the effect of replicating the vertical link which the TEO was intended to address".[12] And he frankly stated the dilemma in which he found himself: "The divestment proposed to meet the TEO" – that is, of Whitbread Brewing – "might not be sufficient to address the competition concerns if the terms of the supply agreement were too close. On the other hand, a supply agreement is probably necessary to help ensure the continued viability of the new brewing company."[13]

One imagines that brewing industry executives had not a scintilla of sympathy with the regulators for the intractable situation in which they now found themselves. Bridgeman's response was not only to pass the current specific problem to the CC, but to express his concern over "the effect, or lack of effect, of the Beer Orders on the current market",[14] and to announce that OFT officials would be considering whether a wider review of the Orders was needed.

The senior management at both Allied and Whitbread, but particularly the former, were regarded as having mishandled the situation in relation to the deal itself; but all this was rendered academic when, following the announcement that it would be investigated by the CC, Whitbread withdrew, leaving the field open to Punch and Bass.

This setback didn't alter the case for the company to leave brewing, particularly after its acquisition in January 2000 of Swallow Group, which had significantly expanded its hotel interests. Just four months later, in fact, Whitbread announced that its brewing business had been sold to the Belgian brewer, Interbrew, owner of the Stella Artois brand, for which Whitbread had been the UK licensee. Thus one erstwhile UK brewer – Courage – had returned to domestic ownership, but a second had fallen into foreign hands.

Then in October 2000 Whitbread published the results of a strategic review, which included the radical proposal to dispose of its 3000+ pubs, and in May 2001 the latter were sold to Morgan Grenfell Private Equity. Although the company retained its well known pub-restaurant brands, such as Beefeater, it was by now almost totally unrecognisable from the company which for centuries had brewed beer and operated pubs. [In 2004 Interbrew merged with the South American AmBev, to create InBev, and in 2008 the latter acquired the US brewer, Anheuser-Busch, renaming itself – as a condition of the deal – Anheuser-Busch InBev.]

Bass withdrawal from brewing

For Bass, the authorities' rejection of its proposed merger with Carlsberg-Tetley marked the end of its ambition to develop an international beer business. It deprived the company of both the substantial domestic base which it regarded as essential for a brewer wishing to grow overseas, and the opportunity to build an international business in partnership with Carlsberg. At the same time, there was considerable interest in acquiring UK brewing assets among foreign brewers, who perhaps took a more optimistic view of the industry's prospects than the UK brewers themselves. And so, after lengthy consideration, Bass decided to sell. An auction process was conducted throughout the first half of 2000, and in June it was announced that Interbrew would purchase the Bass brewing business. The agreement was not conditional upon clearance by the UK competition authorities.

In September Stephen Byers, Secretary of State at the DTI, referred the deal to the CC, which was to report back by December. The four Commission members unanimously concluded that the merger would create, with S&N, an effective duopoly in the UK beer market, which would lead not only to smaller wholesale discounts and higher retail prices, but also to greater emphasis on brand-building, which would harm competing brands and thereby lead to reduced consumer choice. In addition, thanks to the scale and efficiency of their wholesaling and distribution operations, Interbrew and S&N would effectively control the route to market. One of the Commissioners considered that compelling Interbrew to divest itself of the Whitbread brewing business, including the licence rights to Interbrew's lager brand, Stella Artois, would remedy the adverse effects of the merger, but the other three concluded that Interbrew should divest itself of Bass's UK beer business. Stephen Byers, Secretary of State for Trade and Industry, concurred with the latter recommendation, and told Interbrew that the disposal must be made within six months.

Interbrew, however, announced that it would seek a judicial review of the decision, and in May the High Court overruled the Government on a procedural point. It asked the Government to reconsider the matter, and a few weeks later the OFT recommended to the Secretary of State – by now Patricia Hewitt MP – that Interbrew should dispose of most of Bass's brewing assets, including its four breweries in England and a number of brands, including its best-selling Carling lager. Assets to be retained by Interbrew included Bass's Scottish and Northern Irish breweries and the Bass ale brand. Another auction was conducted, and in December 2001, around a year after the CC had reported, the assets in question were sold to the American brewer, Coors. Thus the brewing operations of three of the "big six" UK brewers were now foreign-owned. And those of the other three – Courage, Grand Met and S&N – were combined in one company.

And then there were none

As alluded to earlier in this chapter (with reference to Whitbread), Grand Met had sold its managed pub estate, Chef & Brewer, in 1993, and going into the second half of the nineties, it became progressively more dissatisfied with its participation in Inntrepreneur, the tenanted/leased pub joint venture with Courage. In September 1997 it was announced that the business was to be sold to the Japanese investment bank, Nomura, and the deal was completed in March 1998. Most of the Inntrepreneur pubs were subsequently put into a new Nomura entity, the Unique

Pub Company, which was sold in 2002 to a consortium comprising the leading pub operator, Enterprise Inns, and a number of venture capitalists. In March 2004 Enterprise exercised its call option in respect of the other shareholdings in Unique, making it the biggest pubco in the country.

Following Whitbread's sale of its pub estate in May 2001, it still operated a few hundred Beefeater pub-restaurants, but only Bass and S&N from the original "big six" were still involved in the business of running large numbers of traditional pubs. For Bass, this was one of the two remaining prongs of its strategy – the other being international hotels. By the summer of 2001 it was in fact the world's leading hotel group and, in keeping with a long-held aim, and following the sale to Nomura earlier that year of just under 1000 pubs, it operated some 2070 managed pubs, restaurants and bars. In June the company announced that it proposed to change its name from Bass to Six Continents, and then, in the autumn of 2002, that it was going to split into two separate quoted businesses, InterContinental Hotels Group and Mitchells & Butlers (the latter named after two companies which had come together in 1898, before merging with Bass in 1961).

During the period 1999–2001 S&N had been disposing of its tenanted pubs, mainly to Royal Bank of Scotland, on whose behalf it managed the estate, as well as supplying beer; and then, in November 2003, it sold its 1400-strong managed estate to the unquoted pub operator, Spirit Group. At the same time it had been expanding its brewing business internationally, through acquisitions or joint ventures, most importantly in France, Russia, the Baltic, Ukraine and Portugal. It also purchased the cider maker, Bulmer, in 2003. But in January 2008 the S&N board announced, after three months of negotiations, that agreement had been reached on a joint offer for the company by Carlsberg and Heineken. On 28 April 2008 the sale of S&N was completed, meaning that the brewing operations of every one of the original "big six" national brewers had now gone into foreign ownership. S&N's UK operations went to Heineken, and in November 2009 the name of the business was changed to Heineken UK.

What has happened to the brewing plants operated by the "big six" national companies at the time of the 1986–89 MMC Report is shown in Table 13.1.

Thus out of 39 breweries operated by the "big six" in 1987 25 have closed, while two more are awaiting closure. Of the remaining 12, four are operated by Molson Coors, two by Anheuser-Busch Inbev, two by Heineken and one by C&C Group (the Ireland and UK-based long alcoholic drinks manufacturer). Two of the other three are operated by privately owned companies, S.A. Brain and Theakston, and the other by two entrepreneurs.

Table 13.1 Current Status/Ownership of the "Big Six" Brewing Plants Operating in 1987

Brewery	Status/ownership	Brewery	Status/ownership
Allied-Lyons:		**Grand Met:**	
Alloa	Closed 1998	Edinburgh	Closed 1987
Burton	Molson Coors	Halifax	Closed 1996
Leeds	C-T; closing 2011	London Brick Lane	Closed 1988
Romford	Closed 1992	London Mortlake	A-B InBev; closing 2011/12
Warrington	Closed 1996	Trowbridge	Closed 2000
Wrexham	Closed 2000		
		S&N:	
Bass:		Blackburn	Closed 1991
Alton	Molson Coors	Edinburgh	Closed 2004
Burton	Molson Coors	Manchester	Heineken
Belfast	Closed 2004	Masham	Theakston
Birmingham	Closed 2002	Newcastle	Closed 2005
Cardiff	SA Brain	Nottingham	Closed 1996
Edinburgh	Closed 1992		
Glasgow	C&C Group	**Whitbread:**	
Runcorn	Closed 1992	Castle Eden	Closed 2002
Sheffield Cannon	Closed 1999	Cheltenham	Closed 1998
Sheffield Hope	Closed 1994	Faversham	Closed 1991
Tadcaster	Molson Coors	Magor	A-B InBev
Walsall	Entrepreneurs	Samlesbury	A-B InBev
Wolverhampton	Closed 1992	Sheffield	Closed 1994
Courage:			
Bristol	Closed 1999		
Reading	Closed 2010		
Tadcaster	Heineken		

Source: Authors' research.

Notes

1 SBC Warburg Securities Ltd, "Pub Retailing, Trading Places", April 1995.
2 British Beer & Pub Association, *Statistical Handbook*.
3 Submission from the Director General of Fair Trading (DGFT) to the Secretary of State for Trade and Industry, 27 June 1995, para. 33.
4 *Ibid.*, para. 33.
5 *Ibid.*, paras. 22 and 24.
6 *Ibid.*, para. 7.
7 *Ibid.*, para. 24.
8 Letter from the President of the Board of Trade [as already noted in the text, this is another title by which the Secretary of State for Trade and Industry was sometimes known] to the DGFT, 4 July 1995.

9 Submission from the DGFT to the Secretary for Trade and Industry, 27 June 1995, para. 21.
10 Monopolies and Mergers Commission, *Bass PLC, Carlsberg A/S and Carlsberg-Tetley PLC: A Report on the Merger Situation*, Cm 3662 (1997).
11 Submission from the DGFT to the Secretary of State for Trade and Industry, 19 May 1997, para. 18.
12 Submission from the DGFT to the Secretary of State for Trade and Industry, 1 July 1999, para. 22.
13 *Ibid.*, para. 24.
14 *Ibid.*, para. 27.

Some of the draught beers and ciders on sale in February 2011 in JD Wetherspoon's pub "The Blue Boar" in Billericay, Essex. The complete range comprises seven cask-conditioned ales, nine lagers, two keg ales, two versions of Guinness stout, a stout from a microbrewery, Strongbow cider and three ciders produced by small companies.

The Greene King Brewery at Bury St Edmunds, Suffolk, some 150 years ago.

The Kelham Island microbrewery, Sheffield. The company was established in 1990 and moved into these purpose-built premises in 1999.

Above

Anthony Fuller CBE. As Chairman of the Brewers' Society from 1986 to 1989, he led the industry during the MMC inquiry. He was Chairman of the London brewers, Fuller Smith & Turner P.L.C., from 1982 to 2007.

Right

Sir Ian Prosser was Chairman of the Brewers' Society MMC Steering Committee. He was Managing Director of Bass PLC from 1984 to1987, when he became Chairman and Chief Executive, a post he held until 2000.

Left. Rt Hon Francis Maude MP. At the time of the MMC Report and until July 1989 he was Parliamentary Under-Secretary of State at the Department of Trade and Industry.

Below. The MMC Panel and support staff during a visit to the Henley Staff College. Back row (left to right): Bernard Gravatt, Trevor Williams, Robin Aaronson, Stephen Burbridge, Dan Goyder and Leif Mills. Front row (left to right): Pip Flint, Dick Smethurst, Bob Young. (Photograph reproduced courtesy of Leif Mills). David Thomson isn't in the photograph.

RESEARCH
BREWERS AND DISTILLERS

Published in November 1990, 11 months after the Beer Orders, a City view of the then state of affairs and likely future developments (taken from the cover of a piece of stockbroker's research into the drinks industry). Lord Young was at the time Chairman of Cable & Wireless Plc (C&W).

14
The Regionals React

The end of three large regionals

The 1989 Monopolies and Mergers Commission (MMC) Report had been quite explicit as to the motivation behind its proposal that brewers should be allowed to own only up to 2000 on-licensed premises, namely, its authors' belief that if the tie were broken completely, many small brewers "would withdraw from brewing, concentrate on retailing, and leave the market to domination by national and international brand owners".[1] This was certainly going to be no level playing field, but the possibility that the majors would themselves react in just this way if the 2000 ceiling were implemented, and the effects that their reactions might have on the regionals, apparently weren't considered.

In fact, the 15 years following the Beer Orders would see brewers of all sizes withdrawing from brewing to concentrate on retailing on an unprecedented scale – a change of strategic direction which, with a few tiny exceptions, such as Cooks and Grays (both of Essex), Beards (of Sussex) and Heavitree (of Exeter), had thitherto been unheard of. At the same time, the pace of industry consolidation amongst the regionals through mergers and takeovers accelerated.

In discussion with the authors, Hubert Reid, former Chief Executive of Manchester-based ale brewer, Boddingtons, said that the company had decided to give up brewing even before publication of the MMC Report. This was on the grounds that the ale market was in decline; Boddingtons had a strong brand but not the financial resources fully to exploit it; its pubs, released from the obligation to support the brewery, would be able to offer customers a wider choice of beers; and the company would have the cash to invest more in its pubs and to expand in its chosen areas of diversification, namely, hotels, nursing homes and drinks wholesaling. It entered into serious discussions with three possible buyers of the brewing business, but negotiations were later suspended until the findings of the MMC inquiry were known.

In 1989, however, Boddingtons did sell its brewery and eponymous brand to Whitbread, and just six years later, in November 1995, the remaining business was taken over in an agreed bid by the Warrington-based Greenalls (until 1991 Greenall Whitley), which, as described below, had itself withdrawn from brewing after the Beer Orders. The Boddingtons brewery closed in 2005.

JA Devenish, for decades a sleepy West Country brewer, came to the attention of the City in 1986, when the brewing and pub entrepreneur, Michael Cannon, took control. He quickly closed the Weymouth brewery, and in May 1991 disposed of the company's beer brands and free trade loan book to Whitbread. Two months later he sold the company's other brewery, at Redruth, to the management, but it went into administration early in 2004 and closed in March of that year. In the summer of 1991 Boddingtons had made an unsuccessful bid for the Devenish pub interests, and then two years later Greenalls acquired them.

Meanwhile, Greenalls itself had in February 1991 closed its two breweries, to concentrate – very much like Boddingtons – on pubs, hotels, health and fitness, and drinks wholesaling. Having bought Boddingtons at the end of 1995, Greenalls disposed of the combined tenanted pub estate to Nomura in January 1999 and then in December sold the managed pubs to Scottish & Newcastle (S&N). In February 2001 it got rid of the drinks wholesaling business.

On the way to thus becoming largely a hotelier, the company changed its name in February 2000 to De Vere Group. In January 2006 Lord Daresbury, formerly Peter Greenall, stepped down as Chairman, finally severing all links between the company and its founding family, and the following September the company was taken into private ownership by Alternative Hotel Group. In July 2008 De Vere's Warrington head office was closed, thereby symbolically bringing to an end the story of Greenall Whitley, which had begun brewing in the town in 1787.

In the meantime, S&N had sold its entire managed estate, including the ex-Greenalls pubs, in November 2003 to the venture capital-backed pubco, Spirit Group. The latter was in turn bought back in December 2005 by the publicly quoted pubco, Punch Taverns, from which Spirit had been demerged in March 2002.

Up in the North East, Vaux continued to brew beer for several years longer than Boddingtons or Greenall Whitley, but brewing profits virtually stagnated in the period 1993–98, and in 1995/96 were overtaken by profits from the Swallow Hotels division. Paul Nicholson, then Chairman and Chief Executive, has never claimed that the Beer Orders were responsible for this performance, but the wholesale price wars that broke out among the national brewers after the Beer Orders were nevertheless clearly unhelpful. Vaux's coastal location had in the past hampered its expansion, and it quickly grasped the opportunity provided by the Beer Orders to acquire pubs from the majors. But it didn't have strong enough beer brands to attack the guest beer market. Nicholson was, and remains, an implacable critic of the MMC Report and the Beer Orders, arguing that radical change imposed through government interference was bound to have unintended consequences.

Be all that as it may, by 1995 the question of whether or not to continue brewing had come on to the agenda. Nicholson himself not only felt passionately about the company's heritage, and its social responsibility in a region which had suffered considerable economic hardship, but believed that the difficult times in brewing would not persist indefinitely. But the arrival of new non-executive directors in 1997, together with the appointment in 1998 of Martin Grant from Allied Domecq as Chief Executive, following Nicholson's decision to stand down – but to remain as Chairman – on reaching 60, provided significant impetus to the general rush towards brewery closure. In March 1999 the board decided on closure. Nicholson resigned.

The company changed its name to Swallow Group, and sold its tenanted pub estate to the North East-based, venture capital-backed pubco, Pubmaster. In January 2000 Whitbread made a successful bid for the company, rebranding most of the hotels as Marriott and disposing of the remaining assets. The Sheffield brewery site was developed as flats, and the Sunderland headquarters, geographically and symbolically at the heart of the city, were sold to Tesco.

Emergence of two "super-regionals"

By contrast with Nicholson, David Thompson, of Wolverhampton & Dudley Breweries (W&DB), as it then was, made clear in conversation with the authors that he was far from displeased when he heard news of Sir Gordon Borrie's speech in December 1985. He wasn't to know then of the favourable treatment the regionals would receive, but he was hopeful that the constraints on expansion that he believed the regionals were up against, as a result of the majors' financial muscle in the pub market and Whitbread's ability to thwart takeovers through its "umbrella" shareholdings, would be removed.

He became a lone voice within the Brewers' Society, arguing in the months leading up to the MMC reference that he wouldn't necessarily regard it as a bad thing; and then, when it happened, strongly objecting to the setting-up of a Steering Committee to present the industry's case without agreement having been reached as to what that case should be. Following publication of the Report, he enraged the major brewers by suggesting that the industry should adopt a negotiating stance, but to this day he insists that anyone with the slightest contact with Ministers should have realised that the latter were receptive to negotiation. Thompson thought that some others sympathised with his apparently maverick position, but it seems that, if so, they didn't show it, and, certainly, W&DB was one of only a handful of companies (Greenalls was another) which refused to be associated with the Brewers' Society's advertising campaign against the Report's recommendations.

David Thompson's appointment to the W&DB board in 1980 had already brought about a more aggressive expansion policy, as evidenced by a hostile – and unsuccessful – bid for Birmingham-based Davenports in 1983, and then the secret accumulation in late 1986 of a 4.9 per cent holding in Vaux. By the time of the Beer Orders, in December 1989, Thompson had become Managing Director, and over the next ten years W&DB acquired three leading regional companies, namely, JW Cameron in a trade sale in 1992, Marston's in a contested bid in February 1999, and Mansfield Brewery in an uncontested bid in September 1999.

In 2000 and again in 2001 W&DB was itself the subject of takeover bids, from the private equity-backed pubcos, Noble House and Pubmaster, respectively, escaping from the second bid only by a margin of 3 per cent of the shares. But these interventions certainly weren't allowed to hinder the company's expansion march. Thus in 2003 (by which time Thompson had become Chairman), when the financial performance of Eldridge Pope was seriously deteriorating, despite the sale of its brewing business to the management, W&DB was inevitably one of a number of parties to make an approach. In fact, Michael Cannon eventually acquired the company in October 2004, but in January 2007 he sold it on to W&DB, at close to four times what he had paid for it. The Eldridge Pope brewery closed in July 2003.

In June 2004 W&DB had bought Wizard Inns, a small privately owned managed pub operator, and in January 2005 it had acquired Warrington-based Burtonwood Brewery (by then, in fact, only a pub operator, having in 1998 transferred its brewery to a stand-alone company in return for a minority stake). In May 2005 it bought the AIM-listed integrated Lake District brewer and pub operator, Jennings, and then in July 2007 the small privately owned Ringwood Brewery, situated near the Hampshire/Dorset border. Most recently, in April 2008, W&DB purchased another privately owned company, Refresh UK. This business, which owns the Wychwood brewery in Oxfordshire, had been set up in 2000 to take over the brands of Ushers of Trowbridge, whose brewery had closed that year; and its portfolio now includes the beer brands of Brakspear, which stopped brewing in 2002 and was taken over in 2006. In January 2007 W&DB changed its name to Marston's, and it brews at the former Marston's, Jennings, Ringwood and Wychwood breweries, as well as at Wolverhampton, having sold the Cameron brewery and closed Mansfield.

Comments to the authors by Tim Bridge, who was a director of Greene King at the time of the MMC inquiry and is now Chairman, suggest that

David Thompson hadn't been quite as isolated in his non-confrontational views as some others had represented. Indeed, when it became clear that the regional brewers would be exempt from most of the measures proposed by the MMC, Greene King wrote to local MPs in June 1989 to express its approval of the Government's position. Bridge believes that the industry's Steering Committee was weakened and compromised by conflicts of interest, and feels that the regionals were to some extent cajoled by the majors into collaborating in presenting a united hostile front after the Report, even though the latter's recommendations offered them clear growth opportunities.

Greene King had for many years before the inquiry been remarkably unobtrusive within the industry, concentrating its management effort on culling its tail of remotely situated low barrelage pubs while at the same time exploiting the opportunities offered by rapid economic growth in its East Anglian heartland. But the Beer Orders were for them – to quote Bridge's own word – "transformational", in that they facilitated all that was to follow, leading to the creation of one of the two "super-regionals".

The company's first move after 1989 was to purchase 150 Allied-Lyons pubs, which took it into the more or less virgin – but not too distant – territories of Buckinghamshire, Hertfordshire and Kent. This, together with a number of smaller pub acquisitions, brought about a steady but significant expansion in the company's free trade and distribution network, thereby in Bridge's judgment making feasible a major acquisition. In the summer of 1992 Whitbread Investment Company, as part of the disposal programme forced on it by the Beer Orders, sold Greene King a major stake in Morland, the Oxfordshire brewer of the cult premium ale, Old Speckled Hen, which had an estate of 422 pubs. Greene King immediately made a bid, but it just failed. Then in the summer of 1996 it purchased Magic Pub Company, which had been founded in May 1994 by Michael Cannon with the purchase from S&N of 282 Chef & Brewer pubs.

Thereafter Greene King's acquisitions grew in terms of both frequency and size. In July 1998 it bought the 43 pubs of Beards of Sussex (which had given up brewing in 1959), and then in December of that year the 165-strong Marston's southern pub estate. In August 1999 it made a second – and this time successful – bid for Morland, which had itself acquired Ruddles in 1997 and had just closed the latter's brewery. Within months the Morland brewery had closed. In September 2001 Greene King bought Old English Inns, operator of 136 pubs and small hotels, and then, in June 2002, Morrells of Oxford (which the seemingly ubiquitous Michael Cannon had set up in July 1998 to purchase the brewery – which immediately closed – and tied estate of the original Morrells company).

Greene King's next purchase, in August 2004, was of 432 pubs from the private equity-backed Laurel managed pub operator (originally formed to run ex-Whitbread pubs), and then in July 2005 it took over the Essex family brewer, Ridley's. Two months later it made an agreed bid for the quoted Scottish brewer, Belhaven, and then in September 2006 purchased, also by agreement, the quoted but family-controlled East Midlands-based Hardys & Hansons. These three acquisitions brought in a total of 612 pubs, but both the Ridley's and Hardys & Hansons breweries were quickly closed.

Two other small brewery deals of the post-Beer Orders era are worth mentioning. First, towards the end of 2005 Fuller Smith & Turner announced an agreed bid for the family-controlled Gales, to be followed within months by closure of the latter's brewery. One doesn't know what the vendors' motivation was in deciding to sell, but the decision looks surprising, given that the company had been nominated as Regional Brewer of the Year in 2002, that it had been voted best operator of small tenanted estates in the March 2004 *Publican* newspaper awards, and that beer sales to the free trade had been expanding rapidly. This certainly didn't look like an old family firm struggling to cope with a newly harsh trading environment.

The other noteworthy event was the decision by Young & Co. to abandon its ancient brewery in the London suburb of Wandsworth for redevelopment and in 2006 to establish a brewing joint venture with Charles Wells based at the latter's modern brewery in Bedford; but the value of the Wandsworth site and its unsuitability in logistical terms make this decision easily understandable, and suggest that any connection with the Beer Orders was negligible.

In the wake of the radical and far-reaching developments described above, it seems appropriate to hold a roll-call. At the start of its investigation the MMC identified 11 leading regional brewers, namely, Boddingtons, JW Cameron, JA Devenish, Greenall Whitley, Greene King, Mansfield, Marston's, Robinsons, Thwaites, Vaux and Wolverhampton & Dudley Breweries. Fifteen years later only five still existed as separate entities, namely, the two private – and therefore bid-proof – companies, Robinsons and Thwaites; the former Greenall Whitley, by now renamed and unrecognisable; and the two emerging "super-regionals", Greene King and W&DB (now renamed Marston's).

Of the 40 smaller – referred to as local – brewers mentioned in the MMC Report, by the end of 2006 14 of them had been taken over, of which only three had retained their brewery (all three, it should be said, in the hands of what is now Marston's). Two others, including – as referred to above – Young & Co, remained independent but had closed their brewery. Of the 20 regional and local brewers that had been taken over, 12 had finished up as part of either Greene King or Marston's.

It is clear that if one aim of the Beer Orders had been to benefit consumers by sustaining regional and local brewers, and enhancing their competitive position relative to the majors, then those Orders had failed spectacularly. As Mike Benner, Chief Executive of the Campaign for Real Ale, was moved to observe in the summer of 2005, following W&DB's purchase of Jennings and the Greene King/Ridley announcement: "A new generation of national brewers has been created".[2] He might have added that this had in part been made possible by the revocation in 2002 of the Supply of Beer (Tied Estate) Order and thus the removal of any limit on pub ownership. In any case, during the process there had been corporate carnage.

Growth of the microbrewers

On the other hand, at the same time as all this was going on literally hundreds of new so-called "microbrewers" were coming into existence, in the first place thanks to the guest beer provision within the Beer Orders. Inevitably in what was seen as one of the few growth areas in the industry, which moreover probably attracted a number of enthusiastic amateurs, there were casualties as well as success stories. The total number of microbrewers nevertheless grew from 173 in 1989, the year the MMC Report was published, to 471 in 1998.

In 1999 the number fell back to 425, but stabilised at around this level up until 2002, when the microbrewery sector was given another fillip by the introduction of a system of "progressivity". This had been a feature of the excise duty system in several European countries, under which brewers paid a rising rate of duty on specified levels of output, the benefit applying in some countries to all producers irrespective of size and in others only to those producing up to a maximum specified level. In those countries with the lowest duty rates the benefit of progressivity at the retail level is barely significant, but, as shown below, this is certainly not the case in the UK.

The Society of Independent Brewers (SIBA), which had been formed in 1980 (as the Small Independent Brewers' Association) to promote the commercial and political interests of microbrewers, had argued in its evidence to the MMC for the introduction of progressivity in the UK. The MMC had been sympathetic, but nothing had happened within the context of the Beer Orders. In the April 2002 Budget, however, the Chancellor of the Exchequer, Gordon Brown MP, in response to the urgings of John Bridgeman (acting as an adviser to SIBA after his spell as Director General of Fair Trading), and perhaps recognising an opportunity to make a tax change which would be eye-catching, mildly popular and cheap, announced the introduction of a progressive duty system. In 2004 the system was modified and extended, to provide for brewers producing up to 5000 hls (3050 36-gallon barrels) to pay 50 per cent of the duty rate, and then to receive tapering relief up to a maximum of 60,000 hls (36,662 barrels). In 2004 this concession, at its highest level, was worth 17p on a pint of beer of average strength (4 per cent ABV), including the Value Added Tax (VAT) effect, but subsequent increases in duty and in VAT pushed the maximum benefit in 2011 up to around 25p. Under the UK system brewers producing more than 60,000 hls receive no benefit at all, which, as illustrated below, can produce perverse outcomes.

The theoretical justification for the system is that it compensates small brewers for their inability to obtain the economies of scale available to bigger producers. Whether this is fair or desirable within a free market is a matter of opinion, but the move undoubtedly led over the following few years to a burgeoning in the number of microbrewers. Unsurprisingly, some established brewers, small but too big to benefit from the new system, felt disadvantaged in the guest beer market; and one company – McMullen, of Hertford – announced its intention in 2003 actually to give up some contract brewing in order to reduce output to below the level up to which concessionary duty rates were (then) charged.

Microbrewers produce almost exclusively cask-conditioned ales, and the British Beer and Pub Association (BBPA) has estimated that they account for around 1 per cent of domestic beer sales, which is equivalent to 15 per cent of the cask-conditioned market. In volume terms this would represent around 530,000 hls (325,000 barrels), and with some 700 microbrewers listed by the BBPA at the last count, would imply average output of just 757 hls (460 barrels per annum, or just under nine barrels a week). SIBA itself has claimed that its members account for over 20 per cent of the cask-conditioned ale market, and whether this or the BBPA's 15 per cent is correct, it seems likely that the proportion will continue to grow, given the persistent consumer demand for locally sourced produce of all kinds, and the pride which good licensees seem to take in satisfying that appetite in their beer offering. As it is, according to the BBPA there are now as many breweries in the UK as in the 1940s.

Notes

1 Monopolies and Mergers Commission, *The Supply of Beer: A Report on the Supply of Beer for Retail Sale in the United Kingdom*, Cm 651 (1989), para. 1.25.
2 Campaign for Real Ale press release, 4 July 2005.

15
Pub Companies and Licensees

Rise and fall of the pubcos

The Beer Orders, together with undertakings given to the Office of Fair Trading (OFT) as a result of the Grand Met/Courage deal, obliged the major brewers to release over 11,000 public houses from the tie by November 1992. As Allied-Lyons commented in evidence to the Agriculture Select Committee in 1993, the authorities had given no great thought as to who would buy these pubs.[1] There appears to have been an assumption by the Monopolies and Mergers Commission (MMC) that pub landlords and regional brewers would purchase a large number and, in fact, had been waiting to do so. As it turned out, slightly under half of the pubs were sold or leased to individuals or regional brewers, and rather more went to the new multiple pub operators. It is often said that this marked the beginning of the pubcos, but, in fact, there had already been a number of significant developments in that direction.

Regent Inns, Surrey Free Inns, Inn Leisure (which merged with JA Devenish in 1986), Gray & Sons, Yates Brothers Wine Lodges and – arguably the most successful – JD Wetherspoon were all operating before 1992. Wetherspoon had started life in 1979 and by the end of 1992 was running 44 pubs.

In addition, some of the traditional integrated brewers were starting to question the vertically integrated model. Boddingtons, as we have seen, decided in the late eighties to withdraw from brewing, and although negotiations were suspended until the MMC Report was published, the company duly sold its breweries to Whitbread in 1989, thereby becoming a pubco. Greenalls and Devenish followed a similar route, closing or selling their breweries in 1991, to become pubcos with around 1500 and 550 pubs, respectively.

The pub estates of these companies were mainly run as a combination of managed and tenanted pubs. Other companies, however, had started to enter the pub market with a business model based solely on tenancies, the first being Brent Walker, which in 1988 purchased 386 public houses from

Grand Met. It soon expanded, with the purchase from the Barclay brothers of two small integrated brewers, JW Cameron and Tollemache & Cobbold Breweries, which brought almost 800 pubs into its estate (the breweries were sold). By the end of 1992 Brent Walker had 2026 pubs and had changed the name of its pubs division to Pubmaster. Another tenanted pub operator emerging at this time was the property company, Control Securities. Its first foray into the pub business was through the acquisition of 68 outlets from Allied in 1987, and this was followed by the purchase of a parcel of pubs from Grand Met and the acquisition of the Scottish integrated brewer, Belhaven (which was sold in a management buy-out in 1993 and floated on the stock market in 1996). At its peak Control Securities owned 800 pubs.

Prior to the Beer Orders, Grand Met, one of the "big six" brewers, had also been reviewing its strategy regarding its pubs, and in 1986 had transferred the entire estate to its property division, having concluded that a tied house should be managed like any other property asset. This gave rise to the 20-year Inntrepreneur assignable lease, announced in March 1988, in place of the previous short-term tenancy. The *Morning Advertiser* led with the story, intemperately proclaiming, "Watney [Grand Met's brewing business] yesterday sounded the death knell for the traditional pub tenancy system".[2] By the time the MMC Report came out there were 100 20-year Inntrepreneur leases. Then in 1991, having sold its breweries in the deal with Courage, Grand Met became a managed pubco, owning some 1650 pubs. Meanwhile, Inntrepreneur Estates Ltd (IEL), a 50/50 joint venture company with Courage's parent, Elders, had become a huge tenanted pubco, with some 4350 pubs.

It is clear, then, that a tenanted/leased pubco sector had already been emerging before the Beer Orders came into effect and that some companies had taken advantage of the sale of pubs by the major brewers to expand their estates. As a direct result of the Beer Orders and the enforced untying of pubs, however, a raft of new pub companies suddenly came into being, including, by the end of 1992, companies such as Enterprise Inns, Sycamore Taverns, Century Inns, Discovery Inns, Centric Pub Company and Marr Taverns, which bought or leased groups of pubs from the major brewers. Often the new company negotiated a supply contract with the previous owner of the pubs and it was usual for the acquired pubs to stock the same range of beers as before, simply because the new owners didn't want to upset their regular customers. As some regional brewers were quick to point out, the pubs of the new pubcos were not only tied under a supply contract, but, not being subject to the Tied Estate Order (because they weren't owned by one of the big brewers), their tenants were not entitled to demand a guest beer. These thousands of pubs were thus closed to the regionals, and the supply contract, hitherto virtually unknown in the industry, had become a new form of tie.

The belief that the intent of the MMC was being thwarted was further nourished by the fact that quite a few of the new pubcos were set up by former executives of the big brewers. Thus, for example, former Whitbread executives set up companies to acquire leases of groups of pubs from Whitbread. Although the parties were careful to ensure that the arrangements they entered into didn't contravene the Beer Orders, and, indeed, the OFT was vigilant in this regard, suspicions were aroused when a supply contract, albeit not exclusive, was struck.

It should be noted that the major brewers were distressed sellers, forced to sell or free from the tie a large number of pubs within a short timeframe, and, moreover, at a time of economic recession and depressed property prices. And so, even though the pubs being sold were mostly the poorest performing ones, the fact is that many of them were acquired cheaply, frequently for less than their balance sheet valuation. The scale of transactions was such that by 1994 there were over 100 pubcos, accounting for around 15,000 pubs, some 26 per cent of the total at that time.

Most of the new pubcos operated tenanted or leased pubs only, and their business model was based on two main income steams. First, they derived income from the wholesale profit, sometimes referred to as the "wet rent", which was the difference between the price the company paid for its beer and that at which it sold it to its tenants. The second main income stream was the rent charged for the property, the "dry rent", normally determined at the beginning of the lease and reviewed at regular intervals. Profits could thus be grown by raising rents, often based on turnover, by selling more beer through the outlet, and/or by achieving a higher discount from the supplier and passing on to the tenant none or only some of the gain.

The period 1992–96 was a relatively quiet one for the pubcos, with a number of them gradually expanding by swallowing up smaller rivals. But from 1997 onwards a sea change occurred as the big integrated companies started to sell all or large parts of their pub estates. Most of the pubs affected ultimately ended up in the hands of one or other of the two companies that were to dominate the pubco scene – Enterprise Inns and Punch Group.

Enterprise Inns had started life in 1991, with the purchase of over 300 pubs from Bass, and by the time it floated on the Stock Exchange in 1995 it still had fewer than 500 pubs. It then began to expand rapidly, with the purchases of John Labatt Retail, Discovery Inns, Gibbs Mew, Mayfair Taverns and Century Inns, and by buying blocks of pubs from the major brewers, giving the group an estate of over 3400 pubs by 2001.The Punch Group had begun operating in 1997, when it bought around 1400 Bass pubs, but by 2001, following the purchases of the Inn Business Group and Allied's retail estate, it owned 5000 pubs. Punch was floated on the Stock Exchange in May 2002, changing its name to Punch Taverns. Both companies found that expansion brought benefits of scale, enabling them to spread overhead costs over a larger asset base, and to secure bigger discounts from the brewers.

There was no pause in the consolidation process and by 2004 the "big two" had emerged: Enterprise Inns, with over 8500 pubs, following the purchases of Laurel Pub Company and Unique Pub Company; and Punch Taverns, with over 7000 pubs, following purchases including Conquest Inns and Pubmaster. After Punch's purchase of the Spirit Group of managed pubs in 2005, Enterprise and Punch each owned more pubs than any of the major brewers had before the MMC Report. To fund expansion they relied mainly on debt finance in the case of Enterprise, and securitisation – the creation of securities backed by a cash flow stream, in this instance pub rental income – in the case of Punch. Both companies pursued a course of rapid expansion, with the result that peak net debt levels were £3.8bn for Enterprise, equivalent to 253 per cent of shareholders' funds, and £5.5bn for Punch, equivalent to 342 per cent.

The tenanted pubco business model worked well for the pubco owners for a number of years but from 2007 a host of problems arose. The ban on smoking in pubs was introduced in England in July 2007 (it already operated in Scotland and Wales) and this, combined with recession, shifted consumption away from the pub and into the home, causing a drop in on-trade sales. To add to pubco woes, from 2008 the Government adopted a policy of raising excise duty ahead of inflation. Increasing levels of discounts offered by the brewers had effectively come to an end, putting pressure on pubco margins; property values were falling; and the banking crisis reduced available finance. Suddenly what had been a successful business model was soured, as falling volumes not only led to declines in "wet rent", but made it hard to raise "dry rent", as lessee income came under pressure. The share prices of Enterprise and Punch, having reached 774p and 1379p, respectively, in May 2007, both fell to around 32p in January 2009. In June 2009 the *Daily Mail* remarked, "the pubcos have become dinosaurs with unmanageable portfolios and swamped by debts rather than customers".[3]

To combat these problems the companies suspended their dividends, reduced capital expenditure, sold pubs and started to reduce their debt, and in the case of Punch raised cash with a deeply discounted share placing. At the same time licensees had been experiencing financial difficulties and so the companies felt obliged to offer assistance, estimated in the case of Punch to be equivalent to £1.6 million a month by June 2009.

No changes in beer wholesaling

The MMC had been ambitious to see the advance of the independent wholesaler, which it believed would provide competition to the national brewers. The Agriculture Committee, in its 1993 review of the Beer Orders, specifically recognised that no such advance had occurred, having heard evidence from The National Association of Licensed Trade Wholesalers alleging that brewers were pursuing trading practices that meant the complex monopoly still existed.[4] The situation didn't change over the next few years either, with the result that the OFT, in its own review of the Beer Orders in 2000, observed that independent wholesalers' share of the market had not changed since 1989.

The MMC's thinking had been that the enforced sale of thousands of pubs would create a swath of independent licensees, which wholesalers would be well placed to service. Instead, of course, the majority of the pubs freed from the tie ended up in the hands of pubcos, which found the national brewers to be effective in meeting their needs. Nor did wholesalers find much joy in trying to service the guest beer purchases of the tenants of national brewers. The brewers all stocked their depots with dozens of different ales, so that licensees felt no need to use wholesalers, and, moreover, welcomed the opportunity to have their guest ales delivered alongside beers for which they were tied.

Tenants as pawns

The MMC had also wanted to help tenants, partly because it believed that the relationship between brewer and tenant was inequitable, and partly because it hoped in this way to create a vigorous independent sector that could compete with brewers at the retail level. As we have seen, it therefore recommended the divestment of more than 21,000 pubs owned by the national brewers, and that the interests of all tenants in on-licensed premises should be brought within the provisions of the Landlord & Tenant Act 1954 Part II. The implementation of these remedies, even though modified by the Government, had an impact on tenants that can only be described as dramatic, if not traumatic. It is inconceivable that the authors of the Report anticipated anything like the disruption and anxiety that followed.

Whilst the Government began to get to grips with the Report early in 1989, a mood of uncertainty and worry spread amongst licensees. Concern was sharpest among the tenants of the large brewers, but shrewder licensees within the ranks of the smaller brewers realised that the game was changing. Every tenanted pub of one of the large brewers (around 23,500) was susceptible to being sold, or retained by the large brewer but with new rights and, inevitably, new obligations. For many tenants their pub wasn't only a business, it was also a family home. The National Licensed Victuallers Association was opposed to the Report's more drastic proposals, fearing that they could undermine the viability of the tenanted system. Time and again it reminded Government that it wanted no more than security of tenure.

Within weeks of the Report being published several brewers announced that in a situation of such uncertainty they would freeze or curtail investment in their pubs, but more alarmingly, others issued their tenants with notice to quit. Whether or not issuing notice was something that the brewers could have avoided – and the Agriculture Committee concluded in 1993 that, as far as the large brewers were concerned, compliance with the Orders made it unavoidable[5] – what is certain is that it was unsettling for licensees.

By early 1990 the Government had given effect to its decisions on the MMC Report in the shape of the Beer Orders and the Landlord and Tenant (Licensed Premises) Act 1990. But although a degree of legal certainty had been brought, and with it the fact that the large brewers could retain more tied pubs than the MMC had proposed, implementation of the new regulatory regime would not be completed until November 1992, meaning that tenants were consigned to an extended state of limbo.

During 1990 two events of significance for tenants occurred. First, in May tenants of large brewers gained the right to stock a guest ale and freedom from the tie on non-beer beverages. Most commentators came to regard guest beer as the biggest success of the Orders (the Agriculture Committee in 1993 called it "the sole unarguable success stemming from the Beer Orders").[6] Taken together with the right to shop around for non-beer drinks, it gave tenants of large brewers some welcome benefit, and one not enjoyed by their counterparts in the pubs of smaller brewers.

The second event was the "pubs-for-breweries" deal struck between Grand Met and Courage, announced in March and completed early in 1991. One of the conditions imposed by the Government after an investigation by the MMC was that over 1000 more pubs should be freed from the tie than had been required by the Beer Orders. This may have been positive for competition, but for the affected licensees it symbolised the way in which they would be treated – as pawns in a game. One licensee involved told the authors how virtually overnight he was informed by Courage that his pub in North Kent was to be freed from the tie, a situation for which he felt totally unprepared.

During 1991 and into 1992 the large brewers and IEL concentrated on deciding which pubs to retain, sell or lease free of tie, and on converting standard tenancy agreements to long leases. Although IEL had pioneered the long lease before the Orders came into effect, its mass use dates from the Orders – although the extent to which there is a causal link between the two events remains unclear. The new freedoms available to tenants from May 1990 had to be written into new agreements, and the brewers would naturally seek higher rents to compensate for the loss of income resulting from these freedoms. It was also the case that many tenants *wanted* a different arrangement with the brewer, principally in order to create capital value, which could only occur through a longer term lease. And once tenants won Landlord and Tenant Act protection from July 1992, which preceded the date of the enforced divestment requirement, the brewers' room for manoeuvre would be limited. Given also that the brewers were working to a tight timetable, they came to regard long leases as their preferred option, providing maximum flexibility.

Thousands of tenants were thus confronted with a stark choice: sign up to a lease with a higher rent and a repairing obligation or quit. Again it must be stated that some tenants embraced the new arrangements, and that, as the Agriculture Committee Report made plain, some brewer landlords handled the process with more sensitivity than others. Nevertheless, some distress was undoubtedly caused in the process. As we have seen, Stan Crowther MP told the House of Commons in November 1991 that thousands of tenants had been forced to leave the trade or had felt forced to sign a lease on onerous terms;[7] that, according to Grand Met, 40 per cent of its tenants had left since the Beer Orders; and that, in Crowther's opinion, the same was probably true of the other national brewers. If true, this meant that over 9000 tenants had gone from the trade. Leif Mills, in his Note of Dissent in 1989, had expressed his concern that many tenants who couldn't buy their pubs would become unemployed. Events justified his concern.

The time now came for the brewers to complete the divestment programme and in so doing to end over two and a half years of uncertainty and confusion for individual licensees. How many of the 11,000 pubs affected were sold, as opposed to leased, and who bought them, is not recorded. But the authors estimate that pubcos bought or leased some 6000 pubs, individuals (including sitting tenants) about 3000, and other brewers in the region of 2000.

Licensees who found themselves transferred to one of the pubcos tended at first to be on a tenancy agreement or short lease. The immediate effect for many was that their recently won entitlement to a guest beer was removed and the tie on non-beer drinks reimposed, moving the Agriculture Committee to comment in 1993 that, "It is symptomatic of the confusion surrounding the introduction of the Beer Orders that the two principal provisions, divestment of pubs and the right to purchase guest beers, have acted to some extent at cross-purposes".[8]

Many tenants left the trade in the immediate wake of their pub being transferred to a pubco (and, of course, as Crowther had articulated, many had quit even before this). In conversation with the authors the former chief executive of one small pubco formed in 1992 said that within a year of taking on the pubs all of the original tenants had, for one reason or another, left. It was also a feature of the time, however, confirmed by a senior manager of the tenanted estate of one of the major brewers, that there were plenty of aspiring tenants ready to take on pubs, so that the new operators had no need to try to retain reluctant or under-performing licensees.

For many licensees, shifting from tenure under a national brewer to one under a pubco didn't mark the end of the turmoil, as pubcos consolidated. Several former Whitbread tenants, for example, abruptly found themselves in 1992 in the hands of a new pubco, Trent Taverns, only for that company to be acquired in 1999 by Inn Business, which was itself acquired by Punch later that year. Any tenant surviving this upheaval would thus have experienced no fewer than four landlords in seven or eight years.

John Overton, Chief Executive from 1976 to 1993 first of the National Union of Licensed Victuallers, and then of the National Licensed Victuallers Association (NLVA) when the former changed its name in January 1987, told the authors that in retrospect his overriding view was that his Association had "got it wrong" at the time of the MMC inquiry. He recalled that the old system had offered people of modest means an opportunity to run their own business in partnership with a paternalistic brewer. In fact, according to the evidence given by the NLVA itself to the MMC, relations between tenants and the major brewers had already deteriorated by the mid-eighties, the old concept of partnership had changed, and brewers had started to exploit the tenanted sector with unrealistic rent demands. Even so, Overton felt that the Association had made matters worse with its frequent lobbying in London and Brussels. In the end it got what it thought it wanted – long-term security of tenure and the opportunity to build an asset that could be sold on. But when the full implications of what had happened sank in, including higher rents, responsibility for repairs, and a generally far tougher regime for those who became tenants of pubcos, they didn't like it. The old adage, "Be careful what you wish for, lest it come true", seems pertinent.

The story of one East London licensee, spanning 25 years, illustrates the fast changing world with which the modern licensee now contends. This licensee took over the tenancy of a Bass pub from her father in 1985. In 1989 came the MMC Report and speculation as to whether the pub would be sold, turned over to management, or retained as a tenancy. Efforts to raise loans to buy the pub came to nothing and in 1992 the licensee was offered a 15-year lease. She was pleased to take this on as it provided a business building opportunity. When, in 1997, Bass sold its leased pubs to Punch, the licensee was able to retain the Bass lease – far superior, she says, to the Punch lease – until 2007, when it expired and was replaced with a Punch lease. With a bank loan and investment from Punch the pub was extensively developed, and in 2009 the licensee bought the freehold of the pub. Her father had run the pub for 18 years under a simple tenancy arrangement, but her tenure at the pub has been characterised by change, albeit with a favourable outcome.

The MMC had imagined that many of the pubs to be divested by the national brewers would be bought by smaller brewers, and it would no doubt have been disappointed by an uptake probably of no more than 2000 pubs. There were several reasons for the smaller brewers' lack of interest.

First, many of the pubs on offer were small and of poor quality. The London brewers, Young & Co. and Fuller Smith & Turner, for example, would hardly have been tempted by pubs with sales of perhaps a third of the average of their existing estate. Second, the wiser regional brewers had misgivings about taking on pubs in the strongholds of one of the national brewers. Some threw caution to the wind and paid a price: for example, Thwaites, of Blackburn in Lancashire, which bought pubs in Sheffield, a stronghold for Bass and Whitbread, only to find that its beers were both unknown and unwelcome in Yorkshire; and Charles Wells, of Bedford, which thought it could compete in Birmingham with the mighty duopoly of Bass and Allied. In both instances, of course, it wasn't only the brewers that suffered, but also the tenants, who didn't even have a say in the matter.

The MMC also misunderstood the corporate strategy of some of the family brewers. Many were not motivated by growth for its own sake, they had no public shareholders, and their approach might be described as dynastic rather than corporate. So they were simply not interested in acquiring new assets, or, at least, would do so only if an exceptional opportunity presented itself.

In its construct of the market following the implementation of its recommendations, the MMC also foresaw many former tenants buying the freeholds of the pubs they occupied. It would be wrong to suggest that only a negligible number of such transactions occurred, but they were probably fewer in number than expected, and, indeed, rather more pubs were sold to individual entrepreneurs buying pubs on the open market. One reason why so few tenants stepped forward was that many were unwilling to take on the risk of ownership, but even the more ambitious were aware that the UK had entered a recession, credit was tight and raising finance was impossible. Another problem was that, given the tight timetable under which they were labouring, the national brewers were keener to dispose of pubs in bundles of dozens or hundreds than to embark on a programme of individual sales. Nonetheless there were licensees who bought the pub that they had formerly occupied as tenant. The authors spoke to such a licensee who in 1991 bought his pub in South London from Courage for £200,000, using his house as collateral for a bank loan, later selling the property at a substantial profit for residential development. But, as he pointed out, he was one of the lucky few.

The Crehan case

During the 1990s relationships between lessees and their landlords suffered a serious deterioration, and it wasn't long before the courts became involved, particularly in disputes involving IEL, the most important being that concerning Bernard Crehan.[9] Crehan had entered into agreements with Inntrepreneur in 1991 to take the leases on two pubs, but trading proved very difficult and in 1993 the businesses failed. Litigation between Crehan and IEL began in June 1993, when Courage (Inntrepreneur's beer supplier under the tie) sued Crehan for outstanding monies owed on his beer account. Crehan counter-claimed that his leases, which tied him to Courage, were in breach of Article 81, formerly Article 85, of the European Community Treaty relating to agreements that restricted competition. But proceedings were stayed until 2000 whilst the European Commission deliberated over the standard leases notified by IEL.

Eventually the Commission's comfort letters to IEL (as described earlier) cleared the way for a reference to be made to the European Court of Justice (ECJ) to determine whether Crehan could claim damages under English Law. After further delay, in 2003, and with the assent of the ECJ, Crehan's claim was heard in the High Court. [John Spicer, one of the authors, acted as an expert witness at the hearing.] The Court found in favour of IEL, but the judge concluded that, had it not been for the European Commission's conclusion on Delimitis,[10] namely, that the UK market was not foreclosed to new entrants, he would have awarded damages in excess of £1 million.

The Court of Appeal overturned the High Court's ruling and awarded Crehan damages, not of £1 million but of £131,336. The case was then referred to the House of Lords, and in July 2006, 13 years after the original action, the Lords reversed the Court of Appeal's decision and restored the High Court's decision that the market had not been foreclosed in the early 1990s. Crehan's claim had failed, and with it the hopes for compensation of many other IEL tenants.

The courts may have buttressed the legal position of pubcos, but from 2007 they had to contend with an almost ruinous combination of external factors, resulting in plummeting earnings and plunging stock market values. For many of their lessees the situation became equally, if not more, grave. But, even before this, signs of licensee difficulty and of disaffection with the strategies being pursued by pubcos had started to emerge, as highlighted in the 2004 Trade and Industry Select Committee inquiry.[11] That Committee was not unsympathetic, but didn't intervene, leaving lessees to face the full adverse impact of recession and social change.

Although the Committee was critical of how the leased business model was applied in some instances, it nevertheless acknowledged that not every lessee was unsuccessful. The authors talked to one of the new breed of licensee, an entrepreneur in West London with a tied lease from a regional brewer, who has transformed the business from a failing wet-led pub to a thriving food-led business. Yet it is symptomatic of the enduring difference of interest between landlord and tenant that this success, entirely down to the endeavour and investment of the lessee, was rewarded with a proposed doubling in rent at the time of the first rent review.

The MMC wanted to improve the lot of licensees. So many external factors have intervened in the twenty-odd years since then that the long-term effects of the Beer Orders alone cannot be isolated, rendering any judgment of the Commission's role imperfect. It is unarguable, however, that the years immediately following the Report saw confusion and dislocation that would not have struck so swiftly nor been so severe without the Beer Orders. The biggest victims of this shock were licensees.

Notes

1. Agriculture Committee Fourth Report of Session 1993, *Effects of the Beer Orders on the Brewing Industry and Consumers*, HC 402 p. 60, para. 5.4.
2. *Morning Advertiser*, 14 March 1988, p. 1.
3. *Daily Mail*, 16 June 2009.
4. Agriculture Committee Fourth Report of Session 1993, *Effects of the Beer Orders on the Brewing Industry and Consumers*, HC 402, Appendix 20.
5. *Ibid.*, para. 50.
6. *Ibid.*, para. 29.
7. HC Deb 14 November 1991 Vol. 198 cc1327–34.
8. Agriculture Committee Fourth Report of Session 1993, *Effects of the Beer Orders on the Brewing Industry and Consumers*, HC 402, para. 29.
9. Inntrepreneur Pub Company and others v Crehan [2006] UKHL 38.
10. Stergio Delimitis v Henninger Brau AG, Case C-234/89, 28 February 1991.
11. Trade and Industry Select Committee Second Report of Session 2004–05, *Pub Companies*, HC 128-1.

16
Prices and Choice

Surge in the price of a pint

As we have seen, the Price Commission found that between June 1974 and June 1977 ex-duty beer prices, at both wholesale and retail level, had fallen in real terms; and between December 1977 and May 1979 the Commission found little to object to in the price increases proposed by Allied Breweries, Bass Charrington and Whitbread. The first half of the eighties, however, following the abolition of price controls by the newly elected Conservative Government, saw beer prices – at least in the pub trade – rising significantly faster than retail prices generally. Thus the November 1985 Monopolies and Mergers Commission (MMC) Report into the proposed merger between Scottish & Newcastle and Matthew Brown showed that the average price of non-premium bitter in the public bar, excluding duty and Value Added Tax (VAT), had risen by 81 per cent between July 1979 and July 1985, against an increase of 64 per cent in the Retail Prices Index (RPI),[1] a rise in real terms over six years of just over 10 per cent.

Matters, however, were to become considerably worse for the consumer. Thus in the four years between 1985, the year in which Sir Gordon Borrie stated that he was seriously considering referring the brewers to the MMC, and 1989, the year in which the Commission reported, average prices in the pub of bitter and lager, again excluding duty and VAT, went up in real terms by around 12 per cent and 14 per cent, respectively.[2] Whether or not there was a causal connection between these increases and the activities of the regulatory authorities isn't known, but, coming at such a sensitive time, the increases could be described as provocative, or at best undiplomatic.

The Commission, however, was confident that it had worked out how to improve the consumer's lot. "The majority of us believe that these measures will increase competition in brewing, wholesaling and retailing, encourage new entry, reduce prices and widen consumer choice."[3] What actually happened to prices is illustrated in Tables 16.1 and 16.2, which compare the course of ex-taxes pub prices for bitter and lager over the ten years from 1989, the year of the Beer Orders, with the RPIY (see footnote to Table 16.1).

Table 16.1 Average Pub Price of Draught Bitter, Excluding Duty and VAT, Relative to RPIY*

	Ex-taxes price per pint (p)	(a) Increase	RPIY*	(b) Increase	(a) relative to (b)	Cumulative increase
1989	65.7		113.1			
1990	76.8	16.9%	121.4	7.3%	+8.9%	+8.9%
1991	87.2	13.5%	129.5	6.7%	+6.4%	+15.9%
1992	89.8	3.0%	135.1	4.3%	−1.3%	+14.4%
1993	93.8	4.5%	139.0	2.9%	+1.5%	+16.2%
1994	97.1	3.5%	141.3	1.7%	+1.8%	+18.2%
1995	101.4	4.4%	144.5	2.3%	+2.1%	+20.7%
1996	108.2	6.7%	148.2	2.6%	+4.0%	+25.6%
1997	115.8	7.0%	151.5	2.2%	+4.7%	+31.6%
1998	119.4	3.1%	154.5	2.0%	+1.1%	+33.0%
1999	122.0	2.2%	157.1	1.7%	+0.5%	+33.7%

*RPIY is the Retail Prices Index excluding mortgage interest and indirect taxes. 13 January 1987 = 100.
Sources: British Beer & Pub Association quoting the Office for National Statistics; HM Revenue and Customs; authors' calculations.

Table 16.2 Average Pub Price of Draught Lager, Excluding Duty and VAT, Relative to RPIY*

	Ex-taxes price per pint (p)	(a) Increase	RPIY*	(b) Increase	(a) relative to (b)	Cumulative increase
1989	76.1		113.1			
1990	88.1	15.8%	121.4	7.3%	+7.9%	+7.9%
1991	99.2	12.6%	129.5	6.7%	+5.6%	+13.8%
1992	103.4	4.2%	135.1	4.3%	−0.1%	+13.8%
1993	108.3	4.7%	139.0	2.9%	+1.8%	+15.8%
1994	111.5	3.0%	141.3	1.7%	+1.3%	+17.3%
1995	117.5	5.4%	144.5	2.3%	+3.0%	+20.9%
1996	123.5	5.1%	148.2	2.6%	+2.5%	+23.8%
1997	131.1	6.2%	151.5	2.2%	+3.8%	+28.7%
1998	136.4	4.0%	154.5	2.0%	+2.0%	+31.2%
1999	139.9	2.6%	157.1	1.7%	+0.8%	+32.3%

*See note to Table 16.1.
Sources: As for Table 16.1.

What the tables starkly illustrate is that the implementation of the Beer Orders was accompanied by a further surge in beer prices in the pub. Indeed, the rate of increase accelerated from that which had been seen during the MMC inquiry. Thus in 1990, the year in which the major brewers had to allow tenants to stock a guest beer and to purchase their non-beer requirements from a supplier of their choice, the ex-taxes prices of bitter and lager over the bar rose, respectively, by 8.9 per cent and 7.9 per cent in real terms. In 1991, during which the majors were selling or freeing from the tie thousands of pubs, these prices leapt again – by a further 6.4 per cent and 5.6 per cent in real terms. Over the whole period from 1989, the last year of the old order, to 1993, the first year following full compliance with the Beer Orders, the ex-taxes prices of both bitter and lager rose around 16 per cent faster than inflation. And, as we have seen, prices had already been soaring during the period of the investigation. If the Commissioners and various Ministers and officials had assumed that the big brewers, in their continuing but diminished role as pub operators, would respond to the increase in competition by reducing their prices, or at least by not raising them, they were sorely mistaken.

The authorities may have consoled themselves in the mid-nineties with the thought that, once the industry had settled down, the consumer would finally start to benefit from lower prices. But it never happened. There were two occasions in the first decade of the new century when beer prices actually rose slightly – very slightly – less than the RPIY, but the long-term inflation-adjusted trend was upward, and by 2009, 20 years after the Report, average pub prices of draught bitter and lager (still excluding duty and VAT) had both risen in real terms by slightly more than 50 per cent. What renders these figures even more extraordinary is the fact that wholesale prices were falling, at least for draught beer – by 15 per cent (ex-taxes) in real terms between 1992 and 2000, according to a Brewers & Licensed Retailers Association (BLRA) survey quoted in the December 2000 Office of Fair Trading review of the Beer Orders. Self-evidently, hardly any of this wholesale price reduction was being passed on to the consumer.

A number of studies of the effect on prices of the Beer Orders have been published, one, in 1995, being a technical piece of work by George Garafas, of the Regulatory Policy Institute and of Christ Church, Oxford, entitled "The effects of regulation on prices in the UK brewing industry: an empirical investigation". This concluded that between December 1989 and July 1993 the real ex-taxes price of beer rose by 4.8 per cent as a direct result of the Beer Orders. It must be said that this represents only a small part of the 16 per cent increase referred to above, and therefore that this study may have significantly understated the effect of the Orders. Leaving aside the numbers, it is nevertheless interesting to note that Garafas mainly attributed the increase to the fact that restructuring costs were passed on to the consumer, and that the growth in non-brewer owned pubs exerted upward pressure on prices.

This latter point was in line with the reasoning of another economist, Graham Bannock. He wrote a study for inclusion in a BLRA booklet, in which he argued that the increased volume of beer sold through pubcos and the free trade, as a result of the Beer Orders, had led to higher prices by raising delivery costs. This was because average deliveries ("drop-sizes") were smaller than in the tied trade, brewery managements had less control over delivery days, and delivery distances were longer.[4]

Keyworth, Lawton Smith and Yarrow found in their 1994 paper, "The effects of regulation in the UK beer market", that on the basis of a trend line from 1975 to 1992 the real ex-taxes price of beer in 1992 was 7.3 per cent above trend. They also argued, however, that prices were subject to contra-cyclical influences and that the economic recession of that time partly accounted for this blip in prices. They estimated that, excluding this factor, the deviation from trend was only a little over half of what they had found. In any case, they concluded that price increases associated with the Beer Orders had cost consumers over £500m (at 1992 prices) in the period 1989-92.[5]

In 1998 Margaret E Slade wrote a paper in which she claimed that a break upwards in trend in tied house beer prices occurred in the second half of 1990. Perhaps of greater interest, however, were, first, her finding that free house beer prices showed no evidence of such a shift; and, second, her prediction that a move from traditional tenancies to long-term leases and the creation of pub chains would lead to higher prices.[6]

Academic analysis carried out during the nineties thus seems to demonstrate a linkage between real price increases and the Beer Orders, but this would have come as no surprise to many. As early as 1990 George Yarrow had produced a paper, never published, but likely to have been sent to the OFT, in which he forecast that the large-scale enforced separation of production and retailing would have the effect of pushing up pub prices. He also expected consumers to suffer a loss of amenity and a reduction in the number of pubs.[7]

The Brewers' Society had long argued – and, indeed, did in its evidence to the MMC – that the price of beer in the pub represented the price of a package, consisting of the product itself, the service element and the amenities; and that rising beer prices were partly a function of increased staff costs and spending on amenities. The MMC retorted that the same general point could be made in relation to other retail activities, that the costs of providing such packages across the whole retail sector were reflected in the RPI, and that this therefore couldn't explain why the pub price of beer had risen so much faster than retail prices generally. The point is not worth dwelling on, but common sense suggests that improving the package accounts for a significantly greater proportion of total costs in retail outlets that people visit for pleasure than in premises which people enter in order to make a purchase to be used or consumed elsewhere.

Price and amenity

Before leaving the subject of beer prices, it is worth drawing attention to the widening gap between prices in different outlets that has occurred since the Beer Orders. The British Beer & Pub Association (BBPA) publishes the highest and lowest prices between which 80 per cent of each annual sample falls, thus excluding exceptionally cheap and expensive offerings. These figures – which include duty and VAT – show that the price of the cheapest pint of bitter as a proportion of the most expensive fell from 78 per cent in the year of the Beer Orders, 1989, to 63 per cent in 2009; the figures for lager were 80 per cent and 63 per cent. If this phenomenon is down to the Beer Orders, however, it must be said that the chickens have taken a long time to come home to roost. Thus the ratio for bitter in 1999, ten years after the Beer Orders, was still up at 73 per cent, while that for lager was 78 per cent, the latter representing only a slight widening of the gap since ten years earlier. In fact, the biggest parting of the ways occurred between 2007 and 2009. These figures are summarised in Table 16.3.

Table 16.3 Range of Pub Beer Prices Covering 80 per cent of Sample

Year	Bitter price range	Low as % of High	Lager price range	Low as % of High
1989	84–108p	78	96–120p	80
1999	150–206p	73	175–225p	78
2007	185–265p	70	200–280p	71
2009	185–295p	63	215–340p	63

Source: BBPA quoting the Office for National Statistics; authors' calculations.

Although the pace of widening of the price range has thus been particularly noticeable in recent years, nevertheless John Bridgeman, the Director General of Fair Trading, referred to the phenomenon as early as 2000 in his review of the Beer Orders, pointing out that the pub "offer" had greatly improved and that there was "some trade-off between this and higher prices".[8] He also referred to the "considerable degree of differentiation in the on-trade retail market in response to a significant increase in the demands and sophistication of pub-goers since 1989".[9] And he seemed to accept the industry's assertion that there was now "more correlation between beer prices and levels of amenity offered by outlets such that consumers [had] a greater choice between different price-amenity combinations".[10]

These developments had, of course, already been in train during the eighties, but were arguably given added impetus by the Beer Orders, to the extent that the resulting diminution in the importance of the tie meant that the majors' pubs must earn a commercial return in their own right, rather than largely as an outlet for the company's beer.

10,000 fewer pubs since 1991

There is little doubt in the authors' minds that the Beer Orders have been at least partly responsible for another ill to have befallen the pub user, namely, the decline in the country's stock of pubs. Surprising as it may seem, there are no official statistics in respect of pub numbers. The Home Office stopped collecting the information in 2004, but even before then the only figures available related to all full on-licences, including hotels and so on. Since 1991, however, the BBPA and its predecessor bodies have published annual figures in respect of the numbers of on-licences owned by pubcos and the proportion of all pubs which these account for, from which it is obviously possible to calculate total pub numbers. It should be noted, though, that the numbers which the BBPA has used for total pubs are its own estimates, derived from several different data sources.

Subject to this caveat, it is possible to make the following observations. Between 1991 and 1999 the number of pubs in the UK fell from 62,255 to 61,473, a net reduction of barely two a week, and, indeed, in both 1998 and 1999 the number rose slightly. In 2000, however, it fell, and has continued to do so every year since. Between 1999 and 2006 the rate of net decline was around nine pubs per week, but then the rate accelerated markedly, to around 27 per week in 2007, 38 in 2008 and 45 in 2009 – at the end of which the number stood at 52,495.

The authors believe that the reason why pub numbers held up so well during the nineties is that for several years the Beer Orders had the perverse effect of sustaining in business thousands of pubs which would otherwise have succumbed to the same market pressures that had for years been causing a steady decline in pub numbers. These were the pubs which were poorly located, of uneconomic size, of a low standard of décor and repair, or unequipped to run a food operation. And the factors pressing down on them included the growth in home entertainment, the widening price difference between on- and off-trade prices, the reduction in drinking and driving, and increased competition from venues such as wine bars and restaurants.

In these special circumstances, however, what was a headache for the big brewers was a boon for the pubcos. The problem for the former of being forced by the Tied Estate Order to sell very large numbers of pubs – or lease them free of tie – within a short timescale coincided with a severe recession and plummeting property prices. And the beneficiaries from an environment not only of depressed pub values and rents, but also of falling wholesale beer prices, as the brewers scrambled for sales, were the pubcos. For a number of years the returns, even from the lower-end pubs, were very satisfactory, but, as later became clear, such returns misrepresented the capacity of large numbers of these outlets to survive in harsher circumstances.

As property values began to recover in the second half of the nineties, and as the two largest pubcos, Enterprise and Punch, competed to swallow up the smaller ones, many operators sold out at a substantial profit. And as these two companies expanded, debt levels rose, they demanded more from their properties, and tensions emerged between company and lessee. For a time pubs struggled on, but it couldn't last, and when circumstances combined to produce a severe deterioration in trading conditions, the pubs that without the Beer Orders would long since have closed were finally found out.

The reasons for the travails of the pub industry since 2006 are well known. First, the introduction of a ban on smoking in public places in July 2007 was bound to hit some pubs very hard, given that over 25 per cent of pub users were also regular smokers. This blow was followed by the collapse in financial markets and consumer confidence, together with the credit crunch. And, against this challenging economic background, beer duty was raised between March 2006 and March 2011 by a cumulative 40 per cent. By this time too the scope for squeezing ever bigger discounts out of the brewers had been largely, if not entirely, exhausted.

A survey of pub tenants and lessees conducted on behalf of the House of Commons Business and Enterprise Select Committee in May 2009 showed that the smoking ban and cheap take-home prices were rated by only 14 per cent and 8 per cent, respectively, of the respondents as the principal reason for their financial difficulties; rents or the prices they had to pay their landlords for supplies were cited by 60 per cent.[11] Given that the non-integrated pubcos were largely created out of the ashes of the old industry, and given that by this time pubs tenanted or leased from pubcos accounted for 42 per cent of all pubs, this figure suggests that the terminal financial problems experienced by thousands of pubs over recent years can at least in part be traced back to the Beer Orders.

It is arguable that, 20 years on, the number of pubs isn't far from what it would have been without the Beer Orders, and that the latter's only – albeit undesirable – contribution in this regard was to compress into a few years what would otherwise have taken place over a long period. What should have been an orderly process thus became a confused and chaotic one, to the detriment of both licensees and customers. But this analysis – whilst to some extent valid – ignores the substantial increases in on-trade beer prices seen in the years immediately following implementation of the Orders. Hindsight suggests that not only were these two events directly related (academic research agrees), but so too were the rise in prices and the enormous decline in on-trade beer sales which has occurred since 1989, and which inevitably contributed to the long-term decline in the number of pubs.

Marked increase in brand choice

As quoted earlier, the second principal benefit to the consumer that the authors of the MMC Report foresaw – that is, in addition to lower prices – was a widening of choice of beer, and in some ways their confidence in this respect was vindicated. The Brewers' Society's paper, "The recommendations made by the MMC and their likely consequences", published in the spring of 1989, had reported that the average number of beer brands sold in a sample of 80 pubs in the UK was 16.3, of which 6.5 were draught and 9.8 packaged.

What they didn't show, however, was that, as far as tied houses were concerned, most of the beers on sale in any one pub were from the same brewer. These landlord-produced beers would mainly have consisted of an ordinary cask bitter, a premium cask bitter, a keg bitter and possibly a cask mild; and, in the packaged category, light ale, brown ale, pale ale, strong ale, barley wine, sweet stout, and perhaps a bottle-conditioned ale. Virtually the only beers not produced by the brewer-landlord, in both draught and packaged categories, would have been a couple of lagers – although here, too, a number of brewers produced their own brand – and Guinness stout. In other words, for the typical beer drinker, that is, one who habitually drank the same style of beer, most tied houses effectively provided no choice at all. The Brewers' Society dismissed the notion that consumer choice was affected in this way, while the MMC took the other view, asserting – not unreasonably – that "many consumers consider that there are differences between brands".[12]

It is true that there were many brewers operating in the market, and that it was unusual for the typical beer drinker, at least in an urban environment, not to have a choice between the pubs of at least two different brewers, and sometimes several. Nevertheless, the MMC found that in 1986 one brewer still owned at least half of all the full on-licences in 6 per cent of the 600+ Petty Sessional Divisions (PSDs), at least a third in 29 per cent, and at least a quarter in 52 per cent. On balance, it is fair to say that there was a reasonable degree of pub – and therefore brand choice – in most parts of the country other than the most sparsely populated, but that within individual pubs choice was distinctly restricted, and, as we see below, inferior to what is now available.

In comparing the choice of beers available to the pub customer now with what was on offer before the Beer Orders, a number of fundamental changes in the market since 1989 must be borne in mind. First, the beer market as a whole had by 2009 fallen in volume terms by over 28 per cent, and, second, pubs and other on-licensed premises accounted in that year for only 53 per cent of the beer market, compared with 81 per cent 20 years earlier. Together, these figures mean that beer consumption in on-licensed premises declined by 53 per cent, equivalent to a fall of around 48 per cent per on-licensed outlet. Within the 53 per cent decline, draught lager fell by a third and draught ale and stout by two-thirds, with the result that in 2009 the former accounted for 63 per cent of the draught beer market and the latter for just 37 per cent. Over 7 percentage points of the latter figure, moreover, were accounted for by stout.

In these circumstances it is hardly surprising that many of the erstwhile major ale brands have been sold, abandoned or severely neglected by their now internationally inclined owners. These include Bass Ale, Charrington IPA, Courage Best, Boddingtons, Whitbread Best, Flowers, Ansell's, M&B, Ind Coope and many others. At the same time, numerous regional brands have disappeared with their owners' demise. Against this, however, a number of regional and local brewers have established their ale brands on a national – or at least widely distributed – basis, for example: Adnams (various), Fuller's (London Pride), Greene King (IPA and Abbot), Marston's (Pedigree), Shepherd Neame (various), Timothy Taylor (Landlord), Wadworth (6X), Wells (Bombardier) and Young's (Bitter). In addition, over 700 microbrewers now produce at least one brand each, almost entirely ale.

In 2010–11 the authors conducted a survey of the choice of draught beers – which account for over 90 per cent of total on-trade beer sales – in over 80 pubs that before the Beer Orders were owned by one or other of the national brewers. The survey was slightly larger than the 1989 Brewers' Society survey referred to above, and the sample was constructed so as to represent the geographic composition of the population of Britain.

The survey shows that British pubs today offer on average 8.6 draught brands, comprising 4.9 ales and stouts, and 3.7 lagers. In 1989 the Brewers' Society reported that the pubs in its sample carried an average of 6.5 draught brands, whilst the MMC's considerably larger survey, carried out in 1986, had shown an average of 6.1 brands for tied pubs. The wider offering today may not represent a massive increase in choice, but what makes it remarkable is that it has occurred alongside the 48 per cent sales decline in the average on-trade outlet referred to earlier. What is equally surprising is that, far from a rationalisation of brands having taken place, there has been a multiplication of brands available around the country – at least in draught form. Thus the authors' survey reveals 38 different lagers and over 130 ales and stouts. The most striking aspect of this collection is the number of microbrews now to be seen, with nearly 40 per cent of the pubs in the survey stocking at least one beer produced by a microbrewer. These include a handful of lagers and stouts, but the vast majority are ales, with no fewer than 50 different brews found, most of them on sale in only one pub. Aside from John Smith's, mostly seen in keg form, and – along with Tetley's – one of only two national ale brands found in the survey, no ale was on offer in more than 12 per cent of the sample.

The impressive market penetration achieved by microbreweries must obviously owe something to the Progressive Beer Duty regime, endorsed in

1989 by the MMC, but not introduced until 2002, and in 2011 worth around 25p/pint over other beers. Whatever the reasons for the micros' success, one is struck by the distance that some of the brews have travelled to the point of sale, with beer from Sussex on sale in Blackpool, Cornish brews in Suffolk, and ale from Scotland available in London and *vice versa*. There is less diversity in the range of lagers in pubs, but there are certainly a number of Continental – and even Japanese – brews on sale that would not have been found 20 years ago.

All in all, within the average pub there has been an increase in the number of draught beers on sale, perhaps not dramatic (although some larger pubs offer a choice of as many as 10–15), but nonetheless marked. Very often microbrewers' brands are available for only a short period before being replaced by others, which, of course, is a mixed blessing – a further enhancement of choice for some, but an annoyance for the drinker who takes a liking to a particular brand only to find it gone on his next visit to the pub. The only pubs where choice is routinely restricted, at least as far as ales are concerned, are those owned by local and regional brewers. In such pubs, although there may be a number of ales available, none of them are likely to have come from other brewers.

It seems to the authors that whatever changes have occurred in the choice of draught beer in the last 20 years cannot be fully attributed to the Beer Orders. Other factors have had a role, notably the favourable excise duty regime enjoyed by microbrewers. But the severing of the vertical link between production and retail for many pubs and the fillip provided by the guest beer provision, both brought about by the Orders, were clearly helpful too. Consumers responded positively to wider choice and more pub owners came to see the advantages in meeting that demand.

Notes

1. Monopolies and Mergers Commission (MMC), *Scottish & Newcastle Breweries PLC and Matthew Brown PLC: A Report on the Proposed Merger*, Cmnd 9645 (1985), Table 2.7.
2. British Beer & Pub Association, *Statistical Handbook*; authors' calculations.
3. MMC, *The Supply of Beer: A Report on the Supply of Beer for Retail Sale in the United Kingdom*, Cm 651 (1989), para. 1.32.
4. Brewers & Licensed Retailers Association, "The Case for the Renewal of the Block Exemption Regulation 1984/83: The Need for Property Ties" (April 1996), Annex 4, Graham Bannock & Partners Ltd., "The Distribution Economics of Beer" (February 1996).
5. T Keyworth, H Lawton Smith and G Yarrow, "The Effects of Regulation in the UK Beer Market", Regulatory Policy Research Centre, Hertford College, Oxford (January 1994), p. 28.
6. M Slade, "Beer and the Ties: Did Divestiture of Brewery-Owned Public Houses Lead to Higher Prices?" *The Economic Journal*, 108 (1998).

7 G Yarrow, "Opinion on the Likely Effects of Regulation of the Beer Market", 26 April 1990.
8 Office of Fair Trading, *The Supply of Beer: A Report on the Review of the Beer Orders by the Former Director General of Fair Trading, Mr John Bridgeman*, OFT317 (2000), para. 4.5.
9 *Ibid.*, Annexe E, para. 16.
10 *Ibid.*, Annexe E, para. 88.
11 Business and Enterprise Committee Seventh Report of Session 2008–09, *Pub Companies*, HC 26-1, para. 30, Fig. 2.
12 MMC, *The Supply of Beer: A Report on the Supply of Beer for Retail Sale in the United Kingdom*, Cm 651 (1989), paras. 12.57–58.

17
The Beer Market

Collapse in on-trade beer sales

Between the year preceding the Monopolies and Mergers Commission (MMC) inquiry and the year in which it was completed, that is, between 1985 and 1989, the UK beer market had grown, without interruption, by a little under 6 per cent. As referred to in the previous chapter, however, and as shown in Figure 17.1, between 1989 – the year in which the Beer Orders were made – and 2009 volumes fell by over 28 per cent.

Figure 17.1 UK Beer Sales, 1989–2009

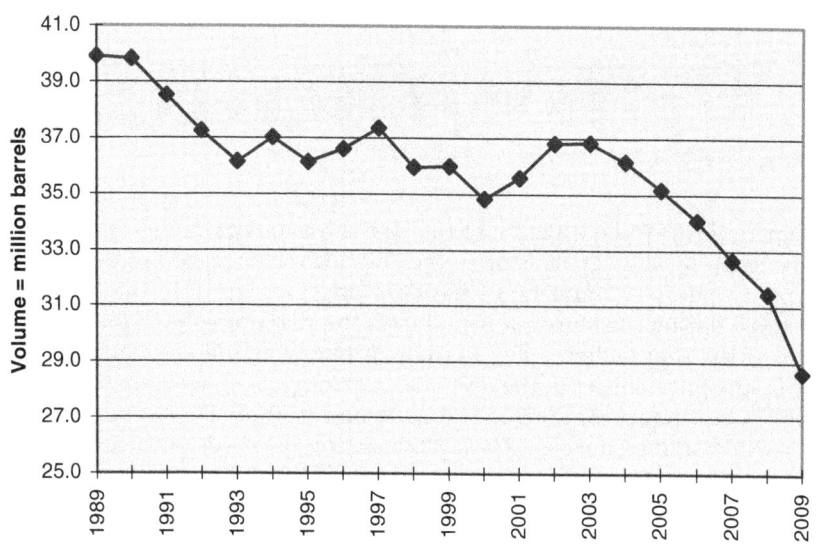

Source: HM Revenue and Customs.

The factors underlying this decline are manifold, and include a drop in the number of people aged 15–24 (beer consumption is traditionally higher among younger people), the inexorable decline of manufacturing industry, health concerns, the move towards going out in the evening to eat rather than to drink, the reduction in the number of pubs and clubs, and the explosion in the popularity of wine amongst all age groups.

The remarkable feature of the 28 per cent decline in beer consumption between 1989 and 2009 is that, as illustrated in Figure 17.2, it consisted of an astonishing drop of 53 per cent in the on-trade (pubs and clubs), partly offset by an even greater increase – 77 per cent – in the take-home trade.

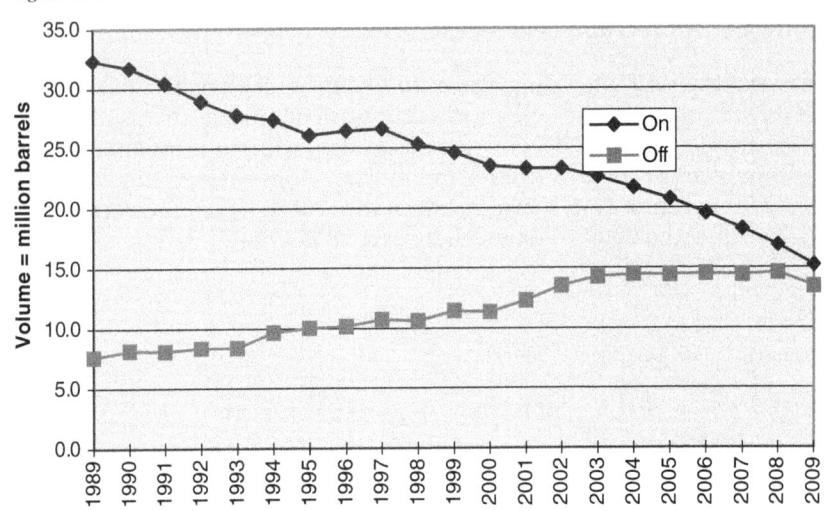

Figure 17.2 Beer Sales in On- and Off-Trade Channels, 1989–2009

Sources: HM Revenue and Customs; British Beer & Pub Association.

There seems to be little doubt that the most important factor exerting downward pressure on demand in the on-trade – as suggested by a comparison of Figures 17.2 and 17.3 – has been price. As shown in the previous chapter, during the four-year period from the year preceding implementation of the Beer Orders, 1989, to the year following full implementation, 1993, the price of beer in the on-trade, excluding taxes, went up by 16 per cent in real terms. By 2009 it had gone up by 50 per cent in real terms. Academic studies have concluded that rising prices in pubs have been caused – *inter alia* – by restructuring costs within the industry, the separation of production from retailing, the general move to long-term leases and the creation of independent pub chains. All of these factors are, at least in some degree, attributable to the Beer Orders.

But as damaging to on-trade beer volumes as those substantial real price increases themselves – as also shown in the two above-mentioned Figures – has been the almost equally substantial drop in the real price of beer sold in the take-home trade. Thus, as shown in Figure 17.3, during the period 1989–2009 on-trade prices, including duty and VAT, rose by 31 per cent in inflation-adjusted terms, while off-trade prices on the same basis fell by 25 per cent. The combined result of the movements in on-trade and off-trade prices is that the ratio of the former to the latter widened from 1.37:1 in 1989 to 2.41:1 in 2009. Put another way, in the space of just 20 years the premium paid for drinking beer in the pub compared with drinking at home went from 37 per cent to 141 per cent. [The 31 per cent increase mentioned above differs from the 50 per cent quoted in the previous paragraph primarily because, as stated, the former includes duty and VAT, which over this whole period (although not in latter years) rose less than the ex-duty price; but also because the higher figure is based on a statistical series which includes only draught beer.]

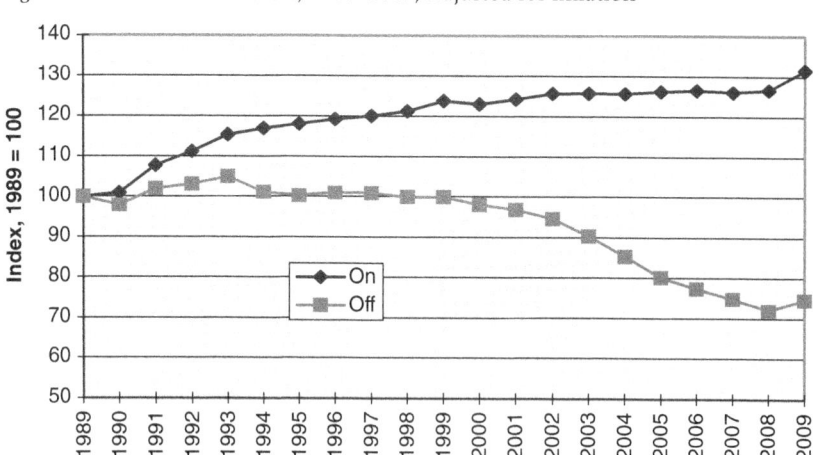

Figure 17.3 Beer Price Indices, 1989–2009, Adjusted for Inflation

Source: The Office for National Statistics. The measure used for inflation is the Retail Prices Index.

Unsurprising as the correlation is between declining off-trade prices and the growth in drinking at home, price hasn't been the only factor at work. Growing affluence has played a major role, partly because of widening ownership of electronic entertainment systems, the proliferation of television channels, and access to computers, and partly because of rising standards of comfort, décor and amenity within the home. The ban on smoking in public places cannot have failed to deter those many customers for whom the combined enjoyment of cigarettes and beer had become one of the main reasons for using pubs. And the huge expansion of takeaway and home delivery food outlets must have played at least a small part in transferring beer consumption from the pub to the home.

Burgeoning wine market

During the period 1989–2009 beer as a proportion of UK alcohol consumption fell from slightly under 57 per cent to less than 38 per cent. Indeed, beer was the only drinks category to experience a volume decline during this period, with spirits rising by 9 per cent; cider by a massive 88 per cent, albeit from a very low base; and wine by an even more impressive 126 per cent. The effect of these movements on the distribution of alcohol consumption amongst the main drinks categories is shown in Figures 17.4 and 17.5.

The reasons for the burgeoning of the wine market are numerous, but increased exposure to the category as a result of foreign holidays has clearly played a very important role. The supermarkets have been quick to capitalise on this by providing a wide range of good quality wines, attractively

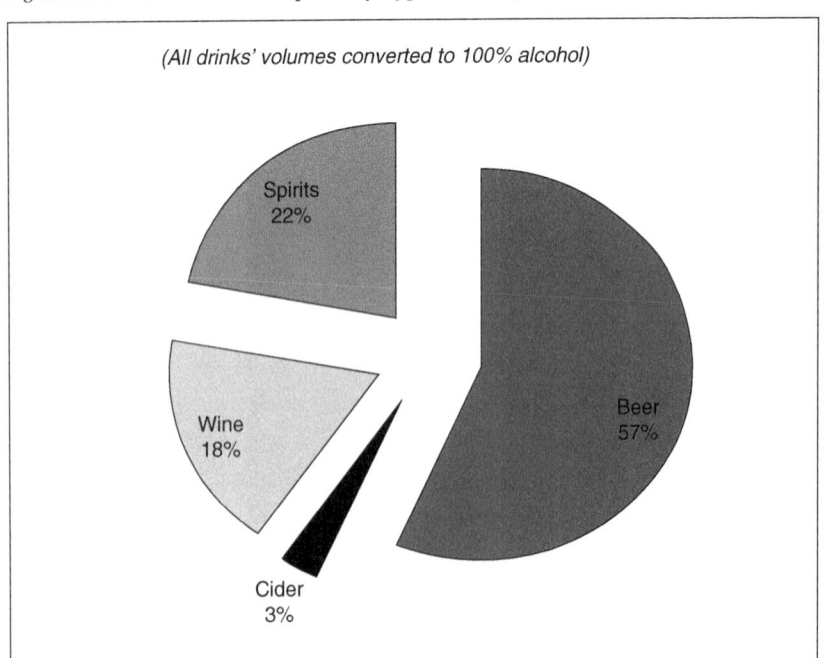

Figure 17.4 Alcohol Consumption by Type of Drink, 1989

(All drinks' volumes converted to 100% alcohol)

- Spirits 22%
- Wine 18%
- Cider 3%
- Beer 57%

Source: Based on British Beer & Pub Association statistics.

Figure 17.5 Alcohol Consumption by Type of Drink, 2009

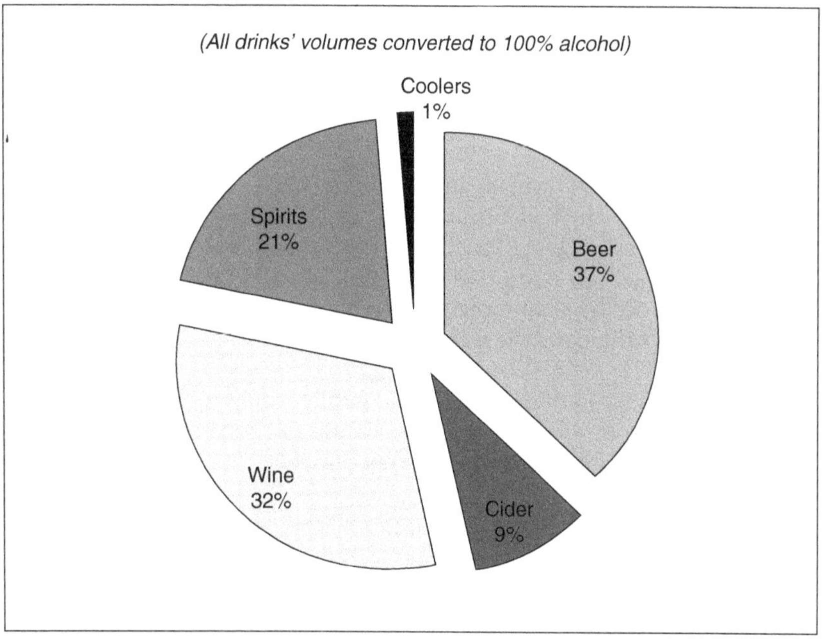

[Pie chart: (All drinks' volumes converted to 100% alcohol) — Beer 37%, Wine 32%, Spirits 21%, Cider 9%, Coolers 1%]

Source: Based on British Beer & Pub Association statistics.

priced and presented, and by removing the mystique which had attached to the product. But while the mystique has gone, wine is still seen as aspirational, even sophisticated, or at least a world away from images of beer-swilling and drunkenness. It has therefore become the product of choice for people in the two segments of the drinks market that are in growth – women acting independently and older consumers. Pubs were slow to seize the opportunities offered by wine, but are increasingly doing so, and more eating out – whether in pubs or elsewhere – has also driven the market.

About one-third of the increase in cider sales in the period 1989–2009 took place in a relatively short period, that is, 2003–07. This was the time during which a major marketing campaign was under way for the Magners brand, closely followed by a relaunch of Strongbow cider, made by Bulmer, which had been acquired by Scottish & Newcastle in 2003.

The role of the Beer Orders

The collapse in the beer market, then, has been driven by the decline in on-trade consumption, and the question at issue here is whether this has been at least partly attributable to the Beer Orders. In October 1988, more than a year before the Orders were made, the Brewers' Society had responded to an addendum to the MMC's Public Interest Letter concerning the options for structural change. Amongst other matters, the Society considered the possibility that public houses might be sold to non-brewer management companies, or what are known today as pub companies, and commented as follows:

> A retail group could not take into account, in the same way as an integrated producer, the benefits at each stage of the supply chain of incremental sales volume. ... The retail group has correspondingly less incentive to sell an extra barrel of beer, and therefore less incentive to offer as good value for money (in terms of the price-amenity package offered to its outlets) as the integrated brewer.
>
> This lower standard of offering to the public would mean that demand for beer sold in on-licensed premises would fall, which would lead to a reduction in the number of on-licensed outlets.[1]

George Yarrow made the point in an unpublished paper that the number of pubs available to the public is an important determinant of the size of the beer market, in that, when a pub closes, it is generally the case that not all the lost volume is recovered by other pubs.[2] And although, as we have seen, the effect of the arrival of the pubcos for several years was to sustain unviable pubs in business, the absence on their part of the economic incentive to pursue the "marginal barrel" meant that, when trading conditions deteriorated, the pubcos were forced to close and sell off large numbers of outlets. In so far as pubcos largely came into being as a result of the Beer Orders, it is thus at the very least arguable that more pubs have closed – and beer volume lost – than if the Orders hadn't been enacted. But with so many other factors having influenced the beer market, it is impossible to isolate this one cause alone.

Pub usage and beer volume are also affected by the standards of amenity and décor on offer – a factor which has probably become more relevant with the improvement in standards in alternative venues, such as restaurants. And some commentators have observed that large numbers of pubs have in recent years suffered from under-investment, attributing this to the business difficulties experienced by pubcos and their lessees. The Campaign for Real Ale, for example, referred in 2009 to the negative effect on pubgoing of, *inter alia*, "reduced expenditure on refurbishment and renovations",[3] citing this as one reason for the rise in the number of pub closures. Many pubs, of course, have received substantial investment, certainly most of those owned by the managed pub operators, but the effect of this has been to put less well maintained pubs at a greater competitive disadvantage. Since no data exist in respect of the total amount or trend of investment in pubs, one can only surmise as to its impact on the size of the beer market today or the relevance of the Beer Orders in shaping the market.

One further factor may also have had a detrimental effect on beer consumption, namely, the disruption caused by the untying operation, following the Beer Orders. This was bound to create uncertainty and anxiety amongst pub tenants and managers, whose livelihoods, careers and even homes were at risk, and it would be unrealistic to think that this uncertainty had no impact upon pubs' operations.

Since the on-trade includes both pubs and clubs, and since at the time of the MMC inquiry the latter accounted for a highly significant 20 per cent or more of the beer market (larger than the take-home trade), it is important to refer to their role in the 53 per cent decline in on-trade volume. They cover a variety of organisations, including working men's clubs, political clubs, sports clubs, leisure centres and night clubs, and the majority are owned by their members. Their retail prices are typically lower than those in pubs, and the gaming laws allow them to have jackpot machines – unlike pubs, which are limited to amusement with prizes machines (AWPs), which accept lower stakes and offer smaller prizes, and are less profitable to the operator.

The number of clubs fell by 20 per cent between 1989 and 2009, clearly in part because of the same economic and social factors that have affected pubs, but also because of the demise of heavy industry, in which many club members worked, improvements in pub amenities, easier access to pubs by families with children, and the growth in eating-out. In addition, the financial background changed. Traditionally, clubs had received trade loans from the brewers, at low or even nil interest, which might have been used to refurbish bars or improve facilities; but this changed after the Beer Orders, perhaps because of the turmoil they created amongst the nationals and because of the accompanying disappearance of many regional and local brewers. In addition, and as the OFT noted in 2000, the practice of

> offering loans appears to be a less popular commercial practice, given the increased competition from the commercial banking sector. Data provided by the BLRA suggest that there has been a trend in recent years toward more monies being repaid than paid out in tied loans.[4]

Other influences

The increase in eating out has almost certainly had an adverse effect on the beer market. Encouraged by improvements in the quality and range of popular catering, many people who in the past would have gone out for an evening of drinking, chatting, playing darts, and perhaps smoking now go out instead to eat. These people are likely to drink wine with their meal, and so the beer they would have consumed on their evening out in earlier times has been lost to the market. Like those who are now happy to spend an evening on the computer, the diners-out may well drink more beer at home than they used to, but, as the statistics clearly demonstrate, not enough to compensate for what they no longer drink in the pub.

Pubs themselves are playing an important and growing role in the eating-out market, at both the budget and luxury ends (the latter manifesting itself in the gastro-pub), and many diners do, of course, consume beer with their meal. But the competition has also increased, through the growth in both restaurant chains and individual restaurants, including the ever popular ethnic Asian restaurants.

Binge drinking, particularly amongst young people, is a problem that has grown over the last 10–20 years, bringing antisocial behaviour into some town centres and generating bad publicity for the pub trade. During the recession of the early nineties many local authorities, keen to regenerate high streets in economic decline, adopted a policy of supporting applications to the licensing magistrates from companies and entrepreneurs willing to take on empty premises for use as bars, and of allowing the grant of Public Entertainment Licences permitting late opening. Very often the result was several competing businesses concentrated into one drinking circuit, fiercely

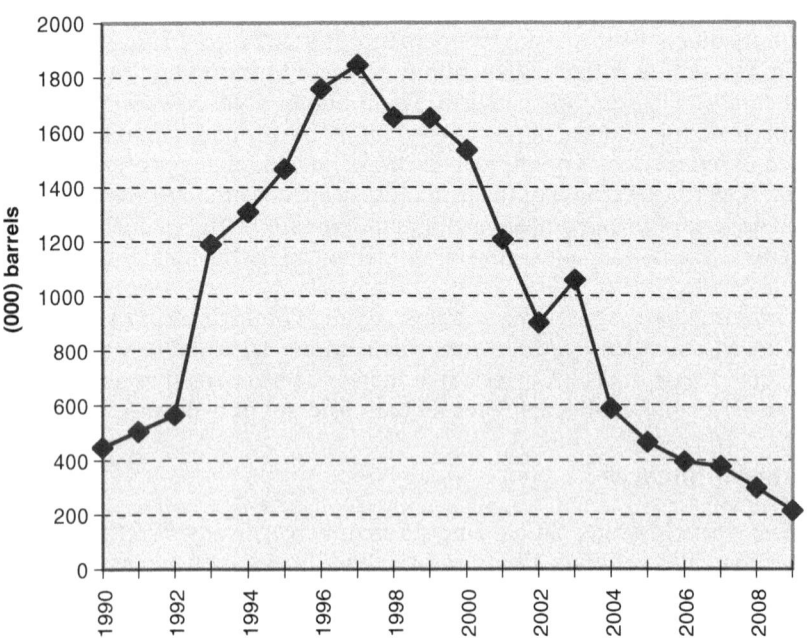

Figure 17.6 Personal Imports of Beer, 1990–2009

Source: British Beer & Pub Association estimates based on cross-Channel passenger numbers and two independent research surveys.

competing on price, particularly as sales came under pressure. Against the background of declining standards of public behaviour across society as a whole, all this seems often to have been a recipe for alcohol-fuelled public disorder. Media coverage of the worst incidents fanned public perception that town centres should be avoided at weekends. Whether, however, the development of drinking circuits and incidents of disorder have on balance affected beer consumption, one simply doesn't know.

A factor previously mooted as being likely to bring about a decline in domestic beer sales was the introduction of the Single European Market, on 1 January 1993, which meant that travellers returning to the UK could bring with them unlimited amounts of dutiable goods, provided that they were for their personal use. With duty on beer in the UK then 29.7p a pint (at 5 per cent alcohol by volume), compared with 4.2p equivalent in France, the volume of beer imported by individuals soared.[5] [See Figure 17.6.] But by 1997 it had already peaked, and since then has been largely in decline, to the extent that during the summer of 2010 the two British supermarket companies that had opened shops in Calais – Sainsbury and Tesco – closed them. Several factors contributed to the decline in personal imports, amongst them tighter control by Customs officers, higher fares, lower beer consumption, more competitive prices in UK supermarkets, and the drop in the value of the pound.

Figure 17.7 shows the combined volume of estimated personal imports of beer and recorded beer sales within the UK, from which it is clear that over

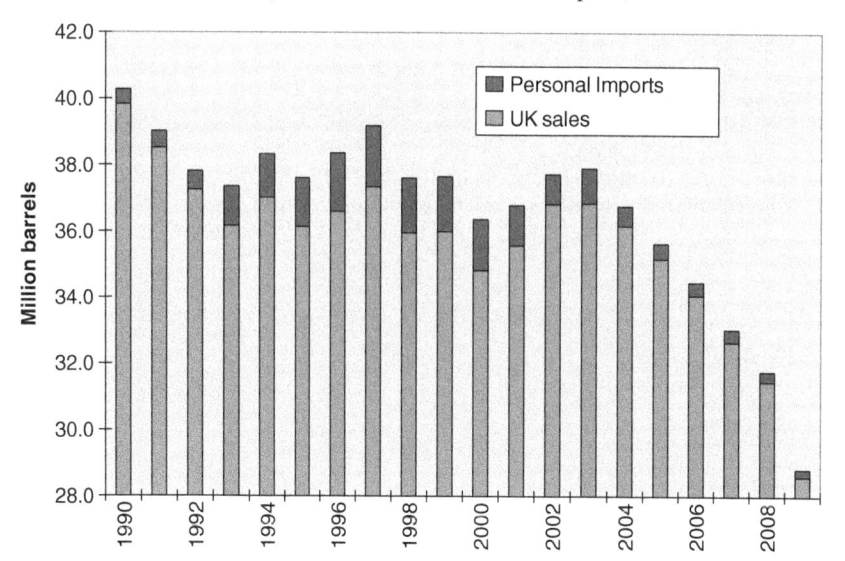

Figure 17.7 Beer Consumption: UK Sales and Personal Imports, 1990–2009

Sources: HM Revenue and Customs; British Beer & Pub Association (figures for personal imports are estimates – see note below previous table).

the long term the trend in domestic sales hasn't been significantly affected by personal imports.

Assessment

By any standard, the 53 per cent fall in on-trade beer volumes between 1989 and 2009 must be described as dramatic. In 2009 consumers were obliged to pay 31 per cent more in real terms to purchase beer in a pub or on other on-licensed premises than they had done in 1989, and there is little doubt that steeply rising prices have played a major part in depressing sales, particularly when beer in supermarkets has become a much cheaper option. In so far as the Beer Orders, as has been shown, have precipitated real on-trade price increases in the 1990s, they must be regarded as having contributed to the sales decline. Further, the Beer Orders have played some part in the fall in the number of clubs, and in recent years – more importantly – in the number of pubs, also affecting sales. The authors have therefore concluded that less beer is sold in the on-trade than would have been sold absent the Orders. But it is obvious too that many other factors unconnected with the Beer Orders, such as the rising popularity of wine, the smoking ban and a myriad of social changes, have combined to contribute to the picture of plummeting sales.

Notes

1. Reply to the Public Interest Letter "Possibilities for Structural Change", October 1988, paras. 1.a.13 and 1.a.14.
2. G. Yarrow, "Opinion on the Likely Effects of Regulation of the Beer Market", 26 April 1990.
3. Campaign for Real Ale, UK Beer Market Super-Complaint, A Fair Share for the Consumer (2009), para. 1.2.
4. Office of Fair Trading, The Supply of Beer, OFT 317 (2000), para. 4.19.
5. Confédération des Brasseurs du Marché Commun; British Beer & Pub Association.

18
The Beer Orders are Revoked

Beer Orders largely irrelevant

On 14 January 2000 John Bridgeman, Director General of the Office of Fair Trading, announced that he would review the Beer Orders. It will be recalled that an earlier review, scheduled for 1993, had been cancelled by Michael Heseltine. In conversation with the authors in 2011 Bridgeman said that he had first begun to have concerns about the relevance of the Orders in the summer of 1996, but that the Secretary of State for Trade and Industry had felt that a review would be premature as more time was needed to see how the pub and beer markets were developing. Then later, when Ministers might have been more responsive to the idea of a review, corporate activity in the sector prevented it, the feeling being that any review undertaken during or immediately after a Monopolies and Mergers Commission (MMC) inquiry would be inappropriate and that in any event a lengthy review could impede corporate activity. Thus it was not until the dust had settled on the Bass/Punch acquisition of the Allied Domecq pubs late in 1999 that a review of the Orders was possible.

The last industry-wide investigation had in fact been carried out in 1995, but in the meantime the OFT had certainly not been ignoring the beer industry. It had continued to monitor the big brewers' compliance with the Beer Orders, and it had also been obliged to consider several potential or actual merger situations involving the national brewers. So when it came to conduct its review of the Beer Orders, the Office was by no means starting with a blank sheet of paper. Its terms of reference were to assess the extent to which the adverse effects which the Orders had been intended to remedy still existed, and, if they were found to persist, to consider whether the Orders were still the appropriate remedy, and, if they were found no longer to exist, to determine whether their revocation would have a benign effect or not.[1]

The OFT's Report was sent to the Secretary of State for Trade and Industry on 31 July 2000, and in the present context is chiefly of interest for its review of changes in the market over the previous decade and for its conclusions on the public interest detriments identified in 1989. The Report's comments on the retail price of beer are particularly important. It was noted that, whilst prices in the off-trade had broadly tracked the Retail Prices Index (RPI) changes, on-trade prices had increased much faster.[2] But, significantly, the Report recognised, at least in part, that the industry had invested heavily in improving pub amenity and that there was perforce some trade-off between price and the overall consumer offering. It even went so far as to say that, in view of the high service element in the price of a pint, a better comparator than the all items RPI might be the service sector RPI, and on this basis the ten-year real price increase was a mere 4 per cent. The sheer range of prices, even in a small area, suggested that price was a relatively unimportant factor in consumer decisions.[3]

Ten years earlier the MMC had shown little sympathy with any discussion of service or amenity, the very arguments now espoused by the OFT. Bridgeman concluded that any detriment regarding retail price no longer required the form of structural regulation offered by the Beer Orders. He further decided that the MMC's concerns about the higher price of lager relative to ale, and regional price differences, were no longer matters of concern, or at least not ones that required intervention.[4]

The MMC had been concerned about the limited independence of tenants, but the OFT stated that the European Commission's recent decision to grant exemptions to the standard leases of Whitbread, Bass, and S&N meant that such agreements couldn't be regarded as anti-competitive. So in this respect, too, Bridgeman concluded that there was no continuing need for the Beer Orders.[5]

He recognised that the practice of brewers offering loans had become less common and that the amount of money out on loan was declining, but in this matter he erred on the side of caution, recommending that loan ties continue to be regulated, to guard against any future market foreclosure.[6] He also observed that the MMC's hopes for the growth of the independent wholesale sector had not been realised, and that in fact its share of the market was virtually unchanged, but he nevertheless recommended that the requirements contained in the Beer Orders for brewers to publish wholesale price lists and not to refuse to supply should remain on the statute book.

Turning to the guest beer provision, Bridgeman declared that the concept and practice of stocking guest beers had grown beyond the immediate and narrow application of the Beer Orders, such that many pubs not subject to the Orders were stocking an enhanced range of ales. With only Whitbread's tenanted pubs [it owned 1700] and recipients of tied loans from Bass, Scottish & Newcastle and Whitbread still benefiting from the provision, he concluded that it had outlived its usefulness and that that part of the Tied Estate Order (TEO) providing for guest beers should be revoked.[7]

Bridgeman saw no need either for the cap on the number of tied pubs that a brewer could own. The number of pubs owned by the national brewers had declined from around 34,000 (43 per cent of all full on-licences) in 1985 to fewer than 10,000 (11 per cent) in 2000, as the brewers had sold pubs in order to comply with the Orders and, in some cases, to satisfy undertakings resulting from merger activity, as well as making some strategic disposals. He felt it unlikely that national brewers would start to buy up pubs again since supply agreements had largely supplanted pub ownership as a way of doing business. He said he was also conscious that the cap could inhibit regional brewers from expanding. Accordingly, and having dealt with the matter of guest beer, he recommended the revocation of the TEO in its entirety.[8]

Before describing the Government's response to Bridgeman's recommendations, it is important to record more fully what he saw as the most significant structural change over the previous decade – the revolution taking place in the retail on-trade. The shape of the market had, he said, changed dramatically, and further change could be expected from the radical overhaul of licensing being proposed (eventually to become law in the Licensing Act 2003).[9] The OFT's analysis suggested a blurring of the boundaries between pubs, bars, restaurants and restricted on-licences. Pubs were competing across a wider front than in 1989, with consumers enjoying much more choice. Many pubs belied the image of "the dingy, male dominated drinking den".[10] More people, particularly the growing number of women visiting pubs, chose non-beer drinks, and factors such as amenity, cleanliness and the provision of food had become more important.[11]

Transfer of power from brewers to retailers

Just as significant for the future was the structural change which the Orders had precipitated and which had seen pub ownership by the national brewers plummet. As Bridgeman pointed out, retail pub chains, independent of brewery ownership, had been the primary beneficiaries of enforced divestment. Most of these companies had signed long-term supply agreements with national brewers, often contracting more than one brewer to supply them. Rapid consolidation amongst pub companies meant that by 2000 the five largest pub companies owned an estimated 26 per cent of all pubs.[12] With consolidation came market place muscle and a transfer of bargaining power from brewer to retailer, as witnessed by the fact that, in contrast to the trajectory of retail prices, wholesale prices had fallen by some 15 per cent between 1992 and 2000.[13] According to the OFT, the impact on the brewers was dramatic. "Margins achieved [by brewers] on sales of draught lager to retail pub chains are zero if not negative", it reported.[14] The manner in which pub companies had come to dominate the relationship between brewer and retail customer was to become a major theme of the next decade.

Stephen Byers MP, Secretary of State for Trade and Industry, received the OFT's Report on 31 July 2000, but it wasn't until December that it was made public and the Minister announced his decision on its recommendations. Bridgeman had proposed that, with three exceptions, all elements of the Beer Orders should be revoked. The exceptions were the regulation of loans, transparency in wholesale pricing, and the prohibition of failure to supply. Byers endorsed Bridgeman's recommended exceptions but decided to retain two further provisions, the guest beer entitlement and the ban on the sale of pubs with restrictive covenants.

Reporting on the decision, *The Independent* harked back to the familiar theme of what it had described as the "humiliating climbdown" by Lord Young in 1989, before going on to argue that no benefit had flowed to the consumer from the Beer Orders, and declaring, "It is hard to resist the conclusion that the power that once resided in the integrated brewers has merely been transferred to the big retail chains, which continue to charge exorbitant prices for beer and everything else that they sell".[15] Criticism of pub companies was to gain momentum such that their behaviour would be scrutinised by three Parliamentary inquiries.

Orders abandoned in their entirety

In December 2002, two and a half years after Byers had received Bridgeman's Report, the Government introduced the Supply of Beer (Tied Estate) (Revocation) Order 2002. The Order was the subject of debate in the House of Commons Standing Committee on Delegated Legislation, the Order being moved by Melanie Johnson MP, Parliamentary Under-Secretary of State for Trade and Industry. She explained that the TEO had become irrelevant. By this time Whitbread had sold its tenanted pubs, so that no pubs whatever were subject to the guest beer provision, and the Government felt sufficiently emboldened to revoke the Beer Orders in their entirety, that is, including the five elements that Bridgeman and Byers had between them recommended retaining. Liberal Democrat members of the Committee opposed the Order saying that both the Campaign for Real Ale (CAMRA) and the Society of Independent Brewers had attacked the change. CAMRA had argued that a new set of Orders was needed "to curb the power of pub chains and global brewers".[16]

The Order was approved and took effect on 17 January 2003. The Supply of Beer (Loan Ties, Licensed Premises and Wholesale Prices) (Revocation) Order 2003 followed, taking effect on 10 February 2003. The Beer Orders had been created amidst controversy and fierce argument, their implementation had caused tremendous upheaval, but they were swept aside a decade later almost unnoticed – to the extent that when, in 2009, the authors interviewed one of the Commissioners involved in the 1986–89 MMC inquiry, he was unaware of their revocation.

Notes

1. Office of Fair Trading, *The Supply of Beer: A Report on the Review of the Beer Orders by the Former Director General of Fair Trading, Mr John Bridgeman*, OFT 317 (2000), Annex C.
2. *Ibid.*, Annex F.
3. *Ibid.*, paras. 4.3 and 4.5.
4. *Ibid.*, paras. 4.4, 4.8 and 4.9.
5. *Ibid.*, para. 4.12.
6. *Ibid.*, paras. 4.21–22 and 4.29.
7. *Ibid.*, para. 4.42.
8. *Ibid.*, para. 4.39.
9. *Ibid.*, para. 2.15, Annex E, paras. 18 and 80.
10. *Ibid.*, Annex E, para. 64.
11. *Ibid.*, Annex E, paras. 16, 17 and 75.
12. *Ibid.*, Annex E, Table E8, quoting The Publican, 10 January 2000.
13. *Ibid.*, Annex E, para. 68, Table 8, and para. 4.6
14. *Ibid.*, Annex G, para. 12.
15. The Independent, 2 December 2000 "Chucking-out time for Lord Young's beer curbs".
16. HC Standing Committee Deb 11 December 2002 cc006–007.

19
Pubcos Move Centre Stage

Limited succour for lessees from Select Committee

Within two years of delivering its report on the Beer Orders, the Office of Fair Trading (OFT) again found itself embroiled in beer and pubs. The Federation of Small Businesses (FSB) had latterly recruited into membership numbers of pub tenants, most of whom had joined the Federation to gain greater lobbying power in tackling what they saw as unreasonable behaviour on the part of their pubco landlords. In pursuit of the interests of these members, the FSB made a complaint to the OFT in 2002.

The complaint alleged a number of ills. Tied tenants paid too much for their beer; rents were too high; pubco support, particularly in tough times, was inadequate; and exclusive purchasing agreements imposed on tenants were anti-competitive. The complaint asked whether there were grounds for referring pubcos to the Competition Commission.[1] The Federation got a fairly dusty response from the OFT: there were, it said, no grounds for a referral.[2]

But the FSB was disinclined to drop the case, and shifted its attack, persuading the Trade and Industry Select Committee in 2004 to investigate the relationship between pubcos and lessees. The Committee received over 400 written submissions, including a number from tenants under conditions of confidentiality, and it held several hearings, at which evidence was given by – amongst others – the OFT, the FSB, the British Beer & Pub Association (BBPA), the Association of Licensed Multiple Retailers (ALMR), the Campaign for Real Ale (CAMRA), and representatives of the major pubcos. The Committee's report was published on 8 December 2004.

Reviewing the development of the beer market since the MMC Report, the Committee found that, whereas in 1989 the "big six" had controlled 75 per cent of beer production, by 2004 just four brewers accounted for 76 per cent. Notwithstanding this concentration, the sector was competitive, it said, noting the complete demise of pub ownership amongst large brewers.[3]

It was, in fact, the seismic change in pub ownership that preoccupied the Committee. In 1989 the national brewers had owned 34,000 – or 57 per cent – of the UK's 60,000 pubs in the UK, and by 2004 they owned none. Meanwhile, the share of pubs owned by regional brewers had fallen from 20 per cent to 14 per cent. Pub ownership had shifted dramatically to non-brewers, or "independents", as the Committee termed them, which now owned 86 per cent of all pubs. Within this category, free houses had remained stable in number, whilst the number of "independent" tenanted/leased pubs, a category practically unknown in 1989, had mushroomed to represent 40 per cent of the total.[4]

Not only had the sector grown from virtually nothing to become the dominant form of ownership, but the pattern of ownership within it had changed rapidly, so that by 2004 two companies, Enterprise and Punch, owned over 8000 pubs each, thereby controlling nearly 30 per cent of all pubs.[5] While highlighting the scale of the largest pubcos, the Committee was careful to conclude that no single company enjoyed a dominant position.

The Committee received evidence from all sides of the argument. Criticism of the pubco model came from – *inter alia* – the FSB, CAMRA, and professionals representing lessees.[6] The FSB described the relationship between pubco and lessee as "the unequal partnership", and suggested that the total available profit was shared approximately 70/30 in the pubco's favour. The nub of the imbalance was that the high prices that lessees were obliged to pay for beer were not sufficiently offset by a below-market rent. Furthermore, pubcos took an unfair proportion of revenue from amusement with prizes machines (AWPs). Pubcos had gained bargaining advantage over the brewers, as John Bridgeman (then Director General of Fair Trading) had noted in his 2000 review, but the margin which had been transferred to the pubcos in the process had "remained with the pubcos...individual tenants have not shared in this market dynamic". Moreover, "the shift in margin has not reached the consumer".[7] Ramming home its negative view of pubcos, the Federation remarked:

> In short, the pubco, an unintended consequence of the Beer Orders, has taken a dominant role in the supply chain, but without, in our view, adding any real degree of value other than to their capital providers. It has supplanted the brewer as the owner of property, leaving little else changed.[8]

A survey was conducted by the *Morning Advertiser* in May 2004, in which 45 per cent of tenants responding said that they would "probably not" or "definitely not" take another lease from their current landlord. The corresponding figures for Enterprise and Punch were even more damning, at 60 per cent and 61 per cent, respectively.[9] Dissatisfaction amongst pubco tenants surely demonstrated, claimed the FSB, that the relationship was unequal.

CAMRA too was critical of pubcos. Their impact on both lessees and the market was negative and it alleged that together they constituted a complex monopoly.[10] The results were unfair rents, business failure, lack of investment, higher retail prices and restricted brand choice. Local brewers had difficulty in getting access to pubco estates, a view echoed by the Society of Independent Brewers (SIBA).[11]

When it came to remedies, the FSB and CAMRA were agreed on several recommendations. They wanted an end to automatic annual rent increases linked to the Retail Prices Index and upward-only rent reviews. Lessees should have a choice of either a tied lease, with a guest beer entitlement and the protection of a statutory code of practice, or a free-of-tie lease, with a commercial rent and lower cost beer. Both the FSB and CAMRA, however, made it plain that they didn't want to see an end to the tie.

The pubcos and the BBPA vigorously defended the pubco business model and its impact on tenants.[12] It provided a low cost, low risk entry to business, offering the lessee the opportunity to build a business and create and realise capital value. The pubco provided support in the shape of procurement benefits, training, and capital expenditure on development projects – approximately £23 million per year in the case of Punch. And lessees enjoyed a greater choice of beers than they had under brewery ownership. Thus Punch said that it sourced beer from 46 national and regional brewers and 35 small brewers. The basis on which rents were set was both fair and transparent. There was no detriment and therefore no need for change.

By the time the Committee had finished taking evidence it was strikingly clear that a large gulf existed between the views of the proponents of the pubco model and their antagonists. The Committee now had the task of judging whether, on balance, the arrangements operated in a way that enabled lessees to compete in the market.

The Committee had received various estimates of the discounts that lessees might receive absent the pubco tie, and they ranged from £40 to £140 per barrel, equivalent to 14–48 pence per pint.[13] The question was whether the smaller discounts received by tied lessees were balanced by countervailing benefits. After much analysis the Committee concluded that "on the basis of the evidence provided to us we feel that the immediately quantifiable cost of the tie is usually balanced by the benefits available to tenants". Just as crucially, it decided that it was not clear that "removing the tie would make tenants better off".[14]

This didn't mean that all was well. To redress any imbalance in the pubco/lessee relationship the Committee made a number of recommendations, centred on updating the BBPA's Framework Code of Practice. It went on, "at this stage we do not think a legally binding code of practice is necessary, but if the industry does not show signs of accepting and complying with an adequate voluntary code then the government should not hesitate to impose a statutory code on it". In a sentence that may have passed unnoticed by many it said "we hope that our successor Committee in the next Parliament will review the situation in the public house industry, in particular whether the code of practice is working".[15]

The Committee made a number of other recommendations, the most important of which were the removal of the AWP machine tie and the ending of upward-only rent review clauses. To the disappointment of the likes of CAMRA, the FSB and SIBA, however, it didn't recommend the introduction of a guest beer provision.[16]

If those opposing the pubco model were disappointed by the Committee's recommendations, they would have been more disappointed still by the reaction of the Government and the OFT. In a response dated 8 March 2005,[17] the Government commented only on the proposal for a revised Code of Practice, saying that it hoped that the industry would respond constructively, but that it doubted that existing legislation gave it powers to impose such a code. The OFT responded separately, asserting that the contractual difficulties faced by tenants and small brewers didn't constitute grounds upon which it could exercise its enforcement powers.[18]

The Committee's inquiry seemed to have been very much a non-event, but as far as the pubcos' opponents were concerned, an important seed had been sown and this would prove to be by no means the end of the matter.

Unequivocal criticism of pubcos in second investigation

In the years immediately following this inquiry the pub industry had several external problems with which to contend. The Licensing Act 2003 came into effect in England and Wales in November 2005, introducing a new bureaucratic regime, intended, the Government said, to be simpler and cheaper for the industry to administer, a claim hotly disputed by the industry. The take-up of the opportunity provided by the Act to extend opening times, although no doubt varying from place to place, was modest across the country as a whole, a Government report in 2008 finding an average increase in trading hours of just 21 minutes a day.[19] The ban on smoking in public places including pubs came into effect in England on 1 July 2007,[20] and although the effect varied from pub to pub, it was generally damaging to business. Antisocial behaviour associated with excessive consumption of alcohol began to command the headlines, with lurid examples making for good copy. Excise duty on beer rose inexorably (and by an unprecedented 9.1 per cent in 2008 alone).[21] For a combination of reasons, on-trade beer sales declined considerably more rapidly than before – by 23.7 per cent in 2004–08 alone – and the rate of pub closures accelerated.

Against this dispiriting background, in June 2008 the Business and Enterprise Select Committee, the successor to the Trade and Industry Committee, announced another inquiry into pub companies. The Committee was chaired by Peter Luff MP. Luff had been Lord Young's special adviser in 1989 and this had given him first-hand experience of government intervention in the industry. He had come to take a jaundiced view of subsequent events, telling *The Publican* in 2009 that the Beer Orders had "manifestly failed".[22]

The Committee intended its inquiry to be no more than a review of the implementation of the recommendations made by its predecessor committee, but the task was to prove more complicated than that. The chief reason was that, as the Committee remarked, "our call for evidence gave us two irreconcilable pictures of the industry".[23] Witnesses disagreed on almost every point, the inquiry took far longer than had been expected, and the report was not issued until 13 May 2009.

The inquiry may have been more complex than the Committee had envisaged, but its conclusions were unequivocal. It recognised that times had become tough for pubs for economic and social reasons beyond the control of pubcos or lessees, and it acknowledged that across the commercial property spectrum tenants rarely praised landlords. The Committee nevertheless firmly concluded that "the imbalance of bargaining power between pubcos and their lessees has produced a system which is biased against lessees".[24]

Some important themes emerged from the report. First, the Committee's analysis of the industry's implementation of the 2004 report's recommendations suggested a less than wholehearted response. Thus, although the BBPA's Framework Code of Practice had been revised quite quickly after the 2004 recommendations and pubcos had removed upward-only rent review clauses,[25] in other areas the pubco response was found to have been wanting. None had removed the AWP machine tie, and a system of inexpensive arbitration was still awaited.

Second, it was clear that since 2004 tenants had become more disillusioned with pubco landlords, and, indeed, that there was now real dissatisfaction and anger on their part. The FSB reported that only 1 per cent of respondents in a survey said that their situation in relation to their pubco had improved since 2004. Frustrated by conflicting evidence, the Committee commissioned its own research, and found that 63 per cent of lessees questioned didn't think that their pubco added any value. The Committee concluded, "pubcos may share the risk with their lessees but they do not share the benefits equitably".[26] This was an indictment that went beyond a failure to pursue adequately the recommendations of the 2004 report and struck at the very heart of the pubco model.

Linked with lessees' growing dissatisfaction was a hardening of opinions on the part of the pubcos' opponents. Since 2004 licensees had become more outspoken and more organised. They were now represented not only by the FSB, but by a new grouping, The Fair Pint Campaign (FPC), a coalition of independent tied landlords supported by sympathetic professionals, which was launched in Parliament on 13 May 2008. The aim of the FPC was no less than the complete ending of the tie. The FSB had had more modest aims in 2004, but it too now wanted to end the tie.[27]

Another notable theme of the report was that the Committee had begun to lose confidence in the reliability of evidence presented by some pubco executives. The pubcos, supported by the BBPA, had put up a solid defence, rebutting criticism point by point, and not yielding any ground. But the report showed that the Committee was not prepared to give the benefit of the doubt to remarks made by senior pubco executives in evidence before the Committee. In a telling conclusion, its report states, "in evidence to us both Mr Thorley of Punch and Mr Tuppen and Mr Townsend of Enterprise Inns made assertions which, on investigation, proved to give a partial picture, or on one occasion were positively false...these repeated slips have undermined the reliability of their evidence".[28]

The Committee's disapproval of pubco behaviour and its feeling that the relationship was unfair led it to make recommendations altogether more robust and wide-ranging than those put forward in 2004. The AWP machine tie should be ended; and again it was recommended that restrictive covenants imposed when a pub was sold should be prohibited. But more important than either of these was the proposal that all existing and future lessees should be offered a free-of-tie contract as an alternative to a tied agreement, something that several parties had advocated in 2004 but which the Committee had at the time shunned. The Committee was sceptical that this would occur voluntarily and recommended that the DTI should consider how best to achieve it.[29]

The Committee didn't confine its recommendations to the position of tenants, but went beyond this into wider competition issues. Reviewing the price of beer in pubs, the Committee was struck by evidence from CAMRA and by a report by stockbroker Morgan Stanley. CAMRA asserted that in the decade to April 2008 pub prices had increased faster than wholesale prices. In other words, margin had shifted from producer to retailer. Morgan Stanley said that in the period September 2007 to April 2008 the average price of a pint of lager had increased more rapidly in leased pubs than in managed pubs, widening a gap that already existed.[30] The suspicion was that pubco price increases to lessees were making leased pubs uncompetitive. CAMRA went on to claim that the pubco market was substantially foreclosed to small brewers.[31]

The Committee believed that evidence of real price increases and restricted choice demonstrated consumer detriment and required remedy. It was not surprising then that it found the OFT's submission to the inquiry underwhelming. The Office stated again that it saw no case to be answered. "We have seen no evidence or complaints that lead us to alter the position we adopted before the Trade and Industry Select Committee in 2004 that there is no significant competition problem in relation to the beer and pub market".³² Faced with this rebuff, the Committee observed, "we are both surprised and disappointed by the OFT's apparent reluctance to investigate whether the pub market is working well for the consumer". It felt that there certainly were competition issues and stated its "provisional view that the tying of beers, other drinks and ancillary products should be severely limited to ensure that competition in the retail market is restored".³³ Conscious, however, that the Beer Orders had had unintended consequences, and not wishing history to repeat itself, it was wary of making any specific policy recommendation. Instead it proposed that the Government should, as a matter of urgency, refer the public house industry to the Competition Commission, thus bypassing the apparently uncooperative OFT.

A few weeks later the Committee issued a short special report,³⁴ which noted two significant developments since it had published its main report. First, it seemed likely that CAMRA would launch a so-called super-complaint to the OFT, and, second, the ALMR was working with an industry group to negotiate voluntary changes in the industry. [A super-complaint is defined under Section 11(1) of the Enterprise Act 2002 as "a complaint submitted by a designated consumer body that any feature, or combination of features, of a market in the UK for goods or services is or appears to be significantly harming the interests of consumers". CAMRA is a "designated consumer body".] The Committee wanted the Government to delay its response to its report until more clarity emerged on these two fronts. The Committee would return to the matter in October, making it plain that it had no intention of letting pubcos off the hook.

Third investigation: OFT still unmoved

The Committee was true to its word, instituting a fresh inquiry in October 2009. By this time its name had been changed again: now it was the Business, Innovation, and Skills (BIS) Select Committee.

CAMRA had launched its super-complaint in July. It required the OFT to fast-track consideration of alleged anti-competitive practices in the pub market which were, CAMRA said, "resulting in higher prices, lower amenity, restricted choice and pub closures".³⁵ It said that unjustifiably high rents and high cost prices for beer were translating into high retail prices, thereby making pubs uncompetitive against supermarkets, causing chronic under-investment in pubs by cash-strapped lessees, and forcing many pubs to close. But, it was quick to add, the answer didn't lie with the abolition of the tie. It favoured intervention to bring about a fairer application of the tie. In this it parted company with the likes of the FSB and FPC, both of which wanted a more radical solution – the end of the tie.

CAMRA might have cited in evidence a paper produced in 2009 by Professor Michael Waterson, in which he argued that, because of what he termed "successive marginalisation", retail prices would generally be higher in a pub owned by a pubco than in a brewer-owned tenanted pub, which in turn would charge more than a brewer-owned managed pub. Support from this academic source seemed to back up the empirical evidence that CAMRA had found at the bar.[36]

As far as the OFT was concerned, the question of solutions was academic, as on 22 October 2009 it rejected CAMRA's case, baldly stating that, "having examined the issues raised...the OFT has not found evidence that supply ties are resulting in competition problems that are having an adverse impact on consumers".[37] CAMRA may not have liked the response, but it couldn't accuse the OFT of inconsistency. Whilst CAMRA was considering its position, several initiatives were taking shape.

The ALMR had set a target date of October for its attempt to "produce a concrete plan for self-reform", but despite some honest endeavour on the part of many, the process ended on 14 October without agreement.[38] It did, however, lead to the formation of a new body, the Independent Pub Federation, which aimed to represent the interests of lessees and consumers, and whose members included ALMR, CAMRA, FPC, FSB, SIBA and the Unite Union – but not the BBPA. The Federation swiftly adopted a manifesto which included the right of lessees to be offered a free-of-tie lease and a guest beer, but with an exemption for companies owning fewer than 500 pubs.

Elsewhere, the BBPA, the British Institute of Innkeeping (BII, the professional body for the licensed retail sector) and the Federation of Licensed Victuallers Associations (FLVA, an organisation looking after the business interests of self-employed licensees) reached a binding agreement on the operation of leased and tenanted agreements. This led to the publication of a new version of the BBPA's Framework Code of Practice on the Granting of Tenancies and Leases.[39] The BBPA said that the new code greatly improved the transparency of tied agreements and that member companies would revise their own codes and submit them to the BII's accreditation body for scrutiny and approval.

Meanwhile, CAMRA, rather than lick its wounds over the OFT's latest rebuff, decided to act, and on 22 December 2009 launched an appeal to the Competition Appeal Tribunal, challenging the Office's decision. CAMRA said that "the OFT's conclusion that there is no restriction on competition in the wholesale market is based on wholly deficient logic, and is unreasonable". CAMRA's boldness was rewarded. On 5 February 2010 it was announced that CAMRA and the OFT had reached agreement whereby the former would stay its appeal until August 2010 and the OFT would invite comments on its earlier decision that there were no competition problems in the pub market.[40]

In an environment of claim and counter-claim, the BIS Select Committee published its report on 4 March 2010. It was unsympathetic to the pubcos and sceptical of some of their claims. Its sympathies lay unmistakably with the lessee. The Committee grudgingly accepted that the BBPA's updated Code of Practice represented a modest step in the right direction. Still, it doubted the industry's "willingness to do enough voluntarily to prevent statutory or regulatory intervention", and proposed that the Committee return to the subject, checking observance of the Code, in June 2011. The Committee voiced other, familiar concerns – the continuing existence of the AWP machine tie and the absence of a satisfactory dispute resolution mechanism. It reiterated its support for the introduction of a free-of-tie option for lessees.[41]

The report ended with a warning. "The industry must be aware that this is the last opportunity for self-regulated reform. If it cannot deliver this time, then government intervention will be necessary". Nor did the OFT escape rebuke. The Office was urged to "look more carefully at the issues involved as it responds to CAMRA's super-complaint for the second time".[42]

The Committee didn't have to wait long for the Government's response. It supported the idea of a June 2011 deadline for full implementation of the Framework Code, and pledged that "if the BIS Committee concludes by then that the Code is not working as well as it should we will consult on putting the Code on a statutory basis". It added that the Code should incorporate both a free-of-tie-option and provision for a guest beer.[43]

The Committee took no more than a few days to react, declaring on 25 March that it was "extremely pleased that the Government...has wholeheartedly endorsed the recommendations contained in our Report. This commitment sends to the pub industry an unambiguous message". The Committee signed off by congratulating itself on its "dogged pursuit of reform for the industry in the next Parliament".[44]

In October 2010 it became clear that the OFT was unimpressed by the Committee's admonishments, when it announced its conclusions on its consultation. It said that the pub sector was competitive and that there were no grounds for further action.[45] CAMRA responded in a typically robust fashion, vowing to keep up the pressure.[46]

[The largest pub-owning companies as at July 2010 are shown in Appendix 19.1.]

That may have been the end of the chapter, but it certainly won't have marked the end of the story. The future of the vertically integrated tied house model remains far from certain. Those who want to see the end of it are organised and determined, but so too are its proponents, who will have been encouraged by the European Commission's renewal of the Block Exemption in April 2010 and the outcome of the OFT's latest consultation.

One thing that hasn't changed over the last few decades is the interest that the tied house model excites in regulators and campaigners. It is safe to predict that this will endure.

Notes

1. Trade and Industry Select Committee Second Report of Session 2004–05, *Pub Companies*, HC 128–1, para. 29.
2. *Ibid.*, para. 30.
3. *Ibid.*, paras. 20 and 23, Table 3.
4. *Ibid.*, Table 2.
5. *Ibid.*, para. 17.
6. AB Jacobs & Co and Ferdinand Kelly Solicitors.
7. Trade and Industry Select Committee Second Report of Session 2004–05, *Pub Companies*, HC 128–1 Appendix 12, paras. 2.8 and 2.10.
8. *Ibid.*, para. 2.12.
9. *Ibid.*, paras. 8.4–8.5.
10. *Ibid.*, Appendix 5, para. 2.4.
11. *Ibid.*, Appendix 26, para. 3.2.2.1.
12. *Ibid.*, Appendices 4, 8, 9, 10, 23 and 24.
13. *Ibid.*, Appendix 17, para. 2.2; Appendix 23, para. 420; and Appendix 12, para. 5.1.
14. *Ibid.*, paras. 188 and 198.
15. *Ibid.*, paras. 204 and 205.
16. *Ibid.*, paras. 61, 129 and 151.
17. Trade and Industry Select Committee Fourth Special Report of Session 2004–05, *Pub Companies: Government's Response to the Committee's Second Report of Session 2004–05*, HC 434.
18. Office of Fair Trading (OFT) response to Trade and Industry Select Committee report, 16 February 2005.
19. The Department of Culture Media and Sport, *Evaluation of the Impact of the Licensing Act 2003* (2008).
20. The Health Act 2006 and Smoke-free (Premises and Enforcement) Regulations 2006 (SI 2006/3368).
21. Business and Enterprise Select Committee Seventh Report of Session 2008–09, *Pub Companies*, HC 26-1 para. 2.4.
22. *The Publican*, 5 November 2009.
23. Business and Enterprise Select Committee Seventh Report of Session 2008–09, *Pub Companies*, HC 26-1, Summary, p. 1.
24. *Ibid.*, Conclusions and recommendations para. 1.
25. *Ibid.*, para. 25.
26. *Ibid.*, paras. 27, 129 and 133.
27. Business and Enterprise Select Committee Seventh Report of Session 2008–09, *Pub Companies*, HC 26-1, memorandum submitted by the FSB – Conclusion.
28. *Ibid.*, para. 9.
29. *Ibid.*, paras. 47, 54, 103, 176 and 138–9.
30. Morgan Stanley, "Leisure and Hotels, Leased Pubcos: Avoid", September 2008.
31. Business and Enterprise Select Committee Seventh Report of Session 2008–09, *Pub Companies*, HC 26-1, paras. 162, 246 and 251.
32. OFT submission to Business and Enterprise Select Committee, 12 November 2008, para. 17.
33. Business and Enterprise Select Committee Seventh Report of Session 2008–09, *Pub Companies*, HC 26-1 para. 174 and Conclusions and recommendations, para. 33.

34 Business and Enterprise Select Committee Third Special Report of Session 2008–09, *Pub Companies*, HC 798 (2009).
35 The Campaign for Real Ale (CAMRA) press release "Super-Complaint prompts OFT Probe into Pub Market – CAMRA Demands a 'Fair Share' for Consumers", 24 July 2009.
36 M Waterson, *Beer – The Ties That Bind*, Warwick Economic Research Papers No. 930, University of Warwick (2009).
37 OFT press release "OFT publishes response to CAMRA super-complaint", 22 October 2009.
38 Business, Innovation and Skills Select Committee Fifth Report of Session 2009–10, *Pub Companies: follow-up*, HC138 paras. 12–13.
39 British Beer & Pub Association press release "Pub Industry Framework Code of Practice", 21 January 2010.
40 CAMRA press release "OFT Re-Opens Inquiry Into UK Pubs Market", 5 February 2010; OFT press release "OFT Opens Consultation on CAMRA Super-Complaint Decision", 5 February 2010.
41 Business, Innovation and Skills Select Committee Fifth Report of Session 2009–10, *Pub Companies: Follow-up*, HC 138 Introduction, paras. 3, 5, 8 and 153.
42 *Ibid.*, paras. 158 and 160.
43 Department of Business, Innovation and Skills *Business, Innovation and Skills Select Committee Follow-up Report on Pub Companies 2009–10: Government Response*, 18 March 2010.
44 Business, Innovation and Skills Committee Eighth Report of Session 2009–10, *Pub Companies: Follow-up: Government Response to the Committee's Fifth Report of Session 2009–10*, HC 503 paras. 3, 5 and 7.
45 OFT press release "OFT Announces Outcome of CAMRA Super-Complaint Consultation", 14 October 2010.
46 CAMRA press release "CAMRA Vows to Keep Up Pressure to Secure Reform of the Beer Tie", 14 October 2010.

20
Summary and Conclusions

The warning signals

Among the stream of official inquiries into the brewing industry in the 20 years preceding the 1986–89 investigation, the Monopolies Commission's 1969 *Report on the Supply of Beer* was the only one which had explicitly been concerned with the industry's operational structure. And it is hard to overstate the significance of the authorities' failure to act on that Report's sole recommendation, namely, that because the licensing system inhibited competition by restricting new entry, it should be substantially relaxed. The result was that one regulatory inquiry after another into the brewers, whatever its specific subject, referred disapprovingly to the tied house system, thereby creating growing – and ultimately irresistible – pressure for reform of the industry.

Nor was it difficult in 1985 for the authorities to identify what appeared to be anti-competitive features of the industry's *modus operandi*. For example, the freedom given to pub tenants by European legislation to buy non-beer products from a supplier of their choice was commonly nullified by more or less subtle pressure from their brewer-landlord. The Government's suggestion that companies should sell each other's draught ales had been successfully resisted by the industry. Many brewers were willing to supply independent wholesalers only with the smaller keg sizes, refused to allow them to collect from the brewery in bulk, imposed conditions in respect of whom they could sell to, and offered smaller discounts than to the brewers' own retail customers. Access to brewers' pubs by independent suppliers of non-beer products and by overseas brewers was severely constrained. And, against a weak market for beer throughout the first half of the eighties, the brewers had been raising prices faster than inflation, often at the same time as their competitors and by the same amount, and during some periods as frequently as at quarterly intervals.

It is true that the brewers had a duty to their shareholders to maximise profits, and that it was not unreasonable for them to believe that that aim would be achieved by maintaining the *status quo*. Those companies also owed it to their shareholders, however, to protect their long-term interests, and it is arguable – and, indeed, with the benefit of hindsight almost beyond dispute – that by ignoring the recurring warning signals coming from government they failed in this duty. Not only the 1969 inquiry but no fewer than four Price Commission investigations in the seventies and a Monopolies and Mergers Commission (MMC) report in 1981 all explicitly criticised the tied house system.

Yet, instead of attempting to get on the front foot by promoting the benefits of the system amongst legislators, regulators and the media, the industry's main response was to complain about the number of times it was being investigated. The Brewers' Society did also publicly express its concerns over alcohol abuse, and, indeed, launched several educational and research initiatives. Since, however, one of its solutions to the problem of alcohol abuse was to restrict the growth in licences to sell alcohol, such concern was unsurprisingly not always seen as wholly disinterested.

At the same time, one of the features of the Thatcher Government – as miners, printers and members of the Stock Exchange all discovered – was a detestation of what it saw as vested interests and restrictive practices. And if the brewers thought that their donations to the Conservative party would buy them influence, they should already have been disabused of such a notion by the increase of over 140 per cent in beer duty which had occurred between 1979, the year the Conservatives came to power, and 1985.

It is hardly surprising, then, that when Guinness complained to the MMC and then to the Office of Fair Trading (OFT) in 1985 about the inaccessibility of the brewers' tied pubs, it received a sympathetic hearing. Indeed, on reading the briefing note supplied by an OFT official to Sir Gordon Borrie in connection with his speech in December 1985 ("DG's Leicester speech: Line to take"), it is hard not to conclude that minds were by that time already made up. Thus the note began with the words, "The Director General is seriously thinking of referring *the monopoly in the brewing industry* [authors' italics] to the MMC" – which are hardly the words of someone with an open mind. Nor did the subsequent letter from the OFT to the Campaign for Real Ale (CAMRA), in which an official requested the latter's views on how the tied house system was affecting competition, and on how it might be ended, suggest a neutral attitude on the part of competition officials. Even more objectionable – indeed, improper – was the OFT's July 1986 letter apprising CAMRA of the potentially price sensitive information that the supply of beer was going to be referred to the MMC, probably on 4 August, and that the OFT would ensure that CAMRA's submission on Grand Met would be passed to the MMC.

"A battle of ideas played out in public"

Three of the six Commissioners who comprised the beer inquiry panel had already participated in at least one earlier investigation into the brewing industry, but the Chairman, Dick Smethurst, had served on two, namely, *Full-Line Forcing and Tie-In Sales* (1981) and the Scottish & Newcastle (S&N) bid for Matthew Brown (1985). The first of these two panels, while admitting that the tied house system was outside its terms of reference, had nevertheless drawn attention to its significance from the point of view of the public interest. The second had included the encomium by former brewing industry doyen, Charles Tidbury, in favour of the regional brewers. During the beer inquiry Smethurst also became Chairman of the panel examining the Elders bid for S&N, which was found to be likely to have serious adverse effects on competition in the industry.

An interesting aspect of the beer inquiry was that it brought together in opposition several graduates and members of the academic staff of Oxford University. Smethurst himself was a fellow of Worcester College, while another member of the panel, Leif Mills, had been at Balliol, as had Robin Aaronson, the MMC's senior economic adviser. Ranged against them, the Brewers' Society team included George Yarrow, fellow of Hertford College; John Vickers, fellow of Nuffield; Jeremy Hardie, an erstwhile fellow of Keble (and a former Deputy Chairman of the MMC); and Derek Morris, a fellow of Oriel. The Brewers' Society's team was, in fact, essentially Oxford's internationally respected Industrial Economics Research Group. Jeremy Lever, the distinguished legal practitioner in European Union and competition matters, who represented the brewers before the MMC, was a fellow of All Souls. Twenty years later Yarrow was, only half-jokingly, to characterise the affair as a battle of ideas played out in public amongst Oxford academics, and, indeed, a former senior brewing executive has recalled forming the impression that Smethurst regarded the hearings, first and foremost, as a stimulating intellectual challenge.

There is still disagreement as to whether the brewers were wise to present a united front to the MMC. Tony Portno, a former director of Bass, is one who believes the industry was wrong to do so. As he eloquently put it in a note to the authors, "Although the brewing industry was very competitive, sometimes aggressively so, the manner in which it chose to respond to the MMC with a single voice through its trade organisation could well have implied the contrary. That virtually the entire industry appeared to sing from the same song sheet must have added very considerably to the MMC's suspicions that the industry was not fully competitive but was more in the nature of a cosy carve-up. I believe that the decision to respond in that way could well have been a major error." Courage evidently not only concurred with this view but thus informed the MMC, who reported that, "Moreover, Courage was concerned that the industry had chosen to project itself as clubbing together to handle what it perhaps understandably perceived to be a threat to its future well-being by making a 'consensus submission'."[1] Whether Courage expected this view to be reported is debatable.

Others felt that, as the industry was under attack, it made sense to respond as an industry; that pooling resources enabled them to hire the best advisers and legal team; and that individual hearings would have brought a risk of differences emerging and being used against them (although individual hearings took place anyway). One intuitively feels that the appearance of a phalanx of highly paid executives and lawyers, backed up by a team of leading economists, and all laden with documents, would not have conveyed a desirable impression. But it must be said that two of the Commissioners, Mills and Bob Young, have told the authors that in their opinion the brewers' case was not compromised by the manner in which it was presented.

Important evidence disregarded

Having been convened in August 1986, the MMC spent over a year fact-finding, and in December 1987 it announced that it had provisionally concluded that a complex monopoly existed within the brewing industry, but no scale monopoly. This finding was based on the arguments that the brewers conducted their business in a similar manner and that by tying the licensees of their pubs and their free trade loan customers for supplies of beer they were acting in such a way as to "prevent, restrict or distort competition" (Fair Trading Act 1973). The Brewers' Society contended that for a complex monopoly to be found to exist it must be shown that competition was actually diminished by the ways in which business was carried on. And George Yarrow, one of the economists retained by the Society, observed that, on the basis of the MMC interpretation, any businesses together supplying more than 25 per cent of a market, which employed vertical trading arrangements, were guilty of operating a complex monopoly.[2] Stephen Cox, who became CAMRA's Campaigns Director in 1989, took a rather more cynical view, writing in 1992 that the term complex monopoly was "so loosely defined in the Fair Trading Act that it could be summarised as 'a situation where the MMC doesn't like what it sees'".[3] In any case, the outcome of this somewhat abstruse debate between the Brewers' Society and the MMC was that the latter confirmed its finding of a complex monopoly.

This finding hadn't in itself implied any detriment to the public interest, but had been a necessary prelude to allowing the MMC to investigate the question of whether the business practices in question did indeed give rise to detriments. This pre-condition having been satisfied, the MMC set about establishing whether the brewers were exploiting the monopoly situation and whether this situation operated against the public interest. A little over a year later the Commission produced its Report, together with the Note of Dissent by Mills, citing 11 facts which operated – or might be expected to operate – against the public interest.

Chapter 12 of the Report – Conclusions – began with an 18-page explication of the Commission's grounds for finding the 11 detriments, which was followed by just one page devoted to "Countervailing benefits". This in turn consisted of a very brief mention of part of the brewers' case for maintaining the *status quo*, with no comment at all from the Report's authors, together with further criticism of the industry's operations. The Commissioners' contention that the benefits of the existing structure of the industry were "significantly outweighed by the detriments"[4] was certainly true in terms of the amount of printing ink expended.

In this same section the Report briefly referred to the three surveys which had been commissioned by the Brewers' Society, and whose validity and conclusions the Commissioners dismissed. One of the Brewers' Society's surveys showed that the ratio of on-trade to take-home beer prices was substantially lower in the UK than in the US, West Germany, France, Italy or Belgium; another demonstrated a preference among international travellers for British pubs over foreign bars; while the third testified to the overall superiority of British pubs in terms of amenity, product choice and value for money. None of the detailed findings of these surveys appeared in the Report's Conclusions, but were relegated to an Appendix.[5]

It was shown in the same Appendix, and mentioned in the body of the Report, that on-trade beer prices were lower in the UK than in most major European markets, but, again, this seemingly not unimportant fact didn't make it into the Conclusions. Nor was it mentioned in the text that those countries where it had been found that the on-trade price premium was considerably greater than in the UK had something in common: there was little or no ownership of retail outlets by brewers. This information could be gleaned only by a close reading of another Appendix, this time the one comprising the Commission's own survey of overseas markets.[6]

The Brewers' Society's evidence showing that the British brewing industry was relatively unconcentrated in international terms was included in the Report,[7] but, again, the reader had to search through the above-mentioned Appendix comprising the international survey to discover that out of a sample of nine leading overseas economies the country with the most fragmented brewing industry – West Germany – also had the highest degree of vertical integration; and that in the two most concentrated markets, Australia and Canada, there was no vertical integration at all. There thus seemed to be correlations not only – as discussed above – between brewer/retailer ties and lower on-trade prices, but between such ties and lower concentration in brewing.

It is hard not to conclude that there was a lack of trust and co-operation between the two "sides" regarding the surveys, which had the unfortunate effect of excluding the findings from the argument. On the one hand, the Brewers' Society was unwise not to have involved the MMC in the commissioning of the surveys, and at fault in not having initiated them till relatively late in the inquiry. On the other, the MMC ought at the start, as part of the due diligence expected from such a body, to have conducted its own surveys. As it was, the Commission went to considerable lengths to refute the findings of the Society's surveys, on detailed technical grounds such as inadequate sample sizes and unrepresentative respondents. Its criticisms were by no means without merit, but they weren't sufficient to invalidate the very clear findings which had emerged in support of the UK's tied house system.

Although the panel rejected the Brewers' Society's surveys, it showed considerable interest in its own review of international markets. Some members of the panel in fact visited the United States, and it is clear from the Report that they were impressed by the important role played by wholesalers there, which they concluded had benefited consumers through low prices. This led them to criticise UK brewers' domination of the wholesaling function and the lack of transparency in their pricing policies. Unfortunately, they failed to distinguish between on-trade and off-trade prices, which, with the latter accounting for 80 per cent of the US market, rendered their finding virtually irrelevant to their consideration of the UK, where off-trade was a mere 15 per cent of sales. Nor did the Commissioners seem to have observed the paucity of brand choice in the US. In fact, it's hardly too far-fetched to suggest that they might as well have been investigating the price of soap powder.

The Report also highlighted the importance of wholesalers in European beer markets such as France, Italy and Belgium, and one has to conclude that the MMC's desire to impose an independent wholesaling sector sprang from admiration for the way it worked in other markets, with no regard for – or perhaps even appreciation of – the unique features of the UK model. When, however, the MMC put forward its list of options for structural change in the brewing industry [see Appendix 5.2], one possibility which didn't appear was that brewers might be required to demerge their wholesaling from their brewing operations.

The outcome was that the Commission's wishes in this matter never even got off the ground. Its recommendation that brewers be required to issue wholesale price lists detailing quantity discounts available to all customers didn't appear in the Beer Orders, perhaps for the very good reason that it was totally unrealistic to expect companies in any industry to make such commercially sensitive information publicly available. In any case, the emergence of the large pubcos, and the ability of the brewers to satisfy the latter's needs efficiently and at very competitive prices, as well as providing an attractive guest beer service to their tenants, rendered the MMC's proposal irrelevant.

The Commission rejected the brewers' argument that improved pub amenities justified beer prices rising faster than inflation, on the grounds that such improvements hadn't been "much greater"[8] than improvements in retailing generally. The vagueness of this assertion was understandable, since, as Mills wrote in his Note of Dissent, "it is a difficult, if not impossible, task to establish whether the price of a pint of beer has increased more than the cost of improving standards and quality of the public houses in which that pint is drunk".[9] Nor did the Commission attach any weight to the related point, also articulated by the Consumers' Association in its evidence,[10] that in deciding whether or not to patronise a particular pub consumers were not influenced primarily by its beer prices, but equally – if not more so – by the amenities, and even intangibles such as the quality of service and personality of the licensee. Social clubs, selling cheap beer in relatively unattractive surroundings, had in recent years been in decline, but this didn't stop the Commission criticising the brewers for all pursuing the same strategy of higher amenities and higher prices, and questioning whether that was what the consumer wanted.[11]

In trying to explain this attitude, one has to concede that it's possible that the majority of the Commissioners genuinely believed, despite the evidence from the clubs, that for "Joe Public" price was all. After all, most of them were probably not regular denizens of pubs (and, indeed, for years afterwards the story was told of the Commissioner who during a fact-finding outing shocked all around with his request in a Liverpool dockside pub for a sweet sherry). In addition, the MMC was generally unaccustomed to dealing with prices that included a service element, particularly when the value of that service element varied between types of outlet. The cynic may conjecture, however, that because considerations of amenity, unlike prices, are not susceptible to precise measurement and analysis, the Commissioners concluded that they couldn't take them into account. On the other hand, only a little over a decade later the Director General of Fair Trading had no difficulty in accepting that there must be some trade-off between prices in pubs and the overall consumer "package" on offer.[12]

As for lager, the MMC (including Mills) could see no justification for the price premium it commanded compared with ale, which it saw as another manifestation of the monopoly at work. It evidently wouldn't accept that the willingness of a customer to pay more for one product than another, on the same premises, was an example of charging what the market would bear, which is a legitimate feature of a properly functioning free market.

A rather odd omission from the Report, though it would perhaps be unfair to blame the Commissioners themselves, is of any reference on the Contents pages to the Note of Dissent. It will be recalled that of the 11 detriments to the public interest which the panel had identified Mills disagreed in the case of five, and, in the case of three others, agreed but considered that the proposed remedies were too drastic. Anyone, however, wishing to read his arguments will find no reference to their existence in the Contents section but will be left to hunt through the Report's 501 pages [they appear on pages 296–303].

The case for continuing evolution ignored

A study of the 1969 and 1989 beer Reports makes abundantly clear that the tied sector had been in decline and the free trade in the ascendant. Thus the brewers' share of ownership of pubs had fallen from 80 per cent to 72 per cent (authors' estimate; the Report said 75 per cent[13]), while their ownership of all full on-licences had gone from 78 per cent to 57 per cent. Even more significantly, the proportion of beer sales accounted for by brewer-owned outlets had dropped from 66 per cent of sales to just 48 per cent. The authors estimate that the "big six" brewers owned on average just under 10 per cent each of the nation's pubs, which hardly suggests unacceptable concentration in pub retailing, let alone a monopolistic situation in the normally accepted sense of that word. The MMC, of course, didn't claim to be dealing with a monopoly in the normally accepted sense, its point being, presumably, that because each brewer restricted choice, the brewers' combined grip constituted a significant barrier to entry, irrespective of their individual market power. The point remains, however, that there had been a substantial shift away from tied trade to free trade over the previous 20 years.

At the hearing between the panel and the Brewers' Society in November 1988 the latter was asked to say how it expected the industry to develop over the next five years in the absence of any changes in government policies. It said, in effect, that it believed that both long established and more recent trends would continue, including, for example, an increase in the number of women- and family-friendly pubs, a fall to well below 50 per cent in the proportion of brewer-owned full on-licences (see previous paragraph), a tendency for pubs to be transferred from the big brewers to the smaller ones, a move towards longer, more arms-length pub leases, and an increase in beer swaps between large and small brewers.[14] This reads almost like a regulator's wish list, and yet as an assessment of the future it was both realistic and credible, the only significant omission, in the authors' opinion – and with the invaluable benefit of hindsight – being that separation of brewing from pub retailing would occur in some companies.

The MMC's failure to request the industry's views on the future until it was reaching the end of its investigations seems surprising, if not negligent. Worse, however, was its apparent failure to take account in its deliberations either of the significant shift from tied to free trade that had already taken place, as described above, or of the Brewers' Society's opinion that not only would this trend continue but other future developments would – although the Society didn't put it in these terms – be such as to benefit the consumer.

Another flaw was the Commissioners' terse consideration of the part played by the licensing laws in local on-trade competition. In three short paragraphs they noted that their 1969 predecessors had called for relaxation of the licensing laws as a means of enhancing competition, and they pointed out that, while there had been a significant increase in the number of on-licences, few of these had been pubs. They recognised that concern over alcohol consumption was likely to inhibit growth in the number of pub licences, and they stressed the importance of eliminating any artificial restraints on the operation of the beer market.[15] And there the matter was left. The Erroll Committee had responded positively in 1972 to the idea of relaxing the licensing system, but in vain; and now, for the second time, the opportunity to encourage competition in a proportionate, uncomplicated and non-interventionist way was to be spurned, on this occasion in favour of upheaval.

The MMC did raise the issue of local concentrations of pub ownership, further action on which (following the pub swaps of the seventies) could have provided another more proportionate and less disruptive way of addressing the detriments that had been identified in the tied system. But having skirted disapprovingly around the subject, the Commissioners declined to make any recommendations – presumably on the grounds that any effective action would have severely damaged the local monopolies (in the conventional sense of the word) enjoyed by many small brewers, with which the MMC made clear it aligned the consumer's interests.[16]

Consequences of MMC's proposals poorly thought through

Given this concern for regional and local brewers, it seems strange that the Commissioners appear not to have considered the probability that, particularly against the background of a declining ale market, the lower wholesale beer prices that they expected to flow – and did flow – from their proposals would seriously damage these smaller companies, causing one after another to give up brewing, or be taken over, or both. The possibility that their recommendations would lead to consolidation amongst the majors, thus further enhancing the latter's competitive advantage over the regionals, apparently – as discussed later – wasn't even foreseen.

Whether the MMC's recommendations in respect of guest beers would, if implemented in full, have had beneficial consequences for the consumer is highly doubtful. Certainly, small integrated brewers – whose viability the authorities considered integral to the consumer interest – would have been damaged by it if Department of Trade and Industry (DTI) officials hadn't restricted qualification as a guest beer to cask-conditioned ales (thus excluding Guinness stout and the nationally promoted lagers). Even after this refinement, small brewers producing unpopular brands would still have suffered a loss of volume in their own pubs.

As it was, they were damaged by another DTI intervention, namely, the limitation of the guest beer right – as well as freedom from the tie on non-beer beverages – to tenants of the "big six". This had the perverse effect of rendering the majors' pubs more attractive to consumers than those of the smaller brewers. Thus a tenant of the local brewer, selling only the local ale, could find himself competing with, say, a Bass tenant who stocked not only the (then) iconic national ale but also perhaps, as a guest beer, a highly regarded regional ale, such as Marston's Pedigree, Wadworth 6X or Fuller's London Pride. A related problem which less frequently – but still occasionally – arose was that of beer drinkers transferring their business from a small brewer's pub to a pub they preferred belonging to one of the majors, who now supplied the small brewer's beer on a guest basis, sometimes at a cheaper price.

In the event, many small brewers saw little point in chasing extremely competitively priced business, which as often as not was "here today and gone tomorrow". Owners of the better known regional brands, however, together with some enterprising local brewers, believed that the opportunities outweighed the disadvantages, and showed considerable commitment to this market, in many cases ultimately building a strong following for their brands. While the guest beer opportunity was thus perhaps not embraced quite as enthusiastically as had been hoped, it was not without benefits to some smaller brewers, as well as to beer *aficionados*.

The other principal benefit that the smaller brewers were expected to enjoy was the opportunity to purchase pubs in a buyers' market, as the majors complied with the MMC's original recommendation that they dispose of around 22,000 pubs. The requirement finally adopted by the Government, that the majors need not sell any pubs but must free from the tie around 11,000, still resulted in thousands of pubs coming on to the market – in fact, ultimately all of them. Research by the authors suggests, however – no official statistics being available – that only around 2000 of these pubs were purchased by regional and small brewers. The reasons for this small take-up were that the pubs becoming available were unattractive in terms of both quality and location; that many local, often family-owned brewers were conservative and simply not interested in expanding (as Mills had warned); that moving into a new trading area would involve local brewers in higher distribution costs; and that many of them judged that their beers wouldn't be popular in areas where other brands were long established.

On the issue of free trade loans, the Commission reversed the opinion it had reached in the *Full-Line Forcing and Tie-in Sales* investigation in 1981, namely, that while the granting of such loans put small brewers at a competitive disadvantage, they were not against the public interest. On this occasion, too, the Commissioners seemed to be in two minds. Thus, "We have no doubt that between the national and a number of the larger regional brewers there is strong competition for the loan-tied trade, and that different brewers may be successful at different times in securing a loan tie to a particular outlet."[17] And it was "a practice entered into by the national and regional and some local brewers".[18] Despite these assertions, the MMC still found that smaller brewers were disadvantaged, and it justified its *volte-face* in concluding that free trade loans were, after all, against the public interest on the grounds that it had conducted "a much wider review"[19] on this occasion than in 1981.

The MMC expected that other buyers of the majors' pubs, in addition to smaller brewers, would be the sitting tenants of those pubs, but, again, the quality of most of the pubs on offer, together with the difficulty at the time of obtaining mortgage finance, particularly for individuals of limited means, meant that only a small number availed themselves of this opportunity. The authors have estimated that around 3000 pubs were bought by individuals, but the available evidence suggests that the majority of these were entrepreneurs from outside the industry rather than the existing tenants. The MMC also thought that groups of licensees might form pub-owning co-operatives, with a view to improving purchasing power, but lack of finance prevented this too.

The final group which the MMC saw as buyers of pubs were businesses, "which will, with the market power derived from the ownership of a large number of properties, be able to obtain beer at substantial discounts".[20] It is hard to think of any other conclusion within the beer Report that was so correct in terms of foresight yet so wrong in terms of estimating the scale and interpreting the effects of what was foreseen. For it seems inconceivable that it ever crossed the minds of the Commissioners that by November 1992, the date by which the major brewers were required to be compliant with the Tied Estate Order, pub companies would own 6000 pubs, and that some ten years later four pub companies (Enterprise Inns, Pubmaster, Punch Taverns and Unique Pub Company) would between them own 17,000.

The Commission had concluded that competition amongst the national brewers to supply the newly enlarged independent retail trade (it was assumed that smaller brewers wouldn't compete) would lead to a reduction in wholesale prices and that this would result in lower prices to the consumer.[21] Certainly, wholesale prices responded to the new market situation. But this proved to be of no benefit whatsoever to the consumer, because pubco managements, judging that there was little to be gained by undercutting what the retail market was self-evidently willing to bear, chose to retain most of the large discounts negotiated with the brewers instead of passing them on to lessees. The on-trade price of beer, which had been rising in real terms during the period of the MMC investigation, was in any case going up even faster, right across the trade, during the period of compliance: in fact, draught beer prices in the pub, excluding taxes, rose by some 30 per cent in real terms between 1985, the last year before the MMC inquiry was announced and 1993, the first year following compliance with the Beer Orders. In the years to follow, as beer sales came under growing pressure, the pubcos' failure to share discounts with lessees more equitably would render many pubs uncompetitive against the managed pub operators, particularly JD Wetherspoon, and in many cases threaten their viability.

As recommended by the MMC, all pub tenants were given the same protection as other business tenants, but tenants were to discover that this protection came at a price. Long leases became the preferred letting arrangement for the large brewers, as they battled against a tight timetable to decide which pubs to keep, which to sell and which to lease free of tie. In this period of uncertainty many pubs were leased free of tie in order to give the brewers the maximum flexibility in deciding their eventual destiny. This meant that, as required under the Beer Orders, the tenant became responsible for the cost of repairs to the property. Moreover, the new freedoms available to tenants, a guest beer entitlement and freedom from tie on non-beer drinks, meant that rents were increased to compensate the brewer for loss of income. This rendered tenancies significantly more operationally highly geared, and thus more vulnerable to a decline in beer consumption. The new business model, effectively forced on many tenants, by no means suited all of them, and large numbers left the trade.

In the latter part of the nineties the pub companies also started imposing on their licensees the new form of lease agreement, and, indeed, anecdotal evidence collected by the authors suggests that pubco leases were even more onerous than the brewers' new leases. The turnover of tenants at that time, whether of brewer-owned or pubco-owned pubs, has never been quantified, but, again, anecdotal evidence, together with sustained coverage in the licensees' *Morning Advertiser* newspaper, and speeches in Parliament – for example, Stan Crowther's assertion that "thousands of public house tenants [had] been forced out of the trade"[22] – suggest that turnover had never been so high in modern times.

A plausible argument can be made that the old tied system had sustained inefficient and unambitious licensees, but such an argument would nevertheless raise the question of whether the changes benefited the consumer. And did the MMC appreciate the misery that its proposals would inflict on so many individuals and their families? It was as well that only around 11,000 pubs – rather than 22,000, as first proposed – were to be freed from tie, and that the option not to have to implement the freeing entirely through disposals – although that's what the brewers ultimately did – was made available. It is hard not to believe that without this change chaos would have ensued.

With an unprecedented supply of pubs on the market, demand in the trade falling and credit starting to become easier to obtain, major consolidation took place amongst the pubcos, leading eventually to the emergence of two "super-pubcos", Enterprise and Punch. As they grew, so did their negotiating position with the brewers improve, and during the long years of national economic growth their aggressive and highly financially geared business model worked so well that investing in Enterprise or Punch seemed like having a licence to print money.

Gearing works both ways, however, and when trading conditions deteriorated further, the poor quality of some of their pubs (the major brewers had initially retained the best), the reliance of their licensees on drink rather than food sales, and the high rents and wholesale prices needed to service their debt combined to produce declines in revenue, profits and spending on pub refurbishment, and increases in financial support for lessees, business failures and pub closures. The MMC clearly cannot be blamed for the very high levels of borrowing that the pubcos took on to finance their growth, which rendered them particularly susceptible to a downturn in trading; but without the MMC's intervention in the industry the opportunity to purchase very large numbers of pubs in a short period almost certainly wouldn't have existed.

Perhaps the greatest weakness of the Report was the absence of any detailed modelling to show how the Commission's recommendations would deliver the outcome it wanted: the final paragraphs of the Report amount to nothing more than a set of expectations. As one Member of Parliament put it at the time, "the most stunning omission from the Report is its failure to examine exactly what effect the proposals will have".[23] In 1995 the Trade and Industry Select Committee, in reviewing the way in which possible monopolies were investigated, used the beer inquiry as one of its case studies, and recommended that all future inquiries should include a "detailed assessment of the result" that the Commissioners foresaw.

The MMC did briefly mention the possibility that, if its recommendations were implemented, some brewers might give up either brewing or pub retailing. Its overriding expectation, however, seems to have been that the brewers, with no regard for their shareholders, would simply tolerate the seriously impaired operating environment with which they were being confronted, and behave according to MMC theory. This meant that the consequences in the real world of what was being proposed were not thought through – a fairly reliable prescription for unintended and unwelcome consequences. Inhabitants of the real world can at least derive some comfort from the fact that, as described below, DTI officials had the sense to advise Ministers to moderate – or abandon – some of the recommendations.

Political expediency and flawed recommendations

Following publication of the Report, attention turned to the Government's reaction. It has been reported that at the press conference called to announce the MMC's findings Lord Young, Secretary of State at the DTI, said that he expected prices in pubs to fall, adding that he imagined members of CAMRA would be drinking Champagne that night.[24] Be that as it may, the Government's ultimate response was to compromise. And no matter how this was presented in public, it is hard not to conclude that the Government had little choice but to retreat from some of the Commission's proposals. First, Young was advised that a Parliamentary majority to approve the measures, in particular the enforced disposal of pubs, could not be achieved in either House. That there was so much opposition amongst backbenchers must at least in part be attributed to the campaign waged by the brewers, who, having desisted from arguing their case in public during the investigation, now went on the offensive.

So the recommendation on pub disposals had to be diluted, and by reducing the number of pubs affected and changing the requirement from disposal to release from the tie the Government defused most of the backbench revolt. The move had the additional benefit of reducing the possibility, which DTI officials – in contrast with the members of the MMC panel – had begun to fear, that many of the large brewers would keep their pubs and give up brewing, thereby leading to further concentration in the latter.

Political expediency thus certainly played a part, but another major factor prompted compromise, namely, the flawed nature of some of the Report's recommendations. Increasingly, it dawned on civil servants that a number of these, far from achieving the goal of increased competition, could have the opposite effect. Exposing small brewers as well as large to the guest beer market, for example, seemed likely – contrary to the MMC's intentions – to weaken the smaller companies' competitive position. The Government thus felt compelled to exempt all but the major brewers from the guest beer requirement – which would now be restricted to cask-conditioned ales – and from the ban on the tying of non-beer drinks (although, as suggested earlier, this exemption was hardly helpful to the smaller companies). And it was clear that many people felt that ending free trade loans by brewers would have had a calamitous effect on social, sports and local political clubs.

There was yet another problem with the recommendations as they stood, and that was Europe. Whatever the merits or otherwise of free trade loans, the uncomfortable truth was that they couldn't be ended without a measure of help from the European Commission, and winning that support, certainly within a reasonable timescale, proved too difficult, probably because of the widespread use of such loans in much of the rest of Europe. The Government also quietly buried the MMC's recommendation that the purchaser of a pub sold by a national brewer in order to comply with the 2000 limit on pub ownership should not be permitted to enter into an exclusive beer supply contract with the vendor of more than one year's duration. Borrie had warned that such a ban would run counter to European regulation, and the Government was wary of confronting Europe, knowing that litigation by the brewers could become a distinct possibility.

One way or another, the Commission had dealt Young a difficult hand, in that it was simply not possible to implement the Report in full. Young's first mistake, as he admitted in later years, had been to say that he was minded to do so. The brewers for their part, with only one or two exceptions, initially rejected all thought of compromise. By the beginning of May, 1989, however, they had privately decided to adopt a more amenable stance – one manifestation of which was that in early June a senior industry executive wrote to Young to offer concessions which he said would be acceptable to the brewers. These were to take effective action on local concentrations of pub ownership; not to compel the regional and local brewers to participate in such action; and to cooperate in a guest beer scheme. This was given short shrift by the Government, which asked instead for voluntary undertakings to comply with the MMC recommendations – which would have delivered what the Government wanted while sparing it a considerable amount of Parliamentary time and political embarrassment.

This in turn was rejected, and by early July Young had decided that the time had come to draw negotiations to a close. It has been suggested that the Prime Minister was becoming impatient. Pub tenants were feeling increasingly insecure. And it was four years since the matter had come on to the OFT's radar. In any case, Young announced that his mind was made up and that discussions with the brewers were at an end, leaving the latter feeling that the consequences of what was about to happen still hadn't been properly investigated.

In his autobiography Young admitted to a second mistake, albeit with a sense of having been naïve – almost hard done by – rather than wrong, namely, in not realising early enough that – as he claimed – Conservative opposition to implementing the MMC's recommendations had nothing to do with the merits of the case but was simply a result of the brewing industry's financial support for local constituency associations. He didn't admit to any further mistakes in this matter, and, indeed, implied that he trapped the brewers into embracing his compromise proposals.[25]

Although Sir Gordon Borrie had urged Young to implement the Report in full, and the latter's own officials were initially slow in spotting the flaws in its recommendations, the fact is that, as Secretary of State for Trade and Industry at the time, Young bears sole responsibility for initiating the process which led to the Beer Orders. There was no statutory requirement nor any political imperative for him to do so, and there was opposition from pub tenants' representatives, the Trades Union Congress, and representatives of the two main political parties in both Houses of Parliament, as well as from the brewers.

The authors do not suggest that Young should simply have ditched the Report, but that he should have used it as a basis for continuing evolution within the industry. There was, for example, widespread support for giving pub tenants greater security and for the idea of cask-conditioned guest beers. And, as we have seen, the industry had offered to act effectively on local concentrations of pub ownership. Together with determined action to end the application of the "need" criterion in granting new entry to the pub market, such a package could have added momentum to the changes which had already been taking place for years, without the systemic shock which the Orders created. But, crucially, Young refused to yield on the over-arching principle of the enforced untying of pubs. And, as a respected business journalist was to observe many years later, he contrived to replace one benign so-called monopoly with two pernicious ones – giant pubcos and giant brewers.

Contradictions and compromise in competition policy

The Beer Orders inevitably had significant consequences for competition policy in the brewing industry. The MMC had concluded from figures provided by individual brewers that if beer were transferred from brewery to managed pubs at the same discount as that given on average to free traders, those pubs would be loss-making. From this they had inferred that integrated brewers made all their profit from making beer; that, in effect, they were subsidising their pubs; and that free traders therefore found it hard to compete with those pubs. Following the meeting of the Commission with the Brewers' Society in August 1988, at which the Chairman outlined an amended version of this hypothesis, the Society had the figures reworked, in respect of the major brewers only. The new figures showed a different picture, but the Report suggests that the Commissioners continued to rely on the original ones. They therefore assumed that, in what they regarded as the unlikely event that the big brewers decided not to remain vertically integrated, they would become pure brewers.

It didn't take long for the scale of the MMC's error in concluding that brewing was more profitable than pub retailing to be exposed. Even before the inquiry had been published, Boddingtons had decided to quit brewing, and shortly after publication of the Report it did so. Within just three months of the Beer Orders being laid, Grand Met announced its intention to follow suit, and within 18 months so had the largest regional, Greenall Whitley, and the smaller JA Devenish. The rush for the exit by three regionals provided hard evidence – had it been needed – that the MMC's naïve efforts to safeguard the smaller companies in the industry were not to be an unqualified success.

Indeed, almost as soon as the Report had been digested, it became commonplace in the City and media to suggest that some – perhaps most – of the big brewers would leave brewing to concentrate on pubs. The authorities, having become aware of this unwelcome analysis, concluded that regulatory policy in the industry should continue to work towards loosening the tie but should not be totally inimical to concentration in brewing. The acquisition of a UK brewer by a foreign company, however, wouldn't be welcome, on political grounds; and nor would any deal involving the largest brewer, Bass.

As the authorities struggled to regulate the corporate activity that the Beer Orders had unleashed, some of these unofficial guidelines had to be abandoned, and, indeed, competition policy throughout the nineties and beyond took on a somewhat random aspect; or, at least, if there was a coherent and consistent thread to policy, the authors have failed to detect it. Of course, matters couldn't have been helped by the fact that during this period the average time in office of a Secretary of State at the DTI was rather shorter than that of a modern football manager: between publication of the MMC's beer report in 1989 and the end of 2001 – during which there was one change of government – no fewer than nine individuals held the post. One wonders how the companies over which they wielded power would have fared in the commercial world if they had changed their chief executives with similar frequency.

Thus the Grand Met/Courage deal was approved, with pub disposals, and with a supply agreement that was actually longer than the companies had proposed; while Allied-Lyons and Carlsberg-Tetley were allowed to merge, with pub disposals and a shorter supply agreement than had been requested. Then S&N was allowed to acquire Courage from Elders, with minimal pub disposals, despite the fact that it gave rise to a beer market share thitherto regarded as unacceptable, and despite the fact that the earlier attempt by Elders to acquire S&N had been thrown out on competition grounds. Bass's wish to acquire Carlsberg-Tetley and Whitbread's planned purchase of Allied Domecq's pubs were both thwarted, but Bass was allowed to acquire part of Allied's pub estate. The Belgian company, Interbrew, bought Whitbread's brewing interests, but having then bought Bass's, it was compelled to divest itself of the latter's principal brands, which were then picked up by Coors, of the US. Finally, the UK interests of Scottish & Newcastle (S&N) – incorporating Courage and Grand Met – were taken over by Heineken, of the Netherlands.

The opposite of what had been intended

Throughout this period compromises had to be reached, and the recurring problem for the regulators was the one explicitly raised by the Director General of Fair Trading in relation to Whitbread's plan, when attempting to acquire Allied's pubs, to float off its beer business as a separate company, with a supply agreement with the enlarged pub estate. On the one hand, he wrote, such vertical integration would replicate the conditions which the Beer Orders had sought to remove; while, on the other, without a supply agreement the stand-alone beer company might not survive, leading to further consolidation.

This opinion amounted to official recognition that the vertically integrated system had sustained a fragmented brewing industry, and obviously sat uneasily with the Commissioners' closing thoughts in their Report, namely, that if no changes were made, a small number of national brewers would increasingly dominate brewing, drinks wholesaling and beer retailing. ("We heartily concur," CAMRA had written in its submission to Lord Young after publication of the Report.[26]) The changes which the MMC saw as necessary to prevent concentration were duly made, albeit in amended and curtailed form, with the result that concentration actually increased, with a few big brewers – but including not one of the original "big six" – coming to dominate brewing and wholesaling.

Before the MMC inquiry was announced, the "big six" integrated brewers had a beer market share of 75 per cent; today four non-integrated brewers – all foreign-owned – have 84 per cent. Three of these four companies are what Michael Heseltine might have favourably described as "national champions": they had the backing of monopoly positions in their home markets, which had given them the scale and confidence to seek to become global players. Bass may well have tried to pursue the same strategy had its planned merger with Carlsberg-Tetley not been thwarted by its own Government.

Some tenuous links still exist between some of the old "big six" and pub retailing. Thus one of them, Whitbread, still has some 370 pub restaurants; another, Bass, lives on in the shape of Mitchells & Butlers, comprising the best pubs in the former's managed house operation, which was floated on the London Stock Exchange in 2002; and Scottish & Newcastle's parent, Heineken, manages tenanted pubs on behalf of their owners. But the fact is that major brewers, far from dominating retailing, as the MMC warned, now own no pubs at all. To the extent that the pub industry is now more fragmented than before, the MMC and DTI between them may be said to have achieved something of what they wanted. But if their aim was to create a more fragmented *traditionally integrated* industry, they failed.

Beer drinkers, pub users, licensees and British brewers the losers

In assessing who won and who lost from the Beer Orders, it must never be forgotten that the point of government intervention in the market – hard to believe though it might seem in this case – is to benefit the consumer. So it is right to state first that this intervention has brought virtually no benefit to the millions of people who enjoy drinking beer in the comfortable ambience of a British pub. Above all, and in the starkest contradiction of the MMC's stated expectation, they have seen a massive and sustained increase in beer prices. But they have also started to witness the closure or deterioration in the physical state of thousands of pubs owned by companies which were created out of the break-up of the national brewers' pub estates and which accumulated unsustainable levels of debt as they consolidated.

Beer drinkers have also seen the demise of some highly regarded and much loved national ale brands, a process which, given the decline in the popularity of ale, might well have happened anyway, but was given further impetus by the takeover of all the major brewers by foreign companies. Thus the "big four" UK brewers now number just two ales – John Smith's and Tetley's (mainly sold in keg form) – amongst their lead brands*, while half a dozen lagers account for virtually all the rest of their output, namely, Beck's, Carling, Carlsberg, Foster's, Kronenbourg and Stella Artois. Similarly, the off-trade would have continued to grow, but the foreign owners' concentration on this segment of the market, consistent with the requirements of their own and most other overseas markets, together with the aforementioned deteriorating state of many pubs, has arguably undermined the UK pub trade. Total beer consumption between 1989 and 2009 declined by 28 per cent, but consumption in the on-trade by 53 per cent. [* Early in 2011 Coors, the American owner of the Carling lager brand, purchased the small cask-conditioned ale brewer, Sharp's, and at the same time started brewing a range of seasonal cask ales of its own.]

Against all this, the wide availability of some regional brewers' brands, such as those of Fuller's, Shepherd Neame, Adnams and so on has provided considerable compensation to ale drinkers, and can be traced back to the Beer Orders. The relatively recent emergence of hundreds of new brews resulting from granting very small brewers a duty advantage has also been a welcome development – although the MMC cannot claim too much credit, having approved of the measure, but not strongly enough to include it in its formal recommendations. The tragedy of this affair for the consumer, however, is that the Government had the opportunity to deliver these benefits – albeit in the face of opposition from the major brewers, and perhaps not without a small cost to the consumer – without blundering into uncharted territory and thereby bringing about the very serious detriments which ensued.

The other principal losers from the Beer Orders were, as described earlier, the tenants of the national brewers, for most of whom their pub was their home as well as place of business. These people at the very least suffered considerable and prolonged anxiety in the wake of the MMC Report, first, as brewers wasted no time in announcing reduced investment in their pubs and issued notices to quit, and then as, over a three-year period, they implemented the Tied Estate Order. Long leases, with increased rents and full repairing responsibilities, were offered by the brewers on a "take it or go" basis, leading to mass departures from the trade. Thousands of those who stayed found themselves transferred to pubcos, which, not being brewers, were under no obligation to allow their tenants/lessees the purchasing freedoms that the Beer Orders had sought to give them. Departures from the trade continued, but with a seemingly inexhaustible supply of optimists prepared to take their places, the pubcos saw no reason to change their business model, which was widely considered to be tilted in their favour. Many of the licensees who somehow survived this turmoil then found themselves involved in recurring changes of ownership, as some pubco operators sold out and others expanded and "churned" their estates.

The brewing companies themselves, of course, were losers. Weakened by the Beer Orders and confused by years of apparent incoherence in government competition policy, not one of the "big six" still exists as an independent brewing entity, and it is probable that by the end of 2012 they will be brewing in just nine locations, compared with 39 in the late eighties. Indeed, by that time the brewing interests of two of the "big six", Allied Breweries and Grand Met, will have ceased to exist in any physical form at all (apart from the brewery at Burton that Allied sold to Bass). Over 20 other companies, including some of the most important regionals, have disappeared into new ownership, where in the great majority of cases their breweries have been demolished for redevelopment. Beer consumption would probably have fallen, and takeovers and internal rationalisation would of course have occurred, without the malign effects of the Beer Orders – but not, one imagines, at the speed and on the scale which have been witnessed.

There have also been some winners in this saga. Greene King and Wolverhampton & Dudley Breweries (now Marston's) have significantly expanded the scale and geographical scope of their operations; and, as mentioned above, a number of the larger local brewers have done significant incremental business by taking their brands outside their traditional trading areas. And a few hundred individuals have been able to set up and sustain a microbrewery business.

The remaining winners are unlikely to have been in the MMC's minds when they framed their proposals. Chief amongst them, at least for several years, were those who created, financed or operated the pubcos. Perhaps a dozen executives from the major brewers left their company, together with a parcel of pubs bought on borrowed money, built a successful operation on the back of declining wholesale beer prices and rising rents, and sold out at a handsome profit to another pubco, for whom the deal made financial sense mainly by virtue of the enhanced purchasing power it provided. Lenders benefited from a secure income flow, while directors and shareholders enjoyed years of growth in dividends and share prices, topped up for the former with attractive share options.

Foreign brewers now contemplating the extent of the decline in the UK beer market have probably come to have second thoughts about the wisdom of buying into it, but they must also be regarded as winners. The traditional British integrated brewing model was not something in which they wanted to be involved, but the Beer Orders ultimately opened the way for them to acquire what they did want, namely, UK brewing and distribution capacity. In this connection it is worth quoting from a paper which George Yarrow wrote in April 1990 to the Brewers' Society:

> With a generosity unmatched by governments elsewhere in Europe, the nature of competition has been artificially changed in a way that reduces the strengths of local producers and increases the strengths of overseas rivals. In particular, the nature of the game has been changed in a way that over time will make it increasingly difficult for UK local and regional brewers to compete effectively. Thus while the MMC Report was initially interpreted in some quarters as a document that was relatively sympathetic to the positions of UK local and regional brewers, the chalice was heavily poisoned.[27]

Finally in this roll-call of the beneficiaries of the Beer Orders come the professionals – the merchant bankers, corporate lawyers, stockbrokers and consultants – who in the prolonged aftermath of the Orders found extremely generously rewarded employment in devising and implementing a string of mergers, acquisitions, corporate restructurings and fund-raising exercises.

The perverse results of interference in the market

Most of the former brewery executives with whom the authors have spoken have expressed the view – with which, perhaps unsurprisingly, none has disagreed – that if the industry had been left to evolve naturally, a weakening of vertical integration, together with consolidation in brewing, would have taken place anyway. Boddingtons, for example, was, as we have seen, already planning to cease brewing even before the MMC Report was published, and the alacrity with which Courage and Grand Met reacted to the Beer Orders suggests that they too were already considering the idea of separation. S&N, with a small tied estate, might well have decided in the fullness of time to concentrate on international brewing and withdraw from domestic pub operation. Other companies would have decided to remain integrated. And although the tied system to some extent allowed companies with weak beer brands to continue to brew profitably, this state of affairs couldn't have lasted indefinitely in a declining ale market, and a number of local and regional brewers would ultimately have followed the Boddingtons example, or been taken over.

But strategic decisions should be made on the basis of purely commercial considerations and according to the judgment of the people best equipped to understand customers' demands and to take such decisions – the managers of each company, answerable to their shareholders. As it was, when the MMC inquiry was announced, corporate activity in the sector virtually came to a stop, and then, following an inordinately prolonged period of uncertainty, much of what should have been allowed to happen over decades, in orderly fashion and according to the demands of the market, was imposed by *diktat*, and implemented hastily, in disorderly fashion, and with only scant understanding of the implications. When interference in the market takes place, as here, on a scale scarcely – if ever – seen in the UK since the great post-War nationalisation programme, at least some of the consequences are likely to be perverse. In fact, virtually all of them were.

The winners and losers from the affair have been discussed above, the former comprising the two largest regional brewers, City professionals, a small number of redundant brewery executives, for a long time the managements and financiers of the pubcos, and foreign brewers. The list of losers embraces consumers, pub licensees and the national brewers. Those facts alone testify to the enormity of the error that was committed by regulators and Government.

How so wrong?

In attributing blame, it is right to ask first whether the brewing industry itself was totally guiltless. The opinion has already been expressed that the Brewers' Society was tactically at fault not to have discussed with the MMC its plans to conduct international surveys of prices, brand choice and customer preferences, particularly since they were likely to produce vital supportive evidence. But, well before this, had there been a case for the industry to answer? Had it either missed or ignored the warning signs? Had it dragged its feet on pub swaps and ale exchanges? Had it been guilty of an abuse of power in – as the MMC alleged – providing financial assistance to local tenants' organisations opposing the granting of new on-licences? The authors believe that all these questions must be answered in the affirmative. Should the brewers have appeared before the MMC as individual companies rather than as a monolithic and wealthy organisation? Over the years, opinions amongst some of the leading participants on this question have changed, but remain divided. Were the problems created by the Beer Orders made worse by a failure on the brewers' part, while the inquiry was in progress, to plan for the kind of damaging changes that were inflicted on the industry? One doesn't know, but the industry certainly managed to convey an impression of unpreparedness.

As to whether the OFT was prejudiced, one can only observe that scrutiny of previously confidential papers from 1985 and 1986 certainly reveals a predisposition amongst officials to establish a case for a reference to the MMC. Was the Report totally balanced? Did it attach due weight to the evidence favouring the industry? The authors' view is that it certainly wasn't and certainly didn't. Did the Report give adequate consideration of the outcomes of its recommendations? Barely. Graham Riddick MP referred in the Commons to the OFT's "dislike of vertically integrated industries", and expressed his surprise that, when consulted about the MMC's recommendations, the OFT hadn't drawn attention to their "obvious flaws". He went on to suggest that "those responsible for the MMC's report were determined to arrive at a preconceived set of conclusions regardless of the realities of the industry and so long as it undermined the vertical integration that they disliked so much...There seems to have been dogma at work."[28]

Did Lord Young himself give the Report the consideration and attention it deserved? The authors think not. It is, of course, natural for politicians to act at least partly politically and to delegate much of the work – both of which Young did. But one cannot help feeling that when the issue in question is of such fundamental and far-reaching importance as this, it should be treated entirely on its merits, irrespective of the politics, and receive careful and lengthy consideration.

Finally, did the investigation and the Beer Orders create once and for all a structure for the brewing and pub industries that would benefit all their stakeholders? In response to this question one can only observe that more than 20 years on there is not the slightest sign of it.

The Commissioners may feel that if their recommendations had been adopted in their entirety, all would have been well. The authors believe, on the contrary, that the confusion and chaos in the industry would have been magnified and the uncertainty caused to licensees would have been intolerable.

Indeed, within months of the Report coming out, more than one MMC member who hadn't been involved in the beer inquiry posed the question to Leif Mills, "How did we get it so wrong?" One is left to speculate as to what they would have said a decade or two later.

Notes

1 Monopolies and Mergers Commission (MMC), *The Supply of Beer: A Report on the Supply of Beer for Retail Sale in the United Kingdom*, Cm 651 (1989), para. 6.39.
2 Brewers' Society, *Report of the Monopolies and Mergers Commission on "The Supply of Beer" – A Critique* (1989), Annex 1, para. 8.
3 Campaign for Real Ale, *Called to the Bar – An Account of the First 21 Years of the Campaign for Real Ale* (1992).
4 MMC, *The Supply of Beer: A Report on the Supply of Beer for Retail Sale in the United Kingdom*, Cm 651 (1989), para. 12.121.
5 *Ibid*., Appendix 5.1.
6 *Ibid*., Appendix 2.2.
7 *Ibid*., para. 5.78.
8 *Ibid*., para. 12.6.
9 *Ibid*., Note of Dissent, para. 29.
10 *Ibid*., para. 10.25.

11 *Ibid.*, paras. 11.73(c) and 11.91.
12 Office of Fair Trading, *The Supply of Beer: A Report on the Review of the Beer Orders by the Former Director General of Fair Trading, Mr John Bridgeman*, OFT 317 (2000), Annex E.
13 MMC, *The Supply of Beer: A Report on the Supply of Beer for Retail Sale in the United Kingdom*, Cm 651 (1989), para. 11.32.
14 *Ibid.*, Appendix 5.4.
15 *Ibid.*, paras. 12.91–12.93.
16 *Ibid.*, paras. 12.126–12.127.
17 *Ibid.*, para. 12.76.
18 *Ibid.*, para. 12.81.
19 *Ibid.*, para. 12.80.
20 *Ibid.*, para. 12.133.
21 *Ibid.*, para. 12.162.
22 HC Deb 14 November 1991 Vol. 198 c1327.
23 HC Deb 08 May 1989 Vol. 152 c698.
24 *The Daily Telegraph*, p. 1, 22 March 1989; Sir Paul Nicholson, *Brewer at Bay* (Memoir Club, 2003), p. 160; *What's Brewing* (newspaper of the Campaign for Real Ale).
25 Lord Young, *The Enterprise Years* (London: Headline Publishing, 1990), p. 319.
26 *The Monopolies and Mergers Commission's Report into the Supply of Beer: The Campaign for Real Ale's Response*, May 1989, para. 1.7.
27 G Yarrow, "Opinion on the Likely Effects of Regulation of the Beer Market", 26 April 1990.
28 HC Deb 14 December 1989 Vol. 163 cc1272–73.

What if...?

Throughout this story a recurring theme has been the adverse effect of the liquor licensing regime on the free operation of market forces in the integrated brewing industry. The system has repeatedly been cited as a barrier to entry and a constraint on competition. Yet until relatively recently the authorities refused to act.

Under the 1964 legislation licences to sell alcoholic beverages were granted or refused by the licensing justices, on whom there was a statutory requirement to consider the suitability of both the applicant and the premises. Frequently, however, they used the discretion that the law gave them also to make a judgment as to whether there was a need within the locality for new licensed premises. In so doing, justices – rather than the market – in effect determined the number of licensed premises in their own area – and, ultimately, nationwide.

Licensees, often supported by the local Licensed Victuallers Association and/or by one or more of the brewers, and sometimes by the police, routinely used lack of need as a pretext for opposing new licences. The need criterion thus became a major barrier to entry to the pub trade, thereby inhibiting competition. An important effect of the restriction on the granting of full on-licences was that they became assets in their own right, providing an incentive for existing owners to protect what was in effect scarcity value. It is hardly surprising that for a long time brewers were unenthusiastic about licensing reform.

As early as 1966 the National Board for Prices and Incomes drew attention to the effect of the licensing system on competition,[1] and in 1969 the Monopolies Commission recommended that the system be substantially relaxed.[2] This bore fruit in the Erroll and Clayson Committee reports,[3] both of which concluded that justices should judge licence applications according to specific criteria – which shouldn't include need. Indeed, to quote Erroll's words once more, "'Need' itself is a meaningless expression which has little or no commercial or economic significance. In our view, the only relevant commercial consideration is that of market demand. A licensing authority is hardly qualified to assess whether such a demand exists, and we see no reason why any licensing process should interfere with the ordinary operation of market forces." Amongst the millions of words that have been written in official reports on the brewing industry, this passage is remarkable for its common sense and the straightforwardness of its language, and one is left to wonder whether the upheaval that was to follow two decades later, and then to continue for several more years, would have been avoided if the Government had acted on it.

Clayson's recommendations, directed at Scotland, were largely implemented, but Erroll's, relating to England and Wales, weren't. This proved to be just the first in a series of failures by the authorities to grasp the relatively straightforward policy lever that licensing represented.

Government couldn't bury the matter, however, and it came to the fore again when the Price Commission, in reviewing the brewing industry in 1977, highlighted the effect of restrictions imposed by the licensing system.[4] The Commission repeated the point in three subsequent brewer-specific reports in the period 1978–79. But these prompts, too, were ignored.

The authors of the 500-page 1989 Monopolies and Mergers Commission (MMC) Report dwelt on licensing for just three paragraphs, concluding that "the present climate of opinion about the consumption of alcohol" stood in the way of reform.[5] Nor, as far as the authors can see, did licensing reform feature in the deliberations of Ministers and officials as they mulled over the MMC's recommendations.

With Young and other Ministers sensitive to accusations of a "climb-down" over the MMC Report, a review of licensing was repeatedly mooted. But nothing happened until 1993, when the Government issued a consultation paper, which proposed that the reasons for refusal of a licence should be codified rather than left to the magistrates' discretion.[6] The following month the Agriculture Select Committee put forward a similar recommendation.[7] All was to no effect. The matter was again quietly dropped.

But this didn't stop determined new operators, principally the JD Wetherspoon chain, chipping away at the concept of the need criterion. In 1992 some case law arose to assist new applicants, in the shape of a judgment, R v Sheffield Justices *ex parte* Meade,[8] of which lawyers were to make frequent use, resulting in licences being granted that might otherwise have been refused. Wetherspoon itself, which converted unlicensed premises such as banks and cinemas to pubs, often had applications rejected, but frequently won on appeal.

In some ways the position was becoming impossible. As recorded by Light and Heenan in 1999:

> The development of the (sometimes ludicrous) methods of proving and refuting need... means that undue complexity now almost certainly

exists. There is a small army of experts who travel the country producing radius maps, demographic analyses, licensing surveys, market research studies, etc.[9]

Meanwhile, another attempt to reform the system had foundered in 1996, when a Home Office report opposing the application of the need criterion was ignored by the Government. The seeds of change were finally sown when in 1998 the Better Regulation Task Force,[10] followed a year later by the Justices' Clerks' Society, recommended the abandonment of the use of the need criterion. With pressure developing on all sides, and with a new Government, with a modernising agenda, in power, major reform was inevitable. And in November 2005, nearly 40 years after the NBPI had first drawn attention to the issue, the concept of need was finally removed, through the Licensing Act 2003.

At the time of the Erroll Report both alcohol consumption and leisure time were increasing, suggesting that there was no lack of room in the market for innovative and attractive offerings in an industry that had been slow to change. And if the Campaign for Real Ale was correct in asserting that greater competition at local level would lead to lower prices and that consumers were looking for wider choice in the pub, then the case for allowing new entrants into the market at retail level looked very strong. In telling Erroll that they opposed more licences the brewers further strengthened the argument. The time had been propitious.

The changes spearheaded by Wetherspoon perhaps provide the best guide to the scale, pace and effect of new entry that might have been seen, had liberalisation flowed from Erroll. Tim Martin, the founder of the chain, opened his first pub in 1979, and by the time of the 1986 MMC inquiry the company had 16 pubs. By the end of 2002 it had over 600, mainly as a result of purchases of single unlicensed sites.

The relatively rapid creation of a business of such scale and power *without* the benefit of licensing reform provides a taste of what that reform might have achieved, had government grasped the nettle earlier. Self-evidently, the opening of successful new pubs across the country couldn't have been achieved without consumer approval (dare one say "need"?). And what Wetherspoon offered was different. The major point of difference was, and remains, value, with beer and other drinks (and increasingly food) offered at previously unheard-of prices, but the chain has become equally well known for its wide, and frequently changing, range of beers. Just as novel was the company's initial policy of offering no music or television in its pubs.

In challenging the *status quo* Wetherspoon forced other pub owners to look to their laurels – something which the rise of the tenanted and leased pubcos, very much creatures of the Beer Orders, failed to do. The story of Wetherspoons (and there were other – albeit smaller – new managed pub companies changing the game in the 1990s) suggests to the authors that if the barrier to entry represented by restrictive licensing had been removed earlier, it would probably have provided the impetus towards the enhanced ease of entry, wider brand choice, lower pricing and greater differentiation of pub offering that the regulators wanted – all without the disorder, waste, misery and consumer detriments that the Beer Orders provoked. A missed opportunity on the grand scale.

Notes

1 National Board for Prices and Incomes, Report No. 13, *Costs, Prices, and Profits in the Brewing Industry*, Cmnd 2965 (1966).
2 Monopolies Commission, *Beer: A Report on the Supply of Beer*, HC 216 (1969), para. 416.
3 Home Office, *Report of the Departmental Committee on Liquor Licensing*, Cmd 5154 (1972); Scottish Office, *Report of the Departmental Committee on Scottish Licensing Laws*, Cmd 5354 (1973).
4 Price Commission, Report No. 31, *Beer Prices and Margins*, 1977.
5 Monopolies and Mergers Commission, *The Supply of Beer: A Report on the Supply of Beer for Retail Sale in the United Kingdom*, Cm 651 (1989), paras. 12.91–12.93.
6 Home Office, *Possible Reform of the Liquor Licensing System in England and Wales* (1993).
7 Agriculture Committee Fourth Report of Session 1993, *Effects of the Beer Orders on the Brewing Industry and Consumers*, HC 402.
8 8 LR 19.
9 R Light and S Heenan, *Controlling Supply: The Concept of Need in Liquor Licensing*, The University of the West of England (1999).
10 The Better Regulation Task Force, *Licensing Legislation* (1998).

Appendix 1.1
The Regulatory Framework

Competition Law: The first piece of legislation relating to competition in the UK was the Monopolies Act 1948, which was followed by the Restrictive Trade Practices Act 1956. The 1966–69 Monopolies Commission (MC) inquiry was held under the terms of the 1948 Act, as amended by subsequent legislation.

This legislative regime was superseded by the Fair Trading Act 1973, which created the Office of Fair Trading, the Monopolies and Mergers Commission (MMC), and the concepts of scale monopoly and complex monopoly, which are defined in Sections 6, 7 and 11 of the Act.

A scale monopoly exists if a single company or group of interconnected companies supplies at least 25 per cent of goods or services of a particular type. A complex monopoly is a situation in which at least 25 per cent of the relevant market is supplied by "two or more persons (not being a group of inter-connected bodies corporate) who whether voluntarily or not, and whether by agreement or not, so conduct their respective affairs as in any way to prevent, restrict or distort competition in connection with the production or supply of goods".

When Sir Gordon Borrie, the Director General of Fair Trading, referred the brewing industry to the MMC in August 1986, he was exercising his powers under Sections 47(1), 49(1) and 50(1) of the 1973 Act.

The Fair Trading Act was superseded by the Competition Act 1998, which brought UK legislation more closely into line with European Union competition law.

European competition law is considered in Appendix 3.1.

Price Legislation – Counter-inflation: Various pieces of legislation restricting price increases were passed in the 1960s and 1970s in attempts to control inflation. These initiatives are described in Chapters 1 and 2.

Resale Prices Act 1964: This abolished – with certain exceptions – Resale Price Maintenance (RPM), the system by which manufacturers could set retail prices. It may be that supermarkets were already disregarding RPM, but the passing of the Act gave them complete freedom to set prices, make special offers, and so on. There has been further legislation, but the basic concept, that RPM is illegal, remains. It has also been declared illegal throughout the European Union.

Licensing Law: Licensing law governs all matters relating to the sale of alcoholic drinks. These include permitted hours of opening for sale, age restrictions on customers and staff, and – most importantly, since no premises can sell alcohol without a licence – control over the grant, refusal and revocation of licences. The way this control has been exercised and its implications for competition are considered in the section entitled "What if...", which follows the final chapter of this book.

At the time of the 1986 MMC inquiry there were several different types of premises selling alcoholic drinks, namely: full on-licences, such as public houses, wine bars and hotels; restricted on-licences, such as restaurants; clubs, both licensed (commercial) and registered (members'); and off-licences, where alcoholic drinks were sold for consumption away from the premises. A fuller description of these outlets is provided in the Glossary.

Between 1969 (the year the MC reported) and 1986 (the year the industry was referred to the MMC) the growth in the number of these different kinds of outlets in the UK was:

Full on-licences: 9 per cent Clubs: 22 per cent
Restricted on-licences: 189 per cent Off-licences: 59 per cent
Source: British Beer & Pub Association, *Statistical Handbook*.

In 1986 – and, in fact, until 2005 – the question as to whether an outlet should have a licence was determined by the licensing magistrates. The above data suggest that they took a more lenient view of applications for a new licence for a restaurant or off-licence than they did of applications for new full-licences. One factor they might take into account – even though not legally required to so – when considering an application for a new licence, particularly for a pub, was the "need" criterion. And if they judged that there wasn't a need within the local area for a new pub, the licence application would be rejected. Clearly, the application of this criterion severely interfered with the normal operation of market forces.

Excise Duty: Although excise duties are applied with the aims of raising revenue and controlling consumption, their impact goes wider than this, in that they can affect the competitive situation, both between brewers of different sizes and between different alcoholic drinks.

Excise on duty on beer is straightforwardly charged on the strength of the product, so that a beer which is twice as strong as another will bear twice as much duty. At the time of the MMC inquiry strength was defined by the beer's original gravity but from 1 June 1993 the measure used has been alcoholic strength. Duty is not levied on beers below 1.2 per cent alcoholic strength.

The MMC recommended in 1989 that smaller brewers should pay a lower rate of duty. This system, known as "Progressivity", is used in several European countries. It was introduced into the UK in 2002, and a description of the system and its impact on inter-brewer competition is considered in Chapter 14.

Excise duties are also levied in the UK on all other alcoholic drinks. Following a judgment by the European Court of Justice in 1984, the ratio of duty on wines not exceeding 15 per cent alcohol by volume to beer duty has been in the ratio of 3.25:1. There are higher rates of duty for stronger (fortified) and sparkling wines.

The Scotch Whisky Association has argued for many years that the UK practice of taxing spirits more heavily in alcohol terms than other drinks is unfair. This argument appears to have been accepted by Government; in 1993, the ratio between spirits duty and beer duty was 1.9:1, but by 2008 it was 1.4:1.

Value Added Tax: Value Added Tax is charged on the duty-inclusive price, thereby creating a tax-on-tax situation.

Landlord and Tenant Act 1954: Because the authorities believed that pub landlords needed to be able to get rid of a tenant quickly if the latter's behaviour was putting the licence at risk, pub tenants had been excluded from the provisions of the Landlord and Tenant Act. The MMC recommended that this situation be changed, and in 1989, as described in Chapter 10, new legislation to this end was introduced.

Gaming Legislation: Pubs are permitted to offer amusement with prizes machines, which accept relatively low stakes and pay out relatively small "winnings". On the other hand, clubs and certain other venues, such as casinos, can have jackpot machines, which can pay out considerably larger sums. Once again, the reason for this is connected with the nature of the pub trade, in that the authorities have always taken the view that consumers don't visit pubs primarily to gamble and that they should be protected from the temptation presented by jackpot machines, and the scope they offer for large losses.

Appendix 1.2
History of Inquiries into the Brewing Industry and Licensing Law

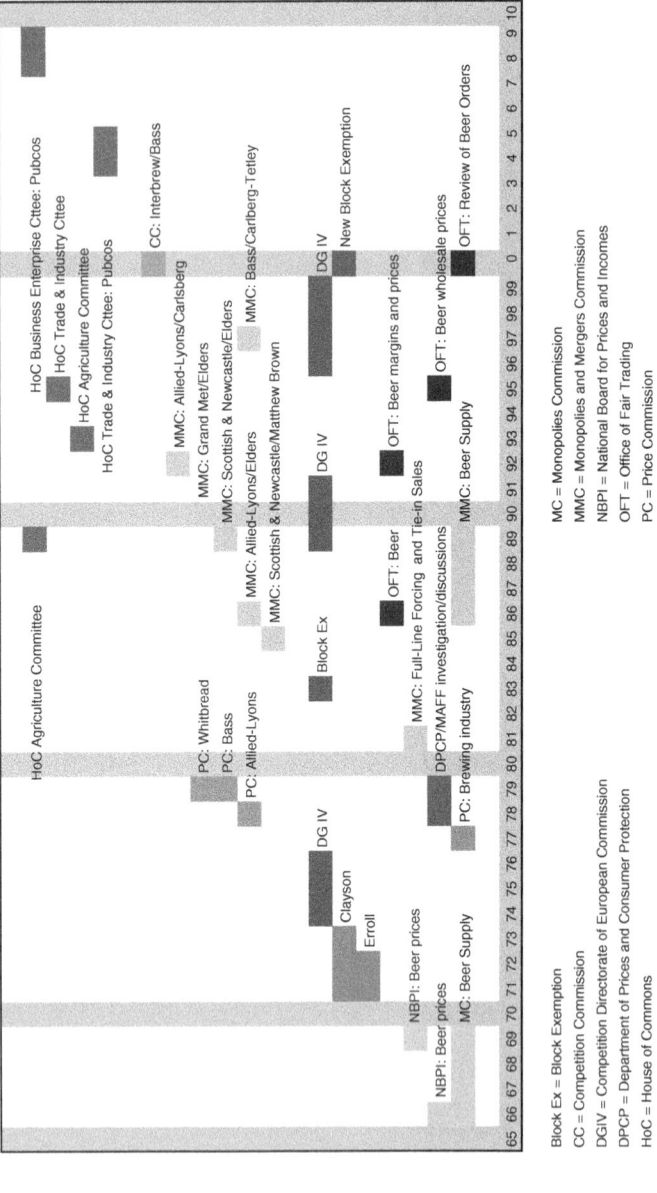

1966–	HoC Agriculture Committee
1967–69	NBPI: Beer prices
1969–71	NBPI: Beer prices
1969–72	MC: Beer Supply
1973–75	Clayson
1975–77	Erroll
1976–78	DG IV
1977–78	PC: Whitbread
1977–78	PC: Bass
1978–80	PC: Allied-Lyons
1980–81	PC: Brewing industry
1981–83	DPCP/MAFF investigation/discussions
1982–85	Block Ex
1986–88	MMC: Full-Line Forcing and Tie-in Sales
1986–89	OFT: Beer
1988–91	MMC: Scottish & Newcastle/Matthew Brown
1988–90	MMC: Allied-Lyons/Elders
1989–91	MMC: Beer Supply
1989	MMC: Scottish & Newcastle/Elders
1991–92	MMC: Grand Met/Elders
1992	MMC: Allied-Lyons/Carlsberg
1993–94	HoC Trade & Industry Cttee: Pubcos
1994–95	HoC Agriculture Committee
1995	MMC: Bass/Carlberg-Tetley
1995–97	OFT: Beer margins and prices
1997–99	OFT: Beer wholesale prices
1999–00	DG IV
1999–00	HoC Trade & Industry Cttee
2000	OFT: Review of Beer Orders
2000–	New Block Exemption
2004	CC: Interbrew/Bass
2008–	HoC Business Enterprise Cttee: Pubcos

Block Ex = Block Exemption
CC = Competition Commission
DGIV = Competition Directorate of European Commission
DPCP = Department of Prices and Consumer Protection
HoC = House of Commons
MAFF = Ministry of Agriculture Fisheries & Food

MC = Monopolies Commission
MMC = Monopolies and Mergers Commission
NBPI = National Board for Prices and Incomes
OFT = Office of Fair Trading
PC = Price Commission

Appendix 3.1
The European Aspect

Competition law

The inquiry by the Monopolies and Mergers Commission (MMC) into the brewing industry, and the subsequent Beer Orders, were not a purely British affair. When the UK joined the European Community (EC) on 1 January 1973, an immediate effect was that where there was conflict between EC and UK law the former took precedence. The European Economic Community (EEC, the so-called Common Market), the European Coal and Steel Community and Euratom had been merged on 1 July 1967 to create the European Communities, with one Commission – the executive arm – and one Council – the political arm, where all member state governments are represented. From the inception of the EEC under the 1957 Treaty of Rome the European Commission had been concerned with removing both tariff and – the more complex – non-tariff barriers to trade, and with improving competition. The Commission viewed the tied house system as a non-tariff barrier to entry (and, more surprisingly, still did so in 1999, ten years after the Beer Orders[1]).

The principles behind competition law in the European Community were not the same as those in the UK, so that British enterprises were subject to two different systems of control. From shortly after the British accession to the Community until the end of the 1980s the Brewers' Society, in order to ensure a full understanding of the Community system, had sought advice from one of its leading competition lawyers, Dr Alfred Gleiss, of Stuttgart. It was only with the passage of the Competition Act 1998 that UK competition law became aligned with that of the European Union (EU).

At the time of the MMC reference in 1986 two Articles of the 1957 Treaty were concerned with competition issues: numbers 85 and 86. Article 86 dealt with the issue of companies that had a dominant market position, but – in contrast to UK legislation, under which a market share of 25 per cent was regarded as constituting a monopoly[2] – the Article didn't quantify dominance in precise terms.

Article 85 dealt with agreements between undertakings, and its first paragraph stated that:

> The following shall be prohibited as incompatible with the common market: all agreements between undertakings, decisions by associations of undertakings and concerted practices which may affect trade between Member States and which have as their object or effect the prevention, restriction or distortion of competition within the common market.

The second paragraph of Article 85 said that all agreements thus prohibited were "automatically void". But the third paragraph stated that the provisions of the first paragraph could be declared inapplicable in the case of "any agreement or category of agreements between undertakings", provided it:

> contributes to improving the production or distribution of goods or to promoting technical or economic progress, while allowing consumers a fair share of the resulting benefit.

Rather than having to deal with individual cases, the Commission has the power under Regulation No 19/65 of 2 March 1965 to issue Block Exemptions, which declare that the prohibition of certain agreements is inapplicable on the grounds described in Article 85(3), above. The first such Block Exemption was EC Regulation 67/67.[3]

Brewers and the Block Exemption

In the early 1970s (as now) there were three categories of brewer-retailer relationships operating in Europe. First, there were those involving no formal agreement, as, for example, in Ireland and Denmark. It is interesting to note that a feature of these two markets was that the biggest brewer – Guinness in Ireland and Carlsberg in Denmark – had a very large market share.

The second category of agreement between brewers and retailers was the loan tie, whereby the owner of an outlet – individual or company – was granted a loan by a brewer, normally on favourable terms, in return for purchasing the latter's beer. Loan agreements were the favoured type of contract in a number of important Continental European markets, including Belgium, Germany and France, but were also used in the UK.

Finally, there was the tenancy agreement, whereby the brewer owned the outlet and let it to a tenant, who was tied for supplies of beer, and often for certain non-beer drinks. Whilst such agreements existed in a number of European countries, the UK was by far the largest user of this arrangement.

When the UK joined the European Community in 1973, agreements between brewers and retailers within the then member states were already covered by a Block Exemption, and UK brewers were provisionally granted the same benefit. [Article 85 had no relevance for brewers' managed – as opposed to tenanted – pubs, since the manager was an employee of the brewing company and there was therefore no agreement between two separate parties.] In 1977 the application of the Block Exemption to brewers' tied house agreements was confirmed in the Concordia case,[4] and the Brewers' Society was to observe a few years later that

> Following the Concordia case, the brewing industry has enjoyed a block exemption for its ties from challenge under Article 85 of the Treaty of Rome as being in restriction of inter-state trade.[5]

Unhappy with the decision in the Concordia case, the European Commission tried unsuccessfully to amend Regulation 67/67, which was due to remain in force until December 1982. In the event, the Regulation stayed in place, unamended, until June 1983, when it was replaced by a new Block Exemption, 1984/83.[6] All agreements concluded after December 1983 would have to comply with its terms in order to receive its benefit, while existing agreements had to be amended by the end of 1988. It was to expire at the end of 1997.

After the opening Recital, Regulation 1984/83 had different sections, or Titles. Title 1 covered exclusive purchasing agreements in general and Title 2 contained special provisions relating to beer supply agreements. The Regulation defined the periods for which the agreements were covered by its terms. In the case of loans the period was limited to five years for contracts for all drinks and ten years for beer only agreements. In the case of tenancies and leases the period was the duration of the tenancy or lease agreement.

The Block Exemption didn't fully resolve the issues, however, and further clarification was required. The first set of guidelines was published on 31 December 1983, but these proved unsatisfactory and another set was issued on 13 April 1984. Even then some matters remained unresolved, for instance, the ways in which individual drinks were to be specified in agreements, as discussed later.

The main features of the Community regime for beer supply agreements after the introduction of the Block Exemption were summarised in a paper presented at a conference in Bordeaux in 1990 by Peter Freeman.[7] Freeman was then a solicitor at Simmons & Simmons, and a specialist in competition law, who had advised the Brewers' Society throughout the 1980s. He said that:

(1) Most agreements for the supply of beer by a brewer to a retailer for resale and consumption on the premises are assumed to be covered by Article 85(1). This is because the "cumulative effect" doctrine [see Henninger Brau case, below] requires each individual agreement to be considered in the context of other similar agreements.
(2) Restriction of competition is assumed to arise mainly from the exclusive purchasing commitment given by the retailer together with the customary restriction on selling competing products.
(3) The Commission is willing to exempt such agreements (either *en bloc* or individually) on the grounds that they promote the distribution of beer and have other benefits.

The Standard Tenancy Agreement

A significant development occurred in the interpretation of the Block Exemption during the MMC inquiry, and it concerned the specification of drinks in the tenancy contract. Thus if, for instance, a contract specified three brands – a bitter, a lager and a stout – and the brewer decided to introduce a new beer (by no means unlikely in the 1980s, as cask-conditioned ales and premium lagers came on to the market) and the new drink was specified by brand, then the tenancy contract would have to be revised. The obvious way to deal with such a situation was to specify the drinks in the tenancy contract by generic type, for example, bitter or lager. This was what Bass proposed in its Standard Tenancy Agreement, which was submitted to the Commission in October 1987, and it would enable the brewer to delete or substitute brands within each specified type.

The Commission announced in 1988 that it intended "to take a favourable position in respect of the agreement",[8] meaning that it could be regarded as a model for others to follow. The Standard Tenancy Agreement specified 13 different types of beer, including no- and low-alcohol beers. The Commission stated that:

> The actual beers supplied to the tenant by the brewery are specified in the brewery's price list which is an integral part of the agreement....The brewery reserves the right to add to or substitute the brands of beer that it supplies to the tenant by amending the contents of its price list from time to time...brands of beer...may be

added or substituted to the price list unilaterally by the brewery without the need for a further agreement only if they are 'specified types' of beer.[9]

Thus the pub owner could change the brands of beer within a given category without the need for a new tenancy agreement. The exclusive purchasing provisions didn't, however, extend to non-beer drinks, with the exception of cider.

The European Commission inquiry into beer

There was consternation in the UK brewing industry when on 16 March 1989 – that is, five days before the MMC Report was published – Sir Leon Brittan, the European Commissioner responsible for competition, announced a Community-wide inquiry into beer. The first few sentences of the press release read as follows:

> In the light of the continuing liberalisation of the EEC beer markets leading to the establishment of the single market in 1992, Sir Leon Brittan, Vice-President of the Commission responsible for competition policy, has decided to carry out a review into the competitive situation in the EEC wide market for beer. This review is intended to enable the Commission to take all measures necessary to ensure that no appreciable competition impediments remain to the opening of national markets in the run up to 1992.[10]

It added that the review would pay "particular attention to the operation of the Block Exemption".[11] In a memorandum received by the Brewers' Society from a correspondent in Brussels it was noted that "British diplomats working on competition policy say that the announcement has come out of the blue". There were immediately suspicions within the industry that the DTI and the Commission's Competition Directorate (DGIV) had been liaising, and that there might even have been direct contact between Lord Young and Sir Leon Brittan. Previously confidential papers now available make clear that there had indeed been contact between the two departments and their leaders.

In June 1989 the Brewers' Society received a questionnaire from the European Commission, asking for replies within some four weeks. It subsequently emerged that the same questionnaire had been sent to the brewing industries of all the member states, in their own language, and that representatives of DGIV had already visited six countries, including Denmark and Ireland, to discuss the review. The Society responded to the questionnaire in two stages: on 29 June 1989 it sent a return covering all the straightforward numerical questions, and then, at the end of August, it sent a further response, together with a paper produced by the Society's advisers making the case for a vertically integrated industry and pointing out how open the UK market was in terms of concentration and imports.

The results of the Commission's survey were announced on 14 June 1990, although the full findings were not published until November 1991.[12] They consisted of four elements. First, the Commission concluded that "no general change is required to the Community rules which govern the tying arrangements between brewers and their outlets", which meant that the Block Exemption remained in place. Its second point was that it would "evaluate whether further measures were needed to take account of the UK market when newly introduced national measures have had time to take effect". Third, the Commission considered that "the Community rules concerning exclusive purchasing arrangements should not apply to small breweries, but that such agreements should be covered by national law". This was the first time that the Commission had indicated that it was thinking of introducing a *de minimis* rule, under which small brewers' exclusive purchasing agreements would not be subject to scrutiny by the Commission under Article 85(1) of the Treaty of Rome. The final element was that "licensing agreements between major brewers will be examined to see whether they were being used as vehicles for market sharing or control of imports".

The Commission estimated from its survey that on the basis of pub ownership and loan-tied business the tied proportion of beer sales in the UK was 62 per cent, compared to Luxembourg's 40 per cent, Belgium's 35 per cent, West Germany's 25 per cent and France's 10 per cent. It was presumably on the basis of these statistics that the Commission was to assert in 1999 that the UK tied house system was a barrier to entry.

Small brewers

As noted above, the Commission hadn't previously said that it was considering special rules for small brewers, but by this time the issue had come to the fore as a result of the Henninger Brau case, which was to provide a landmark ruling. It concerned a dispute between a tenant of a bar in Germany and the owning brewer. The brewer was seeking damages on the grounds that the tenant had failed to meet his obligations, while the tenant argued that the beer contract was at least partly – if not entirely – void because, together with other similar contracts, it affected trade between member states and therefore failed to meet the requirements of the Block Exemption.

The case was referred to the European Court of Justice, which delivered its judgment in February 1991.[13] The Court decided that the relevant market was the distribution of beer through on-licences in Germany rather than the whole of the European Union. It acknowledged that an agreement relating to a single outlet couldn't affect inter-state trade, and that while it was necessary to consider the total effect of all similar contracts, that is, the "bundle effect" (or the Cumulative Effect Doctrine), this was only one factor which had to be taken into account. The Court considered other criteria but concluded that a brewer's tying agreements were only caught by the prohibition contained in Article 85(1) if they made a significant contribution to the closing of the market to new entrants. This was an important judgment, as soon became evident. In a written reply to Ian White MEP,[14] in December 1991 the Commission stated that the judgment supported its conclusion that exclusive beer agreements entered into by small brewers were outside the scope of Article 85(1).

The Commission Notice modifying the Block Exemption for "agreements of minor importance" was published on 13 May 1992.[15] The Commission also announced its opinion that exclusive beer supply agreements did not in general fall under Article 85(1), provided that they met the following conditions:

> The market share of the brewer is not higher than 1% of the national market for the resale of beer in premises used for the sale and consumption of drinks. The brewery does not produce more than 200,000 hectolitres of beer per annum.[16]

The Notice pointed out that these principles applied only if the contracts didn't exceed 15 years for beer only supplies, or seven and a half years for contracts supplying all drinks. In addition, the wording of the notice made clear that in the case of tenancies and leases the period was that of the tenancy or lease agreement. Nothing was said in the Notice about occasional transgressions, but there was an implication that they would be permitted provided they were neither persistent nor significant.

Beer brand licensing agreements

Another aspect of the European Commission statement of 14 June 1990 was that it intended to examine licensing agreements between major brewers to see whether they were being used as vehicles for market sharing or the control of imports. One example of such an arrangement was the production and marketing by Whitbread of Heineken lager, in return for which it paid the Dutch brand owner a royalty.

UK licensing arrangements made good economic sense for overseas producers, partly because they obviated the need to transport a bulky, fairly low value product, with a relatively short shelf life, across the sea. In addition, the brand owner immediately had access to the UK company's distribution and retail facilities and its marketing skills, without having to undertake heavy investment, and with most of the risk borne by the UK brewer. The pub-owning brewers argued that the licensing system for beer also benefited the consumer, in that it enabled them to respond to the changing demands of the market more quickly than might otherwise have been the case – thereby, they added, demonstrating another way in which vertical integration was pro-competitive. The argument against licensing agreements was that they were anti-competitive, in that they reinforced the position of the existing brewers and pub owners, whose power allowed them to prevent or control new entrants.

The Commission's announcement of its intention to examine licensing agreements between UK and overseas brewers inevitably caused concern, but in the event, although nothing was ever formally announced, the idea seems to have been dropped. Nor had the 1989 MMC Report on the UK brewing industry made any reference at all to such arrangements. This was in contrast to the 1989 inquiry by DGIV, and the information collected by the Brewers' Society from its members in connection with this inquiry enabled it to point out to the European Commission that, "Of total lager consumption in 1986, it is estimated that over 35% was brewed under licence from overseas companies, which is a remarkable penetration rate by any standards."[17]

Extensions to the Block Exemption

The Block Exemption remained crucial for UK brewers, and, as its expiry date – 31 December 1997 – approached, the Brewers & Licensed Retailers Association, together with the European brewers, through the Confédération des Brasseurs du Marché Commun (CBMC), argued for its renewal, on the grounds that the system of beer supply contracts worked to the benefit of the consumer, licensee/café owner and brewer. In addition, they argued that beer contracts did not lead to any form of market foreclosure.

The Commission clearly felt overwhelmed by the number of submissions it received, and decided to extend the validity of the Block Exemption as a temporary measure until 31 December 1999. Interested parties continued to make their views known, and in March 1998 the CBMC produced a document entitled *The Brewing Industry and Beer Delivery Contracts*, providing a basis for meetings with Commission officials. The Block Exemption was, in fact, extended further, till the end of May 2000, when it was replaced by another, expiring in May 2010.[18] This in turn has been superseded by a Block Exemption expiring in May 2022,[19] which, so far as the beer agreement is concerned, is substantially the same as its predecessor. [It should be noted that Article 85 became Article 81 with the ratification of the Treaty of Nice

Appendix 3.1   The European Aspect   259

in February 2003. Article 81 became Article 101 in December 2009 as a result of the Lisbon Treaty. Similarly, Article 86 became 82 and then 102.]

Notes

1   OJL (1999)/230/EC, para. 127.
2   Fair Trading Act 1973.
3   JO (1967) 57/849, 22 March 1967.
4   Case 47/76 de Norre v NV Brouwerji Concordia [1977] ECR659.
5   Brewers' Society Annual Report for the year to September 1981, p. 3.
6   Commission Regulation (EEC) No. 1984/83, OJ [1983] L173.
7   P Freeman, Beer: "Tied Houses and Distribution", UIA/UAE Conference, Bordeaux, 25–26 November 1990.
8   OJ [1988] C 285/8, 9 November 1988.
9   Ibid., C 285/6.
10   European Community press release, 16 March 1989.
11   Ibid.
12   XXth European Commission Competition Report: Beer Market Review.
13   Stergio Delimitis v Henninger Brau AG, Case – C234/89, 28 February 1991.
14   Reference No. 28989/91.
15   Official Journal, 13 May 1992, No. C121/2.
16   Ibid.
17   Brewers' Society, "Further Response to the Commission's Questionnaire", August 1989, para. 54.
18   Commission Regulation (EC) No. 2790/1999, 22 December 1999.
19   Commission Regulation (EU) No. 330/2010, 20 April 2010.

Appendix 3.2
Industry and Company Statistics

Table 1 Beer Production and Market Shares in 1985 and Pub Ownership at the End of 1988

Companies	Beer production 000 barrels	Beer production % of total	Tenanted pubs	Managed pubs	Total pubs
Allied Breweries	4,676	12.8	4,479	2,199	6,678
Bass	8,369	22.9	4,770	2,420	7,190
Courage	3,170	8.7	3,673	1,329	5,002
Grand Met	3,210	8.8	4,571	1,848	6,419
S&N	3,889	10.6	1,406	881	2,287
Whitbread	4,020	11.0	4,613	1,870	6,483
Total "big six"	27,334	74.7	23,512	10,547	34,059
Regionals	4,016	11.0	5,214	1,737	6,951
Locals	2,120	5.8	3,590	1,182	4,772
BWTE	3,141	8.6	None	None	None
Total brewers	36,611	100.0	32,316	13,463	45,782

Source: Monopolies and Mergers Commission, *The Supply of Beer*, Cm 651 (1989), Appendices 2.3 and 2.4.

As explained in Chapter 3, the word "pubs" is erroneously used by the MMC in the above table instead of full on-licences, which include other venues where alcohol may be sold for consumption on the premises.

Appendix 3.2 *Industry and Company Statistics* 261

Table 2 National Pub-owning Brewers' Shares of Beer Production in 1985 and Production Facilities as at 30 September 1985

Company	% share of beer production	Number of breweries	Location of breweries
Allied Breweries	12.8	6	Alloa, Burton, Leeds, Romford, Warrington, Wrexham
Bass	22.9	13	Alton, Belfast, Birmingham, Burton, Cardiff, Edinburgh, Glasgow, Runcorn, Sheffield (2), Tadcaster, Walsall, Wolverhampton
Courage	8.7	3	Bristol, Reading, Tadcaster
Grand Met	8.8	6	Edinburgh, London (Brick Lane), London (Mortlake), Manchester, Trowbridge, Halifax
S&N	10.6	3	Edinburgh, Newcastle, Manchester
Whitbread	11.0	8	Cheltenham, Faversham, Hartlepool, Magor, Marlow, Salford, Samlesbury, Sheffield

Sources: Monopolies and Mergers Commission, *The Supply of Beer*, Cm 651 (1989), Appendix 2.4; British Beer & Pub Association, *Statistical Handbook*.

Table 3 Numbers of UK Licensed Premises by Type of Licence, 1986

	Pubs (a)	Other full on-licences (a)	Total full on-licences (b)	Restricted licences (b)	Licensed and registered clubs (b)	Off-licences (b)	Total licences (b)
Number	58,210	22,390	**80,600**	28,390	33,910	49,700	**192,600**
% of all licences	30.2	11.6	**41.8**	14.7	17.6	25.8	**100.0**

Note: A full on-licence authorises retail sale for consumption of intoxicating liquor on or off the premises. A restricted on-licence may be granted for the same purpose in respect of restaurant or residential premises. The distinction between full and restricted licences was ended in 2003, and a premises licence introduced in their place. A licensed club is a commercial enterprise authorised to sell intoxicating liquor to its members, and a registered club is non-profit making and run by its members. An off-licence authorises the sale for consumption away from the premises.

Sources: (a) Authors' calculations; (b) British Beer & Pub Association, *Statistical Handbook*.

Table 4 Beer Consumption and Proportions by Channel of Trade and Beer Type

Year	Beer consumption (000 barrels)	On-trade (%)	Off-trade (%)	Ale and stout (%)	Lager (%)
1971	36,296	90.4	9.6	90.1	9.9
1972	36,895	90.4	9.6	88.3	11.7
1973	38,915	90.4	9.6	85.2	14.8
1974	39,910	90.4	9.6	83.6	16.4
1975	40,722	90.4	9.6	80.3	19.7
1976	41,459	89.5	10.5	76.5	23.5
1977	40,899	89.2	10.8	75.5	24.5
1978	41,656	88.7	11.3	73.1	26.9
1979	42,394	88.0	12.0	70.9	29.1
1980	40,732	87.7	12.3	69.3	30.7
1981	38,901	87.6	12.4	69.0	31.0
1982	37,782	86.5	13.5	67.0	33.0
1983	38,280	85.6	14.4	64.1	35.9
1984	38,127	85.3	14.7	61.1	38.9
1985	37,771	84.4	15.6	59.1	40.9

Source: British Beer & Pub Association, *Statistical Handbook*.

Table 5 Average Price of Draught Bitter in the Public Bars of Managed Houses, Excluding Duty and VAT, Relative to RPI

	Ex-taxes price per pint (p)	(a) Increase	RPI	(b) Increase	(a) relative to (b)	Cumulative change
1973	8.7		93.7			
1974	9.6	10.3%	109.7	17.1%	−5.7%	−5.7%
1975	12.2	27.1%	138.5	26.3%	+0.6%	−5.1%
1976	14.5	18.9%	156.3	12.9%	+5.3%	−0.1%
1977	17.0	17.2%	183.8	17.6%	−0.3%	−0.4%
1978	18.9	11.2%	198.1	7.8%	+3.2%	+2.8%
1979	22.1	16.9%	229.1	15.6%	+1.1%	+3.9%
1980	26.1	18.1%	267.9	16.9%	+1.0%	+4.9%
1981	30.0	14.9%	297.1	10.9%	+3.6%	+8.8%
1982	33.1	10.3%	323.0	8.7%	+1.5%	+10.4%
1983	35.2	6.3%	336.5	4.2%	+2.0%	+12.7%
1984	36.9	4.8%	351.5	4.5%	+0.3%	+13.1%
1985	39.7	7.6%	375.7	6.9%	+0.7%	+13.8%

Sources: Monopolies and Mergers Commission, *The Supply of Beer* (1989), Table 2.55, based on Brewers' Society figures; authors' calculations.

Appendix 3.2 Industry and Company Statistics

Table 6 Average Number of Beer Brands in Tied and Free Trade Pubs, 1987

Beer type	Brewery-owned pubs	Free pubs: loan-tied	Free pubs: no loan
Draught beer			
Bitter	2.5	2.7	3.6
Lager	2.2	1.8	2.1
Stout	0.8	0.7	0.8
Other	0.6	0.5	0.5
Total	6.1	5.7	7.0
Packaged beer			
Bitter	2.8	2.6	2.6
Lager	3.4	3.2	2.7
Stout	1.9	1.8	1.8
Other	2.0	1.9	1.9
Total	10.1	9.5	9.0
Total	16.2	15.2	16.0

Source: Monopolies and Mergers Commission, *The Supply of Beer* (1989), Tables 2.43 and 2.44.

Table 7 Financial Results of UK Brewers' Beer-related Activities

Year	Assets (£m)	Turnover (£m)	Profit before interest (£m)	Return on assets	Profit margin
1983/4	6,100	7,400	788	12.9%	10.6%
1984/5	7,490	8,020	900	12.0%	11.2%
1985/6	8,520	8,680	1,039	12.2%	12.0%

Source: Monopolies and Mergers Commission, *The Supply of Beer* (1989), Table 3.2.

Appendix 3.3
Reference Graphs

Figure 1 Beer Consumption 1960–2009

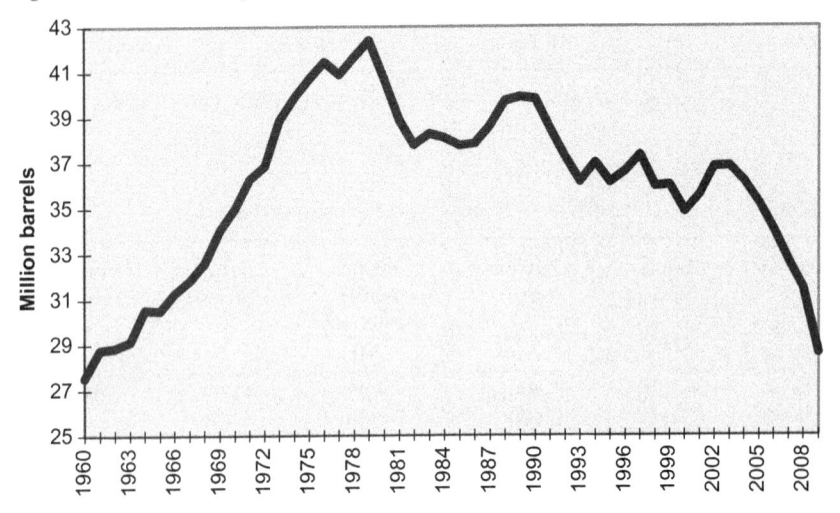

Source: HM Revenue and Customs.

After two decades of more or less continuous growth, beer consumption peaked in 1979, since when it has declined by 33 per cent.

This change of fortune in the beer market is in contrast with the consumption of alcoholic drinks overall, to the extent that beer nowadays accounts for under 40 per cent of alcohol consumption, whereas in 1960 the proportion was 74 per cent. The sector growing most strongly has been table wine.

Within the overall beer market there have been two major trends: the growth in sales through the off-trade and the growth in sales of lager. These trends are shown in Figures 2 and 3.

Figure 2 Beer Consumption 1971–2009 Analysed by Channel of Trade

Source: British Beer & Pub Association.

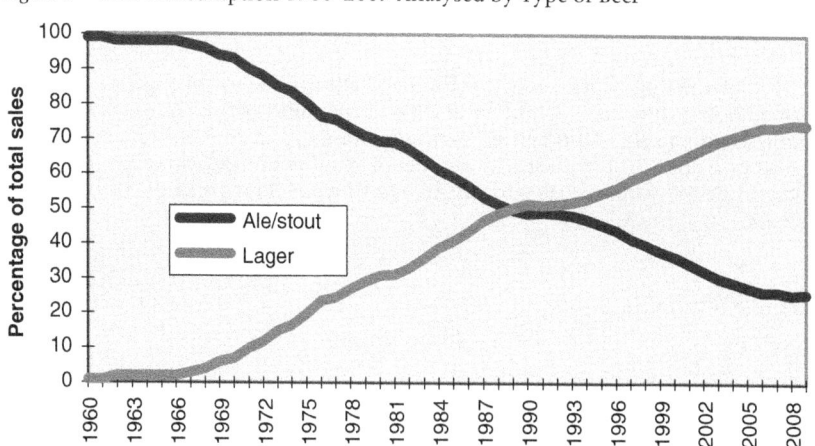

Figure 3 Beer Consumption 1960–2009 Analysed by Type of Beer

Source: British Beer & Pub Association.

Figure 4 shows the numbers of licensed premises in the UK up to 2004 (at which time the method of recording the number of licences changed significantly).

In 1960 full on-licences accounted for 60 per cent of all licensed premises. By 1969, the year in which the Monopolies Commission produced its report on the brewing industry, the proportion had fallen to 52 per cent, and by 1989, the year in which the Monopolies and Mergers Commission reported, the figure had fallen to 41 per cent. Between then and 2004 the proportion rose slightly, to 44 per cent.

Figure 4 Number of Licensed Premises 1960–2004

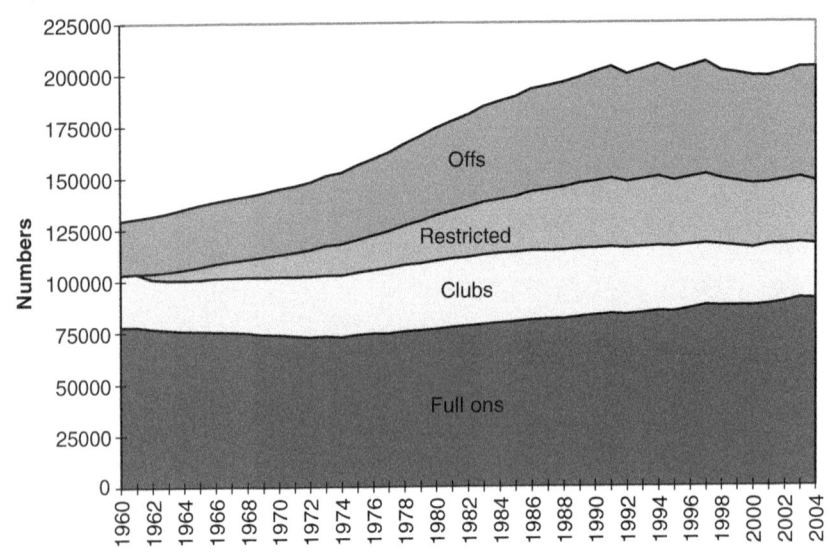

Sources: British Beer & Pub Association; the Home Office and equivalent authorities in Scotland and Northern Ireland.

Over this period of 44 years the UK population grew by 14.3 per cent, from 52.4 million in 1960 to 59.8 million in 2004. The number of full on-licences relative to the size of the population edged slightly upwards, from 14.8 outlets per 100,000 people in 1960 to 15.1 in 2004. The number of all other licences, however, rose from 9.9 per 100,000 people in 1960 to 20.6 in 1990, before falling back slightly, to 18.8, in 2004.

Appendix 3.4
The Participants

Robin Aaronson	Ministry of Defence 1974–80; Economic Adviser to HM Treasury 1980–86; senior economic adviser, Monopolies and Mergers Commission 1986–89; PricewaterhouseCoopers 1989–98 (partner from 1993); Director, LECG Ltd 1998–2009; Member of the Competition Commission 2009–.
Rt Hon. Lord Borrie of Abbotts Morton QC	Called to the Bar 1952; practiced as a barrister 1954–57; Lecturer and Senior Lecturer, College of Law 1957–64; Senior Lecturer, University of Birmingham 1965–68; Professor of English Law, University of Birmingham 1969–76; Director General of Fair Trading 1976–92; Chairman, Advertising Standards Authority 2001–07; Director, Woolwich plc 1992–2000; Director, Mirror Group 1993–99; Director, Telewest Communications Group 1994–2001; Director, General Utilities 1998–2003. Various publications.
Tim Bridge	Greene King 1970–, Director 1977–, Managing Director 1990–94, Chief Executive 1994–2005, Chairman 2005–.
John Bridgeman CBE DL	Alcan Industries 1966–95, Commercial Director UK 1977–80, Managing Director, British Alcan Aluminium plc 1993–95; Member of the Monopolies and Mergers Commission 1990–95; Director General of Fair Trading 1995–2000; Chairman, GPC Europe Ltd 2000–01; Cardew & Co 2001–03; Director, British Waterways 2006–; Board member, British Horseracing Authority 2007–.
Rt Hon. Lord Brittan of Spennithorne QC DL	Called to the Bar 1968; MP, Cleveland and Whitby 1974–83, Richmond 1983–88; Opposition Spokesman on Devolution 1974–76, Employment 1976–79; Minister of State, Home Office 1979–81; Chief Secretary to the Treasury 1981–83; Secretary of State Home Office 1983–85; Secretary of State Department of Trade and Industry 1985–86; Member EU Commission 1989–99, Vice President 1989–93, and 1993–95; Vice President, UBS Investment Bank 2000–; Director, Unilever 2004–. Various publications.

Stephen Burbridge CB	Assistant Principal, Board of Trade 1958–62; Trade Commissioner 1963–65; First Secretary Rawalpindi 1965–67; Principal, Board of Trade 1967–71; Assistant Secretary, Board of Trade 1971–80; Under Secretary, Board of Trade 1980–86; Secretary, Monopolies and Mergers Commission 1986–93.
Sir Bryan Carsberg	Sole practice accountant 1962–64; Lecturer in Accounting LSE 1964–68; Professor of Accounting Manchester University 1969–81; Arthur Andersen Professor of Accounting LSE 1981–87; Director General, Oftel 1984–92; Director General of Fair Trading 1992–95; Secretary General International Accounting Standards Committee 1995–2001; Director, Phillip Allan (Publishers) 1981–92, 1995–2006; Cable and Wireless 1997–2000; RM plc 2002–; Novae Gp plc 2003–; Inmarsat plc 2005–. Various publications.
Dr Christopher Clayson	Edinburgh City Hospital 1929–39; Lecturer in Tuberculosis Department, University of Edinburgh 1939–44; Physician Superintendent, Lochmaben Sanatorium 1944–64. Deceased.
John Elliott	McKinsey & Co 1966–72; Managing Director, Henry Jones (IXL) 1972; Chairman and CEO, Fosters Brewing Group 1985–90; Deputy Chairman, Fosters Brewing Group 1990–92; Chairman, Australian Product Trades Pty. 1992.
Lord Erroll of Hale	MP for Altrincham and Sale 1945–65; Parliamentary Under-Secretary of State Department of Supply 1955–56; Parliamentary Under-Secretary of State Board of Trade 1956–58; President of the Board of Trade 1961–63; Minister of Power 1963–64; President of the London Chamber of Commerce 1966–69; Chairman, Bowater Corporation 1973–84; Chairman, Consolidated Gold Fields 1976–83. Deceased.
Percy ("Pip") Flint	Royal Signals 1941–47; Colonial Administration Services and HMOCS in Nigeria 1948–61; Called to the Bar 1955; ICI 1961–85 (Company Secretary 1981–85). Member of the Monopolies and Mergers Commission 1981–1990. Deceased.
Mike Foster	Courage 1983–1995, Marketing Director 1983–87, Chief Executive 1987–92, Chairman 1992–95; Chief Executive, Inntrepreneur 1995–1998, Chairman, Brakspear 1998–2006; Director, Punch Taverns 2002–10; Chairman, British Beer and Pub Association 1998–2001.
Peter Freeman CBE QC	Called to the Bar 1972; Simmons & Simmons 1973–2003 (Partner 1978); Deputy Chairman,

Appendix 3.4 The Participants 269

	Competition Commission 2003–05; Chairman, Competition Commission 2005–11; Co-founder of the Regulatory Policy Institute and Chairman 1998–2007. Various publications.
Anthony Fuller CBE	Fuller, Smith & Turner 1963–, Chairman 1982–2007, President 2007–; Chairman, Brewers' Society 1986–89; Master of the Worshipful Company of Brewers 1986–87.
Bryan Gould	HM Diplomatic Service: Foreign Office 1964–66; HM Embassy in Brussels 1966–68; Fellow and Tutor in Law, Worcester College Oxford 1968–74; MP for Southampton Test 1974–79; Presenter/reporter Thames Television 1979–83; MP for Dagenham 1983–94; Member Shadow Cabinet 1986–92; Vice Chancellor, Waikato University 1994–2004. Various publications.
Dan Goyder CBE	Assistant solicitor, Allen & Overy 1964–67; Partner, Birketts 1968–83; Consultant 1983–97; Member of the Monopolies and Mergers Commission 1980–97 (Deputy Chairman 1991–97). Deceased.
Bernard Gravatt	Team Leader, Monopolies and Mergers Commission. Deceased.
Edward Guinness CVO	Guinness 1945–89, Director 1971–89, Chairman, Harp Lager 1971–78; Master, Brewers Company 1977–78; Chairman, Brewers' Society 1985–87; Director, Wolverhampton & Dudley 1964–68.
Jeremy Hardie CBE	Fellow and Tutor in Economics, Keble College, Oxford 1968–75; Director, National Provident Institute, 1972–89 (Chairman 1980–89); Partner, Dixon Wilson & Co. 1975–82; Member of the Monopolies and Mergers Commission 1976–83 (Deputy Chairman 1980–83); Director, Alexanders Discount Co 1978–87 (Chairman 1984–87); Director, NAAFI 1981–92 (Chairman 1986–92); Chairman, Alexander Syndicate Ltd. 1982–95; Director, John Swire Ltd 1982–98; Chairman, Radio Broadband Ltd. 1983–85; Chairman, DP Mann Underwriting Agency Ltd. 1983–99; Director, Amdahl (UK) 1983–86; Director, Alexander Laing and Cruickshank Gilts Ltd. 1986–87; Director, Mercantile House Holdings 1984–87; Director, Northdoor Holdings 1989–93; Chairman, WH Smith Group 1994–99; Chairman, Touch Clarity 2001–04; Chairman, Loch Fyne Restaurants 2002–05; Research Associate, Centre for Philosophy of Natural and Social Sciences, London School of Economics 2000–; Chairman, Brasserie Blanc 2005–.

Rt Hon. Lord Hattersley of Sparkbrook	Journalist 1956–64; MP Birmingham Sparkbrook 1964–97; PPS to Minister of Pensions 1964–67; Minister of Labour 1967–69; Opposition Spokesman on Defence 1969–70, Environment and Science 1970–74; Minister of State, Foreign & Commonwealth Office 1974–76; Secretary of State for Prices and Consumer Protection 1976–79; Opposition Spokesman on Home Affairs 1979–83, Treasury and Economic Affairs 1983–87, Home Affairs 1987–92. Various publications.
Rt Hon. Lord Heseltine of Thenford	Director, BW Publications 1961–65; Chairman, Haymarket Press 1965–70; MP for Tavistock 1966–1974; MP for Henley 1966–2001; Opposition Spokesman on Transport 1969; Parliamentary Under-Secretary of State, Ministry of Transport 1970; Parliamentary Under-Secretary of State, Department of the Environment 1970–72; Minister of State for Aerospace and Shipping Department of Trade and Industry 1972–74; Opposition spokesman on Industry 1974–76; Secretary of State for Environment 1979–83 and 1990–92; Secretary of State for Defence 1983–86; President of the Board of Trade 1992–95; Deputy Prime Minister 1995–97. Various publications.
Sir Derrick Holden-Brown	Hiram Walker 1949–54; Managing Director, Cairnes Brewers Eire 1954–60; Grants of St. James 1960–62; Director, Ind Coope 1962–64; Director, Allied Breweries 1967–91 Chairman, Victoria Wine 1964–72; Finance Director, Allied Breweries 1972–75; Chairman and Chief Executive, Allied-Lyons plc 1982–88, Chairman 1988–91; Director, Sun Alliance & London Insurance plc 1977–92, Deputy Chairman 1985–92; Director, Midland Bank 1984–88; Chairman, Brewers' Society 1978–80; Master of the Worshipful Company of Brewers 1987–88.
Peter Jarvis CBE	Unilever 1964–76; Whitbread 1976–97, Sales and Marketing Director, Long John International 1976–78, appointed to the Board 1978, Group Marketing Director 1978–81, Managing Director, International Division 1981–83, Managing Director, Trading Division 1983–85, Group Managing Director 1985–90, Chief Executive 1990–97; Director, Barclays 1995–2001; Chairman, Debenhams 1998–2003; Director, Rank 1995–2005.
Sir Jeremy Lever QC KCMG	Called to the Bar 1957; All Souls College Oxford 1982–84, Senior Dean 1988–; Bencher Grays Inn 1986; Director, Dunlop Holdings 1973–80; Director, The Welcome Foundation 1983–94. Various publications.

Appendix 3.4 The Participants 271

Peter Luff MP	Research Assistant to Peter Walker 1977–80; Head of the private office of Rt Hon Edward Heath 1980–82; Director Good Relations Ltd 1982–87; Special Adviser to Lord Young of Graffham 1987–89; Senior Consultant, Lowe Bell Communications 1989–90; Assistant Managing Director, Good Relations Ltd 1990–92; Member of Parliament for Worcester 1992–97; PPS to Minister for Industry and Energy 1993–96; PPS to Lord Chancellor 1996–97; Member of Parliament for Mid-Worcestershire 1997–; Opposition Whip 2000–05; Chairman Business and Enterprise Select Committee 2007–10; Parliamentary Under-Secretary of State, Ministry of Defence 2010–.
Maj Gen W Mangham CB	Served in the Army 1944–75 (service in India, Malaya, Egypt, Middle East, Cyprus); Ministry of Defence 1976–79; Director, Brewers Society 1980–90.
Richard Martin	Allied-Lyons 1955–91, Chief Executive, Joshua Tetley & Son 1972–78, Vice Chairman, Tetley Walker 1978–79, Chairman, Ind Coope 1979–86, Director 1981–92, Chief Executive 1988–92; Chairman, Brewers' Society 1991–92.
Rt Hon. Francis Maude MP	Called to the Bar 1977; MP for Warwickshire North 1983–92, Horsham 1997–; PPS to Minister of State for Employment 1984–85; Assistant Government Whip 1985–87; Parliamentary Under-Secretary of State, Department of Trade and Industry 1987–89; Minister of State Foreign & Commonwealth Office 1989–90; Financial Secretary to the Treasury 1990–92; Director, Morgan Stanley & Co 1993–98; Director, Asda Group 1992–99; Shadow Chancellor 1998–2000; Shadow Foreign Secretary 2000–01; Chairman of the Conservative Party 2005–07; Shadow Minister for the Cabinet Office 2007–10; Minister for the Cabinet Office 2010–.
John McGrath	UKAEA 1962–65; NCB 1965–67; Ford 1967–71; Jaguar 1971–75; Stone-Platt 1976–82; Grand Metropolitan 1985–97, Group Director, Watney Mann & Truman Breweries 1985–86; Chairman and Managing Director, Grand Metropolitan Brewing 1986–88, Joint Managing Director, IDV 1988–91, Managing Director, IDV 1991–92, Chief Executive, IDV 1992–93, Chairman, IDV 1993–96, Chief Executive, Grand Metropolitan 1996–97; Chief Executive, Diageo 1997–2000; Chairman, Boots Company plc 2000–03; Director, Carlton Communications 2003–04; Director, ITV plc 2004–07.
Leif Mills CBE	Royal Military Police 1957–59; National Union of Bank Employees (later Banking, Insurance and Finance

	Union) 1960–96, General Secretary 1972–96; Member TUC General Council 1983–96 (President 1994–95); Member of the Monopolies and Mergers Commission 1982–91; Council of The Consumers Association 1996–2002; Chairman, Covent Garden Market Authority 1998–2005.
Sir Derek Morris	Fellow and Tutor Oriel College, Oxford 1970–98; seconded as economic adviser to NEDO 1981–84; Chairman, Oxford Economic Forecasting 1984–98; Member of the Monopolies and Mergers Commission 1991–2004, (Deputy Chairman 1995–98, Chairman 1998–2004); Provost, Oriel College, Oxford 2004–. Various publications.
Sir Paul Nicholson LL	Vaux 1965–99, Managing Director 1971–92, Chairman 1976–99; Chairman, Northern Investors Co 1984–89; Director, Tyne Tees 1984–97; Director, Northern Electric 1990–97; Director, Scottish Investment Trust plc 1995–2005; Chairman, Brewers' Society 1994–96. Author of "Brewer at Bay" (2003).
John Overton	Chief Executive, National Licensed Victuallers Association (formerly National Union of Licensed Victuallers) 1976–93.
Dr Tony Portno CBE	Bass 1961–64; Brewing Research Foundation 1964–69; Pfizer 1969–71; Bass plc 1971–98, Quality control and research 1971–76, Director of Research 1976, Director of Britannia Soft Drinks 1983, Director, Bass plc 1985–98, Chairman, Bass Brewers 1991–98, Chairman, Bass Leisure 1996–98, Chairman, Britvic Soft Drinks 1991–98; Director, Gallaher 1997–2005.
Sir Ian Prosser	Coopers & Lybrand 1964–69; Bass 1969–2000, Finance Director 1978–84, Deputy Chairman 1982–87, Managing Director 1984–87, Chairman and Chief Executive 1987–2000; Chairman, Six Continents 2000–03; Chairman, Intercontinental Hotels 2003–04: Director, the Boots Company 1984–96; Director, Lloyds TSB 1988–99; Director, GSK 1999–2009; Director, BP 1997–2011; Chairman, Brewers' Society 1992–94.
Rt Hon. John Redwood MP	Investment Adviser, Robert Fleming & Co, 1973–77; Director, NM Rothschild & Sons 1977–87; Head of Prime Minister's Policy Unit 1983–85; Parliamentary Under-Secretary of State, Department of Trade & Industry 1898–90; Minister of State, Department of Trade & Industry 1990–92; Minister of State, Department of the Environment 1992–93; Secretary of State for Wales 1993–95; Opposition Spokesman on Trade and Industry 1997–99; Opposition Spokesman on the Environment 1999–2000; Shadow Secretary of

Appendix 3.4 The Participants 273

	State for De-regulation 2004–05; Director, Norcross PLC 1985–89, Chairman 1987–89; Chairman Hare Hatch Holdings Ltd., 1999–2008; Director Concentric plc 2003–; Director Pan Asset Capital Management 2007–.
Hubert Reid	Executive Director, Hugh Baird & Sons 1958–77 (Director from 1971); Director, Boddingtons 1975–95, Assistant Managing Director 1980–84, Managing Director 1984–85, Chief Executive 1985–95, Chairman 1995; Chairman, Royal London Mutual Insurance Society Ltd 1996–2005; Director, Enterprise Inns 1997– (Chairman 1999–); Director, Ibstock plc 1995–99 (Chairman 1997–99); Director, Wace Group 1996–99; Deputy Chairman, Majedie 1999–; Director, Bryants Group plc 1993–2001 (Chairman 2000–01); Director, Greenalls 1996–97; Director, Taverners Trust 1996–, Chairman 2004–; Director, Michael Page 2003–.
Sir Stephen Richards	Called to the Bar 1975; Standing Counsel to the Director General of Fair Trading 1989–91; First Junior Treasury Counsel, Common Law 1992–97; Assistant Recorder 1992–96; Recorder 1996–97; Judge of High Court of Justice 1997–2005; Lord Justice of Appeal 2005–.
Nicholas Ridley	Brims & Co Ltd 1950–59; Director, Heenan Group Ltd 1961–68; Director, Ausonia Finance 1973–79; Director, Marshall Andrew Ltd 1975–79; MP for Cirencester and Tewkesbury 1959–93; Minister of State Foreign and Commonwealth Office 1979–81; Financial Secretary to the Treasury 1981–83; Secretary of State for Transport 1983–87; Secretary of State Environment 1987–89; Secretary of State Department of Trade and Industry 1989–90. Deceased.
Peter Robinson	Slater Healis & Co Solicitors 1955–56, Frederic Robinson 1957–, Company Secretary 1957–62, Board Director 1962–, Chairman 1978–.
Ernest Saunders	Managing Director, Beecham Products International 1966–73; Chairman European Division, Universal Stores 1973–77; President, Nestlé 1977–81; Guinness plc 1981–87, Chief Executive 1981–87, Chairman and Chief Executive 1986–87; President, Stambridge Management 1992–.
Richard Smethurst	Fellow and Tutor, St Edmund Hall Oxford 1964–67; Worcester College Oxford 1967–91, Fellow, Tutor and Lecturer 1967–76, Director, Department of External Studies 1976–89, Supernumerary Fellow and Chairman of Board 1989–91; Economic Adviser to HM Treasury 1969–71; Policy Adviser, Prime Minister's Policy Unit

	1975–76; Member of the Monopolies and Mergers Commission 1978–89 (Deputy Chairman 1986–89); Provost Worcester College Oxford 1991–; Pro Vice-Chancellor, University of Oxford 1997–.
David Thompson	Conservative Research Department 1975–76; Whitbread 1976–77; Wolverhampton & Dudley (later Marstons) 1977–, Managing Director 1986–2001, Chairman 2001–; Director, Persimmon plc 1999–.
David Thomson	Lazard Bros & Co 1956–86, Director 1965–86; Director, Richard Daus & Co, Frankfurt 1974–81; Director, Applied Photophysics 1976–87; Member of the Monopolies and Mergers Commission 1984–94; Director General, BIEC 1987–90; Chairman, Kleinwort Emerging Markets Trust 1993–2002; Deputy Chairman, Permanent Insurance Co 1995–97; Director, Wesleyan Assurance Society Ltd 1997–2000; Director, Foreign & Colonial European Investment Trust 1998–2002.
Chris Thurman MBE	London Chamber of Commerce 1963–65; IBM 1965–67; Society of British Aerospace Companies 1967–70; Economist/Statistician, Brewers' Society 1970–99. Various publications.
Alan Tilbury CBE	Bechuanaland Government Secretariat 1954–66, Legal Secretary 1956–63, Attorney General 1963–66; Attorney General of Botswana 1966–69; Brewers Society 1969–92, Assistant Secretary (Legal) 1969–, Legal and Parliamentary Secretary, General Secretary, Director General 1990–93. Deceased.
Sir John Vickers	Financial Analyst, Shell UK 1979–81; Fellow All Souls College, Oxford; Executive Director, Chief Economist, Monetary Policy Committee, Bank of England 1998–2000; Office of Fair Trade 2000–05, Director General 2000–03, Chairman 2003–05; Warden, All Souls College, Oxford. Various publications.
Professor George Yarrow	Emeritus Fellow of Hertford College, University of Oxford; Founder, and Director of the Regulatory Policy Institute Oxford 1990–; Board member of OFGEM 2005–09; Director, DY Ltd 2000–; Adviser to CAA, OECD, European Commission, and World Bank.
Bob Young	IBM 1969–71; Rolls Royce Motors 1971–81; Vickers 1981–85; Managing Director, Crane Ltd 1986–88; Chief Executive, Plastics Division McKechnie plc 1989–90; Member of the Monopolies & Mergers Commission 1986–92; Member No. 10 Policy Unit 1983–84; Consultant, Coopers & Lybrand 1993–98; Director, PricewaterhouseCoopers 1998–2000; Principal, LECG Ltd 2000–04; Principal, European Economic Research Ltd 2004–.

Appendix 3.4 The Participants 275

Rt Hon. Lord Young of Graffham DL	Great Universal Stores 1956–61; Chairman, Eldonwall 1961–74; Chairman, Manufacturer's Hanover Trust 1974–84; Minister without Portfolio 1984–85; Secretary of State for Employment 1985–87; Secretary of State Department of Trade & Industry 1987–89; Deputy Chairman of the Conservative Party 1989–90; Chairman, Cable & Wireless 1990–95; President, Institute of Directors 1993–2002; Chairman, Young Associates plc 1996–.

Appendix 5.1
Companies, Organisations and Others Making Submissions to the Monopolies and Mergers Commission (MMC)

The Brewers' Society

National Brewers (6)
Allied Breweries Ltd (subsidiary of Allied-Lyons)
Bass PLC
Courage Ltd (subsidiary of Elders IXL)
Grand Metropolitan PLC
Scottish & Newcastle Breweries PLC
Whitbread and Company PLC

Whitbread Investment Company PLC

Regional Brewers (10)
Boddingtons' Breweries Ltd
JA Devenish PLC
Greenall Whitley PLC
Greene King and Sons PLC
Mansfield Brewery PLC
Marston, Thompson and Evershed PLC
Frederick Robinson Ltd
Daniel Thwaites PLC
Vaux Breweries PLC
The Wolverhampton & Dudley Breweries PLC

Local Brewers (29)
Adnams & Company PLC
J Arkell & Sons Ltd
George Bateman & Son Ltd
Daniel Batham & Son Ltd
SA Brain & Co Ltd
WH Brakspear & Sons PLC
Eldridge Pope & Co Ltd
Elgood & Sons Ltd
Everards Brewery Ltd
George Gale & Co Ltd
Gibbs Mew PLC
Hall & Woodhouse Ltd
Hardys & Hansons PLC
Holdens' Brewery Ltd
Joseph Holt PLC
Hydes' Anvil Brewery Ltd
King & Barnes Ltd
Maclay & Co
Mitchell's of Lancaster (Brewers) Ltd
Morland & Co PLC
Morrell's Brewery Ltd
JC & RH Palmer Ltd
TD Ridley & Sons Ltd
Shepherd Neame Ltd
Samuel Smith Old Brewery (Tadcaster)
Timothy Taylor & Co Ltd
Wadworth & Co Ltd
Charles Wells Ltd
Young & Co's Brewery PLC

Brewers without a Tied Estate (3)
Carlsberg Brewery Ltd
Guinness PLC
Northern Clubs Federation Brewery Ltd

Brewers – Non-members of the Brewers' Society (4)
Reepham Brewery
The Pilgrim Brewery
Smiles Brewing Co Ltd
Whitby's Own Brewery Ltd

Appendix 5.1 Companies, Organisations and Others Making Submissions

Manufacturers of Non-beer Drinks (6)
HP Bulmer Holdings PLC
The Taunton Cider Company PLC
Merrydown Wine PLC
Showerings Ltd (subsidiary of Allied-Lyons)
Coca Cola and Schweppes Beverages Ltd
Rodwells Ltd

Independent Drinks Wholesalers (3)
National Federation of Beer Bottlers
National Association of Licensed Trade Wholesalers
The National Wine Buying Group

Trade Bodies (2)
National Licensed Victuallers Association
National Association of Licensed House Managers (invited to give evidence but none submitted)

The MMC also had the results of its survey of 1395 licensees.

Associations (3)
The Campaign for Real Ale Ltd
Consumers' Association
The Small Independent Brewers' Association

Trades Unions (2)
Transport and General Workers' Union
General, Municipal and Boilermakers and Allied Trades' Union

Consumers (80)
74 individuals
4 MPs (mostly on behalf of constituents)
2 proprietors of small businesses

Source: Monopolies and Mergers Commission, *The Supply of Beer: A Report on the Supply of Beer for Retail Sale in the United Kingdom,* Cm 691 (1989), chapters 5–10.

Appendix 5.2
Options for Change

In the second addendum to the Public Interest Letter, dated September 1988, the Monopolies and Mergers Commission (MMC) listed a number of possible scenarios that it was considering in relation to structural change and invited the Brewers' Society to comment upon them. The changes were subsequently reproduced in Chapter 5 of the MMC Report *The Supply of Beer*, starting after paragraph 5.194 on page 152 and finishing before paragraph 5.237 on page 163. The possible changes put forward by the MMC for comment are listed below:

1(a) No company or member of a group of companies which brews beer should be permitted to own, lease or otherwise control full on-licensed premises in the United Kingdom.
1(b) No company or group of companies which brews beer should be permitted to own, lease or otherwise control more than a maximum of, say, 500 full on-licensed premises in the United Kingdom.
1(c) No company or group of companies which brews beer should be permitted to own, lease or otherwise control more than, say, 25 per cent of the full on-licensed premises in any PSD in the United Kingdom.
1(d) No company which brews beer should be permitted to own, lease or otherwise control full on-licensed premises in the United Kingdom, although other companies in the same group should be allowed to do so providing the company owning, leasing or controlling premises purchases its beer requirements at the wholesale list price applicable to it and publishes separate accounts.
1(e) No company or group of companies which brews beer should be permitted to operate, as directly controlled managed houses, more than the greater of, say, 50 in number or 25 per cent of the total on-licensed properties it owns or leases as directly controlled managed houses save when at [date] the company had a percentage of managed houses which exceeded these figures when appropriate transitional arrangements would be applied.
2(a) Tenants of companies or groups of companies which brew beer should be allowed to buy whatever products they wish (whether beer, other drinks or other supplies) from any supplier.
2(b) Tenants of companies or groups of companies which brew beer should be allowed to purchase from any supplier or suppliers, but tenancy agreements could specify which brands of beer the tenant must buy.
2(c) Tenants of companies or groups of companies which brew beer should be allowed to purchase up to three draught beers from suppliers of their choice, without restriction on the brand purchased and quantities sold, and display these beers for sale. The brewer could continue to tie the tenant for his other beer requirements.
2(d) Tenants of companies or groups of companies which brew beer should be allowed to purchase all drinks other than beer from suppliers of their choice, irre-

spective of the terms offered and the brand or brands purchased. The brewer could continue to tie the tenant for his beer requirements.

2(e) Leases or tenancy agreements should not impose any particular restrictions in respect of AWP or similar equipment and landlords should not be able to require tenants to pay them any proportion of the profits or other sums in respect of such equipment.

3(a) No company or group of companies which brews beer should be allowed to offer or guarantee loans to owners or tenants of on-licensed premises.

3(b) No company or group of companies which brews beer should be allowed to offer or guarantee loans carrying an interest rate below, say, bank base rate to owners or tenants of on-licensed premises.

3(c) No company or group of companies which brews beer should be allowed to offer or guarantee loans to owners or tenants of on-licensed premises on terms which require the borrower to purchase any amount of any product from the lender.

3(d) No company or group of companies which brews beer should be allowed to offer or guarantee loans to owners or tenants of on-licensed premises ("the borrowers") on condition that the borrower purchases a minimum barrelage of beer, or any percentage of his total beer requirements exceeding, say, 50 per cent by volume from the lender.

4(a) No company which brews beer should be permitted to sell on-licensed premises or premises recently used as on-licensed premises on condition that the purchaser buys any amount of any product from the vendor.

5(a) Tenants of on-licensed premises should be brought within the provisions of the Landlord and Tenant Act 1954 Part II.

5(b) A new Code of Practice under the auspices of the Office of Fair Trading should be introduced for tenancy agreements and leases of on-licensed premises to include tenure of at least five years, the assignment of tenancies with the benefit of goodwill, and access to legally binding independent arbitration. At the end of their lease or tenancy, tenants should be in at least as favourable position regarding renewal of the lease or tenancy as tenants who came within the Landlord and Tenant Act 1954 Part II or its successors.

6(a) Discounts for on-licensed sales should be related to cost and brewers should not be permitted to deal with any customer on terms other than set out in the brewers' wholesale price lists which should be published. The brewers' wholesale price lists of products for sale in on-licensed premises should include details of discounts available and their relation to the size of individual deliveries and to location of deliveries. The price lists should include prices for collection from the brewery or distribution depot. If there are loans at favourable interest rates the brewers' wholesale price lists should state the terms on which those with loans can buy.

6(b) Brewers should publish their wholesale price lists of products for sale in on-licensed premises with details of discounts available (including over-riders) and their relation to the size of individual deliveries, and to place of delivery. The price lists should include prices for collection from the brewery or distribution depot. If there are loans at favourable interest rates the brewers' wholesale price lists should state the terms on which those with loans can buy.

7(a) Brewers should supply any customer, including wholesalers with their whole range of beers, at the prices and with the discounts set out in their wholesale price lists. Restrictions on the customers to when purchasers could re-sell or the re-sale price should not be permitted. Any charges that are made, such as for kegs, should be made on the same terms to all customers.

7(b) Brewers should supply any customer including wholesalers with their whole range of beers at the prices and with the discounts set out in their wholesale price lists. Wholesalers who sell to "tied" customers may be required by the brewers' terms of sale to provide on request information on the volumes of "tied" products supplied to individual customers who have accepted legally binding ties. Any charges that are made, such as for kegs, should be made on the same terms to all customers.

Appendix 19.1
Major Pub-owning Companies as at July 2010

Company	Pubs
Punch Taverns PLC	7676
Enterprise Inns PLC	6128
Greene King PLC	2417
Marston's PLC	2076
Mitchells & Butlers PLC	1983
Admiral Taverns	1805
Wellington Pub Company	830
JD Wetherspoon PLC	742
Trust Inns	600
Pubfolio	500

Source: British Beer & Pub Association, *Statistical Handbook*.

Bibliography

A Abbott, K Lawler and M Ling, 'An Empirical Analysis of the Effects of the Monopolies and Mergers Commission Beer Orders (1989) on the UK Brewing Industry', *Applied Economics*, 30 (1998), 145–9.

Agriculture Select Committee Fourth Report of Session 1988–89, *Supply of Beer*, HC 528.

Agriculture Select Committee Fourth Report of Session 1993, *Effects of the Beer Orders on the Brewing Industry and Consumers*, HC 402.

Better Regulation Task Force, *Licensing Legislation* (1998).

Brewers & Licensed Retailers Association, *Statistical Handbook*.

Brewers' Society, *Beer Prices and Margins – Response to the Price Commission* (1977).

Brewers' Society, *The Recommendations Made by the Monopolies and Mergers Commission and Their Likely Consequences* (1989).

Brewers' Society, *Report of the Monopolies and Mergers Commission on 'The Supply of Beer' – A Critique* (1989).

Brewers Society, *Statistical Handbook*.

British Beer & Pub Association, *Statistical Handbook*.

Business and Enterprise Select Committee Seventh Report of Session 2008–09, *Pub Companies*, HC 26-1.

Business, Innovation and Skills Select Committee Fifth Report of Session 2009–10, *Pub Companies: Follow-up*, HC 138.

Business, Innovation and Skills Select Committee Eighth Report of Session 2009–10, *Pub Companies: Follow-up: Government Response to the Committee, Fifth Report of Session 2009–10*, HC 503.

Campaign for Real Ale, *Called to the Bar – An Account of the First 21 Years of the Campaign for Real Ale (1992)*. ISBN 1 85249 0659.

Campaign for Real Ale, *UK Pub Market Super-Complaint: A Fair Share for the Consumer: Memorandum to the Office of Fair Trading* (2009).

Competition Commission, *Interbrew SA and Bass PLC: A Report on the Acquisition by Interbrew of the Brewing Interests of Bass PLC*, Cm 5014 (2001).

Department of Culture, Media and Sport, *Evaluation of the Impact of the Licensing Act 2003* (2008).

Department of the Environment, *Drinking and Driving – A Report of the Departmental Committee* (1976).

G Garafas, *The Effect of Regulation on Prices in the UK Brewing Industry: An Empirical Investigation*, The Regulatory Policy Institute, Oxford (1995).

T Gourvish and R Wilson, *The Brewing Industry 1830–1980* (Cambridge University Press, 1994). ISBN 0 821 45232 5.

Home Office, *Report of the Departmental Committee on Liquor Licensing*, Cmnd 5154 (1972).

Home Office, *Possible Reform of the Liquor Licensing System in England and Wales* (1993).

T Keyworth, H Lawton Smith and G Yarrow, *The Effects of Regulation in the UK Beer Market*, Regulatory Policy Research Centre, Hertford College, Oxford (1994).

T Knowles and D Egan, 'The Changing Structure of UK Brewing and Pub Retailing', *The International Journal of Wine Marketing*, Vol. 13 No. 2 (2001).

R Light and S Keenan, *Controlling Supply: The Concept of Need in Liquor Licensing*, The University of the West of England (1999).
Monopolies and Mergers Commission, *Allied-Lyons PLC and Carlsberg A/S: A Report on the Proposed Joint Venture*, Cm 2029 (1992).
Monopolies and Mergers Commission, *Bass PLC, Carlsberg A/S and Carlsberg-Tetley PLC: A Report on the Merger Situation*, Cm 3662 (1997).
Monopolies and Mergers Commission, *Carbonated Drinks: A Report on the Supply by Manufacturers of Carbonated Drinks in the United Kingdom*, Cm 1693 (1991).
Monopolies and Mergers Commission, *Elders IXL Ltd and Allied-Lyons PLC: A Report on the Merger Situation*, Cmnd 9892 (1986).
Monopolies and Mergers Commission, *Elders IXL and Grand Metropolitan PLC: A Report on the Merger Situations*, Cm 1227 (1990).
Monopolies and Mergers Commission, *Elders IXL Ltd and Scottish & Newcastle Breweries PLC – A Report on the Merger Situations*, Cm 654 (1989).
Monopolies and Mergers Commission, *Foreign Packaged Holidays: A Report on the Matter of the Existence or Possible Existence of a Complex Monopoly Situation in Relation to the Supply in the United Kingdom of Agency Services by Travel Agents for Tour Operators in Relation to the Marketing and Supply of Foreign Packaged Holidays*, Cmnd 9879 (1986).
Monopolies and Mergers Commission, *Full-Line Forcing and Tie-in Sales*, HC 212 (1981).
Monopolies and Mergers Commission, *Greyhound Racing: A Report on the Supply in Great Britain of the Services of Managing Greyhound Tracks*, Cmnd 9834 (1986).
Monopolies and Mergers Commission, *Scottish & Newcastle Breweries PLC and Matthew Brown PLC: A Report on the Proposed Merger*, Cmnd 9645 (1985).
Monopolies and Mergers Commission, *The Supply of Beer: A Report on the Supply of Beer for Retail Sale in the United Kingdom*, Cm 651 (1989).
Monopolies and Mergers Commission, *The Supply of Petrol: A Report on the Supply in the UK of Petrol by Wholesale*, Cm 972 (1990).
Monopolies Commission, *Beer: A Report on the Supply of Beer*, HC 216 (1969).
National Board for Prices and Incomes, Report No. 13, *Costs, Prices, and Profits in the Brewing Industry*, Cmnd 2965 (1966).
National Board for Prices and Incomes, Report No. 136, *Beer Prices*, Cmnd 4227 (1969).
National Economic Development Office Brewing Sector Working Group, *The Outlook for the Brewing Industry; Market Prospects and the Implications for Employment* (1983).
P Nicholson, *Brewer at Bay* (Co. Durham: Memoir Club, 2003). ISBN 184104 069X.
Office of Fair Trading, *The Supply of Beer: A Report on the Review of the Beer Orders by the Former Director General of Fair Trading, Mr John Bridgeman*, OFT 317 (2000).
Price Commission, *Allied Breweries (UK) Limited – Brewing and Wholesaling of Beer and Sales in Managed Houses*, HC 415 (1978).
Price Commission, *Bass Ltd – Wholesale Prices of Beer and Prices in Managed Houses*, HC 109 (1979).
Price Commission, Report No 31, *Beer Prices and Margins* (1977).
Price Commission, *Whitbread and Company Limited – Wholesale Prices and Prices in Managed Houses of Beer, Wines, Spirits, Soft Drinks and Ciders*, HC 110 (1979).
Scottish Office, *Report of the Departmental Committee on Scottish Licensing Laws*, Cmd 5354 (1973).
M Slade, 'Beer and the Tie: Did Divestiture of Brewer-Owned Public Houses Lead to Higher Beer Prices?' *The Economic Journal*, Vol. 108 (1998).
Trade and Industry Select Committee Fifth Report of Session 1994–95, *UK Policy on Monopolies*, HC 240.

Trade and Industry Select Committee Second Report of Session 2004–05, *Pub Companies*, HC 128-1.
Trade and Industry Select Committee Fourth Report of Session 2004–05, *Pub Companies: Responses to the Committee's Second Report of Session 2004–05*, HC 434.
M Waterson, *Beer: The Ties That Bind,* Warwick Economic Research Paper, University of Warwick (2009).
D Young, *The Enterprise Years* (London: Headline Publishing, 1990).

Glossary and Abbreviations

(Words in the right hand column in bold indicate a separate entry within the glossary.)

Term	Abbreviation	Description/definition
Adjournment debate		A general, open-ended, debate in the **House of Commons** in which no vote is taken.
Agriculture Committee		**Select Committee** of the **House of Commons** concerned with agriculture, fisheries and food matters.
Agriculture Minister		A Government minister at **MAFF**.
Annual General Meeting	AGM	Yearly meeting of the members or shareholders of a club or company.
Alternative Investment Market	AIM	Sub-market of the London Stock Exchange mainly populated by smaller companies and more lightly regulated than the main market.
Alcohol by volume	abv	Measure used to assess the alcoholic strength of drinks. Other terms used are "% vol", and "alc vol".
Alcoholic drink		Any drink having an alcoholic strength of at least 1.2% **abv**.
Ale		Traditional British beer, such as bitter, mild, light, pale, export and brown ale.
Association of Licensed Multiple Retailers	ALMR	Trade association for independent pub and bar operators.
Amusement with prizes machine	AWP	Gambling machine requiring no skill. Sometimes known as a fruit machine.
Article 85 {later (81), later (101)}		The Article of the **Treaty of Rome** (and its successors) that deals with certain relationships between individual undertakings which are prohibited if they prevent, restrict or distort competition between Member States. This article catches, *inter alia*, tenancy agreements. However, some agreements (such as pub tenancies) are specifically permitted under the **Block Exemption**.
Article 86 {later (82), later (102)}		The Article of the **Treaty of Rome** (and its successor treaties) that deals with the concept of a dominant market position.

286 *Glossary and Abbreviations*

Term	Abbreviation	Description/definition
Assistant Secretary		A senior grade in the Civil Service, now more commonly titled Divisional Director.
Backbencher		An **MP** who does not hold government office or is not a front bench spokesman in the **Opposition**.
Barrel	Brl	Traditional measure of volume used in UK brewing industry. 1 barrel = 36 gallons, 288 pints, 1.637 **hectolitres** or 1.395 US barrels. Can also refer to casks and kegs which contain **draught beer**.
Barriers to entry		Obstacles that make it difficult to enter a given market and which therefore often hinder competition.
Beer		Generic term covering all beers such as **ales**, **stout** and **lager** as well as **NAB** and **LAB**.
Beer Orders		The two **Statutory Instruments** giving effect to government decisions arising from the 1989 MMC Report.
Better Regulation Task Force		A non-governmental public body set up in 1997 to advise government on action to reduce unnecessary or disproportionate regulation. Replaced in 2006 by the Better Regulation Executive.
"Big six"		Another term used for the **national brewers** at the time of the 1989 Report.
Block Exemptions {67/67; then 1984/83; then 2790/1999; and then 330/2010}		The Block Exemptions declare the prohibitions of certain agreements by **Article 85** (and its successors) inapplicable where the agreements give economic or technical benefits. Among the agreements to benefit from this exemption are **tenancy agreements**.
Board of Trade		Government Department with responsibility until 1970, *inter alia*, for industrial policy, trade, consumer protection and monopolies. Replaced in 1970 by the **DTI**.
Brewers & Licensed Retailers Association	BLRA	Successor body in 1994 to the **Brewers' Society**. Superseded in 2001 by the **British Beer & Pub Association**.
Brewers of Europe		Successor body to the **CBMC**.

Glossary and Abbreviations 287

Term	Abbreviation	Description/definition
Brewers' Society	BS	Trade association representing brewing companies and some **pub companies** until 1994.
Brewery conditioned beers		Technical term for beers which have been subject to processes such as filtration, pasteurisation and carbonation. Often sold as "**keg**" beers.
British Beer & Pub Association	BBPA	Successor body in 2001 to the **Brewers & Licensed Retailers Association**.
British Institute of Innkeeping	BII	The professional body for the licensed retail sector.
Brewer without tied estate	BWTE	A term used by the **MMC** to cover companies which brewed beer but owned no pubs, such as Guinness, Carlsberg and Northern Clubs Federation.
Campaign for Real Ale	CAMRA	A membership organisation set up in 1972 to defend the continued production of **real ale**. The body representing the beer consumer and pub goer.
Cask-conditioned beer		Correct term for **real ale**. A draught beer which continues to condition naturally in the cask and has not undergone any secondary process such as carbonation.
Chancellor of the Duchy of Lancaster		A senior ministerial office in the government.
Chancellor of the Exchequer		The title held by the Cabinet minister responsible for all economic and financial matters.
Chief whip		A **Member of Parliament** appointed by the leader of the party to which he or she belongs and given responsibility for the discipline of the other **MPs** in that party, and in particular for ensuring that they attend and vote in the **House of Commons** according to the wishes of the party leadership.
Clubs		See **licensed clubs** and **registered clubs**.
Code of Practice on Tenants' Security		A series of voluntary undertakings by brewers to give pub tenants a degree of security, including a system of appeals and arbitration.

288 Glossary and Abbreviations

Term	Abbreviation	Description/definition
Committee of Registered Clubs	CORCA	An organisation representing affiliated non-profit making private members' clubs in England and Wales.
Competition Commission	CC	Successor body to the **MMC**. Created in 1999. Conducts inquiries into mergers, markets and major regulated industries in the interests of competition.
Complex monopoly		Defined in the **Fair Trading Act 1973** as a situation in which at least 25 per cent of the relevant market was "supplied by two or more persons who, whether voluntarily or not, so conduct their respective affairs as in any way to prevent, restrict, or distort competition".
Confederation of British Industry	CBI	The foremost lobbying organisation for UK business, promoting the interests of its members.
Confédération des Brasseurs du Marché Commun	CBMC	The federation of national brewer trade associations in the **European Union**. Superseded by the **Brewers of Europe**.
Consumers' Association	CA	Independent campaigning body, now trading as "Which?"
Competition Directorate	DGIV	Competition Directorate of the **European Commission**.
Department for Business, Enterprise and Regulatory Reform	DBERR (or BERR)	Government department that in June 2005 replaced the **DTI**, assuming its responsibilities but with the addition of regulatory reform. Replaced by **DBIS** in June 2009.
Department for Business, Innovation and Skills	DBIS	Government department that in June 2009 replaced **DBERR**, also assuming the responsibilities of the Department for Innovation, Universities and Schools (DIUS).
Department for Culture, Media and Sport	DCMS	Government department responsible since 1997, for, *inter alia*, the arts, broadcasting, the press, museums and galleries, gambling, tourism, and, from 2001 to 2010, liquor licensing.
Department for Environment, Food and Rural Affairs	Defra	Government department with responsibility for policy and regulation of the environment, food and rural affairs.

Glossary and Abbreviations 289

Term	Abbreviation	Description/definition
Department of Prices and Consumer Protection	DPCP	Government department responsible from 1974 to 1979 for consumer protection, weights and measures, consumer credit, the **Price Commission** and the **Office of Fair Trading**.
Department of the Environment		Government department responsible from 1970 to 1997 for a mixed portfolio of issues including housing, planning, local government and environmental protection.
Departmental Committee on Liquor Licensing		Committee established in December 1970 by the **Home Office** to examine licensing laws in England and Wales; chaired by Lord Erroll.
Departmental Committee on Scottish Licensing Laws		Committee established in December 1970 by the **Secretary of State** for Scotland to examine licensing laws in Scotland; chaired by Dr Christopher Clayson.
Deputy Secretary		A senior grade in the Civil Service, reporting to the **Permanent Secretary**.
Director General of Fair Trading	DGFT	The public official heading up the **OFT**.
Draught Beer		Beer dispensed from large containers, such as kegs and casks.
Dry rent		A below-market property rent charged to tenants by the brewer owning the pub, in conjunction with **wet rent**.
Department of Trade and Industry	DTI	Government department responsible, from 1970 to 2005 for, *inter alia*, trade, company law, employment law, consumer law and competition policy. Replaced by **DBERR**.
Duty-free		Purchases of alcoholic drinks and other goods by individual travellers on which no import duties are payable. Discontinued between the EU Member States in July 1999.
Duty-paid		Alcoholic drinks and other goods on which duties have been paid in the country of purchase. All goods brought in by individual travellers travelling between EU Member States are duty-paid.

Term	Abbreviation	Description/definition
Early Day Motion	EDM	A formal motion submitted to Parliament for debate. Few EDMs are debated, but are submitted for reasons such as publicising the views of a Member of the **House of Commons**, or drawing attention to specific events or campaigns.
Erroll Committee		See **Departmental Committee on Liquor Licensing**.
EU Regulation		A Regulation promulgated by the European Commission having the force of law in each Member State. The **Block Exemption** is such a Regulation.
European Commission		The executive arm of the **European Union** responsible for implementing the decisions of the European Parliament and the Council. The Commission is organised by department, or DG, each with specific responsibilities. The officials and Commissioners are drawn from the Member States.
European Court of Justice	ECJ	The highest court in **the European Union (EU)**. It is charged with interpreting European Law and ensuring its equal interpretation across all Member States.
European Economic Community; European Community	EEC / EC	Established by the 1957 **Treaty of Rome** with the objective of bringing closer economic integration, including a single market, amongst its six founding Member States. Now called the **European Union**.
European Treaty		A set of different Articles, which have the force of law in each Member State. The original Treaty was the **Treaty of Rome**; the current version is the Lisbon Treaty.
European Union	EU	The **European Community** became the European Union in 1993, at which time there were 14 Member States. This economic and political union is now composed of 27 Member State countries and operates through a system of supranational independent institutions including the **European Commission** and the **European Court of Justice**.

Term	Abbreviation	Description/definition
Excise duty		Duties which are specific to defined products, such as alcoholic drinks.
Fair Trading Act 1973		Act of Parliament which established the **Office of Fair Trading** and defined **scale** and **complex monopolies**. Superseded by the Competition Act 1998, it also gave the government powers to take remedial action.
Federation of Licensed Victuallers Association	FLVA	Members' organisation protecting the interests of self-employed licensees.
Federation of Small Businesses	FSB	Membership group which promotes and protects the interests of the self-employed and owners of small firms.
Flexible opening hours		The result of changes in the licensing laws allowing **pubs** to apply to vary their opening hours.
Fortified wine		A wine which has been fortified, or strengthened, with the addition of brandy. Usually over 15% **abv**.
Free trade		That part of the market represented by licensed properties not owned by brewers. See also **free trade outlets**.
Free trade outlet		Licensed retail outlet not owned by a brewery company.
Full on-licence		Retail outlet with a licence to sell alcohol to the public for consumption on or off the premises.
Guest beer		A legal entitlement of the tenants of big brewers, introduced by the Tied Estate Order, permitting them to stock one brand of cask-conditioned draught beer from a supplier other than their landlord.
HM Government	HMG	Her (or His) Majesty's Government, a frequently used term for the **UK** Government.
Hectolitre	Hl Hls	International measure of volume, a part of the metric system. It equals 100 **litres**. 1hl = 22 gallons or 0.611 **barrels**.
Her Majesty's Revenue and Customs	HMRC	Government department concerned, *inter alia,* with the collection of **excise duty**.

Term	Abbreviation	Description/definition
Home Office		Government department responsible for immigration and passports, drugs policy, crime, police, alcohol policy and licensing. From 2001 until 2010 responsibility for alcohol licensing resided with the **DCMS**.
Home Secretary		Government minister in charge of the Home Office.
Horizontal integration		The amalgamation of companies in the same industry and at the same stage of production.
House of Commons		Elected lower House of the UK Parliament.
House of Lords		The unelected Upper House of the UK Parliament whose members consist of Hereditary Peers (sitting by virtue of birth), Life Peers (appointed by government) and the bishops of the Church of England.
Independent Family Brewers of Britain	IFBB	Organisation founded in 1993 to represent the interests of family owned and managed brewing companies.
International Monetary Fund	IMF	Intergovernmental organisation that oversees the global financial system.
Keg beer		Another name for **brewery conditioned beer**.
Lager		Worldwide, the most popular type of beer. Normally lighter in colour than ales or stout, and usually served at a lower temperature.
Lease agreement		An agreement between a brewing company or **pubco** and someone running a **pub**. It is usually for a longer period of time than the traditional **tenancy agreement**.
Lessee		An individual or a company having a lease from a brewing company or **pubco**.
Licensed club		Established by the 1961 Licensing Act, a commercial enterprise, operated by individuals or a company, selling alcoholic drinks to members.
Licensed outlet		An outlet licensed to sell **alcoholic drink**. Until the 2003 Licensing Act all licences were approved by **licensing magistrates** (also known as licensing justices), but licensing is now the responsibility of local authorities.

Glossary and Abbreviations 293

Term	Abbreviation	Description/definition
Licensee		The holder of a licence to sell alcohol in specified licensed premises.
Licensing agreement		An agreement between two major brewers whereby a UK brewer agrees to produce and distribute in the UK a foreign brewer's beers and to pay a royalty to the brand owner.
Licensing Courts		Courts specially convened to consider licensing application and renewals. They were composed of local **licensing magistrates**.
Licensing magistrates (or justices)		Local magistrates who became members of the **Licensing Courts** and were charged with administering the licensing system locally.
Litre	l ls	The standard volume measure of the metric system. 1 litre = 1.76 **pints**.
Litres of pure alcohol	LPA	Measurement of volume derived by converting alcoholic drinks into terms of 100% alcohol.
Local brewer		Brewing company operating in a relatively small area, within the proximity of its brewery.
Local concentration/ monopoly		A situation whereby one brewer owns a substantial proportion of **full on-licences** in a given area. The definitions of proportion and area were different over time.
Low Alcohol Beer	LAB	Beer having a strength between 0.05 and 1.2% **abv**.
Made-wine		Wine not of fresh grape; at one time had substantial sales in the UK.
Managed pubs		Pubs owned by a brewing or **pub company** which are managed by an employee of the owning company.
Market and Opinion Research International	MORI	A market research company.
Member of Parliament	MP	Elected member of the **House of Commons**.
Member of European Parliament	MEP	Elected member of the European Parliament.
Microbrewer		Very small brewing business, whose annual output is typically a few hundred barrels.

294 *Glossary and Abbreviations*

Term	Abbreviation	Description/definition
Minister of State		A government minister responsible to the **Secretary of State** within a particular department.
Ministry of Agriculture, Fisheries and Food	MAFF	Government department responsible for agriculture, fisheries and the food industry, including the beer industry. Replaced in 2001 by the Department for Environment, Food and Rural Affairs (**Defra**).
Monopolies and Mergers Commission	MMC	Created by the Fair Trading Act 1973 and replaced in 1999 by the **Competition Commission**, the independent body that investigated monopolies that might be created by company mergers or takeovers. It also investigated companies, industries or local authorities suspected of operating in a non-competitive way.
Monopolies Commission	MC	Predecessor organisation to the **MMC**. Created in 1948 as an independent tribunal to investigate potential monopoly situations. It was granted power to review mergers in 1965.
Morning Advertiser		Newspaper specialising in news and issues relating to the licensed trade. At the time of the Report it was published six times a week.
National account		A multi-outlet on- or off-trade business or organisation in which supply terms and arrangements are negotiated centrally.
National Association of Licensed House Managers	NAHLM	The Association representing the interests of public house managers.
National Board for Prices and Incomes	NBPI	The Board was established in 1965 with the aim of helping to control inflation.
National brewers		At the time of the 1986–89 MMC inquiry, Allied-Lyons, Bass, Courage, Grand Metropolitan, Scottish & Newcastle and Whitbread. Also called the "**big 6**".
National Economic Development Council	NEDC	Tripartite body established in the early 1960s to help promote economic growth. Composed of representatives from industry, trade unions and government. Discontinued in 1979.

Term	Abbreviation	Description/definition
National Licensed Victuallers Association	NLVA	Successor body to the **NULV**.
National Union of Licensed Victuallers	NULV	Body established to represent the interests of tenants and other licensees.
Need criterion		Criterion frequently used by **licensing magistrates** in the past to determine whether an application for a new licence was justified by market need.
No alcohol beer	NAB	Beer of less than 0.05% **abv**.
Off-licence		A licence for the sale of alcohol to be consumed off the premises. Also, premises licensed in this way.
Off-trade		That part of the licensed trade represented by outlets licensed to sell alcohol for consumption off the premises.
Office of Fair Trading	OFT	Non-ministerial government body, established in 1973, which enforces consumer protection and consumer law, acting as the UK's economic regulator.
On consumption		Alcoholic drinks consumed in on-licensed premises, such as **pubs**, hotels, inns, restaurants, and **clubs**.
On-licence		A licence for the sale of alcohol to be consumed on the premises. Also, premises licensed in this way.
On-trade		That part of the licensed trade represented by outlets licensed to sell alcohol for consumption on the premises.
Opposition (The)		Properly, the Official Opposition. The political party with the second largest number of seats in the **House of Commons**.
Parliament		In the UK this consists of two Houses: The **House of Commons** and the **House of Lords**.
Parliamentary Under Secretary of State		The lowest of three tiers of government minister in the **UK**, junior to both a **Secretary of State** and a **Minister of State**.
Permanent Secretary		The most senior Civil Servant in a government department.

Term	Abbreviation	Description/definition
Permitted hours		Specified hours during which a particular licensed premise may retail alcohol.
Personal imports		Beer and other drinks imported by individual travellers. Such imports might be **duty paid** or **duty free**.
Petty Sessional Division	PSD	Administrative area covered by a **Licensing Court**; may or may not have been identical to local authority districts. Discontinued by the Licensing Act 2003.
Pint		Traditional measure for the retailing of **draught beer** in the UK. 1 pint = 0.57 **litres**.
Price Commission	PC	Body set up in 1973 to control inflation. It had powers to recommend or reject applications for price increases made by companies. Abolished in 1979.
Principal Officer		A grade in the Civil Service at the time of the MMC inquiry, generally reporting to an **Assistant Secretary**. Now obsolete.
Progressivity		System whereby small brewers pay lower rates of **excise duty**.
Pub companies (Pubcos)		Non-brewers owning pubs. Either former brewing companies or companies established specifically to operate pubs.
Pub swaps		Arrangements by which brewers exchanged public houses with the aim of reducing **local concentrations**.
Public bar		The lowest priced bar in a **pub** having more than one bar.
Public house (pub)		An outlet licensed for sale of drinks for consumption on the premises and the traditional venue for drinking draught beers.
Real ale		Popular name for **cask-conditioned beer**.
Reciprocal trading arrangements		Contractual arrangement whereby two parties agree to sell the products of the other party.
Regional brewer		Brewer operating over a substantial area of the country (several counties) and possibly having more than one brewery.

Term	Abbreviation	Description/definition
Registered club		Non-profit making organisation run by its members.
Resale price maintenance	RPM	System whereby manufacturers set retail prices. Now illegal in the UK and EU.
Research Bureau Ltd	RBL	A market research company.
Restaurant licence		Licence introduced in the 1964 Licensing Act permitting the sale of alcoholic drinks to people having meals. Discontinued by the 2003 Licensing Act.
Restricted on-licence		Licence introduced in the 1964 Licensing Act permitting the sale of alcoholic drinks to people staying in hotels or having meals.
Restrictive covenant		A condition placed on the sale of a former **pub** by a brewer or **pubco** preventing its use as a **public house**.
Retail price index	RPI	Official price index whose purpose is to measure movements in UK retail prices, and hence inflation.
Retail price of beer		The price of beer paid by customers in **pubs**, **clubs**, **off-licences** and similar locations, *cf* **wholesale prices**.
Scale monopoly		Defined at the time of the MMC inquiry, under the **Fair Trading Act 1973**, as a situation where a single company or group supplied at least 25 per cent of goods or services of a particular type.
Select Committee		A Committee in the **House of Commons** consisting of at least 11 MPs. There is a Committee for each Government Department examining the spending, policy and administration of that Department.
Secretary of State		A Cabinet Minister in charge of a government department, such as the DTI.
Shadow spokesman		A member of the **Opposition** who shadows or marks an individual member of the Government. Together, Shadow spokesmen form the Shadow Front Bench.

Term	Abbreviation	Description/definition
Society of Independent Brewers	SIBA	Successor in 1995 to the Small Independent Brewers Association, a membership organisation representing the interests of small and microbrewers, whose abbreviated name it retains.
Spirits		Covers many different drinks categories, the best known being whisky, gin, vodka, rum and liqueurs.
Statutory Instrument		The principal form in which delegated or secondary legislation is made in Great Britain.
Stout		A dark beer which may be sweet or bitter in taste. Guinness is the best known brand.
Supply agreement		Contractual agreement whereby a retailer agrees to purchase certain products from a supplier at defined prices and for a defined period of time.
Table wine		A drink from fresh grape being between 8.5% and 15% **abv**.
Tenancy agreement		The agreement between the owner of a **pub** (brewer or **pubco**) and a tenant.
Tenanted pub		**Pub** owned by a brewer or **pubco** which is let to a tenant.
The tie		Contractual arrangement whereby the tenant or lessee of a licensed property is obliged to purchase certain products for resale from the owner of the property.
Tied estate		Pubs and other outlets owned by brewing companies or pubcos.
Tied house system		At the time of the **MMC** inquiry the vertically integrated system by which brewers owned **pubs**, whether **managed** or **tenanted**.
Treaty of Rome		The 1957 Treaty that established the **European Economic Community**.
Trades Union Congress	TUC	Organisation representing all affiliated trades unions in the UK.
Value added tax	VAT	A sales tax. In the case of alcoholic drinks it is levied on the duty-inclusive price.

Glossary and Abbreviations

Term	Abbreviation	Description/definition
Vertical Integration		The integration of successive stages of the production and marketing process under the ownership of a single company or entity.
Wet rent		A premium above the free market price for beer charged to pub tenants to compensate the brewer for a below-market **dry rent**.
Whitbread "umbrella"		See Whitbread Investment Company.
Whitbread Investment Company	WIC	Company set up to acquire some of the shares held in small brewers by Whitbread under its "umbrella" policy. Taken over by Whitbread in 1993.
Whitehall		An area of central London where most of the UK government departments and ministries are located. Frequently used, as in the context of this book, to describe the overall government administration.
Wholesale price of beer		The price of beer as it leaves the brewery or the price charged by an independent **wholesaler**.
Wholesaler		Company which operates in the distribution chain between manufacturers (such as brewers) and retailers (such as **pubs**).
Wine		Includes **fortified wine**, **made-wine** and **table wine**.

Index

Aaronson, Robin   51, 54, 223, 267
Adnams   34, 136, 144, 145, 192, 239
Agriculture Select Committee   116–17, 125, 142–4, 173, 176, 179, 246
alcohol
  anti-alcohol lobby   16, 69
  consumption   15, 67, 80, 198, 199, 229, 247, 264
  problem, misuse, abuse, concern   8, 15, 16, 67, 69, 80, 221, 222, 229 *see also* binge drinking
ale(s)   22, 23, 31, 32, 38, 39, 59, 76, 85, 97, 137, 156, 165, 191, 192–3, 221, 227, 229, 230, 239 *see also* cask-conditioned ale(s)/beer(s)
Allied (Allied Breweries; Allied-Lyons; Allied Domecq)   4, 5, 11, 27, 29, 34, 49, 52, 68, 78, 109, 153, 169, 240
  acquisitions in 1960s and 1970s   27
  bid by Elders IXL and MMC inquiry 1986   29, 51, 128
  Campaign for Real Ale allegation of dominance in Chilterns area 1976   24
  compliance with Beer Orders 1992   133–4
  deal with Pubmaster 1992   134
  evidence to Agriculture Select Committee 1993   144, 173
  exchange of pubs 1978   22, 23
  failed bid for Boddingtons 1970   4
  formation of Allied Breweries 1961   2, 3
  investigation by Price Commission 1977   24–5, 184
  meeting with Francis Maude June 1989   109
  notification to Price Commission of planned price increase 1977   24, 25, 32
  ownership of pubs in Birmingham noted in MC Report 1969   11
  proposed merger with Carlsberg in the UK and MMC inquiry 1992   132–4, 142, 237
  proposed sale of pub estate to Whitbread 1999   158–60, 237
  sale of interest in Carlsberg-Tetley to Bass 1996 and MMC inquiry   156–7
Alternative Hotel Group   166
amusement with prizes machines (AWPs)   70, 80, 201, 211, 213, 214, 215, 218, 251
Anheuser-Busch   135, 160, 162
Ansells   3
Arkell   52
Arthur Andersen   64
Arthur Bell   67
Association of Licensed Multiple Retailers (ALMR)   144, 210, 216, 217
Aylesbury Brewery Company   24

Bain & Company   43
Bannock, Graham   186
Barclay brothers   174
Barclay Perkins   2
barriers to entry   7, 19, 20, 55, 61, 70, 149, 221, 228 *see also* new entrants
Bass (Bass, Ratcliff & Gretton; Bass, Mitchells & Butlers; Bass Charrington)   23, 26, 27, 34, 35, 36, 47, 49, 52, 104, 109, 134, 135, 137, 156, 157, 158, 160, 223, 230, 237, 238, 240
  acquisition of Allied Domecq's share of Carlsberg-Tetley 1996 and MMC inquiry   156–7
  compliance with Beer Orders 1992   134–5
  concentration of pubs noted by Monopolies Commission 1969   11
  European Commission exemption for lease 1999   149

Index   301

evidence to Agriculture Select
    Committee 1993   137, 144
exchange of pubs 1977   22
formation of Bass Charrington   3, 4
investigation by Price Commission
    1979   25, 33, 184
lease notified to European
    Commission 1996   148, 206
market share growth strategy 1992
    135
meetings with Ministers and officials
    1989   109
MMC Report on proposed acquisition
    of Carlsberg-Tetley and Bass
    response 1997   87, 156–7, 237
sale of beer assets following
    Competition Commission
    rejection of Bass/Interbrew deal
    2001   161
sale of beer business to Interbrew and
    Competition Commission inquiry
    2000   160–1, 237
shareholding in Taunton Cider
    Company   46, 68, 78
Beards   165, 169
Beckett, Margaret   157, 158
"beerage"   1
beer brands   38, 52, 56, 59, 167, 168
  Ansell's   192
  Bass Ale   192
  Becks   239
  Boddingtons   192
  Carling Black Label   2, 60, 239
  Carlsberg   156, 239
  Charrington IPA   192
  choice of/range of   32, 38, 39, 59, 62,
      80–1, 96, 97, 129, 165, 191, 242
  Courage Best   192
  Double Diamond   4
  Flowers   192
  Foster's   29, 239
  Fuller's London Pride   192, 230
  Greene King Abbot   192
  Greene King IPA   192
  Guinness   39, 46, 59, 66, 78, 229
  Harp   66–7
  Heineken   158, 162, 258
  Ind Coope   192
  John Smith's   192, 239
  Kaliber   43, 66, 67, 75
  Kronenbourg   239
  M&B   192
  Marston's Pedigree   192, 230
  Old Speckled Hen   169
  Red Barrel   5
  Stella Artois   158, 160, 161, 239
  Tankard   5
  Tartan   5
  Tavern   5
  Tetley Bitter   156, 239
  Timothy Taylor Landlord   192
  Wadworth 6X   192, 230
  Wells Bombardier   192
  Whitbread Best   192
  Worthington   4
  Young's Bitter   192
beer consumption/sales   36, 37, 38, 46,
    52, 58, 60, 64, 65, 66, 129, 141, 152,
    170, 172, 190, 191, 195–8, 201, 203,
    228, 232, 239, 240
Beer Orders   49, 116, 165, 166, 167,
    168, 169, 170, 171, 226, 231, 232,
    235, 236, 237, 238, 239, 240, 241,
    242, 243
  cost of, estimate by Agriculture Select
      Committee 1993   144
  criticism of in Adjournment Debate
      November 1991   139
  drafting of 1989   121
  Early Day Motion concerning
      December 1991   124
  effect of, review by Agriculture Select
      Committee 1993   125, 142–4
  effect on beer prices   185
  effect on beer sales   199–201
  effect on choice of beer brands   193
  review of by OFT 2000   205–8
  revocation of 2003   208
  see also Supply of Beer (Loan Ties,
      Licensed Premises and Wholesale
      Prices) Order and Supply of Beer
      (Tied Estate) Order
beer production   1, 35, 36, 37, 39, 63, 65,
    74, 75, 76, 82, 94, 104, 210, 260, 261
Beesley, Professor ME   133
Belhaven   34, 170, 174
Benner, Mike   170
Benskin's   2
Better Regulation Task Force   247
"big six", see brewers, "big six"
binge drinking   202
Blennerhassett Report   16

302 *Index*

Block Exemption   63, 81, 88, 89, 93, 94, 95, 103, 106, 111, 113, 116, 146, 148, 218, 254–5, 256, 257, 258–9
  see also European Community Regulation (EEC) No 1984/83
Board of Trade   4, 7, 10
Boddington, Ewart   41
Boddingtons   3, 4, 27, 34, 136, 153, 165–6, 170, 173, 236, 241
Borrie, Sir Gordon, Director General of Fair Trading   41, 44, 48, 49, 51, 73, 87, 105–6, 115, 184, 235, 249, 267
  address to Campaign for Real Ale AGM 1992   142
  advice to Secretary of State regarding MMC Report 1989   87–9, 103, 105
  letter to Brewers' Society August 1985   32, 41, 51
  letter to MMC August 1986   49
  meetings with Brewers' Society 1986   44, 49
  speech to Leicester Chamber of Commerce December 1985   41, 42, 43, 44, 167, 222
  see also Office of Fair Trading
Brain, SA   163
Brakspear   3, 136, 168
Brent Walker   173–4
Brewer at Bay   54 *see also* Nicholson, Sir Paul
brewers
  "big six"   2, 3, 4, 23, 27, 34, 35, 46, 47, 97, 115, 129, 161, 162, 163, 174, 210, 228, 230, 238, 240
  integrated/pub-owning   2, 4, 23, 27, 43, 53, 64, 66, 67, 68, 69, 76, 97, 119, 129, 134, 173, 174, 200, 208, 229, 236, 238, 241
  local   23, 58, 61, 70, 74, 75, 77, 78, 79, 82, 85, 105, 109, 110, 115, 133, 141, 170, 192, 201, 212, 229, 230, 231, 235, 240
  major/national   23, 24, 28, 33, 35, 38, 39, 43, 45, 46, 52, 58, 61, 66, 69, 70, 75, 78, 79, 81, 82, 84, 86, 88, 89, 92, 93, 104, 110, 122, 125, 131, 137, 139, 140, 141, 142, 144, 159, 167, 173, 175, 180, 201, 212, 231, 234, 239
  micro-   34, 74, 75, 171–2, 192–3
  open letter to Lord Young 26 April 1989   105
  overseas   33, 61, 221, 239, 240–1, 242, 258
  regional   23, 24, 27, 28, 34, 35, 45, 52, 58, 61, 66, 74, 75, 77, 78, 79, 82, 85, 97, 105, 111, 115, 133, 135, 141, 169, 170, 192, 201, 212, 229, 230, 231, 235
  small Scottish   170
  without tied estate   33, 34, 58, 65–6, 73, 75
Brewers & Licensed Retailers Association (BLRA)
  evidence to Trade and Industry Select Committee 1995   145
  support for extension of Block Exemption 1997   258
  wholesale price survey 2000   186
  see also Brewers' Society *and* British Beer & Pub Association
Brewers' Society   11, 12, 13, 21, 23, 24, 32, 35, 38, 52, 53, 54, 55, 56, 57, 62, 63, 64, 65, 79, 81, 82, 92, 95, 97, 103, 106, 108, 109, 110, 111, 112, 115, 123, 140, 167, 187, 222, 223, 224, 228, 236, 241, 242, 253, 256, 258
  advertising campaign April–May 1989   106, 107, 108, 168
  Annual General Meeting December 1985   41
  Annual Report 1985   41
  Annual Report 1989   56, 107
  briefing note on position of tenants and Tied Estate Order September 1991   125
  Council   11, 52
  engagement with the OFT in the run-up to MMC reference 1985–6   44, 45, 47, 48, 49
  Executive Committee   11, 52
  MMC Steering Committee established 1986   52, 167, 169
  response to MMC's Public Interest Letter April 1988   56, 200
  response to Price Commission inquiry and Report 1977–8   20
  response to setting up of Price Commission inquiry 1977   19

Index   303

Statement on 1969 MC Report   11–12
surveys conducted and submitted to
    MMC 1986–89   26, 38, 58, 59,
    60, 61–2, 80–1, 94, 225–6
Tenants' Code of Practice   77, 83, 96,
    113, 123
"Leading Leisure in Britain" February
    1989   96
"Recommendations made by the
    MMC and their likely
    consequences" 1989   93, 95
"Report of the MMC on the Supply of
    Beer: a Critique" 1989   93–5, 98,
    111–12
"The Tied House System" note 1978
    21
see also Brewers & Licensed Retailers
    Association and British Beer &
    Pub Association
brewing capacity   7, 8, 33, 35, 55, 74,
    75, 95, 96, 97
Brewing Sector Working Group of the
    National Economic Development
    Council   15
Brickwoods   27
Bridge, Tim   168, 169, 267
Bridgeman, John   156, 158, 159, 171,
    205, 206, 207, 208, 211, 267
Bristol Brewery Georges   3
British Beer & Pub Association (BBPA)
    11, 36, 37, 38, 66, 152, 172, 188,
    189, 215, 217
    defence of pubcos to Business and
        Enterprise Select Committee   215
    evidence to Trade and Industry Select
        Committee 2004   210, 212
    Framework Code of Practice   212,
        214, 217, 218
    see also Brewers' Society and Brewers &
        Licensed Retailers Association
British Institute of Innkeeping   217
Brittan, Sir Leon   89, 103, 105, 256
Brittanic Assurance   28
Britvic Soft Drinks (Britvic Corona)   33,
    78, 79
Brown, Gordon   122, 171
Brown, Matthew   3, 27–9, 33, 43, 128,
    184, 223
Bullard & Son   3
Bulmer, HP   33, 45, 46, 55, 68–9, 78,
    109

Burbridge, Stephen   53, 55, 268
Burtonwood   124, 168
Business, Innovation and Skills Select
    Committee inquiry into pubcos
    2009   216
Business and Enterprise Select
    Committee inquiry into pubcos
    2008   190, 213–16
Byers, Stephen   159, 161, 208

C&C Group   162
Cameron, JW   27, 168, 170, 174
Campaign for Real Ale (CAMRA)   44,
    49, 83, 108, 109, 114, 141, 170,
    222, 224, 234
    allegation of dominance in Chilterns
        area by Allied-Lyons 1976   24
    allegation of dominance in Norfolk
        by Grand Metropolitan 1986   46
    appeal to Competition Appeal
        Tribunal   217
    comment on reduced expenditure
        in pubs 1999   200
    evidence submitted to MMC Supply
        of Beer inquiry   55, 70, 78
    evidence to Agriculture Select
        Committee inquiry 1993   143
    evidence to Business and Enterprise
        Select Committee 2008   215
    evidence to Trade and Industry Select
        Committee inquiry 1995   145
    evidence to Trade and Industry Select
        Committee inquiry 2004   210,
        211, 212, 213
    letter to Lord Young concerning
        MMC Report 1989   97–8, 238
    meeting with Ministers and officials
        regarding MMC
        recommendations 1989   109
    super-complaint 2009–10   216–17, 218
Canadian Breweries   2
Cannon, Michael   166, 168, 169
Carlsberg   34, 58, 66, 132, 133, 142,
    156–8, 254
Carlsberg-Tetley Ltd (CTL)   132–3,
    156–8, 237, 238
Carsberg, Sir Bryan   148, 154, 268
cask-conditioned ales(s)/beer(s)   4,
    24, 79, 84, 97, 110, 137, 172, 229,
    234, 236, 239, 255
Castle, Barbara   5

304 Index

Centric Pub Company   135, 174
Century Inns   135, 153, 174, 175
Charles MacKinley   27
Charles Wells   124, 135, 170, 181
Charrington   3
Chef & Brewer   155, 158, 161, 169
choice   42, 49, 62, 65, 78, 82, 85, 92, 104, 111
  between pubs   58, 70, 78, 191
  of brands   44, 46, 83, 84, 226
  within pubs   11, 32, 38, 58, 59, 70, 97, 99, 165, 191–3, 225, 228
cider   11, 33, 45, 46, 59, 68, 74, 78, 79, 85, 110, 198
Clayson, Dr Christopher   13, 268
Clayson Report   12–16, 245–6
Clore, Charles   1, 2, 3
club(s)   20, 21, 58, 79, 95, 104, 108, 111, 112, 196, 201, 227, 234, 249, 250
Coca Cola Schweppes Beverages Ltd   78
Committee of Registered Clubs   109
Competition Act 1998   249, 253
Competition Appeal Tribunal   217
Competition Commission report on proposed sale of Bass's beer interests to Interbrew 2001   160–1
Concordia case   254
Confédération des Brasseurs du Marché Commun (CBMC)   258
Confederation of British Industry (CBI)   18
Conquest Inns   176
Conservative Government   9, 15, 16, 18, 32, 41, 87, 89, 93, 101, 103, 104, 105, 108, 109, 110, 111, 112, 113, 114, 115, 116, 117, 169, 184, 222, 230, 233, 234, 238, 242
consolidation   1–4, 20, 22, 27, 35, 39, 44, 70, 165, 176, 207, 222, 229, 240, 241
Consumers' Association (CA)   108
  evidence to MMC Supply of Beer Inquiry   55, 70, 78, 227
  evidence to Trade and Industry Select Committee 1995   145
  meeting with Francis Maude 1989   109
  reaction to MMC Supply of Beer Report   99–100

Control Securities   174
Cooks   165
Coors (Molson Coors)   158, 162, 237, 239
Cottrell, Michael   52
Counter-Inflation legislation   18
Courage (Courage, Barclay & Simonds)   4, 11, 12, 34, 35, 52, 104, 135, 174, 178, 181, 182, 223, 237, 241
  acquisition by Scottish & Newcastle 1995   152–6, 237
  evidence to Agriculture Select Committee 1993   144
  exchange of pubs 1970/1   12
  exchange of pubs 1977/8   22
  formation of Courage, Barclay & Simonds   2, 3
  "pubs-for-breweries" deal with Grand Met and MMC inquiry 1990   129–32, 237
  representations to OFT 1991   140
  shareholding in Taunton Cider Company   46, 68, 78
  sold to Elders IXL 1986   128
  sold to Imperial Tobacco 1972   27, 128
  see also Elders IXL and Inntrepreneur Estates Limited (IEL)
Cox, Stephen   224
Crehan, Bernard/the Crehan case   181–3
Crosland, Anthony   9
Crowther, Stan   124, 125, 126, 127, 139, 179, 231, 232

Daily Express   93, 115
Daily Mail   93, 176
Darby, Charles   137
Daresbury, Lord   166
Davenports   168
Delimitis case   182
Departmental Committee on Liquor Licensing see Erroll Report
Departmental Committee on Scottish Licensing Law see Clayson Report
Department of the Environment   105
Department of Trade and Industry (DTI)   10, 29, 44, 49, 89, 103–8, 110–12, 114, 116, 121, 123, 142–3, 139, 154, 155, 161, 215, 229, 230, 233, 234, 237, 238

Devenish, JA   166, 170, 173, 236
De Vere Group   166 *see also* Greenall Whitley
DG IV   63, 252
Diageo   27
discounts *see* prices, beer, discounts
Discovery Inns   174, 175
Distillers Company Limited   44, 67
Dobson, Iain   97
drink/driving   16
drunkenness   15, 16, 199 *see also* alcohol problem *and* binge drinking
Drybrough   3
Dutton's   4
duty   10, 33, 37, 61, 68, 69, 76, 83, 98, 144, 171, 172, 197, 213, 222, 230, 250

Early Day Motion (EDM)   103, 124, 125, 127, 139
Elders IXL   29, 51, 140, 223, 237
  acquisition of Courage 1986   128
  proposed deal with Grand Met and MMC Report 1990   130–1
  proposed merger with Scottish & Newcastle and MMC Report 1989   52, 104, 128–9, 154, 237
  see also Courage
Eldridge Pope   52, 109, 168
Ellerman Lines   27
Elliott, John   104, 268
Enterprise Inns
  acquisition of Unique Pub Company 2004   176
  acquisition of Laurel Pub Company 2001–02   176
  evidence to Trade and Industry Select Committee 2004   215
  expansion of   175
  purchase of pubs from Bass 1991   175
  share price   176
  see also pub companies/pubco(s)
Erroll Report   13–14, 15–16, 31, 32, 229, 245–6, 247
Erroll, Lord   13, 14, 15, 16, 268
European Commission (EC)   48, 63, 88, 89, 96, 97, 105–6, 111, 113, 116, 146, 148, 182, 206, 218, 234, 253–8
European Community Regulation (EEC) No 1984/83   31, 32, 47, 63, 68, 77, 78, 81, 82, 83, 88, 93, 116, 148, 254 *see also* Block Exemption
Evans, Jonathan   155
excise duty *see* duty
"progressivity"/sliding scale   171
exclusive supply agreement(s)   88, 106 *see also* supply agreement(s)

Fair Pint Campaign   214
Fair Trading Act 1973   24, 49, 55, 56, 73, 80, 82, 87, 155, 224
Federation of Licensed Victuallers Associations   217
Federation of Small Businesses (FSB)   210, 211, 212, 213, 214, 215, 217
Financial Times   92, 105, 114
Flint, Percy   51, 268
Flowers   3, 4 *see also* beer brands
Forth, Eric   107
Foster, Mike   268
Freeman, Peter   53, 54, 255, 268
free trade   6, 8, 14, 27, 47, 64, 69, 99, 169, 170, 228, 236
  loans   25, 26, 33, 44, 46, 55, 56, 69, 79, 94, 95, 97, 98, 101, 110–11, 113, 224, 230, 231, 234 *see also* loan tie(s)/loan-tying
Fremlins   3, 4
Fuller, Anthony   49, 52, 109, 141, 269
Fuller Smith & Turner   34, 52, 170, 181
full-line forcing and tie-in sales   26 *see also under* Monopolies and Mergers Commission

Gales   133, 170
Garafas, George   186
Gibbs Mew   175
Gould, Bryan   106, 114, 116, 269
Government *see* Conservative Government *and* Labour Government
Goyder, Dan   51, 53, 54, 269

Index

Grand Metropolitan (Grand Metropolitan Hotels) 2, 34, 35–6, 49, 52, 77, 106, 109, 122t, 152, 153, 154, 161, 174, 179, 236, 237, 240, 241
  acquisitions of Truman Hanbury & Buxton 1971 and Watney Mann 1972 27
  allegation by CAMRA of abuse of monopoly in Norfolk 1986 46
  evidence to Agriculture Select Committee 1993 144
  MMC Report on proposed deal with Courage October 1990 130–2
  "pubs-for-breweries" deal with Courage 1990 129–30, 140, 173, 178
  sale of Chef & Brewer 1993 155, 158
  see also Watney *and* Inntrepreneur Estates Ltd (IEL)
Grant, Martin 167
Gravatt, Bernard 51, 53, 269
Grays 165
Greenall Whitley 4, 12, 23, 27, 34, 45, 68, 109, 120, 166, 168, 170
Greene King 34, 45, 52, 67, 68, 111, 133, 135, 136, 168, 169, 170, 240
guest beer (provision) 83, 85, 86, 87, 88, 95, 98, 99, 100–1, 106, 107, 110, 113, 114, 115, 120, 137, 145, 167, 171, 172, 193, 206, 208, 213, 226, 229–30, 232, 234, 236
Guinness 4, 28, 33, 34, 35, 46, 58, 73, 109, 222, 229, 254
  approach and submission to OFT regarding tied house system 1985–86 42–3, 45, 222
  meetings with Ministers and officials concerning MMC recommendations 1989 109–10
  named as part of complex monopoly in Supply of Beer Report 1989 55, 73
  participation in Harp Lager consortium 1977 67
  representations to MMC regarding S&N bid for Matthew Brown 1985 28, 34, 42–3, 222
  submission to Supply of Beer inquiry 1986–89 53, 55, 65–8, 75, 78
  whisky interests 67
  see also beer brands

Guinness, Edward 41, 49, 269
"Guinness Affair" 43–4

Hall & Woodhouse 109
Hamilton, Neil 143
Hanson Trust 128
Hardie, Jeremy 53, 64, 223, 269
Hardys & Hansons 34, 135, 170
Harris, Lord 111
Hattersley, Roy 18, 20–1, 22, 23, 270
Heath, Edward 18
Heavitree 165
Heineken (Heineken UK) 162, 237, 238 *see also* beer brands
Heseltine, Michael 133, 143, 154–5, 156, 205, 238, 270
Hewitt, Patricia 161
Hiram Walker 29
Hoffman, Lord 146
Holden-Brown, Sir Derrick 23, 49, 270
Home Brewery 128
Hope & Anchor 2
horizontal integration 55, 104
House of Commons 110, 116, 179, 190, 208, 234

Imperial Tobacco 27, 128
Ind Coope 2, 3 *see also* beer brands
Ind Coope Tetley Ansells 3
Independent Pub Federation 217
industrial relations 22, 23
Inn Leisure 173
Inntrepreneur 20–year lease 1988 77
Inntrepreneur Estates Limited (IEL)
  comfort letters received from European Commission regarding leases 1998 149, 182
  formation of 130
  lease notified to European Commission 1992 146
  sale to Nomura 1998 149, 161–2
  withdrawal of application for exemption for standard lease 1997 148
  see also lessee(s)
In Place of Strife 5
Interbrew (InBev; Anheuser-Busch InBev) 87, 160, 161, 237
International Distillers & Vintners (IDV) 27, 33
International Monetary Fund 5

Jarvis, Peter   52, 106, 270
Jenkins, Roy   14
Jennings   168, 170
John Labatt Retail   175
John Smith's   4, 27 *see also* beer brands
Johnson, Melanie   208
Joseph, Max   1

keg beers   4
Keyworth, Lawton Smith and Yarrow   187
Kimball, Lord   111

Labour Government   9, 14, 18, 20–1, 22, 32, 157, 221
lager   37, 38, 39, 43, 59, 60, 66–7, 70, 74, 75, 76, 78, 79, 85, 86, 95, 96, 98, 110, 229 *see also* price(s), beer
Landlord and Tenant (Licensed Premises) Act 1990   122 *see also* tenant(s)
Landlord and Tenant Act 1954   77, 83, 105, 110, 111, 113, 119, 123, 250 *see also* tenant(s)
Lang, Ian   155, 156–7
Laurel Pub Company   169, 176
Lawson, Nigel   114
lease(s)
  free of tie   137, 178, 189, 212, 217, 232
  long, advent of   125–6, 178–9, 232, 239
  of Inntrepreneur Estates Limited   144, 146, 148, 149
  see also lessee(s)
Leicester Chamber of Commerce   41
lessee(s)   126, 135, 136, 146–7, 176, 190, 210–12, 214, 215, 216, 217, 218, 231, 232, 233, 240 *see also* lease(s)
Lever, Jeremy QC   53, 54, 223, 270
licence(s)
  off-   20, 36, 61, 65, 69, 74, 78
  on-   8, 9, 13, 21, 31, 36, 58, 60, 61, 74, 76, 80, 82, 92, 99, 177, 189, 191, 204, 207, 228, 229, 245
  restricted   21, 65, 74, 207
licensee(s)   6, 10, 21, 38, 66, 70, 82, 98, 100, 112, 172, 176, 177, 178, 179, 180, 181, 182, 183, 224, 227, 231, 232, 233, 240, 242, 243, 245

Licensing (Scotland) Act 1976   14
licensing agreement(s) (between brewers)   33, 258
licensing
  Act 2003   207, 213, 247
  authority(ies)   13, 14, 31
  law(s)   11, 13, 21, 25, 26, 42, 80, 123, 142, 144, 229, 249–50
  magistrate(s)/justice(s)   8, 13, 70, 99, 202
  system   6–7, 8, 12, 31, 32, 70, 75, 99, 143, 221, 229, 245, 246
  see also Clayson Report *and* Erroll Report *and* "need" (criterion) *and* opening hours
Light and Heenan *Controlling Supply: the Concept of Need in Liquor Licensing*   246–7
Lilley, Peter   125, 126, 131
loan tie(s)/loan-tying   36, 78, 82, 83, 85, 86–7, 99, 106, 107, 111, 114, 144, 231 *see also* free trade
Local Authority Administrative Area(s)   12, 22
local brewer(s) *see* brewers, local
Long John International   27
Lorimer's   27
Luff, Peter   105, 214, 271

Macgregor, John   124
Macmillan, Harold   1
Magic Pub Company   169
Mangham, Desmond   44, 49, 54, 271
Mann, Crossman & Paulin   2
Mansfield Brewery   27, 168, 170
Market and Opinion Research International (MORI)   58–9
market foreclosure   206, 258
market share(s)   4, 12, 24, 34, 35, 39, 46, 58, 68, 78, 130, 131, 132, 135, 152, 153, 154, 155, 228, 237, 238, 253, 260t
Marr Taverns   135, 174
Marston's   3, 27, 34, 133, 136, 168, 169, 170, 240 *see also* Wolverhampton & Dudley Breweries
Martin, Richard   52, 109, 271

Martin, Tim 247
Maude, Francis 123, 271
  Adjournment Debate 8 May 1989 108
  meetings with Brewers' Society, brewers and other interested parties May–June 1989 109, 110
  statement to House of Commons concerning MMC recommendations 8 June 1989 110
Maudling, Reginald 12
Mayfair Taverns 175
McGrath, John 52, 106, 109, 271
McIntosh, Anne 116
McKinsey 134
McMullen 172
Mellor, David 15–16
Merrett Cyriax 12
microbrewers *see* brewers, micro-
Mills, Leif 51, 53, 54, 73, 84–7, 92, 95, 103, 111, 223, 224, 225, 227–8, 230, 243, 271
mineral water(s) 8, 11, 26, 83
  see also soft drinks
Ministry of Agriculture, Fisheries and Food (MAFF) 49, 100, 105, 116
Mitchells & Butlers 3, 162, 238
  see also Bass
Monopolies Commission (MC) 7, 9, 11, 14, 22, 24, 42
  Supply of Beer Report 1969 4, 7–9, 11, 12, 31, 32, 36, 42, 46, 48, 49, 58, 70, 74, 122, 221, 229, 245
Monopolies and Mergers Commission (MMC), 45, 47, 49, 93, 95, 97, 116, 141, 142, 144, 145, 146, 147, 148, 153, 154, 155, 167, 171, 173, 175, 176, 177, 178, 180, 181, 182, 206, 222, 227, 229, 230–2, 233, 234, 235, 236, 237, 238, 239, 242
  investigation into the supply of petrol 140
  proposed Allied-Lyons and Carlsberg A/S joint venture 1992 87, 122, 132–3, 142
  proposed merger of Bass and Carlsberg-Tetley 1997 87, 156–8
  proposed merger of Elders IXL and Allied-Lyons 1985 29, 51
  proposed merger of Elders IXL and Grand Metropolitan 1990 35, 130–2, 135, 140, 178
  proposed merger of Elders IXL and Scottish & Newcastle 1989 51, 104, 128–9, 223
  proposed merger of Scottish & Newcastle and Matthew Brown 1985 27–9, 33, 42–3, 51, 128, 223
  Report on Full-Line Forcing and Tie-In Sales 1981 26, 28, 33, 46, 51, 79, 97, 223
  Report on Carbonated Drinks 140
  see also Supply of Beer inquiry 1986–89 *and* Supply of Beer Report 1989 *and* Competition Commission
monopoly(ies) 20, 24, 32, 42, 70, 78, 227
  complex 48, 53, 55, 58, 66, 73–4, 75, 76, 79, 80, 83, 84, 92, 93, 96, 99, 112, 114, 222, 224, 228, 236, 238, 249
  local 20, 98, 229
  scale 58, 73, 224, 249
Morgan Stanley 215
Morland 3, 34, 136, 169
Morning Advertiser 100, 108, 109, 111, 112, 174, 211, 232
Morrells 109, 169
Morris, Derek 53, 62, 223, 272

national account(s) 36, 65
National Association of Licensed House Managers (NAHLM) 100
National Association of Licensed Trade Wholesalers 177
National Board for Prices and Incomes (NBPI) 5, 6, 7, 9, 10, 18, 19, 32
National Licensed Victuallers Association (NLVA) 69–70, 77, 92, 100, 106, 109, 124, 125, 126, 139, 143, 177, 180
National Union of Licensed Victuallers (NULV) 55, 123, 180
"need" (criterion) 13, 14, 16, 31, 70, 236, 245, 246, 247 *see also* licensing *and* Light and Heenan

new entrants/competitors/participants 6, 7, 8, 80, 99, 182, 247, 258
  see also barriers to entry
Newbery, Professor DMG 157
Newton, Tony 113, 114
Nicholson, Sir Paul 52, 54, 109, 141, 166, 167, 272
Nimmo, J 4
no alcohol/low alcohol beer(s) (NAB/LABs) 43, 67, 74, 75, 83, 95, 99, 110
Noble House 168
Nomura 149, 161, 162, 166
Northern Clubs Federation Brewery 34, 69, 73
Northern Ireland 12, 55, 66

Office for National Statistics 38
Office of Fair Trading (OFT) 23, 24, 31, 41, 73, 98, 210, 222, 242, 243
  advice to Secretary of State on Supply of Beer Report 1989 87–9
  allegations of collusion amongst brewers 1986 47
  announcement of inquiry into brewers' wholesale pricing policy 1995 146
  announcement of results of consultation on pubcos 2010 218
  announcement of results of inquiry into brewers' wholesale pricing policy 1995 148
  development of case for MMC reference 1986 42–4, 45–7
  evidence to Business and Enterprise Select Committee 2008 215–16
  letter to Campaign for Real Ale advising decision to refer 1986 49
  letter to Campaign for Real Ale requesting views on tied house system 1985 44, 222
  letter to MMC referring beer industry 1986 49
  letter to the Government regarding pub exchange programme 1985 24
  letters to Brewers' Society 1986 44–5, 48, 49
  meeting with Department of Trade and Industry officials regarding effects of Beer Orders 19 August 1991 139
  monitoring of pub exchanges 1981 23
  paper recommending reference to MMC 1986 46
  response to report of Trade and Industry Select Committee 2004 213
  response to super-complaint by Campaign for Real Ale 2009 217
  response to Whitbread offer for Allied Domecq pub estate 1999 158–9
  review of beer market 1991–92 127
  review of Beer Orders 2000 205–8
off-trade 45, 61, 62t, 69, 77, 196f, 197, 226, 239 *see also* prices, beer
Old Bushmills 27
Old English Inns 169
on-trade 21, 28, 33, 36, 37, 49, 133, 152, 190, 192, 196, 201, 213, 225, 226, 229, 231 *see also* prices, beer
opening hours 8, 13, 14, 15, 16 *see also* licensing *and* Erroll Report *and* Clayson Report
overseas beer markets 111, 239
  Australia 29, 35, 116, 225
  Belgium 56, 62t, 71, 225, 226, 254, 257
  Canada 35, 60, 225
  Denmark 35, 59t, 61t, 254, 256
  France 35, 59t, 61t, 62t, 162, 203, 225, 226, 254, 257
  Ireland 59, 61t, 254, 256
  Italy 62t, 225, 226
  Japan 35, 193
  Netherlands 35, 237
  United States of America 35, 56, 62t, 71, 86, 225, 226
  West Germany 59t, 61t, 62t, 225
Overton, John 180, 272

Palmar, Sir Derek 49
Paramount 136
Parliamentary debates 111, 114, 119
Pay Board 18
Peston, Lord 112
Petty Sessional Division(s) 99, 191
Phipps & Co. 3

310 *Index*

Portno, Tony   52, 223, 272
Preston, Jeffrey   154, 155
price(s), beer
  discounts   47, 56, 69, 74, 79, 82, 83, 98, 119, 135, 141, 152, 161, 212, 221, 226, 231, 232
  effect of Beer Orders on   185–6
  ex-taxes/ex-duty   19, 37, 38, 184, 185t, 186, 187, 197, 231–2, 262t
  free trade   6, 11, 64, 94
  lager   19, 38, 55, 74, 76, 184, 185t, 186, 188t, 227
  off   61, 78, 189, 197, 226
  on   39, 61, 94, 99, 189, 190, 196, 197, 225, 226, 231
  on/off ratio   61, 62, 80, 225
  public bar   5, 6, 9, 10, 37, 38, 76, 184, 262t
  regional variations   19, 47, 55, 70, 74, 75, 76, 85, 99
  retail   6, 10, 19, 25, 45, 46, 47, 49, 58, 60, 68, 70, 74, 75, 76, 77, 79, 82, 93, 104, 112, 141, 184, 206, 212, 217, 231, 234
  review of by Business and Enterprise Select Committee 2009   190
  rises/increases   5, 6, 9, 10, 18, 19, 20, 24, 25, 33, 37, 39, 47, 52, 99, 116, 140, 141, 142, 143, 184, 187, 196, 197, 204, 215, 221, 231, 239
  transfer   55, 63, 65
  wholesale   6, 8, 9, 10, 19, 24, 25, 63, 64, 65, 68, 74, 75, 76, 77, 82, 84, 85, 98, 120, 121, 135, 146, 147, 148, 186, 189, 208, 231, 233, 240, 279
Price Code   19, 20
Price Commission (PC), Price Commission Act 1977   18, 19, 20, 24, 25, 26, 29, 32, 33, 184, 222, 246
Prosser, Ian   52, 54, 272
pub(s)   4, 7, 10, 12, 15, 21, 22, 24, 25, 28, 58, 59, 60, 62, 66, 67, 68, 69, 70, 71, 80, 82, 84, 85, 86, 87, 92, 94, 95, 100, 104, 105, 165, 178, 189, 207
  amenity in   5, 8, 21, 58, 59, 60, 62, 63, 65, 74, 76, 86, 96, 112, 187, 188, 200, 206, 207, 225, 227, 228, 229, 230, 232, 233
  children in   8, 13, 14, 201
  closures of   46, 95, 96, 97, 98, 108, 111, 200, 213, 216, 233
  divestments/disposals   7, 11, 42, 47–8, 82, 83, 85, 86, 88, 89, 92, 97, 98, 101, 106, 108, 109, 111, 113, 114, 115, 179, 230, 232, 234, 237, 239
  exchanges   12, 18, 22, 23, 24, 32, 41, 47, 229, 242
  food in   60, 65, 189, 202, 207, 233
  leased   134, 136, 161, 175, 232
    see also lease(s) *and* lessee(s)
  local concentration(s) of   11, 12, 22, 23, 24, 31, 41, 46, 54, 69, 70, 78, 98, 99, 112, 130–1, 145, 229, 236,
    see also monopoly(ies)
  managed   6, 8, 19, 24, 25, 35, 36, 37, 38, 42, 45, 52, 62, 64, 65, 74, 76, 78, 130, 131, 134, 158, 162, 166, 217, 232, 236, 260t, 278
  numbers   4, 12, 36, 58, 63, 122t, 189, 190, 207, 211, 260t, 261t, 281t
  purchase of by small brewers from big brewers   137, 179, 180, 181, 228
  purchase of by tenants from big brewers   136, 137, 179, 181
  smoking in   99, 176, 190, 197, 213
  tenanted   6, 8, 35, 36, 52, 62, 65, 74, 76, 78, 140, 141, 162, 166, 173, 174, 177, 211, 217, 238, 260t
  values   13, 189, 190
  see also tied estate *and* tied pubs
pub companies/pubco(s)   8, 82, 93, 95, 96, 97, 99, 135, 137, 141, 143, 147, 166, 167, 168, 169, 173–6, 179, 180, 182, 189, 190, 200, 207, 210–18, 226, 231, 232, 233, 240, 242, 248, 281t
  beginnings of   173
  Business and Enterprise Select Committee inquiry 2008   213
  Business, Innovation and Skills Select Committee inquiry 2009   216
  business model of   175, 176, 182, 212, 213, 233, 240
  role of former executives of big brewers   137, 175
  Trade and Industry Select Committee inquiry 2004   182, 210, 215
pub tenants, *see* tenants
Publican   137, 170, 214
public bar   5, 6, 37, 38

public interest   9, 20, 26, 28, 29, 32, 33, 42, 47, 49, 53, 55, 56, 64, 65, 74, 76–80, 81, 82, 84, 85, 86, 97, 98, 100, 129, 223, 224–5, 230
  see also Supply of Beer inquiry 1986–89, Public Interest Letter *and* Supply of Beer Report 1989
Pubmaster   134, 136, 153, 167, 168, 174, 176, 180, 211, 212, 231
Punch Taverns (Punch Group)   158, 159, 166, 175, 176, 231, 233
  debt financed expansion/securitisation   176
  evidence to Trade and Industry Select Committee 2008   215
  floated on Stock Exchange 2002   175
  purchase of Allied Domecq's pub estate 1999   205
  purchase of pubs from Bass 1997   175, 180
  purchase of Spirit Group 2005   166, 176
  share price   176

Raison, Timothy   15
Redwood, John   123, 124, 126, 272
Refresh UK   168
Regent Inns   173
regional brewers   24, 28, 34, 77, 78, 82, 97, 111, 121, 133, 135, 141, 147, 170, 174, 223
Regulatory Policy Institute   186
Reid, Hubert   165, 273
rent(s)   10, 18, 21, 70, 77, 85, 120, 125, 126, 141, 189, 190, 232, 233, 239, 240
  "dry"   6, 25, 175, 176
  review(s)   83, 113, 212, 213, 214
  below-market   6, 10, 21, 75, 147, 211
  upward only increase(s)   212, 213, 214
  "wet"   6, 8, 25, 175, 176
Research Bureau Limited   59, 60, 61
restrictive covenants   11, 12, 31, 32, 80, 83, 84, 88, 98, 106, 119, 120, 208, 215
Restrictive Trade Practices Act 1956   47, 249
Retail Prices Index   10, 19, 20, 37, 69, 76, 184, 206

Richards, Stephen   53, 273
Riddick, Graham   108, 116, 243
Ridley, Nicholas   12, 116, 121, 123, 273
Ridley's   170
Ringwood Brewery   168
Robinson, Peter   52, 273
Robinsons   27, 170
Ruddles   3, 169
R v Sheffield Justices 1992   246
Ryder, Richard   116

Saccone & Speed   27, 33
Sam Smith   109
Saunders, Ernest   43, 44, 273
Scorpio Inns   136
Scotland   2, 9, 12, 13, 14, 15, 16, 69, 129, 157, 161, 176, 193, 246
  see also Clayson Report *and* Licensing (Scotland) Act 1976 *and* Secretary of State for Scotland
Scottish & Newcastle (S&N), Scottish & Newcastle Breweries   2, 4, 23, 27, 28, 34, 36, 47, 67, 68, 78, 82, 104, 128, 129, 130, 134, 136, 144, 152, 157, 159, 161, 162, 169, 199, 206, 237, 238, 241, 260t, 261t
  acquisition of Bulmer 2003   162
  acquisition of Courage 1995   153–5, 156, 237
  acquisition of Home Brewery 1986   128
  compliance with Beer Orders 1992   136, 137
  European Commission exemption for lease 1999   149
  evidence to Agriculture Select Committee 1993   144
  formation of Scottish & Newcastle 1960   2
  lease notified to European Commission 1996   148, 149
  proposed merger with JW Cameron 1984   27
  proposed merger with Elders IXL 1989   51, 52, 129, 153, 154, 223, 237
  proposed acquisition of Matthew Brown 1985 & 87   27, 28, 29, 33, 43, 51, 128, 184, 223
  purchase of Greenall Whitley's managed houses 1999   166

Scottish & Newcastle (S&N), Scottish & Newcastle Breweries – *continued*
  sale of managed pubs to Spirit Group 2003   162, 166
  sale of tenanted pubs   162
  takeover by Heineken/Carlsberg   162
"Scottish lobby"   155, 157
Scottish Office   155, 157
Sears Holdings   2
Secretary of State for Prices and Consumer Protection   18, 19
Secretary of State for Scotland   13, 155
Secretary of State for Trade and Industry, President of the Board of Trade   9, 12, 73, 81, 82, 83, 87, 108, 112, 113, 114, 116, 121, 125, 126, 131, 133, 143, 145, 154, 155, 158, 161, 205, 208, 233, 235, 237
securitisation   176 *see also* Punch Taverns
Select Committee
  Agriculture   116, 125, 142–4, 173, 246
  Business and Enterprise   190, 213
  Business, Innovation and Skills   216
  Trade and Industry   145, 210, 215, 233
Sharp's   239
Shepherd Neame   34, 52, 133, 135, 136, 192, 239
Sheppard, Allen   49
Shore, Peter   114
Showerings   27, 33, 78
Silkin, John   20, 22, 23
Simmons and Simmons   53, 54
Slade, Margaret E   187
Smethurst, Dick   26, 28, 51, 53, 54, 79, 129, 223, 273–4
Smiles   69
Society of Independent Brewers/Small Independent Brewers' Association (SIBA)   108, 109, 171, 172, 208, 212–13, 217
soft drinks   20, 26, 27, 33, 46, 59, 77, 78, 79, 83, 84, 85, 101, 110 *see also* minerals
Spicer, John   142, 182
Spirit Group   162, 166, 176
spirits   7, 8, 11, 20, 25, 26, 27, 29, 33, 45, 46, 59, 67, 77, 79, 83, 110, 198, 199, 250
Spring Inns   149
Squires Gin   33

Steward & Patteson   3
Stones   27
Strong   3, 4
stout   35, 38, 39, 43, 45, 46, 59, 66, 68, 191, 192
Summerskill, Dr Shirley   14
supermarket(s)   36, 60, 61, 64, 65, 198, 203
supply agreement(s)   7, 82, 88, 96, 106, 119, 120, 130, 131, 132, 133, 134, 140, 141, 142, 143, 148, 153, 155, 159, 207, 237, 255
Supply of Beer inquiry 1986–89   26, 38, 39, 51, 52, 53, 54, 55, 56, 60, 61, 62, 63, 64, 65, 66, 67, 68, 69, 70, 71, 73, 81, 123, 128, 145, 165, 167, 168, 169, 170, 171, 180, 205, 221, 223, 226, 228, 231, 232, 233, 238, 242
  Beer Brands Costs and Profits Study   64
  commissioning of efficiency studies   52
  countervailing benefits   80, 81, 225
  hearings   53–4
  market research studies   52
  Options for change   56, 278–80
  overseas markets, analysis of, visits to   56, 226
  Public Interest Letter (PIL), Addendum to Public Interest Letter   53, 55–6, 64, 74, 200
  questionnaires   52, 56, 64
  search of Brewers' Society offices   53
  Segmented Costs and Profits Study   64
  visits to UK breweries   52
Supply of Beer (Loan Ties, Licensed Premises and Wholesale Prices) Order 1989 (LTO)   116, 121 *see also* Beer Orders
Supply of Beer Report 1969, *see under* Monopolies Commission
Supply of Beer Report 1989   36, 39, 65, 67, 68, 69, 71, 73–84, 88, 89, 92–101, 103–11, 113–17, 119, 120, 122–5, 128, 130, 139–41, 145, 146, 165, 167–71, 173, 174, 176–8, 183, 191, 225, 226, 227, 228, 229, 230, 231, 232, 233, 235, 236, 238, 241, 242, 243

Index 313

Adjournment Debate in House of
   Commons 8 May 1989 108
Europe 88
examination of Report by Trade
   and Industry Select Committee
   1995 145
Note of Dissent 73, 84, 87, 95,
   103, 111, 179, 225, 227, 228,
   230
principal finding(s)/conclusions 73,
   95, 100, 103, 107, 108, 225, 230,
   231, 233, 234, 236
public interest (detriment) 65,
   74–84, 100, 105, 108, 206, 224,
   227, 229
recommendations 82, 83, 87, 88, 92,
   93, 95, 97, 98, 99, 100, 101, 103,
   104, 105, 106, 107, 108, 109, 110,
   111, 113, 114, 115, 119, 145, 165,
   168, 227, 229, 232, 233, 234, 235,
   239, 243
regional pricing of beer 77, 99
return on capital 75
tenants, position of 82, 87, 95, 101,
   113, 139
wholesale price lists 77, 82, 83, 98,
   101, 121, 206, 226
Supply of Beer (Tied Estate) Order 1989
   (TEO) 121, 125, 134, 136, 142,
   159, 171, 174, 189, 206, 208, 231,
   239 *see also* Beer Orders
Surrey Free Inns 173
Swallow Group 160, 166, 167
   see also Vaux
Sycamore Taverns 133, 174

take-home 21, 46, 133, 152, 190, 197,
   225
Taunton Cider Company 33, 46, 68,
   78
Taylor, Eddie 1, 2, 3, 29
Taylor, John 155
Taylor Walker 2
Tied Estate Order *see* Supply of Beer
   (Tied Estate) Order 1989
tenancy/tenancies/tenancy
   agreement/tenanted pubs 11, 26,
   31, 63, 76, 77, 83, 92, 95, 96, 97,
   101, 104, 111, 113, 119, 123, 126,
   141, 149, 166, 173, 174, 180, 187,
   232, 235, 255–6, 257, 279

tenant(s) 6, 8, 10, 11, 19, 21, 25, 26,
   31, 33, 38, 55, 68, 71, 75, 79, 80,
   82–3, 84, 85, 98, 99, 101, 103,
   110, 120, 136, 137, 140, 141,
   143, 147, 148, 190, 206, 210,
   212, 221, 230, 231, 235, 236, 239,
   240
   arbitration for 77, 124, 125, 139
   compensation for 101, 124, 125,
      182
   conversion to long leaseholders 77,
      178, 180
   effect of consolidation of pubcos
      on 179, 180
   notice to quit 113, 124, 125, 126,
      178
   of Inntrepreneur Estates Ltd (IEL)
      181, 182
   security of tenure 70, 77, 95, 96,
      101, 105, 109, 114, 119, 122,
      123, 177, 180, 232, 236
   see also Landlord and Tenant
      Act 1954 *and* Landlord and
      Tenant (Licensed Premises)
      Act 1990
Tennent, J&R 3
Tetley Walker 3
Thatcher, Margaret 26, 32, 37, 113,
   222, 235
Theakston 162
The Economist 55
The Enterprise Years 103, 115 *see also*
   Young, Lord
The Independent 208
The Daily Telegraph 93
The Times 92, 115
Thomas, Lord 111
Thompson, David 110, 167, 168,
   169, 274
Thomson, David 51, 274
Thorley, Giles 215
Threshers 27
Thurman, Chris 44, 54, 145, 274
Thwaites 23, 27, 135, 170, 181
Tidbury, Charles 28, 34, 223
Tilbury, Alan 44, 49, 54, 274
tied house system 6, 7, 8, 9, 20, 21,
   22, 25, 31, 32, 33, 41, 42–4, 48,
   49, 58, 65, 66, 70, 74, 82, 85, 88,
   93, 221, 222, 223, 226, 229, 232,
   241

tied house system – *continued*
  advantages/disadvantages 7, 8, 9,
    11, 19, 20, 21, 22, 25, 32, 33, 41,
    42, 44, 48, 49, 55, 58–63, 65–70,
    80, 81, 107, 225
  tied estate 2, 11, 26, 28, 33, 46, 54,
    85, 86–7, 120, 122, 133, 153, 159,
    169, 241
  tied pubs/houses 20, 26, 38, 44, 46,
    47, 48, 55, 69, 99, 109, 120, 122t,
    222
  tied trade 8, 27, 94, 152, 228
Tollemache & Cobbold 12, 23, 27, 174
Townsend, Simon 215
Trade and Industry Select Committee inquiry into monopoly reports 1995 145, 233
Trade and Industry Select Committee inquiry into pub companies 2004 182 *see also* pub companies/pubco(s)
Trades Union Congress 5, 18, 84, 101, 235
Trent Taverns 180
Truman (Truman Hanbury & Buxton) 4, 12, 27
Truro, Bishop of 111
Tuppen, Ted 215

Unique Pub Company 176, 231
United Breweries 2, 3
Unite Union 217
Ushers 3, 132, 168

Vaux 3, 4, 27, 34, 45, 52, 109, 135, 136, 141, 166, 168, 170
vertical integration 19, 48, 53, 55, 62–3, 75, 77, 80, 86, 87, 94, 96, 97, 104, 131, 139, 141, 144, 145, 154, 224, 225, 236, 237, 238, 241, 243
Vickers, John 53, 223, 274
Victoria Wine 27, 270

Waelbroeck, Professor Michael 106, 115
Waterhouse, Rachel 99
Waterson, Professor Michael 216
Watney (Watney Combe Reid; Watney Mann; Watney Mann & Truman) 2, 3, 4, 12, 23, 27, 174
  acquisition by Grand Metropolitan Hotels 1972 2, 27
  acquisitions in 1960 3
  formation of Watney Mann 1958 2
  hostile bid from Sears Holdings (Charles Clore) 1959 2
  see also Grand Metropolitan *from 1972*
Webster 27
Wetherspoon, JD 173, 232, 246
Whitbread 3, 4, 23, 26, 27, 28, 34, 36, 52, 106, 132, 134, 135–6, 137, 152, 153, 158–60, 161, 162, 167, 175, 180, 206, 238, 260t, 261t
  acquisition of local brewery companies in 1960s 4
  compliance with Beer Orders 1992 135–6
  disposal of pub estate 160, 162, 208
  European Commission exemption for lease 1999 149
  evidence to Agriculture Select Committee 1993 144
  inclusion within Beer Orders' definition of a "brewery group" 120, 121
  interest in acquiring Courage 1994 153, 156
  lease notified to European Commission 1994 146, 148
  notification of planned price increase to Price Commission 1979 25
  presentation to backbench Trade and Industry Committee 1989 107
  proposed purchase of Allied Domecq's pub estate 1999 158–60, 237
  purchase of Boddingtons beer business 1989 166, 173
  purchase of Swallow Hotels 167
  sale of beer business to Interbrew 2000 160, 161
  takeover of Whitbread Investment Company 1993 136
Whitbread Investment Company (WIC) 28, 97–8, 120–1, 136, 169
Whitbread "umbrella" 3, 28, 98, 136, 167
White, R 27
wholesaler(s)/wholesaling 7, 8, 19, 27, 39, 54, 55, 62, 64, 65, 66, 69, 74, 75, 76, 79, 83, 84, 85, 94, 119, 132, 133,

140, 157, 161, 166, 176–7, 184, 206, 221, 226, 238, 279
Wiggin, Sir Jerry   142
Williams, Lord   111, 114, 116
Willis, Norman   101
Wilson & Walker   3
Wilson, Harold   5, 18
wine(s)   7, 8, 11, 19, 25, 26, 27, 33, 59, 77, 79, 83, 110, 198–9, 204, 250
Wizard Inns   168
Wolverhampton & Dudley Breweries (W&DB)   4, 27, 34, 47, 67, 110, 167, 168, 170, 240 *see also* Marston's

Yarrow, George   53, 61, 62, 64, 93, 94, 95, 96, 97, 111, 112, 140, 187, 200, 223, 224, 241, 274
Yates Brothers Wine Lodges   173
Young & Co   34, 170, 181
Young, Bob   51, 129, 224, 274

Young, Lord   73, 87, 88, 89, 93, 97, 99, 101, 103–17, 121, 123, 145, 208, 214, 233, 234, 235, 236, 238, 243, 246, 275
  announcement of Government's decisions 10 July 1989   113
  meeting with brewers 15 May 1989   109
  meeting with chairmen of large brewers 6 July 1989   112
  meeting with Guinness 16 May 1989   110
  meeting with John Elliott April 1989   104
  meeting with Sir Leon Brittan April 1989   89, 105, 256
  speech inviting alternative remedies to MMC recommendations 3 May 1989   107
  succeeded at Department of Trade and Industry by Nicholas Ridley 1989   116